Applications of Consumer Behavior

Applications
of Consumer Behavior:
Readings and Exercises

Gail Tom

California State University, Sacramento

Prentice-Hall, Inc., Englewood Cliffs, N.J. 07632

Library of Congress Cataloging in Publication Data
Main entry under title:

APPLICATIONS OF CONSUMER BEHAVIOR.

 Includes bibliographical references.
 1 Consumers—United States—Addresses, essays,
lectures. 2. Consumers' preferences—United States—
Addresses, essays, lectures. 3. Market surveys—United
States—Addresses, essays, lectures. I. Tom, Gail K.
HC110.C6A8 1984   658.8'342   83-9629
ISBN 0-13-039248-0

Editorial/production supervision and
  interior design: Richard C. Laveglia
Cover design: Wanda Lubelska
Manufacturing buyer: Ed O'Dougherty
Page layout by Peter J. Ticola, Jr.

Printed in the United States of America

10 9 8 7 6 5 4 3 2 1

ISBN 0-13-039248-0

Prentice-Hall International, Inc., *London*
Prentice-Hall of Australia Pty. Limited, *Sydney*
Editora Prentice-Hall do Brasil, Ltda., *Rio de Janeiro*
Prentice-Hall Canada Inc., *Toronto*
Prentice-Hall of India Private Limited, *New Delhi*
Prentice-Hall of Japan, Inc., *Tokyo*
Prentice-Hall of Southeast Asia Pte. Ltd., *Singapore*
Whitehall Books Limited, *Wellington, New Zealand*

To My Parents
Who have been a constant source
of support, understanding,
and encouragement

Contents

Chapter 19 Consumerism: Militant Consumer Behavior 333

Cross-Reference Table for *Applications in Consumer Behavior: Readings and Exercises*

Text	Part I	Part II	Part III	Part IV
1. Assael: *Consumer Behavior and Marketing Action*	Chs. 1, 18	Chs. 9, 10, 11, 12, 13, 14	Chs. 5, 6, 7, 8, 18	Chs. 2, 4, 15, 16, 17, 19, 20, 21, 23
2. Berkman and Gilson: *Consumer Behavior Concepts and Strategies,* Second Edition	Chs. 1, 3	Chs. 4, 5, 6, 7	Chs. 8, 9, 10, 11	Chs. 12, 13, 14, 15
3. Block and Roering: *Essentials of Consumer Behavior,* Second Edition	Ch. 1	Chs. 3, 4, 5, 6	Chs. 7, 8, 10, 15	Chs. 2, 9, 11, 12, 13, 14, 17, 18
4. Cohen: *Consumer Behavior*	Ch. 1	Chs. 2, 3, 4, 5, 6, 10	Chs. 7, 8, 9, 10, 11, 12	Chs. 13, 14, 15, 16, 17, 18, 19, 20
5. Engle and Blackwell: *Consumer Behavior,* Fourth Edition	Ch. 1	Chs. 3, 4, 5, 6, 7	Chs. 8, 9, 19	Chs. 2, 10, 11, 12, 13, 14, 15, 16, 17, 18, 21, 22
6. Hawkins, Coney, and Best: *Consumer Behavior*	Ch. 1	Chs. 4, 5, 6, 7, 8, 9, 14	Chs. 11, 12, 13	Chs. 3, 10, 15, 16, 17, 18, 19
7. Kerby: *Consumer Behavior*	Ch. 1	Chs. 19, 20	Chs. 3, 4, 5, 6, 7, 8, 9, 10, 11, 12, 13, 14, 15, 16	Chs. 17, 18
8. Loudon and Della Britta: *Consumer Behavior Concepts and Applications*	Chs. 1, 2, 3, 4, 5	Chs. 6, 7, 8, 9, 10, 11	Chs. 13, 14, 15, 16, 17, 18	Chs. 12, 19, 20, 21, 22
9. Runyon: *Consumer Behavior and the Practice of Marketing,* Second Edition	Chs. 1, 2, 3, 18	Chs. 5, 6, 7, 8	Chs. 9, 10, 11, 12, 13, 14	Chs. 15, 16, 17
10. Reynolds and Wells: *Consumer Behavior*	Chs. 1, 2	Chs. 3, 4, 5, 6, 7, 8, 15	Ch. 9	Chs. 10, 11, 12, 13, 14
11. Shiffman and Kanuk: *Consumer Behavior,* Second Edition	Ch. 1	Chs. 8, 9, 11, 12, 13	Chs. 2, 3, 4, 5, 6	Chs. 7, 10, 14, 15
12. Walters: *Consumer Behavior,* Third Edition	Chs. 1, 23, 24	Chs. 16, 17, 18, 19, 20, 21, 22	Chs. 9, 10, 11, 12, 13, 14, 15	Chs. 5, 6, 8, 25, 26, 27
13. Williams: *Consumer Behavior Fundamentals and Strategies*	Chs. 1, 9	Chs. 7, 8, 11, 12	Chs. 3, 4, 5, 6, 11, 12, 13, 15	Chs. 2, 10, 14, 15, 16, 17, 18
14. Woods: *Consumer Behavior*	Chs. 1, 2	Chs. 5, 13, 14	Chs. 6, 7 (Parts 1 and 2), 8, 9, 10, 11, 12, 13	Chs. 8, 19

Preface

With origins in the mid-1960s, the development of the study of consumer behavior as a formal discipline is a recent arrival in academics. Within this short period of time, the burgeoning literature in consumer behavior clearly evidences the contributions the study of consumer behavior has made and promises to make to business organizations, public agencies, and nonprofit organizations.

The importance of the study of consumer behavior to marketing is demonstrated by the evolution of the goals and emphasis in marketing. From its original foundation as a branch of applied economics, with emphasis on production, to a management discipline, stressing an orientation to increase sales, marketing has evolved to its current characterization as an applied behavioral science with a focus on understanding the behavioral implications of the elements of the marketing mix. In short, marketing has evolved to the realization that it must take its marching orders from the consumer, because the consumer is the arbiter of success.

The criticality of understanding consumer behavior applies not only to marketing strategy planning, but is of equal importance to nonprofit organizations' policy development and to public policy formation. Whether the orientation of the organization is profit or nonprofit, public or private, its efficiency, effectiveness, and very survival depend to a large extent upon its ability to understand consumer behavior.

The complexity of consumer behavior requires the adoption of an inter-disciplinary orientation to its study with contributions from psychology , sociology, anthropology, economics, marketing, consumer science, and political science. This eclectic approach makes the study of consumer behavior rich, varied, and dynamic, but at the same time unwieldy and difficult for the student to integrate and apply.

This all too frequently produces an artificial schism between the academic world and the real world. The student is a member of both, but separates what is learned in the classroom from what is experienced in the real world on a daily basis. The purpose of this anthology of readings and exercises is to bridge the gap that exists between what is between the covers of a consumer behavior textbook and its occurrence and application in the real world. It is intended to be an educational tool to supplement and complement consumer behavior textbooks. The purpose of this collection of readings and exercises is to allow the student the opportunity to be an active, creative participant in the learning process.

The anthology is divided into four parts:

1. The study of consumer behavior: introduction and overview.
2. Social and cultural influences on consumer behavior.
3. Intrapersonal influences on consumer behavior.
4. Consumer decision making.

Each topic is preceded by an overview of the articles and exercises included.

The readings in this book have been selected according to the following criteria:

1. The articles illustrate real-world applications of the theories and concepts introduced in textbooks.
2. The articles strengthen and deepen the students' understanding of basic principles and concepts.
3. The articles are readable.
4. The articles encourage class discussions and integration of material.
5. The articles encourage the students to appreciate the potential contributions of consumer behavior to profit, nonprofit, government organizations and to themselves as consumers.

The exercises have been designed with the following objectives in mind:

1. To allow the student to experience the application of the concepts and principles introduced in the text.
2. To allow the student to conduct "experiments" that will allow him or her to develop an understanding of how the principles were derived.
3. To understand the usefulness of what they are learning to problem solving.

These exercises are of three types. Some of the exercises are designed to be integrated with the instructors' lectures as an illustration or application of a concept or principle. A second type of exercise is designed for small group discussion and participation. The third type of exercise is more "experimental" in nature and is designed with the intent of giving the student a sampling of behavioral research methodologies and techniques. These three types of exercises provide options in the selection and combination of those exercises that are most appropriate for the goals and objectives of a particular consumer behavior course.

Gail Tom

Acknowledgments

The fruition of this book is the result of the efforts of many people. I am grateful to my students whose enthusiastic interest and insightful inquiries provided me with impetus and motivation for this book. I am indebted to my teachers, Howard Schutz and Margaret Rucker for introducing me to and sparking my interest in the study of consumer behavior.

Many individuals contributed to the completion of this effort. I am appreciative of the valuable administrative support contributed by Dale Tom and Alice Tom. I extend my appreciation to Mary Krieg for her cheerful and efficient help. I thank Elizabeth Classon, Acquisitions Editor; Rick Laveglia, Production Editor; Gert Glassen, Supplemental Books Editor; Paul Feyan, representative, and the many people at Prentice-Hall.

I acknowledge the authors, advertising agencies, and companies for their permission to include their work in this book. I extend my gratitude to: Harold H. Kassarjian, Carol A. Scott, University of California, Los Angeles; Michael A. Belch, San Diego State University; Michael K. Mills, University of Southern California; Jerry C. Olson, Pennsylvania State University; Robert B. Settle, San Diego State University, for their valuable suggestions and constructive comments in the drafts of this book.

Finally, to my husband Calvin Tong and my son Ryan Tom Tong, I give thanks for their love, support and joy.

1

Understanding the Consumer

Consumers are the central focus of the marketing concept. They are the pivotal point, the Rosetta Stone, around which marketing revolves. An understanding of consumers is paramount to the success of marketing efforts.

In the article "Why Barbie Is a Hot Item after 21 Years," James V. Healion discusses the reasons for the incredible long-lasting success of Mattel's Barbie Doll. Barbie's success rests with Mattel's ability to understand consumers. She symbolizes American dreams and cultural values, and as American cultural values and dreams change, so, too, does Barbie's personification of them.

Dean Rotbart's report of the increasing use of licensing in the article "Licensing Boom Envelopes U.S. Industry as Makers Search for a Competitive Edge" demonstrates that in some cases, the symbolic, psychological, and subjective properties of products are of greater overriding importance to the consumers than the products' tangible, physical, and objective attributes.

WHY BARBIE IS A HOT ITEM AFTER 21 YEARS

One major chain store buyer rejected her outright 21 years ago because she was too sexy. Within a year, Barbie was the most popular doll in town.

The same store's 1980 Christmas catalog devotes 2½ pages to Barbie and husband-doll Ken, their clothing and accessories, their six-room, two-story "Dream House," their 3½-foot backyard swimming pool and cabana.

Mattel Inc. has sold more than 120 million Barbie and Barbie family dolls since 1959 when it felt the Sears, Roebuck rejection at the New York Toy Fair was bye bye Barbie.

Ella King Torrey, an art history major at Yale University, has spent more than a year researching the Barbie doll phenomenon. The idea for Torrey's study originated with a joking male friend, but she grasped its potential right away.

When Yale gave her a year to pursue the project under its "Scholar of the House" program, she contacted the Hawthorne, Calif., manufacturer and talked to Ruth Handler, who had founded Mattel with her husband, Elliot. Handler said: "Toys don't last 21 years. Dreams do."

Barbie, for many, has been the American dream girl.

"She's purely a reflection of popular taste. People buy only what they want," said the Indiana-raised Torrey, who is two years older than the doll.

Like the dream doll, she is blonde and long legged. "But," she laughed, "I don't think that explains my attraction to the subject matter."

"Why Barbie Is a Hot Item after 21 Years," James V. Healion, *Sacramento Bee,* November 19, 1980. Reprinted by permission of United Press International.

She said the manufacturer doesn't anticipate trends. It makes no changes in the doll or her surroundings until they become a cultural fact. Her explanation for its commercial success: As cultural standards change so does the doll.

Big changes were in the making as America entered the 1960s:

University of California president Clark Kerr said college students would be easy to handle.

Roman Catholic bishops rejected the assertion American Catholics would eventually use contraceptives.

Some people believed blacks wouldn't demonstrate.

All were wrong. Apathy and conformity were dead.

In the toy world, the baby doll with the pudgy legs and oversized head was being replaced by an 11½-inch sexpot. Barbie was a new kid on the block—and what a kid!

Her bust, waist and hip measurements were the equivalent of a woman whose dimensions were 39-21-33. The company said they were dictated by wardrobe considerations.

"There had been other fashion dolls and fashion accessories for conventional girl dolls," says Ted Erickson, editor of "Toy & Hobby World," a trade magazine. "Barbie was a big revolution, a full-figured adolescent girl doll with a bosom. They took a category that was inconsequential and made it into a whole product category"—the fashion doll.

In 1956, when the Handlers were visiting Zurich, they saw a doll—more of an adult gag item than a child's toy. Their daughter, Barbie, liked it right away.

She was the comic strip heroine "Lilli," a single, sexy blonde career girl distinguished by her dizziness in the office and personal life.

Barbie Handler had been playing with paper dolls from an American comic strip whose heroine was another career girl, "Tillie the Toiler." Like most dolls, all you could do with Lilli was display or carry her.

Barbie had 22 outfits when she made her debut. Now she has 49 in three price ranges and vast accessories. The dream girl does all sorts of things. She has gone fishing, skating, skiing, swimming, bicycling, jogging and roller-disco dancing.

She goes camping, horseback riding, even clam digging. She has practiced ballet, played golf, croquet and tennis. She has gone surfing and sailing.

She has been a ballerina, nurse, baby sitter, career girl, designer, Olympic athlete, actress, astronaut and doctor—the last eventually shelved because it didn't sell. Women apparently weren't being perceived in physicians' roles. Some say Barbie is sexist.

"Yes, she's terribly sexual, and overtly sexual. Her sexuality is defined by things like curvy legs and large breasts. But that is still part of the cultural image. Until that changes, Barbie isn't going to change," Torrey said.

"In the '60s, Barbie came to represent American culture as the heroine. Rarely before in American history has the culture accepted a woman as its ideal.

"She received a great deal of attention in the '60s as the American dream. Then in the '70s women came into their own and sort of realized their own potential. I think the two are in some way related.

"I don't think Barbie herself affected the woman's movement. But I think the ability to see the woman as the ideal in the '60s and the '70s was an example of the growing awareness of women themselves," she said.

Today, she says the doll's world is defined increasingly by her lifestyle accessories. She has a 10-speed bicycle, a dune buggy, several sports cars, a camper, a beach bus, a motor home, a catamaran, a yacht, a private plane, a real garden, a swimming pool and 11 houses. Also 46 friends.

There's even an encyclopedia of Barbie dolls, with price guide, published by Gazette Books of Kermit, Texas, for collectors.

The doll has had four different faces and more than 40 subtle facial variations. The popular notion blonde is better was discovered by Mattel in the early '70s. Since then it has produced blonde Barbies almost exclusively.

Barbie was among the first toys advertised on television, which has been a big factor in its success.

Not all mothers recall her advent kindly. "I didn't think Barbie was a doll for kids," one said. "It was a money machine for Mattel. They'd come out with one outfit on television and the next thing you know, there'd be another."

Torrey says, "You can tell by the years, really, where the popular mind is in America by just examining the various artifacts and accessories that are included in Barbie's dream world."

In the 1960s she was a big girl in a small town. She went to proms, barbecues and dated. A college education was vivid in the American dream. Sears was soon marketing the Barbie Doll campus, which was free of the usual encumbrances, books.

It was discontinued. "You don't see that kind of accessory or artifact in Barbie's world again. It's sort of an interesting statement in what our country values," Torrey said.

By 1974, the doll was on her way to becoming a superstar, a celebrity. She drives what's called a "Starvette." She's involved in a stage show that looks like a mini version of the Academy Awards.

"She's becoming much more glamorized and much less a specific idol. She's gained a lot of real estate, which is something she didn't have originally and she's getting more accessorized," Torrey said.

In 1967 she was given the face of a 16-year-old. It replaced a far more sophisticated face. Her clothes changed, too.

The transformation coincided with the youth generation coming of age.

LICENSING BOOM ENVELOPS U.S. INDUSTRY AS MAKERS SEARCH FOR A COMPETITIVE EDGE

Bugs Bunny, a nice enough rabbit, actually has a sharp commercial instinct. And Fred Flintstone's cherubic smile masks a definite acquisitive streak.

Little Orphan Annie, for her part, is building a financial empire soon to rival that of opulent Daddy Warbucks.

Licensing is the thing; all of those cartoon characters are being lucratively merchandised by their owners—and not without notice by other marketers. Manufacturers around the country are turning to cartoons and other licensable properties, including movie and television personalities, corporate trademarks and designer brands.

The hope is to endow new or existing products with a competitive edge. In some cases, the licenses have proved to be deadly effective marketing tools, to the delight of companies trying to get a foothold in new markets and the despair of firms that have seen licensed competitors peck away at their established name-brand products and market shares.

STARTING AT BREAKFAST

A popular cartoon character's likeness may grace everything from breakfast cereal to gold jewelry, occasionally generating retail sales for the licensees of $100 million or more. Products using American Greeting Corp.'s Strawberry Shortcake character reached that level last year. Similarly, Columbia Pictures Merchandising, a division of Columbia Pictures Industries Inc. that owns licensing rights for the coming movie "Annie," says its licenses should generate $100 million in sales after "Annie" products hit the market.

"Licensing has taken over the world," complains a spokeswoman at Binney & Smith Inc., the maker of Crayola crayons, Silly Putty and other children's items. "Kids don't really care about our putty, they care about their favorite characters," she says.

The company says it was forced to roll back wholesale prices 25% on Silly Putty last year to woo back children and parents who had abandoned the perennial market leader for such recent competitors as Bugs Bunny Putty, Spiderman Putty, Hulk Putty and others.

Over the past three years, says David Hewitt, Binney & Smith's activities division product manager, Silly Putty's market share has slipped to about 50% from about 60%, largely because of inroads made by new licensed competitors. Mr. Hewitt estimates that Bugs Bunny Putty, made by privately held Henry Gordy Inc., Yonkers, N.Y., has grabbed 15% of the $4 million to $5 million putty market. A Henry Gordy official declined to divulge the specifics of his products' market shares, saying they rise and fall regularly with the popularity of character licenses.

In children's vitamins, the proliferation and popularity of licensed products has become so pronounced that some well-established brands are falling victim. "Our research indicates that characters have a lot to do with interest in vitamins," says a spokeswoman for Miles Laboratories Inc. "The preference is so clearly for cartoon characters that we are phasing out Chocks (brand) vitamins."

Chocks, which was introduced in 1960, for many years was the leader in the U.S. children's chewable-vitamin industry, which has annual sales of $50 million to $60 million, the spokeswoman says. However, the company's own Flintstones vitamins, introduced in 1969 (with essentially the same formulation as Chocks), stole the market from Chocks and much of the competition. The company's Bugs Bunny vitamin, introduced in 1971, still carries the name Chocks in small lettering on it. However, Miles plans to drop the Chocks name entirely in the U.S.

HOW TO GET HURT

In some other industries, such as children's sleepwear, manufacturers who don't license may not survive. "Ninety nine and nine tenths percent of everything I make is licensed merchandise," says Louis Bates, president of Bates Nitewear Co., Greensboro, N.C. The figure 10 years ago was 5%.

"Anyone who isn't licensing in children's sleepwear today is being hurt very badly," says Mr. Bates. His company, he says, holds 21 licenses, including, among the most popular, the Burger King Whopper.

The U.S. licensing industry dates back at least to the 1930s, when Walt Disney began selling the rights to some of his characters, and it has grown steadily, with a big expansion in the last few years. About $10 billion in retail products were sold in 1980 with the aid of licenses, with manufacturers paying about $500 million in royalties, according to the Licensing Letter, a trade publication.

A YOUTH MARKET

Arnold R. Bolka, publisher of the Licensing Letter, says more than 1,000 licensors or agents peddle licenses, and "tens of thousands" of companies use them. The majority of licensed products are for children and young adults—about a third of all licenses are for cartoons—but Mr. Bolka says the adult market has been growing, with the inclusion of such items as designer jeans.

St. Regis Paper Co., which concluded it needed to "add some excitement" to its otherwise "fairly prosaic" line of school, home and office products, tried licensing for the first time last year with Strawberry Shortcake. The license "had a tremendous impact in terms of our sales and our customers' sales," says Sanford G. Scheller, vice president and divisional general manager of the consumer products division. This year, St. Regis added Ziggy, Holly Hobbie, Mini-Page and Dungeons and Dragons licenses to its fold.

Licensable properties evolved from the success of popular characters or personalities. Nowadays, it is increasingly common for licensors to create new characters, and then create a demand for them. Strawberry Shortcake was just such a "test tube" licensing property.

With increasing frequency, the fates of some TV shows or motion pictures depend on whether they have characters or other material that are licensable. "There is no question people look at scripts for their licensing potential," says Lester Borden, vice president and general manager of Columbia Pictures Merchandising. Some producers will go so far as to have a marketer evaluate a movie's licensing potential before making a decision on whether to produce the movie, he adds.

Exercise 1

Brand Images: Marketing Creations

OBJECTIVES: 1. To demonstrate the interrelationship between marketing and consumer behavior.
2. To illustrate the impact of marketing efforts on the creation of brand images.

For both of the following products, describe your image of the brand's or product's uses and purposes. Then turn to the following pages, which present each product's present-day image and present ads, and its past image and past ads.

Listerine

Fleischmann's Yeast

1. Listerine was previously positioned as a solution for dandruff. Today Listerine is positioned as a mouthwash.
2. In the 1930s and 1940s, Fleischmann's Yeast proclaimed its many health benefits. For example, Fleischmann's Yeast was positioned as an aid to digestion and as a treatment for acne. This is in great contrast to Fleischmann's current position as an ingredient in the making of baked goods.

Reprinted with permission from Warner Lambert Company.

Sister, it can "BLITZ" you!

Start now with LISTERINE ANTISEPTIC

Those distressing flakes and scales can put you in plenty wrong socially, and can raise hob with the health of your scalp and the looks of your hair.

If you have the slightest symptom, better start now with Listerine Antiseptic and massage. It's easy. It's delightful. *And it treats the infection as infection should be treated... with quick germ-killing action.*

Kills "Bottle Bacillus"

Listerine Antiseptic kills mil-

lions of the "bottle bacillus" (Pityrosporum ovale) which many dermatologists say is a causative agent of the trouble.

Almost at once flakes and scales begin to disappear. Your scalp feels healthier and your hair looks healthier.

Listerine Antiseptic is the same antiseptic that has been famous for more than 60 years in the field of oral hygiene.

In a series of tests, 76% of dan-

druff sufferers showed complete disappearance of, or marked improvement in, the symptoms of dandruff after 4 weeks of twice-a-day Listerine Antiseptic treatment. Lambert Pharmacal Co., St. Louis, Missouri.

As a precaution ...
As a treatment ...

LISTERINE ANTISEPTIC and MASSAGE

IT'S NEW! Have you tasted the zippy MINT flavor of today's Listerine TOOTH PASTE with 27% more Lusterfoam?

Reprinted with permission from Warner Lambert Company.

Exercise 2

Market Segmentation

OBJECTIVES: 1. To demonstrate the use of market segmentation to satisfy consumer needs and wants.
2. To illustrate the application of the consumer orientation principle of the marketing concept.
3. To show the importance of the symbolic, intangible, and psychological components of products to consumers.

Analyze each of the following brands of toothpaste for (1) the objective and symbolic attributes that it highlights and (2) the consumer needs and benefits that it attempts to meet and fulfill for its target market.

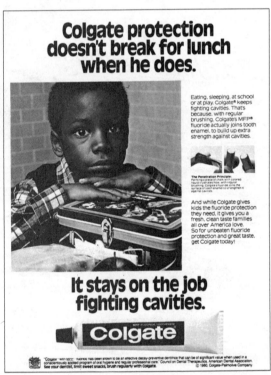

Reprinted with permission from Colgate-Palmolive Company.

Reprinted with permission of Lever Brothers, Co.

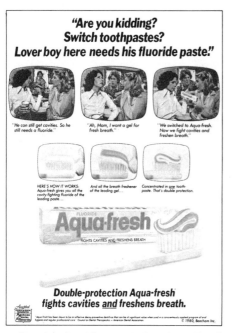

Reprinted with permission from Beecham Products.

Reprinted with permission of Lever Brothers, Co.

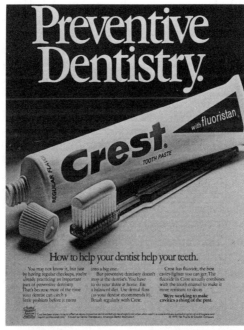

Courtesy of the Procter & Gamble Company.

2

Researching Consumer Behavior

Focus group interviews, consumer surveys, motivation research, laboratory experiments, intensive panel studies—marketers leave no stone unturned in their quest to understand consumer needs and desires. But finding out what the consumers want or need is not easy. Consumers may not be able to articulate their desires. In other cases, inhibitions may suppress the expression of true desires.

The following articles present a sampling of the breadth and depth of the research tools that marketers use to study consumer behavior. Some of the tools are qualitatively oriented, and others adopt a quantitative perspective. Both have their advantages and disadvantages. Their usefulness to consumer behavior research is complementary.

In the article "Long Lunch Produced the 'Greasies': Key Role of Research in Agree's Success Is Told," the role of research in every step of the development and marketing of Agree Shampoo and Agree Cream Rinse is told. Through the use of focus groups, concept studies, concept product studies, product testing, advertising testing, extended-use testing, a laboratory test market, and a test market, research identified the opportunity, helped define the target user, helped define the positioning and strategy, and helped define the attributes and features the product should have.

"Psyching Them Out," by Roger Ricklefs, discusses the application and controversy surrounding the use of motivational research techniques. Ernest Dichter, a leading practitioner of qualitative motivational research, explains, for example, that larger doorknobs are instrumental in selling homes because they provide a means to caress the house.

LONG LUNCH PRODUCED THE "GREASIES": KEY ROLE OF RESEARCH IN AGREE'S SUCCESS IS TOLD

"The most successful new product introduction in the history of Johnson Wax" was how two marketing research executives of the company (formally S. C. Johnson & Son, Racine, Wis.) referred to the debut of Agree Creme Rinse and Agree Shampoo.

The appraisal was made before the recent Midwest Research Conference sponsored by the AMA's Chicago Chapter. The joint presentation was made by Frederic D. Nordeen, marketing research manager, and Neil DeClerk, associate marketing research manager.

"Marketing research was involved every step of the way," Nordeen said, recalling that Agree Creme Rinse, launched

"Long Lunch Produced the 'Greasies': Key Role of Research in Agree's Success Is Told," *Marketing News,* January 12, 1979. Reprinted from *Marketing News,* published by the American Marketing Association.

in 1977, has taken a 20% share of the market for its category and is No. 1 in unit volume.

Agree Shampoo, for which advertising didn't start until last August, also is "on target and doing very well," DeClerk said.

Marketing research at Johnson Wax, Nordeen said, "helped identify the opportunity, define who our target user should be, define our positioning and strategy, and define the physical features and performance attributes" of the Agree products.

"As positions and strategies were fine-tuned, as formulas were developed, and as advertising was written, we tested to make sure that we stayed on track," DeClerk said.

"We did a lot of work. We fielded more than 50 individual research projects from late 1975 until national introduction of Agree Shampoo this past summer. There were focus groups, concept studies, concept product studies, product testing, advertising testing, extended use testing, a laboratory test market, and a test market.

"I can't tell you how much we spent, but two research suppliers retired. If Fred and I had been on commission, we wouldn't have to be here today," he said. "But we were serious, and we were thorough."

"Finally, when we were ready, we put it all together with finished product and a detailed marketing plan and we tested them—first in a laboratory test market, then in a controlled store test market," Nordeen said.

"Johnson Wax had been flirting with the personal care business since the mid-1960s, when a technical breakthrough led to Edge, a truly superior men's shaving cream," he said. "Today, Edge is a strong No. 2 brand in its field—and gaining.

"Edge, our first success, and even our personal care product failures, taught us two simple lessons:

1. "We could profitably market a personal care product possessing a 'product plus,' and
2. "We could *not* profitably market a 'me-too' product.

"This commitment to the 'product plus' philosophy by Johnson Wax means we will only market new products demonstrably superior to competitive ones and recognizable as such by consumers," he said.

"With Edge, we'd had our appetite whetted for the personal care business, and we wanted more.

"And, when we looked over the field, it quickly became apparent that women's hair care was an area of interest. It was big, growing, and it fit our R&D abilities and marketing skills. In 1970, we began to explore the area."

"Over the next three years, we explored and eliminated several hair care products," DeClerk said. "We considered:

1. "Hair dressings (the category wasn't growing),
2. "Hair coloring (we didn't have the technological base), and
3. "Hair sprays (but changes in style and practices were trending women away from hair sprays)."

"This left shampoos and creme rinse/conditioners, and work began in the early 1970s which has led to Agree Creme Rinse and now to Agree Shampoo," Nordeen said.

"Before we decided to develop these products, marketing research's part had been fairly passive. We were called upon to establish market sizes and trends and generally review the attitudes of users and nonusers. But, once targets were set, marketing research assumed a more active role."

"In 1971, before we had begun to concentrate on shampoo and creme rinse, a mail panel study of hair care practices was conducted among a large national probability sample of women," DeClerk said. "It provided a broad background of knowledge of hair care practices, characteristics of women's hair, and user and nonuser data.

"And it gave an early indication of some directions of change. Compared to some 1965 background data, it showed women were shampooing more frequently, were more likely to use creme rinses and conditioners, and to a greater extent than in the past, perceived themselves to have oily hair," DeClerk said. "Oiliness, the mail panel showed, was the No. 1 problem."

"Agree Shampoo and Agree Creme Rinse at first were on parallel development paths," Nordeen said. "Originally it had been planned that the shampoo come first, with the creme rinse to follow.

"But, since you can't always schedule R&D success and the creme rinse was ready before the shampoo, it was introduced first, in 1977, and quickly was a success."

Both products, DeClerk said, were targeted toward "greasies.

"How did we get to 'greasies'?

"We knew patterns were changing, oily hair was a problem, and more a problem among the young: the prime target, the most frequent users, and the most receptive to new ideas."

"In 1973 and 1974, we fine-tuned our approach to this market," Nordeen said. "We conducted many focus groups among all types of women, but increasingly we came to zero in on the young.

"This was a new experience for us at Johnson Wax. We were used to researching the attitudes and behavior of the housewife," he said.

"Now we needed to talk to her daughter, to understand teenage girls—some as young as 13—and reach them with both qualitative and quantitative research. This was a new (and more expensive) approach for us.

"Using focus groups to further our understanding of users' problems and perceptions—and also to get early reactions to some product concepts—we found that we were on the right path. The oiliness problems were major, and our ideas were regarded as important by the potential users."

"But," DeClerk said, "While the marketing research was telling us that we were working in interesting areas, R&D wasn't having as much luck.

"After many months of trying, it became apparent that the new technology just wasn't going to work for the shampoo, and we returned to ground zero.

"And, in a major disappointment, the Agree Creme Rinse formula failed to beat its major competitor in internal R&D testing. It was back to the drawing board."

"Then R&D came through on the creme rinse, developing a formula with no oil except for the fragrance, less than 0.25%," Nordeen said. "This made our communication to the consumer easier.

"It was during this time that (over a long lunch) 'Helps stops the greasies' was born."

So Agree Creme Rinse took the lead and ultimately would beat the shampoo to market. But shampoo development continued. It had its own R&D team and was making good progress toward a formula. Since Agree Creme Rinse had established the brand's positioning, shampoo work became more focused, DeClerk said.

"Early in 1975 we were into copy development," he said. "Some focus groups conducted at that time gave us our first exposure to our ultimate theme. These groups gave us insight into the virtues of several alternative 'reasons why' a shampoo would keep hair cleaner longer.

"They showed that users would be uncomfortable with heavy 'scientific' reasons. The communication task was really a simple one—to talk about cleaning.

"But, we certainly didn't stop with focus groups," he said. "We conducted quantified concept tests among target users."

The two researchers showed a "good example of a bad concept," an ad with "a laundry list of benefits, something for everyone. And it turned people off with 'special ingredients,'" DeClerk said.

Creative development now began in earnest, and the first of the commercials was written, Nordeen recalled. In the summer of 1975, the first shampoo commercial was rough produced and tested.

"At that time," he said, "we were on an early wording of our ultimate claim. We promised Agree would help keep hair cleaner longer. But after testing, it was back to writing copy.

"With the successful introduction of Agree Creme Rinse and its establishment of the term 'the greasies' as part of the language, our claim was modified to 'helps stop the greasies—between shampoos,'" Nordeen said. "Actually 17 new commercials have been tested using copy testing methods that offer us the best blend of measures of communication, motivation, and diagnostic help.

"We are finding, as time passes, that the motivation and communication scores are falling into predictable ranges, but that the diagnostic analysis of the ratings and open-end responses are providing valuable guidance. The commercials have been getting better as we learn more.

"By late 1975, the lab was making progress on the shampoo. A first formula was blind-tested against a target competitor and was significantly preferred," he said.

"This was the first of what ultimately was a series of more than 20 of these studies among 8,000 women—testing Agree and its formula refinements against the nine leading competitors, which were doing about 60% of all shampoo business. We were determined to have a 'product plus.'"

"Our test design used a blind-paired comparison among members of a mail panel," DeClerk said. "We placed products with 400 women and had them use each for two weeks. At the end of the use period, a telephone interview determined their preferences overall and their ratings on 15 to 20 performance attributes. And we asked open-end questions for supporting diagnostics."

Nordeen emphasized that they "early established the strategy for Agree Shampoo, defined our target, and consistently tested against the strategy. Product tests made sure the product delivered the right benefits to the right people—that the product was superior in the areas we claimed.

"Ad development and testing always made sure we were expressing our strategy well to those we wanted to reach. With all this behind us, we were ready to put the package together and get our first reactions to the total brand," he said.

"Up to now marketing research had been testing elements of the total product—performance positioning, advertising—but in the meantime product management was developing the marketing plan," DeClerk said.

"From now on our concern was mainly with the plan, not so much the individual pieces," he said.

The first real test of the plan, according to Nordeen, was a lab test market, a technique that simulates the awareness, trial, and repurchase sequences by using a finished commercial and final label product and by providing a shopping situation in a simulated store, actual use, and simulated repurchase.

"Various assumptions can be made for levels of distribution, levels of ad effectiveness in building awareness, variations in the purchase cycle, and effects on trial of different sampling plans. We find it a valuable tool to test the effects of different combinations of marketing assumptions. We have confidence mainly because of a good track record with the model," Nordeen said.

"For example, our model predicted Agree Creme Rinse's test market share almost dead on and was only slightly lower than the ultimate national share.

"Then, because we sweetened the national plan to include more media and more sampling, we got better distribution than we'd fed into the program. In fact, when the model was rerun with results from our national introduction it came within a point of the real share."

"The Agree Shampoo lab test market was conducted in Fresno, Calif., and South Bend, Ind., two of the markets in which Agree Creme Rinse had been test marketed," DeClerk said.

"By using these cities, where the first Agree had been sold for more than a year, we were able to simulate the real-world time lapse between the introductions. This was key, since much of the shampoo's story and its appeal would play off the creme rinse's image.

"Frankly, we were nervous," he said. "We had committed more money to Agree Creme Rinse than to any other product we'd introduced, and now we were planning to go even further out on the limb with shampoo.

"But, we needn't have worried. The model predicted a share which met the objectives of the marketing plan. We got good trial based on advertising. We had good repurchase and retention rates. Our

sampling program worked. And the model let us test various mixes of two different size samples.

"We wound up using a lower-cost sample in a mass co-op mailing, reserving a more expensive 2-oz. trial-size bottle for individual mailings to smaller numbers of identified target users.

"We had a 'go' for our national plan," DeClerk said.

"But, we're a cautious bunch," Nordeen said. "The women had only used the product for four weeks. Maybe they'd tire of it. Maybe there were some negatives. Maybe the basic promise, 'Helps stop the greasies between shampoos,' would lose its appeal.

"So, just before we started the lab test market, we began an extended-use study. We went back to Fresno and South Bend, the markets where Agree Creme Rinse had been test marketed, and we placed fully labeled, market-ready product.

"We placed the product with women who had read a print ad describing Agree Shampoo and who were willing to pay real money to buy a bottle.

"These women were meant to simulate real-world triers. They understood the promise. They were motivated to buy and presumably would use the product with the same expectations as real-world trier would," Nordeen said.

"These women were called back at four-week intervals over 16 weeks and re-supplied with product during the test if they wished to continue.

"There were very few who dropped out—hardly any for product-related reasons. They rated the product at each of the four callbacks on a long list of attributes.

"The ratings never varied; the actual ounces used were measured, and there was no slowdown in use. No long-term negatives showed up; the brand even seemed to gain strength as time went by.

"Now we were ready for test market," DeClerk said. "Actually, we'd begun planning the test market months before—even before the lab test market. But the good lab test market results gave us the green light to spend quite a bit of money on bottle and cap molds and on making and filling equipment.

"But, we couldn't be ready for test market until late summer or early fall of 1977," he said.

"Caution told us not to start a test market late in the fall. Previous experience with holiday season test marketing made us wary, and we elected to start a test market in January, 1978."

"We had faced a basic decision months before on what kind of test market we needed—on what the test market objectives were," Nordeen said.

"Our decision was easy. We had a sales success with Agree Creme Rinse and we knew we'd have no trouble getting distribution of Agree Shampoo. So sales ability wasn't the question; there was no need to sell in.

"What we needed was carefully to measure consumer response to the execution of the marketing plan. Therefore," he said, "we elected to conduct a controlled store test."

"For a change," DeClerk said, "we had some time to plan. The delay from fall, 1977, to January, 1978, allowed us to gather good base data and to use it to specify store patterns of shelf location, facings, prices, and promotional support.

"In effect, we went—store by store—through the stores we were going to audit and executed in each store what the response to the Agree Shampoo marketing plan would likely be.

"We even built some inefficiencies into our test market," he said. "For example, not all stores had both sizes of all types, and not all stores participate in promotions. So, in effect, we were simulating trade response to the market plan."

"The proposed national plan was translated to test market in South Bend and Fresno," Nordeen said. "Because we were in a controlled store test we got instant distribution, and the ad and promotion timetable could begin on the same day we stocked shelves.

"During the test market we duplicated the gross-rating-point (GRP) levels of the national television plan. We simulated magazine coupon ads via newspaper inserts. We dropped co-op samples to the proper number of households. And we mailed single trial-size bottles to a list of the younger target users.

"We were careful not to overkill. We were interested in the true share, not how high we could make it," Nordeen said.

"We test marketed in the two Agree Creme Rinse test markets because the shampoo and creme rinse are companions and we needed to test the shampoo in a mature creme rinse situation. We had food, drug, and mass merchandiser stores in our panel, and we ran a tightly controlled test," DeClerk said.

"In all of these stores, we maintained a specified shelf location, a specified price, a specified item array, and a specified number of facings," he said. "Each store was visited regularly, some as often as three times a week, to insure that the plan was being followed."

"Store audits," Nordeen said, "were conducted and reported monthly, with adjustments made to compensate for the 100% distribution of the audit panel and for the super-efficiency of controlled store shelf management.

"The reduction factor we use for 'controlled store effect' is 15% (that is, 85% of the volume achieved in this special situation). This number, we have found, accurately reflects this special attention," Norder said.

DeClerk added that the test market was not only a vehicle for measuring sales and share but also enabled the company to test elements of the marketing plan on the firing line.

"We conducted qualitative studies among both purchasers and nonpurchasers as well as quantitative studies to measure how many and what kind of households got our sample and how many went on to purchase.

"We measured rates of awareness and trial at 8, 13, and 26 weeks, and we probed for the attitudes toward the advertising and the product. In each of these studies we were measuring performance against an objective, a goal detailed in the marketing plan," he said.

"The net of all of our test market experience was positive," said Nordeen. "We achieved our share goals, our rates of awareness and trial were satisfactory, and our sampling worked. We were ready to go. And we did.

"In our first year, we will spend more than $30 million in advertising, sampling, couponing, trade deals, and public relations," he said. There's a lot riding on Agree Shampoo, but early results are favorable.

"We got excellent distribution very early and the product is moving off the shelves at the rate we expected. We're confident we have a success."

"Marketing research will have had a real part in the success of Agree Shampoo. We helped identify the opportunity, helped define the target user, helped define the positioning and strategy, and helped define the attributes and features the product should have," DeClerk said.

"Finally we tested the marketing plan. We did all of these things, maybe not in as neat an order as in the textbooks, but we did them."

PSYCHING THEM OUT: ERNEST DICHTER THRIVES SELLING FIRMS RESEARCH ON "HIDDEN EMOTIONS"

"All right, now pretend you're a typewriter," the researcher tells a young typist.

The woman flings herself on the floor, lies on her back and stretches out her arms.

"Are you a man or a woman?" asks the researcher.

"A woman."

"What are you doing?" the man asks.

"I'm waiting for somebody to type on me," she replies.

To some people, this may seem like simply a bizarre exercise in play acting, but to Ernest Dichter, a pioneer in motivational research, it is full of significance. It suggests that many office workers sub-

consciously consider typewriters not as mundane machines but rather as passive "receiving" objects, he says. "Type me, fly me, it's the same idea," Mr. Dichter maintains.

Interviews and testing show that many typists really want to regard their typewriters as "feminine" and yielding objects, Mr. Dichter claims. Following these interpretations, a major typewriter producer is planning a model with a "more concave keyboard in a receiving configuration," the 65-year-old psychologist adds.

Such research is a typical task for Mr. Dichter, who has spent a career influencing the advertising you see and the purchases you make. As a leader of the "qualitative" school of motivational research, he believes that the real reason people buy one product over another is often a deep-seated emotion. Only probing the consumer's psyche in depth will reveal it, he thinks.

DOORKNOBS AND SOCK DRAWERS

Why do big doorknobs help sell a house? Why do some men become irrationally hostile when their sock drawers are empty? Such are the questions that intrigue researchers like Mr. Dichter.

Some critics condemn this whole psychological approach as devious manipulation of the buyer's emotions and sexual instincts. They say, too, that if Mr. Dichter's theories were ever conclusively confirmed business would de-emphasize product quality and simply rely on psychological appeals to sell goods. Engineers, production managers, traditional marketing people and many others in business would consequently find their own importance diminished, these critics think. In a different vein of criticism, many advertising research men think Mr. Dichter's samples are simply too small and his methods too subjective to yield reliable results.

"Dichter's ideas are just fascinating, but to call his sort of studies scientific research, I'd have to be nuts. I just don't take the guy's work seriously," says one advertising research executive. Others say his theories are simply nonsense.

Yet the maverick methods have made Mr. Dichter a fortune. "I have $2 million now, so I guess that makes me a millionaire, at least a small one," he says cheerily.

Indeed, even critics conceded that after a slump during the 1960s, the psychological research that Mr. Dichter favors now is enjoying a revival. One big reason, they say, is simply that this research is comparatively cheap. Whatever the case, in the past two or three years Du Pont, Alcoa, General Mills, Procter & Gamble, Colgate-Palmolive, Johnson & Johnson, Schenley Industries and dozens of other well-known companies have commissioned studies from Mr. Dichter's Institute for Motivational Research. The institute has annual volume of $600,000 and profits of $80,000 to $100,000.

"DO YOU REMEMBER WHEN . . . ?"

Mr. Dichter started his unusual career shortly after he and his wife emigrated from Vienna in 1938. Arriving in New York with a doctorate in psychology from the University of Vienna and $100 in cash, he got a job in market research. He says he soon became disillusioned with the traditional approach.

"I found that if you simply ask people directly why they bought a given car, they'll usually give you about the same answer—regardless of the car," he says. Everybody likes to think he is acting on a sensible reason like "low depreciation."

So Mr. Dichter soon began working on his own, and in 1946 he opened the Institute for Motivational Research. He also began to develop indirect methods of inquiry. In one early study, he hypothesized that people attach great importance to their first car. It is a "puberty symbol" signifying that "at last you can get away from your parents and be on your own," he says.

The findings led to a Plymouth advertising campaign that played up the theme, "Do you still remember when . . . ?" The ads showed an old car and linked it with the new Plymouth models. Plymouth was "very satisfied" with the results of the campaign, a Chrysler Corp. spokesman says.

In a study for the American Red Cross blood donor program, interviews conveyed the fear among men that if they gave blood they would be "emptied out" and drained of their virility. "When we asked them how much blood they would lose in the process, some thought it would be half a gallon or more," Mr. Dichter recalls.

Then researchers showed these male respondents a picture of a man standing erect and of another man standing in a stooped, wilted position. The men overwhelmingly identified the stooped individual with giving blood, again corroborating the fear that being a blood donor threatens potency, Mr. Dichter recalls.

Of course, blood banks take only a pint of blood, and the body normally reconstitutes the loss rapidly. "But," says Mr. Dichter, "there is clearly a psychological relationship between semen and blood—a feeling that blood is a special fluid." Largely because they're unafraid of impotence, women are much braver about giving blood than men, he maintains.

Many people find such interpretations far-fetched. But people who accept the basic beliefs of modern psychologists find them quite plausible. Mr. Dichter recommended that blood-donation centers stress the idea that giving blood is a "manly" thing to do. "By lending blood, you are really in a way fertilizing, giving life to many other people, he suggested.

CARESSING A HOUSE

The psychologist also found that even a commonplace object like a doorknob has a surprising emotional significance to buyers. "The doorknob offers the only way you can caress a house; you can't caress the walls," he says. "The way a product fills a hand is very important. How a handle does this will make an engineer prefer one technical product over another—and he doesn't even realize it," Mr. Dichter says.

During part of a baby's embryonic development, the thumb fills the palm of the hand, Mr. Dichter says. The new-born infant thus exhibits a strong desire to grasp objects, possibly to fill the palm of the hand again, the psychologist adds. As he sees it, the same instinct later prompts a subconscious tendency to judge a house by its doorknob or a tool by its handle. Mr. Dichter says those findings and theories prompted a California lockmaker to enlarge the doorknobs it manufactured.

Even men's socks can inspire passion, Mr. Dichter asserts. "We find that any empty sock drawer is a symbol of an empty heart," Mr. Dichter said in a study for Du Pont's hosiery section. "When the husband finds that his sock drawer is not overflowing, he interprets his wife's neglect as symptomatic of her lack of consideration, concern and love."

Consumers often don't recognize the "emotional significance" of products they buy, Mr. Dichter says. Most men prefer a strong aftershave lotion and offer a rational explanation for this choice, such as a desire to "close the pores," he says. The real reason, he claims, is that most men subconsciously consider shaving a symbolic emasculation. Therefore, they want to submit themselves to a mild degree of physical pain in order to reassert their virility, Mr. Dichter would have you believe.

While subconscious emotions can affect preferences for products, they also can distort perception of reality, Mr. Dichter claims. For instance, Institute interviews show that housewives quite commonly think it takes 25 to 30 minutes to go through a supermarket checkout line, he says. (It actually averages about three minutes.) "The supermarket is the childhood dream; everything seems free—until you get to the woman who takes the money," he explains. "While standing in the checkout line, one is really waiting to be punished, so it seems like a long time" he adds with a straight face.

CASKETS WITH LOCKS

In a study for Forest Lawn Cemetery in Los Angeles, Mr. Dichter found that often the bereaved subconsciously don't fully accept the death and have a strong desire to deny its reality. "People prefer large plots so that the deceased will have room to move about," he maintains. Moreover, many mourners have a strong preference for caskets with locks. "Many people fear that the dead will get out," Mr. Dichter says.

More than 4,000 studies such as these have made Mr. Dichter's Institute the most famous organization in its field and one of the largest. With a full-time staff of 50, the Institute operates offices in Germany and Switzerland as well as here.

The Institute charges $10,000 to $60,000 for a complete study, depending largely on the amount of interviewing the client wants. However, pilot studies using a sample of under 100 people may cost as little as $3,000. If you want a consultation with Mr. Dichter himself, it will cost $1,500 to $2,000 a day, compared with $600 to $750 five years ago.

Last year, Mr. Dichter sold the Institute to Lehigh Valley Industries Inc., a conglomerate based in New York, but he remains as president. He indicates that with salary, book royalties and other income, he earns well over $50,000 a year.

Mr. Dichter says money is a big factor in motivating his own behavior. (Can't we make that another couple hundred? he says, haggling enthusiastically with a client over a fee that already exceeded $3,000.) Mr. Dichter recalls: "I was very poor in my childhood, so I still suffer from insecurity. My wife, who comes from a middle-class family and is much more secure, is always asking me when I will stop worrying about going hungry."

Mr. Dichter says he had to quit school at age 14 to help support his family. "My father was a traveling salesman. He never got any where in life and was against my studies," he adds.

Continuing his academic life on the side, Mr. Dichter worked as a window dresser, secretary and tailor, tried writing novels and poetry and at one point, even wrote an advice-to-the-lovelorn column for an Austrian Catholic housewives' magazine. At another stage, he worked as a private tutor and taught French to the pupil's parents during their dinner. "That way, I got a free meal too," he recalls. Eventually, Mr. Dichter became fascinated with psychology, earned his doctorate and was on his way.

"HIDDEN PERSUADERS"?

Mr. Dichter has attracted voluminous criticism, especially from those who lambast him as the archtypical "hidden persuader" who plays on our emotions. "I will admit that we are utilizing the promise of self-enhancement," answers Mr. Dichter. "You want to call it sex? All right, you're welcome to it!" He claims that not more than 5% of his recommendations are based primarily on sex. "But if sex plays a role, I'm not a prude. Sex is here to stay—I hope," he says.

"Besides, none of my techniques is 'hidden.' I've written books on them," he adds. "The half-way intelligent customer knows he is being sold. We're not holding a gun to the customer's head. I don't feel bad, and I don't think I'm using any below-the-belt techniques," he says.

Others fault Mr. Dichter's methods. "The American market is just too diverse to yield results on a small sample," says Alvin A. Achenbaum, senior vice president for marketing services (including research) at J. Walter Thompson Co., the advertising agency.

Mr. Achenbaum also thinks the heavily psychological approach is excessively subjective. "You get three different psychologists, and you get three different answers," he contends. "In my opinion, if you can't attach a number to a relationship, you haven't said anything about it."

Mr. Achenbaum concedes that Dichter-style or "qualitative" research is growing considerably, but this is because there have been both a recession and a "tremendous inflation in research costs," he says. "Everybody tried to save a buck, so qualitative work has grown," he says. "A quantitative survey with 2,000 interviews can cost $80,000 or $90,000, but for $1,500 an (advertising) agency can put together a 40-page report. So you figure it out," he says. "Until a guy gets burned, it's very popular."

A quantitative study relies on a large sample and heavy use of statistical analysis. To take a simple example, researchers might ask 2,000 consumers to rate factors they consider important in a coffeepot, such as the richness of the coffee produced, the ease of operation, and the reputation of the maker.

This method allows researchers to test a large, scientifically chosen cross-section of a given market. But Mr. Dichter thinks the direct question approach is inadequate because consumers themselves often don't understand the underlying psychological factors that, he contends, really make them buy the product.

The "qualitative" research that Mr. Dichter favors depends on "depth" or "quality" in a small number of interviews. In a typical study, the Institute conducts about 100 initial interviews, each running from around 30 minutes to an hour, says Charles Wortham, a senior project director. Then the Institute gives psychological tests to another 100 or more consumers to verify the findings, he adds.

Though the samples are comparatively small, many businessmen find the studies get useful results. Take Du Pont's hosiery section, which has commissioned two Institute studies in the past several years. "In both cases we also used complicated statistical research, and in both cases the statistics confirmed Dr. Dichter's findings," says Frank G. Oswald, the section's advertising manager. (Many companies use both quantitative and qualitative studies.)

But the statistical studies, which cost three or four times as much, were far more difficult to understand, the Du Pont official adds. "Besides, we've definitely gotten insights from Dr. Dichter's studies that we just wouldn't get from statistics," he says.

Exercise 3

Motivation Research

OBJECTIVE: To provide a "taste" and "feeling" for qualitative research.

In this exercise you are asked to use a projection instrument, the Thematic Apperception Test (TAT). First look at the picture below for 15 seconds. Then turn the page and write an anonymous identification number on the page and write the story that the picture suggests.

Just look at the picture briefly (ten to fifteen seconds), and write the story it suggests.

Instruction to writer: Write the story the picture suggests to you below.

Writer's Identification Number _____

Upon completion of the story, your instructor will collect the papers and randomly distribute them to the members of the class.

Instructions to interpreter: What can you say about the writer of the story you have received? What types of products and brands would this writer own? Write your reactions and interpretations below.

Interpreter's Identification Number _____

Upon completion of your interpretations and reactions, your instructor will collect the papers and return them to the writer.

Just look at the picture briefly (ten to fifteen seconds), and write the story it suggests.

Instruction to writer: Write the story the picture suggests to you below.

Writer's Identification Number _____

Upon completion of the story, your instructor will collect the papers and randomly distribute them to the members of the class.

Instructions to interpreter: What can you say about the writer of the story you have received? What types of products and brands would this writer own? Write your reactions and interpretations below.

Interpreter's Identification Number _____

Upon completion of your interpretations and reactions, your instructor will collect the papers and return them to the writer.

Exercise 4

Laboratory Research

OBJECTIVE: To provide an opportunity to conduct quantitative behavioral research.

This exercise requires you to carry out an experiment to determine the extent to which consumers taste with their eyes.

MATERIALS NEEDED FOR THIS EXPERIMENT

1. Commercial chocolate pudding mix.
2. Food coloring.
3. Sampling cups.
4. Tasting spoons.

PROCEDURE

1. Make the package(s) of chocolate pudding according to the package directions.
2. Divide the pudding into three separate bowls.
3. Leave the first bowl as is. To the second bowl add a brown food coloring. To the third bowl add a darker brown food coloring. (Brown food coloring can be made by mixing blue, red, and yellow.) The puddings are labeled C, M, and D. respectively.

COLLECTING THE DATA

1. Present consumers with a sample cup of each of the three puddings simultaneously. They should be labeled C, M, and D.
2. Ask the consumers to taste the pudding cups and answer the questionnaire.

Collection of the data may be accomplished with groups of consumers or on a one-to-one basis. Sampling may be nonprobability or probability.

ANALYSIS OF THE RESULTS

1. Collect the questionnaires.
2. Tabulate the results.
3. Rank order the following:
   a. Question 1: Consumers' preference for the pudding samples
   _____ _____ _____
   b. Question 2: Consumers' perception of the chocolateness of the pudding samples _____ _____ _____
   c. Question 3: Consumers' judgment of the smoothness of the pudding samples
   _____ _____ _____
   d. Question 4: Consumers' judgment of the consistency of the pudding samples
   _____ _____ _____
   e. Question 5: Consumers' texture preference of the pudding samples
   _____ _____ _____
   f. Question 6: Consumers' buying intentions _____ _____ _____

More advanced analysis such as chi square is appropriate.

INTERPRETATION OF THE RESULTS

1. Does the color of the pudding influence the consumers' perception for the pudding? chocolateness? smoothness? consistency? texture? or buying intentions?
2. Discuss the marketing implications of the results of your study.

QUESTIONNAIRE

We are testing consumer acceptance of three types of chocolate pudding. Please taste the three pudding samples and answer the following questions. Circle the response that applies.

1. Which of the pudding samples do you prefer?

    M   D   C

2. Which pudding sample tastes more chocolaty?

    M   D   C

3. Which pudding sample tastes smoother?

    M   D   C

4. Which pudding sample has greater consistency?

    M   D   C

5. Which pudding sample has the best texture?

    M   D   C

6. If these puddings were all priced the same, which would you buy?

    M   D   C

3

Economic and Demographic Influences on Consumption

The demographic structure and economic trends of the nation significantly influence consumer behavior and marketing strategy. Consumer spending power is heavily determined by the nation's economic climate, and demographic variables define the markets' structure. The articles in this section illustrate the impact of demographic and economic variables on consumer behavior and marketing strategy formation.

One of the most significant demographic trends in the United States is the aging of the "baby boom" children, those children born shortly after World War II until the mid-1960s. These baby boom children currently make up about one-fifth of the American population and are the largest age group in the United States. As they move into the 35 to 44 age group in the next ten years, they promise to cause a bulge in big spending. The marketing implications of the aging postwar babies is the subject of the article, "The Over-the-Thrill Crowd."

Economists and psychological economists agree that what consumers do unquestionably has enormous impact on the economy. However, they disagree on the importance of understanding what consumers think. Psychological economists believe that surveying consumers' attitudes is necessary to understanding and forecasting the economy, whereas economists do not. The growing influence and controversy of including surveys of consumers' attitudes to understand and accurately forecast the economy are discussed in the article "The Economist Who Polls Consumers."

31

THE OVER-THE-THRILL CROWD

Age, alas, has caught up with the kids of the baby boom. Now, one in every three Americans are products of the population surge that began right after World War II and lasted until the mid-1960s. According to the Conference Board, a blue-ribbon business research body, the aging of this generation "will be the single most important economic stimulant of the 1980s."

The oldest of these postwar children are already 34, and over the next ten years they will cause a bulge in the big-spending 35 to 44 group. The number of Americans in this bracket will jump from 28 million to 40 million by the end of the decade, and they will be pocketing $1 out of every $4 in personal income, up from $1 of every $5 at present. By 1990, the average household income for people in this group will be close to $30,000 in real terms, and their total spending power will have grown by 70%. Because of their numbers and affluence, the aging baby boomers are being avidly courted by sellers of all sorts of goods and services. Says William Hull, research director for the J. Walter Thompson ad agency: "Anything that people in this group does is hot, and companies are therefore riding along with them into middle age."

They are entering an age when their outlays normally will be heavy because they will be buying and outfitting homes and educating their children. But this typical spending will be even more exuberant because the baby boomers are themselves the children of inflation, born with credit cards in their mouths and oriented toward spending rather than saving. They are part of the instant-gratification, self-indulgent Me generation, which has a taste for high-priced gadgets and little interest in self-denial.

The increased spending of the 35 to 44 group is expected to give a mighty lift to such key segments of the economy as housing, furniture, appliances, apparel, autos and financial services. Already this group spends 50% more than the average consumer for furniture and one-third more for appliances. John Widdicomb Co., a top-of-the-line furniture manufacturer, has increased its advertising to attract these people, while Chicago's John M. Smyth Co. retail furniture chain has expanded its interior decorating services to appeal to the more sophisticated customer entering early middle age.

Ford Motor Co. managers estimate that the 35 to 44 age group, with its interest in outdoor leisure pursuits, buys 25% of all vans and pickups. These consumers want fuel-efficient cars—but also fancy extras like air conditioning and stereo. Says Louis W. Stern, marketing professor at Northwestern University: "That age group wants the outward visible

things that say, 'I have made it and I want to live comfortably.'"

These people are major users of credit, taking out mortgages to acquire their bigger houses and urban condominiums and installment loans to furnish them. Maurice Mann, vice chairman of A. G. Becker, a brokerage firm, has warned savings and loan officials to anticipate "massive demand" for mortgage lending in the 1980s "as a result of the postwar babies seeking shelter." Insurance executives are looking at the group as an ever expanding market for homeowners' and life policies. Bankers are catering to their desire for convenience by opening more and more centers that can manage all aspects of a customer's personal finances.

As the baby-boom generation is growing older, the youth cult is gradually fading. Says J. Walter Thompson's Hull: "Ten years ago, everyone wanted to be young, but now people just want to stay active and attractive." Tennis clubs, exercise salons and racquetball courts are proliferating, largely because physical fitness has become a priority, not to say mania,

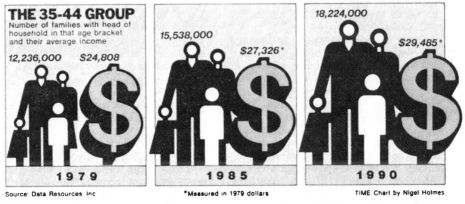

THE 35-44 GROUP
Number of families with head of household in that age bracket and their average income

12,236,000 $24,808   **1979**

15,538,000 $27,326*   **1985**

18,224,000 $29,485*   **1990**

Source: Data Resources Inc   *Measured in 1979 dollars   TIME Chart by Nigel Holmes

Reprinted by permission from *Time,* The Weekly Newsmagazine; Copyright Time Inc., 1979.

with yesterday's youth. Reports Denise Bourcq, manager of Chicago's Gloria Marshall Figure Salon: "The majority of women we see are between 30 and 45." Even Geritol, that elixir of the sunset years, has aimed for some time now at a younger, still attractive woman who wants to hold on to her health.

Some more mature faces are showing up in ads to match the aging of the audience. Revlon's Lauren Hutton wonders in magazine ads what to do about her skin now that she is over 30 (her answer: use Ultima II creams), and the One-A-Day vitamin girl is no longer a teen but a woman pushing 30.

Companies are bringing out new products or repositioning existing ones specifically for these older consumers. Says Roy Johns Jr., a vice president at Levi Strauss & Co.: "As the baby-boom kids continue up the age ladder, either we will go with them or somebody else will." Thus Levi's has already sold some 15 million pairs of new, wider jeans "cut to fit a man's build with a little more room in the seat and thigh," as the ads say. The jeans have spawned a whole rack of clothes for the aging male body, ravaged by roast beef and gravity.

Mattel, the California toy company, is trying to hang on to the kids who have mellowed into grownups. Its Barbie doll has been joined by a line of electronic toys for adults. The $500 Intellivision, a computer that plugs into a TV set, will play roulette, compute income taxes and do estate planning. Winemakers are also preparing to reap a rich harvest as the Pepsi generation trades its aluminum pop tops for corkscrews. By 1985 domestic wine is projected to be a $6 billion industry, up from $3 billion today. "Sales of the better wines can only be described as spectacular," says Alin Gruber, senior vice president of Sonoma Vineyards, "and the most important reason for it is that people who started with pop wines are moving up."

It is precisely this advance to more sophistication and affluence, as well as sheer numbers, that will make the 35 to 44 age group such a potent force in the economy of the 1980s. People with products to sell are getting the message: Age—at least early middle age—is more attractive than youth.

THE ECONOMIST WHO POLLS CONSUMERS

The way many economists see it, what consumers *do* unquestionably has enormous impact on the economy, but what consumers *think* is another matter. The practice of measuring consumer attitudes is not held in especially high regard within the profession. The Commerce Department does not even include "consumer sentiment" among its dozen leading economic indicators—much to the dismay of Jay Schmiedeskamp, who, as director of Consumer Attitudes at the University of Michigan's Survey Research Center, has made a career of probing the consumer's psyche.

Nonetheless, Schmiedeskamp is enjoying a considerable triumph these days.

Reprinted with the special permission of *Dunn's Review,* April 1976, Copyright 1976, Dunn & Bradstreet Publications Corporation.

Although the economics establishment continues to give him the brush-off, he and his colleagues have been winning greater respect among businessmen, politicians and journalists. Currently, some 100 subscribers—including banks, brokerage houses and major companies—shell out $800 and up a year for the consumer surveys put together by Schmiedeskamp and his staff.

Schmiedeskamp's eminence goes back to the fall of 1973. While most economists were predicting a short and shallow slump to be followed quickly by a robust recovery, his surveys were showing that the confidence of consumers in the ability of government to contain inflation was tumbling at an alarming rate. Convinced that consumers would hoard their dollars under those circumstances, he forecast a recession.

"PSYCHOLOGICAL ECONOMICS"

The painful accuracy of that prediction proved to be a vindication not only of Schmiedeskamp but of George Katona, the imaginative scholar who pioneered consumer surveying and helped found the Michigan Center thirty years ago. Now in semiretirement, Katona carries the title of economist-in-residence at the center. A refugee from Nazi-occupied Europe, Katona carried out an investigation for the U.S. government during World War II to find out what Americans would do with their war bonds—cash them in or hold them—once the war was over. In so doing, he created his own discipline: "psychological economics."

What Katona's theory comes down to is this: Conventional economists acknowledge that in building an econometric model (a mathematical computer picture) to forecast how the economy is going to behave, it is essential to feed into the formula data on such *quantifiable* items as consumers' personal income and tax schedules; but Katona maintains that simply knowing how much money consumers have in their pockets does not tell the economist whether or not it will be spent. Important questions are left open, he argues. For example: If consumers fear that the rate of inflation is going to accelerate within the next year, will they rush out and buy new television sets now before prices go up, creating excess demand that actually contributes to the inflation they fear? Or will they put off the purchase of TV sets indefinitely, save their money to cover the higher prices ahead for food and other essentials and, by not spending, precipitate a recession?

The only way to find out, says Katona, is to ask consumers themselves. Thus, four times a year, the center dispatches interviewers into communities stretching from Eugene, Oregon, to New Paltz, New York, to talk to 1,500 consumers representing economic strata from ancestral wealth to ghetto poor—and also including the *nouveau* poor, as the middle class unemployed have come to be known. They ask such questions as: Are you better off now than you were a year ago? Do you think you will be better off a year from now? Will the country in general have good times or bad times in the next twelve months? Is the next twelve months a good time to buy a new car? Is the government doing a good job with its economic policy? Do you think interest rates will go up?

Back in Ann Arbor, Schmiedeskamp and a dozen or so colleagues compute a consumer sentiment index with the aid of a simple formula. The percentage of pessimistic answers is subtracted from the percentage of optimistic replies; the number 100 is added to prevent the answer from being a negative number, which would be awkward to work with. If 50% of the replies are optimistic and 50% are pessimistic, the index is 100. The natural mood of the country is apparently at least a shade on the glum side, because the norm over the years has been about 95.

One practical application of the index is that it turns out to be a useful guide to what is likely to happen in the stock market. Although the connection has only been recognized for the past two or three years, fluctuations in the index since 1952 have corresponded so closely to the price changes of Standard & Poor's industrial average that a peak and subsequent sharp decline in the index is likely to foretell that stock prices are about to peak and fall as well. "The connection is a logical one," notes Joseph H. Ellis, vice president in the investment research department of Goldman, Sachs & Co. "If you are sampling consumers, you are also sampling the 78 million people in the labor force, and they often sense a decline in economic activity because of such things as layoffs and less overtime several months in advance of a market decline."

Among the subscribers to the Michigan survey are such major producers of durable goods as General Electric, Ford, General Motors and RCA. For $800 a year, subscribers receive the consumer index score after each quarterly survey and a lengthy written evaluation of what the data mean. For an additional $400 and up a year, they are entitled to personal consultation with Schmiedeskamp to get deeper analyses on how intensely consumers feel about particular issues. Discovering the passions that underlie the answers, Schmiedeskamp believes, is the essence of consumer surveying. As questionnaires flow in from the field, he pores over them with the enthusiasm of a detective-story fan, seeking out words, phrases and patterns of logic—or illogic: one respondent assumed that because the housing industry was distressed, he could buy a home at a bargain—that will serve as clues to how consumers think and thus how they are likely to behave.

As noted, despite the surge of interest in consumer surveying, many economists—particularly academic and government economists—have serious reservations about its value. For one thing, they charge that consumer surveyors are inclined to exaggerate their findings and make doomsday predictions because gloom is marketable. They also believe that consumer surveying has not added as much to the sum of knowledge as it once seemed to promise. Finally, since interpreting the data is an art, not a science, the results cannot be easily fitted into an econometric model, a decided deficit in an era when modeling is the preeminent means of forecasting.

Still, Schmiedeskamp has a follow-ing among some of the country's most influential business leaders, including Henry Ford II.

MONEY AND NUMBERS

Schmiedeskamp concedes that surveys could dig deeper into consumer attitudes and provide more information, but says that he is limited by his budget. Each additional minute of time it takes to complete a questionnaire adds as much as $3,200 to the cost of the survey in interviewers' wages alone.

The charge that Schmiedeskamp finds most frustrating is that surveying consumer sentiment is incompatible with econometrics. "This profession is completely carried away with numbers," he complains, his voice rising with irritation. He insists that he is not an opponent of econometrics but that it provides only half the answer and must be joined with psychological economics if forecasting is to become truly reliable. "The marriage of the two is my ultimate aim," says Schmiedeskamp.

Until that happy day, Schmiedeskamp will probably remain on the periphery of the economics establishment—even, it appears, at the University of Michigan. Although technically a part of the university, the center is financed separately, out of its own earnings, and is located on a commercial street two blocks away from the main campus.

Schmiedeskamp is convinced that in time his fellow economists will come to recognize that it is impossible to anticipate the future without consulting consumers. "The difference between the opinions of economists and the opinions of consumers is that, by saving or spending, consumers can make *their* forecasts come true," he sums up dryly. Until his fellow economists do come around to that way of thinking, Schmiedeskamp does have at least one consolation: When it came to calling one of the most important economic events of the decade, he was right and they were wrong.

Exercise 5

Marketing to Changing Americans

OBJECTIVE: To show the interrelationships that exist between demographic structure and consumer behavior by:
1. Demonstrating the changes in the American demographic structure, and
2. Marketers' responses to these changes.

The following advertisements are marketing responses to changes in American demographics. For each set of advertisements for each product, indicate (1) the changes in the positioning of the product, and (2) the demographic trend that is implied.

Reprinted with permission from Johnson & Johnson Baby Products Company.

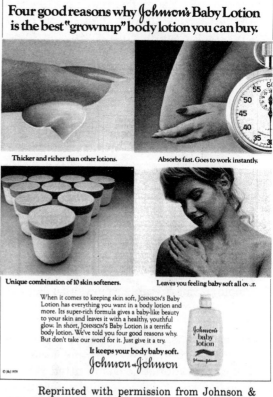

Reprinted with permission from Johnson & Johnson Baby Products Company.

We discovered a recipe that helps Molly get more of the iron she needs...

...just mix Gerber rice cereal with apple juice.

Like each of the more than 30 million babies we've helped feed since we began, Molly needs iron. And we've found a particularly good-tasting way to help see that she gets more of it.

Gerber Rice Cereal has always been a good iron supplement for breast and bottle-fed babies. But we know that babies can absorb more iron when the cereal is mixed with vitamin C fortified baby juice (like Gerber apple juice), instead of milk or water. It's a complex biological effect, and one that took years of study to identify. But Molly thinks the result is great tasting. And when Molly is happy and healthy...well, we're happy, too.

Gerber
Babies are our business...
and have been for over 50 years.
Gerber Products Company, Fremont, MI 49412

We've learned a lot about food because we care a lot about babies.

Reprinted with permission from Gerber Products Company.

Expecting? Or a new mother already? Whichever the case, this note from a mother to her daughter-in-waiting may give you some baby-care confidence:

Mrs. Dan Gerber
Mother of Five

"My dear—you should read all the baby-care rules you can. But when your baby comes be a natural mother . . . instinct will help tell you how to apply them to your child. All the rules do not fit all babies and even the best need a little stretching sometimes."

Feeding facts
In addition to the milk or formula your baby gets in the beginning, he (or she) will soon embark on two other early-food experiences: juice and cereal. (Fruit or meat may also be starters.) Gerber offers properly prepared nourishment in all these categories.

Why special juices?
Because they provide vitamin C . . . a necessity in any baby's diet, because it helps build strong bones and teeth. One can of any Gerber Strained Fruit Juice will give your baby over 100% of the recommended daily allowance.
Gerber Orange Juice or Apple Juice are usually the starters. Juice combinations (and there are several) provide flavor variety later.

For a good start on solid food
Gerber Baby Cereals are enriched with iron for its blood-building quality; B-vitamins to help build appetite and growth. Five delicate flavors . . . all smooth as can be and easily digestible when mixed with milk or formula.

Dan Gerber explains nutritional research
"Whether in Pediatric Clinics, University Laboratories, or in our own Research Center, Gerber supports dozens of scientific studies. Successful projects have resulted in putting rice polishings back into Gerber Rice Cereal. Rice polishings are a natural source of the important vitamin-B complex. Another helped develop a strain of squash with a higher vitamin-A value. Another established a highly nutritious meat base formula for milk-intolerant babies.
"Things like these are hidden values that make Gerber Foods worth their weight in goodness and nourishment."

Review: Gerber prepares infant formulas and over 100 baby foods. Comfortable, durable babywear, too.

Babies are our business...our only business!
GERBER BABY PRODUCTS, BOX 33, FREMONT, MICHIGAN

Reprinted with permission from Gerber Products Company.

Reprinted with permission from Levi Strauss & Company.

WHY IN THE WORLD WOULD MISS AMERICA NEED BRACES?

Shirley Cothran Barrett was Miss America in 1975. Her smile was as beautiful then as it is now.

So, why would Shirley need braces? Her condition was similar to one shared by millions of Americans. A health problem was hiding behind very acceptable teeth.

Shirley was fortunate. Discomfort led her to orthodontic care. Many people, however, don't realize danger signs: crowded teeth that are difficult to clean; teeth that may "drift" and tip in too much space; teeth that show abnormal wear; clicking of the jaw or actual pain.

It's estimated that two out of three adults carry a problem that should be treated. One out of four of those is potentially serious.

When your family dentist recommends you see an orthodontist, he's spotted a danger sign. He's sending you to a specialist with the extended training to treat your problem properly.

It's important to understand that the scope of orthodontic treatment reaches beyond attractive smiles to building the health of the mouth. Shirley's a shining example of that.

You may wish to check the availability of orthodontic insurance where you work. It's surprisingly economical. For more information on orthodontics for adults and children, write the American Association of Orthodontists, 460 N. Lindbergh Blvd., St. Louis, MO 63141.

WE SHAPE HEALTH, NOT JUST TEETH.

American Association of
Orthodontists
In cooperation
with The
Canadian Association
of Orthodontists

Reprinted with permission from the American Association of Orthodontists.

4

Cultural and Subcultural Influences

The social and cultural environment is the larger framework within which consumers function. The sociocultural environment provides reference points that impart meaning to our behaviors and cognitions. The influences of the sociocultural framework are so encompassing and their impact so subtle that their effects on our behaviors and thoughts are "natural." However, when the sociocultural frame of reference changes, so too does the meaning of "natural."

It is necessary for the marketer both to understand and to incorporate this realization in his or her marketing plans. What is natural, right, and desirable may be unnatural, wrong, and undesirable to others within a different sociocultural framework. The articles in this section have been selected to illustrate this point.

Once, in the nineteenth century, Americans were a nation of pork eaters. Today beef is the most popular meat. In the article "How Beef Became King," Marvin Harris and Eric B. Ross analyze the social, economic, and technological forces that led to the cultural preference for beef over pork and the abhorrence of dog meat.

David A. Ricks, Jeffrey S. Arpan, and Marilyn Y. Fu, in the article "Pitfalls in Advertising Overseas," recount some humorous but costly errors committed by American businesses overseas because of a failure to appreciate cultural differences.

HOW BEEF BECAME KING

Although vegetarians are becoming either more numerous or more vocal, there's no sign that the nation as a whole is eating less beef these days. Americans consume more than 100 pounds per person per year (see table), much of it in the form of oddly misnamed hamburgers. That's twice as much as pork, the second most popular meat. Moreover, beef in the form of steak is our favorite prestige food. Coast to coast, rare, medium, or well done, it honors those who serve it and those who eat it far more than pork or lamb. To special guests at home or in a restaurant, we offer steak or perhaps prime ribs, seldom ham steaks, less often pork chops or mutton, and never, never horse or dog meat. In America, steak is to meat what Cadillac is to cars.

"How Beef Became King," Marvin Harris and Eric B. Ross, *Psychology Today,* October 1978. Reprinted from *Psychology Today* Magazine. Copyright © 1978, Ziff-Davis Publishing Company.

Like most cultural practices, American beef-eating seems natural until we lift our gaze beyond the smoke of our own barbecues. Throughout the Far East, hundreds of millions of people have never tasted beef and have not the slightest desire to try it. In Hindu India, steak is as unthinkable as dog chops in the United States. Less well known is the fact that the Chinese, who are not averse to eating dogs now and then, find the idea of slaughtering cattle to eat steak rather appalling. As anthropologist Martin Yang reports, "It would be insulting, or at least improper, to offer beef to a guest at an honorable dinner." The honorable host offers pork instead.

"There is no disputing taste" is an old but misleading maxim. Everybody's food preferences ought to be respected, but there is much to dispute when it comes to explaining why we have them. It's easy to dismiss food preferences as quirky, inscrutable traditions that science can never understand: Americans like hamburgers and steak, and that's that. But with the price of meat setting records at the supermarket, some of us prefer to shop around for a slightly more edifying theory.

The whole question of American meat preferences has recently been raised by anthropologist Marshall Sahlins at the University of Chicago. Sahlins sides with those who feel that the search for the practical, mundane causes of cultural lifestyles is futile. Our liking for beef and our abhorrence of dog meat, he argues, "is in no way justifiable by biological, ecological, or economic advantage." It is really a cultural convention that originated thousands of years ago when Indo-European ancestors identified cattle with virility because cattle represented "increasable wealth." This traditional "sexual code of food," Sahlins contends, is not determined by any practical benefits associated with eating beef rather than other meats. Further, our beef preference arbitrarily shapes the conduct of American agribusiness and distorts the exploitation of American resources along fundamentally irrational lines. Its consequences "extend from agricultural 'adaptation' to international trade and world political relations."

We don't eat dogs, Sahlins explains, because they remind us of people. Cows seem human to Hindus; dogs seem human to Americans. So the people of India bestow all sorts of privileges on their cows, while Americans treat canines as if they were members of the family. If India is the land of the sacred cow, concludes Sahlins, the U.S. is the land of the sacred dog.

Our research leads us to very different conclusions. The preeminence of beef in the United States is a recent, temporary development that has little to do with an-

cient Indo-European cattle cults. It grew out of specific economic and technological changes brought on by the attempt to maximize the benefits and minimize the costs of meat production in the face of shifting ecological and demographic considerations. These costs and benefits also lie behind the American abhorrence of dog meat as well as other apparently inscrutable food preferences.

The U.S. has not always been the land of big steaks. Before 1875, pork was the preferred daily meat, and ham was the choice for honored guests. Even as late as 1950 (see table, this page), pork was a bit more popular than beef. It is true that cattle were reared and consumed in substantial numbers from Colonial times onward, and in regions such as New England and the Louisiana prairies, cattle hides and salted, barreled beef formed the basis of important local industries. But nowhere did cattle rival hogs as a source of meat. Whites in the antebellum South consumed three times as much pork as beef. In his

Beef versus Pork: Recent Trends

U.S. Per-Capita Consumption, in Pounds*		
Year	Beef	Pork
1977	125.9	61.5
1976	129.4	58.2
1975	120.1	54.8
1974	116.8	66.6
1973	109.6	61.6
1972	116.1	67.4
1971	113.0	73.0
1970	113.7	66.4
1965	99.5	58.7
1960	85.1	64.9
1950	63.4	69.2
1920	59.1	63.5

*Figures, from the U.S. Department of Agriculture, represent carcass weight—how much the meat weighed at the packinghouse. The National Livestock and Meat Board estimates that, allowing for bone, fat, and cooking losses, we actually ate about 44 pounds of beef and 22 pounds of pork per person last year.

book *Hog Meat and Hoecake,* historian S. B. Hilliard writes that "this preference for pork came to be a distinctive element of Southern culture and as a food item pork completely eclipsed all others."

New Englanders were only slightly less pork-conscious. As historian H. S. Russell put it, "From the viewpoint of the family larder, the most necessary farm animal was the hog; few meals of this period anywhere were complete without some pork product." The importance of pork during the antebellum period—when the good life was "living high on the hog"—has left its mark on American speech habits. Americans still talk about "bringing home the bacon," not "bringing home the steak," and accuse politicians of "pork barrel" rather than "beef barrel" legislation.

One reason for the early preeminence of pork is strictly biological. Under favorable conditions, the pig converts plants into flesh far more efficiently than any other domesticated animal. Pigs transform about 35 percent of what they eat into live weight, compared with only 11 percent for cattle; they also have larger litters. Moreover, the hog is a creature that likes to root about for nuts and other tidbits buried in the forest floor. As long as there were extensive forests, American settlers could let their pigs feed themselves during most of the year. But what really made the hog king was the fact that American homesteaders produced more corn than the sparse human population could eat. At first, this surplus was most profitably converted into whiskey (hence the origin of bourbon as the distinctive American contribution to the world of hard liquor).

When the federal government decided to make whiskey one of its principal sources of tax revenue, frontier farmers found it more profitable to turn surplus corn into meat rather than alcohol. From then on, as the corn belt moved steadily westward across the Appalachians and beyond, so did the hog belt. By 1830, the corn-hog complex had reached the Ohio Valley, and Cincinnati, known as Porkopolis, was the major source of pork for the Eastern Seaboard as well as for the overseas trade via New Orleans. It was in Cincinnati that the technical pattern for the American meat-packing industry was first established. Workers stood in place, mechanically performing specialized operations as the pig carcasses moved past them suspended from overhead monorails. Henry Ford is usually credited with creating the assembly line in Detroit in 1913, but the prototype of Henry Ford's assembly line was Cincinnati's pig disassembly line, operating well before the Civil War.

When the corn belt moved still farther west, accompanied and spurred on by furious railroad building, Chicago replaced Cincinnati as the nation's principal meat-packing and transshipment center. But, despite Carl Sandburg's characterization of Chicago as "Hog Butcher to the World," beef, not pork, was destined to be the city's real glory.

Up to this point, about 1860, cattle suffered from two disadvantages as a source of mass-produced meat. Because the pig was a more efficient converter of corn into flesh, pork was cheaper to produce. There was also the problem of preservation. Early meat-packers had to rely on salting as the principal way of getting the meat to market in edible condition. And pork took to salting far better than beef, which was stringier to begin with. These advantages kept pork the favorite American meat until physiology, geography, and technology combined forces to move beef ahead.

Cattle have one distinct physiological advantage over swine: as ruminants, they are outfitted with a series of stomachs adapted to eating grass; pigs, for all their omnivorous tastes, cannot digest grass. Beyond the Mississippi lay great expanses of semiarid grasslands only marginally suited for corn production, where cattle rather than pigs could more efficiently convert plants into meat. Cattle could also be driven over long distances and made to swim broad rivers to get to market; pigs are poor swimmers and notoriously hard to drive.

The cattle had another advantage, as well as some drawbacks. Herds of long-horned breeds descended from stock released by some Spanish settlers roamed southern Texas in a semiwild condition before the Civil War. But because the Eastern market was inaccessible, the animals were valued chiefly for their hides rather than their flesh. The railroads, spreading out from Chicago, soon changed all this. Where the cattle trails crossed the tracks, Chicago-based entrepreneurs built stockyards and towns virtually overnight.

As soon as Illinois livestock-shipper J. G. McCoy learned that the trail from Texas would cross the tracks being laid through Kansas at Abilene, he ordered holding facilities for 3,000 head built within 60 days. By the end of the year 1867, starting from scratch, McCoy shipped 35,000 head from Abilene to Chicago. By 1871, over 700,000 head of range cattle were being shipped by rail to the packing houses in Chicago and elsewhere, and cattle-ranching was spreading across the plains from Texas. But the stupendous potential of the Western rangelands as yet remained untapped. Most of the cattle raised on the Great Plains still reached the Eastern consumer in the form of barreled, salted beef. The more desirable fresh beef was available only at exorbitant prices by

shipping live animals all the way from Chicago, and slaughtering them at the neighborhood butcher shop.

In the late 1860s, George Hammond delivered the first fresh Chicago beef stored on ice to the Boston market. Since Hammond's beef touched ice, it was discolored and met with consumer resistance. A few years later, Philip Armour and Gustavus Swift, founders of the huge meat-packing companies that still bear their names, introduced refrigerator cars that chilled the meat by circulating air over ice. In October of 1882, *Harper's Weekly* reported that Swift's "Chicago dressed beef" arrived in New York in cars whose doors opened directly in front of a refrigerated wholesale storage building. The overhead trolley in the car linked up with the trolley in the building (kept at the same temperature as the car) and the carcass was transferred from one to the other "without being removed from the hook on which it was hung when killed."

Thus, by taking advantage of the unexploited rangelands, recently cleared of buffalo and Indians, and by using assembly-line processing, efficient rail transport, and intensive capitalization, the giant packers undersold the local butchers and captured the Eastern markets. Swift's first shipment depressed the price of beef $4 per hundredweight, leading *Harper's* to declare, "The era of cheap beef has begun for New York."

Beef's reputation in the U.S., it seems, did not arise from some ancient, arbitrary code in which beef stood for virility, but from practical production and marketing breakthroughs that made fresh beef affordable by the urban consumer. Beef won out over pork principally because the available grasslands made it cheaper to mass-produce fresh beef than fresh pork. If pigs could still have been raised by the old system of semiwild forag-ing, fresh pork might have competed with fresh beef for the urban market. But by the 1870s, the corn belt had moved out of the forested regions—in fact, much former wilderness had been cleared for farm-land—and the mass production of pigs had come to depend almost entirely on feeding them corn and other farm products. While cattle were fattened on corn just before slaughter, the rangelands provided vir-tually free food during the animals' years of maximum growth.

Based on the same analysis, we can resolve the matter of America's sacred dogs rather briefly. Dogs are carnivores and hence thrive best on meat, not grass, nuts, or grain. So why should packers pro-duce meat by fattening dogs on meat that humans can eat? Actually, the only place where dogs have been mass-produced for human consumption was in pre-Colum-bian Mexico, by the Aztecs. But the Aztecs, who bred a special hairless variety of dogs for this purpose, did not have pigs, cattle, sheep, or any other efficient sources of ani-mal flesh. Making the best of matters, the Aztecs not only ate specially bred hairless dogs, but human babies and captured en-emy soldiers as well.

American dogs are not only hairy; they are also expensive animals, carefully bred for specialized functions that other animals cannot perform as well. Right now, their main job is to scare off intruders and provide company in an increasingly urban, crime-ridden, and lonely society. Our taboo on dog flesh, therefore, merely expresses in symbolic form the high value we place on these functions, as well as the more traditional ones dogs exercised when they helped men hunt or herd other animals.

Just as geographical, physiological,

and technological factors explain the de-velopment of America's current prefer-ence for beef, so contemporary economic and ecological considerations will change our tastes in the future. Actually, the orig-inal economic bonanza of open-range cat-tle-ranching was a short-lived phe-nomenon. Rising land prices caused by the continuous advance of farms into the mar-ginal areas of the Great Plains, and over-grazing during the boom years of ranching in the early 1880s, soon obliged ranchers to use more intensive methods of stock-raising. Competition for the Eastern mar-ket also led to the replacement of the hardy but stringy longhorns with less hardy but tender Herefords. With the cut-back in rangeland and increasing use of more expensive breeds, more and more of the weight gain of beef cattle came to de-pend on alfalfa, corn, soybeans, and other planted crops. Current feedlot operations, in which calves are force-fed a rich diet of energy-expensive grains, vitamins, and hormones, and brought to maturity within eight months, constitute an ever-more wasteful form of production.

Thus, just as much of America's housing and travel preferences depend on no-longer-cheap supplies of petrochemi-cals, our beef-eating ways now stand at odds with sound ecological and economic principles. Cattle have lost much of their cost advantage over swine and other more efficient sources of animal protein (such as poultry-farming and dairying) and Amer-ica's taste for meat must sooner or later swing back to pork and dairy products, and include vegetable sources of protein as well.

We can speculate about the fate of beef-eaters like ourselves on the basis of what happened in older civilizations. High per-capita beef consumption has always been associated with low-density populations, pioneering in natural or artificially created grasslands. The Indo-European Vedic-speaking peoples of ancient northern India, and the ancestral Chinese of the Yellow River basin, were both at first cattle-raisers and avid beef-eaters. As their populations grew and farming was intensified, cattle became too expensive to be raised for meat. They were needed as plow animals, to help the croplands feed people rather than animals.

In China, pork gradually became the preferred meat, because pigs could be raised more efficiently than cattle on household wastes and agricultural by-products. In northern India, the fierce summer heat, the monsoons, and periodic droughts made the pig a poor choice. So, as population density increased in the Gangetic plain, India turned to dairying as the major source of animal protein. It soon became a cardinal religious principle of Buddhism and Hinduism to protect the supply of draft animals by prohibiting the slaughter of cattle and the consumption of beef. Thus, out of the same Indo-European tradition to which Sahlins erroneously attributes the American taste for beef, a civilization arose in which beef-eating is the greatest sin. Nothing so drastic is likely to happen to us. But we are bound to lose our taste for big fat steaks just as surely as we are bound to lose our affinity for big fat cars.

PITFALLS IN ADVERTISING OVERSEAS

International trade and investment operations are fraught with risk and uncertainty. In fact, the problems encountered by
managers of foreign operations are often
more difficult than those encountered in
domestic operations, and in many instances they have threatened the very survival of the firm.

Many managers fail to realize this,
and investors frequently underestimate
the difficulties associated with overseas
operations. Domestic success is no guarantee of predictable performance in a different environment. Many successful domestic firms have made plans for foreign
investments that have missed their mark
so widely that these companies have been

unable to take advantage of opportunities
in even the most promising markets.

When actual results differ widely
from planned results, it is often difficult to
judge whether the cause was an initial
conceptualization error or one of failing to
adapt adequately to the environment.
Whatever the timing of the decision, however, the basic root of the troublesome uncertainty is most likely the presence of an
additional culture in the decision making
framework. Different customs, attitudes,
and needs render many of a firm's normal
procedures inapplicable or untransfera-
ble. Awareness of and sensitivity to these
often subtle cultural differences may be
the major determinant in the success of an
international business venture.

Research in this area can identify
critical factors in the environment which
have caused problems for outsiders in the
past so that others can avoid making simi-

lar mistakes. This particular research reports investigations and analyses of actual blunders made by executives in advertising and other aspects of international business. All blunders are publicly documented as having been made by real companies in real countries. Taken as a group, they offer some important lessons for international business in the future.

Essentially, a blunder was judged to have occurred if the problem was foreseeable, but a solution was either poorly prepared or entirely overlooked and a significant negative result occurred. Thus, the incorrect translation of an ad into embarrassing wording which would cause adverse reaction would qualify as a blunder, but it would not if the ad had poked fun at a public figure who died shortly after the ad's release. The question of foreseeability is admittedly a crucial one. Every attempt was made to include only examples where the negative result could have been avoided with reasonable foresight and effort.

FINDINGS

Advertising blunders are the most varied and colorful. From the seemingly minute errors of a faulty word in advertising copy, to major problems arising from failing to conduct a thorough market study before committing hundreds of thousands of dollars to a multinational promotional campaign, these blunders have been extremely damaging to the erring firm. Although the circumstances surrounding each situation differ, the core of the problems are primarily due to these few factors: a tremendous optimism about a particular product or product line, vast confidence in business know-how and past success formulas, and failure to fully understand and appreciate the foreign environment.

To illustrate, some advertising blunders are presented which, although somewhat humorous, were often critically injurious to the firms involved.

General Motors made an embarrassing mistake when, in Flemish, "Body by Fisher" translated as "Corpse by Fisher" (Mazze, 1964). In a similar case, Schweppes Tonic Water was rapidly dehydrated to "Schweppes Tonica" in Italy, where "il water" is the idiomatic expression for a bathroom. An American airline operating in Brazil proudly advertised plush "rendezvous lounges" on its jets, only belatedly discovering that "rendezvous" in Portuguese meant a room hired for love-making. Pepsi's familiar ad, "Come Alive with Pepsi" had problems in Germany because the translation of "come alive" meant "come alive out of the grave." Obviously, the ad had to be reworded (*Ad Age,* 1966).

Colgate-Palmolive made an expensive mistake when it introduced its Cue toothpaste in French-speaking countries. Colgate maintained its trademark without knowing that "Cue" was a pornographic work in French (Martyn, 1964).

Faulty laundry soap advertising can clean out sales, as one company discovered in French-speaking Quebec. The firm had come up with numerous new point-of-sale material describing the fantastic cleansing powers of its detergent, boasting that it was particularly suited for the really dirty parts of the wash—"les partes de sale." Sales rapidly declined and the firm later found out to its chagrin that the phrase was comparable to the American idiom "private parts" (Winick, 1961).

Linguistic anomalies are but one class of blunders in advertising. One of Unilever's highly popular detergents was sold under the trademark Radion in Germany, but the product in nearby Austria sold under a different brand name. Although Germany and Austria are independent and distinct in national characteristics, their physical closeness and language similarity permit the use of communications media—such as magazines, television and radio—common to both nations' audiences. In particular, German media hold a substantial geographical spread in Austria, and the great majority of Austrian housewives are exposed to German advertising in magazines and on television. However, the Austrian exposure to Radion proved a waste since boxes of Radion could not be found on the shelves of Austrian retailers—and its Austrian counterpart could not be immediately recognized by the consumers (Elindor, 1965).

LACK OF CULTURAL AWARENESS

Although the preceding examples are actual cases of management errors in advertising, they are not the most typical. In fact, most international advertising blunders occur because of a failure to fully understand the foreign culture and its social norms. This can take many forms, ranging from blatant rejection of existing customs and tastes to innocent insensitivity to the environment. One well-intended company, for example, brought upon itself the indignation of foreign participants of its promotional campaign when it elected to use for favors simulated old coins with "$1 billion" engraved on them (*Business Abroad,* 1966). The participants resented the omnipresence of the dollar sign. Germans preferred to see DM, the French the franc, etc. What began as an innocent but well-intended promotional gadget became

interpreted as a reflection of the pompous U.S. superiority and all but nullified the efficacy of the promotional campaign.

Advertisements that somehow fail to reflect the local lifestyle often wind up as wasted effort. When General Mills made its attempt to capture the English market, its breakfast cereal package showed a freckled, red-haired, crew-cut grinning kid saying, "See kids, it's great!"—a promotional package that could not be more typically American (McCreary, 1964). General Mills failed to recognize that the British family is not as child-centered as the U.S.; the stereotype U.S. boy and near banal expression had no appeal to the more formal and aristocratic ideal of the child upheld by the English. As a result, the cereal package repelled the British housewife and wound up untouched on retail shelves.

Similarly, a certain American manufacturer of beauty products decided to court French consumers by using some of the lustrous and arresting advertisements that so successfully captured the American audience (Lenormand, 1964). Unfortunately the advertising missed its audience. The French women did not identify themselves with the exceptionally attractive models because the advertising had been too exaggerated and lacked sufficient realism to elicit the audience's self-identification with the models. The beauty products did not cause Paris to rave and rant, and French women did not choose them.

Another cosmetics firm tried unsuccessfully to woo the Japanese with a lipstick ad campaign that had quite an appeal in Italy (*Business Abroad,* 1967). The ad featured a statue of Nero coming to life with a freakish grin as he saw a girl wearing their particular brand of lipstick. The advertisement struck no accord with the Japanese consumers. Nero was alien to them, the grin was grotesque, and the ad simply had no trace of those characteristics that appealed to the Japanese women. Sham Law, president of the New York consulting firm S. Lall and Associates, had this comment: "The success of an ad in Japan depends largely on the use of a proper appeal. The hard sell is considered extremely impolite. Japanese consumers respond best to ads that emphasize the product's practical advantages."

Warner Lambert's Listerine has also had its share of advertising problems (Diamond, 1969). In Thailand, Warner Lambert filmed commercials about Listerine fashioned after the well-known U.S. TV commercials showing a boy and girl, overtly fond of each other, one advising the other to use Listerine for curing bad breath. Sales remained minimal and company executives were puzzled by the turn of events. Finally, Charlie Tse, Warner Lambert's Southeast Asia area manager noted the catch: such public portrayal of boy-girl relationships was objectionable to the Thai people. The Thai commercial was carefully and quickly adjusted—this time to show two girls discussing Listerine. The ad caught on and increased sales confirmed the effectiveness of the modifications.

Admen have encountered other unusual situations unique to Thailand. A well-known marketer of eye glasses initiated a campaign to promote its spectacles (Carson, 1967). To attract attention, ads and billboards showing cute pictures of animals wearing eye glasses were used. Despite the apparent charm of the portrayals, sales failed to materialize. The marketer only belatedly discovered that Thais regarded animals as a lower level of creation and were unattracted to advertising using animal themes. Similarly, the widely acclaimed Exxon ad, "Put a tiger in

your tank," failed to elicit favorable reaction in Thailand (Miracle, 1968). Tigers were simply not symbols of power and strength there.

Additional examples further illustrate the need for careful examination and analysis of marketing labels and advertisements before using them in foreign markets.

A prominent international manufacturer of water recreation products was perplexed when its Malaysian distributors requested that they stop shipment of its products (Carson, 1967). It turned out that in this area where a large number of the people are illiterate, color and shapes served as an important communication medium for the illiterate. Green, to these people, was the symbol of the jungle with its dangers and diseases. Unfortunately for the manufacturer, its international emblem, prominently displayed on its products, was green and people shied away from products stamped with such a fearful omen.

Pepsodent's promise of white teeth was especially inappropriate in many regions of Southeast Asia where betel-nut chewing was an elite habit and black teeth a symbol of prestige (Martyn, 1964). The "wonder where the yellow went" slogan didn't help out either.

As another example of what can be done incorrectly in advertisements, consider the following advertisement which had prominently appeared in magazines and newsmedia of Quebec, Canada (Winick, 1961). A woman, comfortably dressed in shorts, could be seen playing golf with her husband. The caption boldly indicated that the housewife could carefreely enjoy a day on the golf course and still quickly prepare a delicious evening meal for the family by serving the advertised canned fish. Literally everything turned out wrong in this ad. Anthropologists strongly recommended changes because every element shown represented a violation of some aspect of French-Canadian life: Wives were not likely to be golfing with their husbands; women seen in shorts, especially on a high-class golf course, were socially unacceptable, and to top it all, French-Canadians simply did not serve that particular kind of fish as the main course for the evening meal!

It's possible to export what's a good thing in one country to a totally different environment and wind up with no gain. In the following case, the mistake was one of overdoing a good thing in a different situation.

Dow Breweries introduced a new beer, Kebec, in 1963. To highlight the French-Canadian national overtones for the beer, an advertising campaign was especially planned for such emphasis. But in its broad and liberal use of French-Canadian symbols, certain nationalistic emblems were inappropriately included. Loud protests from the public denouncing the company's "profane" use of "sacred" symbols forced Dow to withdraw the campaign within 15 days. The error was unintentional, yet the drastic consumer reaction proved very dear to Dow (Elkin, 1969).

BiNoca similarly offended the Indian public with a seemingly innocuous ad (*The New York Times*, 1967). The ad, placed in certain leading local newspapers, showed an attractive though apparently nude young woman lavishly dousing herself with BiNoca's talcum powder. The following caption was placed on the layout, casually covering strategic portions of her body: "Don't go wild—just enough is all you need of BiNoca talc." The public, accustomed to conservative traditional standards of morality, found the ad indecent, publicly distasteful, and offensive.

IMPLICATIONS

The importance of having an adequate "cultural sensitivity" on the part of decision-makers involved in international operations is well borne out by the findings of this study. Unicultural managements making all the decisions regarding advertising in different cultures seems a high risk strategy. Multicultural participation in the planning, decision making, execution, and evaluation stages of an advertising program appears to be a better procedure. Effective use of local foreign nationals would have prevented many, if not all, of the blunders reported in this study—especially those done because the advertisement was translated too literally.

Those knowledgeable in the field of international advertising have advised that the need is to translate basic appeals, not necessarily the literal. No matter how different people are in different countries, one fact remains: there are certain basic appeals that are common to all people, although they may not always be expressed in the same words. The key is to identify and respect the differences in point of view and sensitivities to nuances. Basic appeals can be successfully employed everywhere.

References

Advertising Age, May 9, 1966, p. 75.

Business Abroad, When Marketing Abroad: Remove Your Star Spangled Glasses, May 2, 1966, p. 14.

Business Abroad, How to Get Madison Avenue "Sell" into Japanese Ad Campaign, October 30, 1967, pp. 26–29.

Carson, David. *International Marketing: A*

Comparative Approach. New York: John Wiley & Sons, Inc., 1967.

Carson, Margaret. Admen in Thailand, Singapore Find Unusual Problems, Novel Solutions. *Advertising Age,* November 27, 1967, pp. 3 ff.

Diamond, R. S. Managers Away From Home. *Fortune,* August 15, 1969, pp. 56 ff.

Elindor, Erik. How International Can European Advertising Be? *Journal of Marketing,* April 1965, p. 7.

Elkin, Frederick. Advertising Themes and Quiet Revolutions: Dilemmas in French Canada. *American Journal of Sociology,* July 1969.

League, Frederick A. Why Companies Fail Abroad. *Columbia Journal of World Business,* July-August 1968, p. 55.

Lenormand, J. M. Is Europe Ripe for Integration of Advertising? *International Advertising,* March 1964, p. 14.

Martyn, Howe. *International Business, Principles and Problems.* New York: Collier-Macmillan, 1964.

Mazze, Edward M. How to Push a Body Abroad Without Making It a Corpse. *Business Abroad,* August 10, 1964, p. 15.

McCreary, Edward A. *The Americanization of Europe.* New York: Doubleday & Co., 1964.

Miracle, Gordon E. International Advertising Principles and Strategies. *MSU Business Topics,* Vol. 16, Fall 1968, p. 29.

The New York Times, "Nude in Talc Ad Offends in India," April 29, 1967, pp. 36 ff.

Pryor, Millard H. Planning in a World-Wide Business. *Harvard Business Review,* January-February 1965, p. 130.

Skinner, Wickham. Management of International Production. *Harvard Business Review,* September-October 1964.

Winick, Charles. Anthropology's Contributions to Marketing. *Journal of Marketing,* July 1961, p. 53.

Exercise 6

Cultural Norms

OBJECTIVE: To provide an opportunity to experientially understand the meaning of norms by asking you to break everyday norms.

The purpose of this exercise is to give you a first-hand experience of the definition of *norms*—culturally defined behavior patterns. What is acceptable or unacceptable behavior in a given situation is defined by the culture. You may not be aware of the American norms that govern your behavior. Only when these norms are broken does it become apparent that what is normal behavior in one culture may not be normal in another culture. In this exercise, you are asked to break the following American cultural norms:

1. Ride an elevator but upon entrance do not turn around. Face your fellow passengers.
2. Take a seat next to someone in the library or cafeteria, even though there are empty chairs all around the table and other empty tables.
3. Stand about 4 inches away from someone in a conversation (a friend and/or a stranger). Maintain your 4-inch distance.
4. If you ride the bus, ask someone for his or her seat.

You may choose to complete this exercise individually or in small groups (three maximum). If you choose to complete this in groups, one person should enact the behaviors and the other person(s) should be "unobtrusive" observers. Interchange roles among the members of the group.

You may have difficulty completing this exercise. Give it the "college try," but if it proves overwhelmingly difficult, a reaction to attempting this exercise and a description of your experiences in trying to carry it out will satisfy the requirements of this exercise.

Exercise 7

American Cultural Values

OBJECTIVES: 1. To demonstrate that the value system of people heavily directs their consumption behaviors.
2. To show that value systems change over time and that these changes are interrelated with consumer behavior and marketing activities.
3. To provoke thought on the nature of the intertwining cause-effect relationship that exists between advertising and cultural values by examining advertisements for their statement of cultural value(s).

Advertising is an ubiquitous and institutionalized aspect of the American culture. In the long run, advertising may influence American cultural values, while in the short run it mirrors cultural values. In this exercise:

1. Analyze each of the following advertisements for their implicit reflection of cultural values.

Reprinted with permission of Generex Drug Corporation.

Reprinted with permission of the Hanes Corporation.

Courtesy of the Procter & Gamble Company.

Reprinted with permission from the Boeing Commercial Airplane Company.

Reprinted with permission from the Ford Motor Company.

5

Social Stratification

Whether consumers prefer to shop at Woolworths or I. Magnin, decorate their homes with artificial flowers or art nouveau, or spend an evening at a boxing match or at an opera is to a large extent related to their social class. People's social class greatly influences their tastes in products, retail outlets, and services, as is shown in the following articles.

The article "Living Room Decor Tells All" reveals that the consumers' social class influences how they furnish their living rooms.

In the article "Soles on Fire," Alan Cartnal tells how the PRIMO ladies— the "nouveau riche" and the "old wealth"—go about attiring their feet.

In the article "An Authority Tells Why Status Symbols Keep Changing," Paul Blumberg describes the characteristics of status symbols and analyzes the economic and social values that underlie the creation and change in status symbols.

LIVING ROOM DECOR TELLS ALL

How you furnish your living room is more than just a matter of personal taste. It is also a dead giveaway of your income, social standing, religion, politics and ancestry. A sophisticated person could categorize another person pretty completely just by taking a good look at his living room.

Generally, families that had had money for several generations favored the traditional styles whereas families that had just become prosperous went in for more modern trappings.

Lower-middle-class and working-class families tended to have little style but they did have characteristic differences from other groups.

One example which was particularly

significant was called the "migration of the TV set."

The TV is never seen in upper-class living rooms, although it may have been common there 20 years ago. It has migrated to studies, dens, bedrooms or recreation rooms. Placing the TV in a prominent place in the living room is typical of a working-class family.

So are religious paintings, and the more vivid and striking they are, the more characteristic they are of lower-class taste.

Another working-class sign is the presence of dogs, especially mutts and the commoner breeds. (Afghan hounds and borzois are all right in the upper-class living room and French poodles are okay for those who are just "making it.")

Working-class houses have living-room curtains with floral designs.

Lower-middle-class houses have translucent curtains.

The Nouveaux riches have curtains with geometric designs.

The old rich have plain curtains— and they don't call them "drapes."

The lower middle class has living rooms crowded with bulky overstuffed furniture.

The working-class living room is comparatively bare, because they can't afford to pile things into the room. The newly prosperous, who like modern things they see in magazines, also have bare living rooms but it's part of their style. They also go in for abstract painting, sunburst clocks and solid-color wall-to-wall carpeting.

The lower middle class likes artificial flowers in its living rooms, as well as antimacassars, Bibles, small religious statues, family photographs, and bowling trophies.

Persons who have had money furnish their living rooms with traditional French, English or American Colonial pieces, usually mixed. They like representative art such as landscapes, still lifes and oil portraits.

They have fireplaces and grand pianos. Their knick-knacks may be Royal Doulton china, compared to the abstract glass sculptures of the modern new rich, the bowling trophies of the lower middle class and the religious paintings of the working class.

SOLES ON FIRE

Item: Spending close to $50,000 on ready-to-wear and accessories may seem a bit extravagant, but to Deborah (Mrs. Winthrop) Rockefeller Jr. of Arkansas it's all in two days' work. She, a friend and a couple of bodyguards walked into Donald J. Pliner's Right Bank Shoe Company in Beverly Hills the other day and stacked up mounds of purchases, including 69 pairs of shoes, mostly Maud Frizon, at an average price of $130; fifteen pairs of $275 Frizon boots; twenty Frizon bags; eleven Trussardi bags; several pairs of leather chaps at $200 a pair; and 37 pairs of special-order boots at $285 per.

"It's hard to find great shoes and clothes in Arkansas," said Rockefeller,

"Soles on Fire," Alan Cartnal, *New West Magazine,* November 6, 1978, pp. 63–70. Reprinted with permission from the November 6, 1978 issue of NEW WEST. Copyright 1978 by NEW WEST.

who wears lots of Indian jewelry with her white garbardine suit. "I come here once a year to buy things."

The people at the Right Bank Shoe Company didn't enjoy that particular story. "That dumb Dale Kern, the West Coast bureau chief for *Women's Wear Daily,* didn't get the story straight," scoffs David Green, 31, the shoeman to the stars who masterminded one of the greatest shopping sprees of the century. "They did a kind of New York, bitchathon put-down of it all. I mean, it was the most exciting day of my life. It was the ultimate high. I shook for four days. I couldn't even lift a shoe box. I mean, Debby Rockefeller, who is truly a heavy of the heavyweights when it comes to shopping, flew here in her Lear Jet. And she didn't wear a gabardine suit—these people were just too big a snob to say she was wearing polyester. I mean, sometimes you can't judge a book by its cover, doya-knowwhatimean? This woman is sooooo beautiful. A wonderful, fabulous lady and they made her sound dumb or something. I should be so dumb. This woman rented two suites at the Beverly Wilshire Hotel—one for herself and one for her shoes. I sold her $22,000 worth of boots, shoes and accessories in three hours. It's got to be a landmark in capitalism."

That's right. Supersalesman Green waits on everyone, all the right people, from Cher to Natalie Wood Wagner to Tina Turner to Marisa Berenson to Britt Ekland. "You see," he says, strutting like a gentleman-in-waiting to the new upwardly mobile royalty of California inside the outrageously discolike showroom of the Camden Drive shoe store, which has even surpassed the renowned Polo Lounge as the playground of the rich and celebrated, "I'm in the women's business. You see, women are just like my dogs. They want to have their feet excited. They want somebody to twinkle their toes. I think all women are wonderful—but the most wonderful of them all are the top 2 percent. The heavyweight spenders. These women are at the pinnacle of our society—yes, these women should be placed on the highest of pedestals. Those dumb reporters don't understand that this store is a religion. *A religion.* We don't just sell shoes—we *transform* women. We change lives."

All the time, Green's mind is calculating. Calculating like no other mind since that of Sinclair Lewis's Babbitt. He makes elaborate charts. On his chart he lists his current top 30 spenders, often adding bullets by the names of the climbers to shopping-spree fame.

Right now, he says, Cher and Barbra Streisand are fighting for top position.

David Green's Top 30 Shoe Spenders

$50,000 a Year or Less

1. Barbra Streisand
2. Cher
3. Deborah Rockefeller
4. Marlo Thomas
5. Britt Ekland
* 6. Marisa Berenson
7. Bettina Bancroft (mystery woman)
8. Jeanne Martin (former Mrs. Dean Martin)
9. Ali MacGraw
10. Tina Turner

$20,000 a Year or Less

11. Minnie Riperton
12. Eydie Gorme
13. Cheryl Cooper (Mrs. Alice Cooper)
*14. Carole Bayer Sager
*15. Natalie Wood Wagner
16. Phyllis George
*17. Jaclyn Smith
*18. Kate Jackson
19. Farrah Fawcett-Majors
20. Bernadette Peters

$10,000 a Year or Less

*21. Billie Jean King
22. Stacey Winkler (Mrs. Henry Winkler)
23. Pam Grier
*24. Brooke Hayward
25. Sara Dylan
26. Suzanne Pleshette
*27. Joyce DeWitt (actress, *Three's Company*)
*28. Suzanne Somers
29. Mrs. Michael Landon
*30. Maureen McCormick (*The Brady Bunch*)

*Asterisks indicates increase in sales in last six months.

"Cher doesn't need dope," says Green. "She gets high on shoes. No, she doesn't sniff coke or smoke dope or anything like that. This sweetheart is addicted to shoes." As for Barbra, he doesn't wait on her. Streisand, he says, gets the special treatment—the ultimate shoe coronation—the Right Bank shoe store is loaded into automobiles and transported in a caravan to her current court in her Holmby Hills hideaway.

"I know that some people might object to these women spending as much as $30,000 a year on shoes, and somebody eating a TV dinner might object," says Green, who is getting higher and higher by the minute—transported to a shoe Oz, so to speak. "But let them be. We are living in a new age. The age of self-expression. Women like Cher and Barbra—these wonderful women—do not want to look like anyone else. I treat them like ladies when I wait on them. I would kiss their feet. All right! These are not just women—these are the PRIMO ladies."

The Right Bank? Well, who ever heard of it besides the haut monde and tout le monde and people who care about the shopping sprees of the new going-for-the-goodies brigades? People have heard about I. Magnin and Bullock's Wilshire, S. F.'s Wilkes Bashford and, if they are really savvy (and read lots of trashy newspapers or books), Gucci and Giorgio on Rodeo Drive. After only two years of existence as a shoe store (the Beverly Hills clothing store of the same name is seven years old), this tiny shop on Camden Drive is creating major shock waves in the world of fashion. My God, the customers: movies stars, jigglies, former models and just your average rich wife to the crème de la crème of the corporate structure are flocking down and, lordy, are they having fun. The Right Bank has more than 27,500 women on its customer list, and more are coming by the minute.

Some fashion bigwigs are not charmed by the encroachment of the supercharged, higher-than-high sexual sell in the new statusphere of the California shopping dream. "You can't compare pizza to caviar," scoffs Dr. Aldo Gucci, who has made a fortune off of conservatism and uniform designs. But the shoe world is sitting up and taking notice. "This Donald J. Pliner is becoming the biggest name in shoes in the world," says Maud Frizon, the goddess of European sexy shoes (often called haute hookers in the trade), who sells up to 12,000 pairs of her sexathongs each year at Right Bank at over $140 a throw, and has a whole factory in Italy producing shoes just for Pliner. "When he comes to Europe, the shoe-salon doors are thrown open. He can have his pick of the great shoes of the world. The man is only 34 years old and he's like the Andy Warhol of shoes. He's the pop artist of pumps."

And this emporium of sex, sensuality, spending sprees, high-grade and low-grade gossip, this monument to the new social climbing through shoes, is not just your average high-chandeliered, let's-be-ladies-and-gentlemen, Old-World-charm store. You can spot Cher pulling up in front of the Right Bank in a Jeep. Mrs. Robert Stack in a bathing suit. ("She potentially could be one of the heavyweights of the heavyweights," says Green. "She only dropped $1,000 the other day, but we'll work on her and get her up to maybe $20,000 a year.") European fashion groupie and sometime actress Marisa Berenson checking out the chaps in pencil-thin jeans. All three Charlie's Angels flying in on shopping sprees. Get it. This store has replaced tennis, Gothic novels and hairdressers on the Beverly Hills circuit.

Disco, jazz, pop and classical music on specially made $500 tapes play constantly. (Repetitive rhythm is very important in keeping women on their toes, so to speak.) Mannequins in the shoe store's windows, are sometimes nude—X-rated windows, as they're called in the fashion trade. Pliner has designed the store so that everything is recyclable to your home—

the lamp from Italy, the living-roomlike furniture, the exotic palms. And if you need a $320 gold coke spoon and vial or some expensive, right-on dope paraphernalia at $250 a crack, they've got that, too.

Pliner is selling youth, good times and sex—an unbeatable combination where the newly rich are concerned. One society lady, for example, just discovered the store a week ago and has dropped more than $20,000 since her great discovery. Where's a not-so-poor little girl in the age of constant change supposed to go for a little class in El Lay—Thrifty? How is she going to learn to be a Primo Lady? She goes where the big names go. And the word is out in the right circles—get your credit cards down to the Right Bank. Pliner has not only got the high, high European brands—Pasquali, Maud Frizon, Stèphane Kèlian (mostly designed especially for Pliner and his collectors)—but he's also made money with all this fun shoe biz. The Right Bank (clothing and shoes) grossed over $3 million last year, and the shoe store alone is expected to do $2 million in business this year. Pliner modestly considers it to be the highest-grossing small shoe store in the world.

Pliner doesn't want to be known as a shoeman. God forbid. Cashing in on fashion went out with Halston and all those other big-name designers who sold out for money and became impersonal objects. No. This guy thinks he's an artist. Not only does he think he's an artist, he also thinks that fashion stores have replaced art galleries and self-help therapy groups as the art form of the seventies. In the Age of Success, no one sees the inside of people's pads or judges people by their art or book collections. Now, says Pliner, what you see is what you get. And what we see are clothes and shoes "Fashion should make us smile," says Pliner, a former art student who hails from Chicago where his father went bankrupt selling "cheapie" shoes. Pliner thinks that shopping sprees are heavily related to sex. "I don't care whether it's someone of the same sex or the opposite sex," he says. "But when I think of an evening well spent it usually ends up in bed." Because of such theories, *Playboy* featured his shoes in a shock-therapy layout on hooker shoes which everyone in the fashion world is still stuffing into their Vuitton suitcases.

Pliner believes that the whole world is now aware of the movements and periods of fashion. "People today couldn't care less about merchandise. They want design. We've had our riots. Our protest period. Now what's emerging is fashion as self-expression. No one wants to be the same. They want to be different. Ten years ago I started with my Hair period. I didn't cut my hair to express my freedom. And my store started as a rebellion against fashion. It was all glitter and rhinestones. Then I went into my Pop Art period. I did clothes with prints of cows to herald the boycott of meat. I was enjoying myself. Making fun of our own society. I broke loose of the fashion establishment. Now, I guess I'm in my Throwing-a-Party period. The one thing that it'll never become is a uniform—right now people are getting free of that. They want pleasure—and I sell it."

Service! Trucks of clothes and shoes go floating up to the mansions of the top 30 spenders. Green, the selling stud, is off to Las Vegas to take five pairs of shoes and three pairs of boots (worth $3,500) to Tina Turner.

Service! The best women (the women who have proved that they are true members of what could only be called a private club of shoe collectors) are called into the store, where they are able to order shoes six months in advance by looking at Polaroid pictures of a design. (Farrah loves to do it that way.)

Service! The salesmen know tastes and quirks. They know their customers. They know their customers' credit card numbers (so the women don't have to go to the trouble of producing their plastic), their birthdays (for little presents), their husbands' birthdays, what they have purchased for the last two years. And every woman receives "love letters" (incredible acknowledgments of her beauty and taste) each time she makes a purchase.

"These guys sell like dope dealers," says Pamela Draper, a former *Cosmopolitan* magazine cover girl, now an actress. "I go into that store saying I will not spend more than $100 and I always end up spending much more money than I intend. They treat each woman like Cinderella. If you've got an insecurity, they play on it. They give you coffee, Perrier, wine. They hide your shoes so you can't walk out of the store. It's like everyone's having a party. And you go on a spree. You go crazy. I've never seen such ambition—not even in actresses on the make."

But there are things—deeper, darker secrets of selling—that not even the dear collectors know about the store. David Green explains: "Now, when a lady comes in and I say to the other salesman, 'You're wanted on line 34,' that is a termination of a customer. That means, you are waiting on a dog. The lady is told very nicely that we are out of merchandise in her size. Because we find that many ladies do nothing but waste our time. I mean, they are crazy. They order seven shoes and return them

the next day. A lot of them wear them out one night and return them the next day. Hey, this is Beverly Hills—the user capital of the world. These ladies, these 34s, have become so notorious that we simply have to kick them out. But kindly, of course.

"On the other hand, there's 68. That's 34 doubled and that means you've got a fox. That means you've got a potential superheavyweight. I mean, they could be number one. Mrs. Robert Stack walked in and I didn't know who she was. So I hear 68 and I go bananas. I mean, I had analyzed her—she had diamonds, the Rolex watch, the beautiful personality—the warmth of that wonderful woman. I sat her down, took her shoes off—it's very important that when you take their shoes off, you hide them. Because they can't walk out of the store without shoes. I mean, Mrs. Stack—those diamonds and that Rolex, which must have cost $2,000, made me see decimal points. And I love money. I love my country—but cash is serene."

Bettina Bancroft, one of the top ten and a lady of total mystery who doesn't allow the RBSC boys in her living room, drops by the store often, considering it the supreme hang-out. She doesn't care much whether she's a Primo Lady or not. She has sized up the success of the store pretty well. "See this shoe?" she says, pointing to a spike-heeled number that might have been worn by Elizabeth Taylor in *Butterfield 8*. "I wore it on Hollywood Boulevard the other day and two ladies of the night stopped me and said, 'Baby, you sure got some fine lookin' shoes.' Right then I knew I'd gone to the right store."

AN AUTHORITY TELLS WHY STATUS SYMBOLS KEEP CHANGING

Q Professor Blumberg, what's happening to "status" in America?

A What seems to have happened in the postwar period—roughly till 1973—is that, with the gradual spread of affluence, the material things which people previously used as status symbols have lost some of their effectiveness. Ironically, as America became more prosperous, it became less materialistic, that is, less preoccupied with material things as badges of status.

Q What kinds of things are important today?

A Don't misunderstand me; there's still a lot of conspicuous consumption

around. Just look at recent Christmas ads from any fashionable store.

But I do see a changing emphasis in the last few years—away from the conventional status symbols, away from what you can buy to what kind of a person you are: cultural tastes, activities, esoteric interests and hobbies. In the realm of things: ceramics, pottery, antiques and handmade one-of-a-kind objects—things that show good taste rather than high cost.

Q Just how do you define status and status symbol?

A Status symbols are marks of distinction. They set you apart from others. Status seeking itself is very widespread because it's really an extension of ego needs for respect, and the desire to be admired and thought well of.

Now, the key to status symbols is the idea of scarcity. If a status symbol is something that sets you apart from and above others, then obviously it has to be scarce. If everybody's got it, it's no good. Once there's an abundance of anything, it becomes useless as a status symbol. Look what's happening to the status value of a college degree as it becomes widely distributed.

Q If there were a scarcity of glass beads, would they then acquire the status of diamonds?

A Probably not. Something must be socially desirable as well as scarce to become a status symbol. Someone with an unusual tropical disease doesn't gain status simply because of the rarity of his condition.

Now, what happened in the United States since World War II was that a great many Americans were able to purchase consumer goods of all kinds—automobiles, appliances, furnishings and so on. They were able to acquire what one sociologist has called the American "standard package" of goods and services. Now, please understand, I'm not celebrating the achievement of the affluent society. After all, we still have 26 million officially defined poor, and millions more economically deprived. Nevertheless, in the postwar period, the availability of this "standard package" increased greatly. So today, if perfectly ordinary people can display big cars and expensive consumer goods, then obviously these things are no longer effective status symbols.

I think you can see very clearly what's happened by looking at the American automobile market in the last 15 years. When automobiles became very widespread, when almost any family could have almost any American car, when someone driving an Oldsmobile or even a Cadillac was nobody special—at that point, cars lost much of their ability to con-

fer status. In a sense, Detroit became a victim of its own success.

Then, about 1960, as a consequence, we saw the beginning of the domestic compact and the unostentatious imports like the Volkswagen. The Volkswagen phenomenon, in fact, can be traced to the loss of the automobile as a status symbol, as people began buying cars for function rather than for show.

Q Might people then start riding bicycles to work?

A They might. Environmentalism in recent years has been a real force working against the old principle of conspicuous consumption. In the old days the advice was, "Drive the biggest car and buy your wife the most exotic fur." Today, environmentalism tells us, "Buy the smaller car, save the fuel, clean up the atmosphere, and buy your wife a cloth coat or fake fur and save the endangered species."

Q Is a rebellion developing against ostentation?

A Well, besides environmentalism, there are many things about American life which work against conspicuous display. There's America's earthy "plain folks" tradition, a kind of rough-and-ready egalitarianism which frowns on pretensions. There's also the youth principle. Looking young, dressing young and so on contradicts the impulse to look rich. So the casual dress and style of the young filter up to the middle-aged and middle class.

Q Is there then a particular age or social group that is setting the pace for these trends?

A According to conventional theory of how fashion spreads through society, the upper class sets the style. Then, because these people are seen as successful and personifying the most respected values in society, their styles trickle down to the middle and working class. That still does happen on occasion. The so-called Gucci style or "status stripe," for example, has trickled down from very expensive leather goods to cheap imitations.

But in the last 10 or 15 years, it hasn't worked this way very much at all. When you look at important styles of the last decade or so—blue jeans, work shirts, denims, beads, long hair and the whole costume associated with the youth movement of the '60s—you have, instead of a trickling down from the top, a kind of percolating up from the bottom.

Q Broadly, what do these trends in fashion styles tell us about the American people?

A They demonstrate, I think, a certain confusion about American values these days. Recently, people have looked, not to the top of society for guides to behavior and dress, but to the bottom or to anti-establishment values. It reflects troubled times and a questioning of official values. Harris Polls taken over the last 10 years show falling public confidence in the leadership of government, large companies, labor, organized religion and so on, reflecting the social turmoil the country has passed through since about 1960.

You can see, I think, that status symbols are not merely frivolous cocktail-party conversation pieces, but are sensitive barometers of scarcity and affluence in society, and also reflect changing social values.

"'SOCIAL REGISTER' IS ALIVE AND WELL"

Q Are wealth and birth no longer passwords to status?

A There's something about our "aristocracy" of wealth and birth that clashes with American values. American society stresses achievement, not inheritance—Horatio Alger and all that. Wealth and birth emphasize the past and tradition, whereas most Americans are future-oriented and look not so much to tradition but to innovation and change. Then, of course, the elitism of the old upper class clashes with America's egalitarian tradition.

Of course, the social position of people of birth and wealth is still intact. The "Social Register," for example, which is the closest thing America has to an official listing of our "best" families, is still alive and well. In fact, it has just now become national—publishing one volume for the entire country, instead of individual volumes for each city—symbolizing, perhaps, a kind of national unity among old upper-class families.

Q Do the very wealthy enter the search for status symbols, or is that confined to the less affluent?

A The old rich, of course, have the reputation for subtlety of display and understatement, marking the confidence of those whose families have been comfortably ensconced for generations. Obviously, the old rich don't have to prove anything to anybody. They can wear 15-year-old suits and drive 20-year-old cars. The new rich, of course, have a reputation for vulgar display—the strainers and strivers showing off their credentials which are usually disdained by the older families.

But I think there are also differences lower down. More-educated, more-sophisticated middle-class people, as well as the stable working class, tend, I feel, to be less ostentatious. The less-sophisticated middle class, plus newly affluent minorities and immigrants, continue the traditional display of cars, furs, jewels and spending sprees for weddings and other affairs.

Of course, a lot of compulsive spend-

ing, even for expensive things, has nothing at all to do with status seeking, but is
merely a form of diversion, an antidote for
boredom. The old expression is accurate:
"The difference between men and boys is
mainly the price of their toys."

**Q How has the recession and in-
flation affected status and status symbols in America?**

A I think 1973 will be seen as a wa-
tershed year in American history—the
end of the postwar era. That year marked
the oil embargo, growing shortages followed by double-digit inflation, and so on.
The drive toward the affluent society became stalled. Real wages have actually
fallen since the early '70s. Poverty is not
declining. Real GNP [gross national prod-
uct] has grown very slowly in the past
several years. For the first time in this
century, we've had unfavorable trade bal-
ances, and our economy is no longer as
competitive vis-à-vis Europe and Japan as
it was during the postwar period. All of
this has certainly had an effect on our
standard of living and on the traditional
American sense of optimism about the
future.

Inflation is a particularly serious
problem here because it begins to put
things out of reach again for middle and
low-income families. Certainly the most
important item here is housing. With the
average new house now around $50,000,
the typical American family is simply
being priced out of the housing market.

If this continues, we may be moving
toward the creation of a two-class society:
those who own their own single-family
houses, and those who, because of inflation, are relegated to apartment-house
rentals. That would be a devastating blow
to the American dream of a house for every
family.

Now, if the inflationary spiral that

developed in the last few years continues—not only in housing, but in soar-
ing costs of automobiles, college education, vacation travel and so on—these
things are going to become scarce again,
and become the basis for new status
symbols.

**Q So you would then come back
full circle to the old material things as
the source of status—**

A Yes. That's exactly my point. Back
to square one.

But everything depends on what
happens to the economy. If income begins
to rise again, if inflation is brought under
control, then material status symbols will
continue to diminish in importance. If,
however, we're locked into shortages and
prohibitive costs for the average family,
then ordinary things will again become
the basis of status.

WHERE STATUS SYMBOLS DON'T WORK

**Q Can status symbols survive at
all in an urban-oriented society?**

A It's very difficult. Status symbols
work better in a small community where
everybody's known to everybody else.
Most people in the city are strangers to one
another, making status hard to identify.
What happens then is that status symbols,
instead of being attached to persons, become attached to larger entities like
neighborhoods, clubs, churches and so on.
You may not know who I am, but if I tell
you I live in Scarsdale [New York City
suburb], you can immediately put a status
tag on me.

Another thing that has happened to
status in the anonymous and transient
city environment is that "visuals," often
unrelated to class position, become very

important: how attractive you are, your poise and presence in public places. Or other superficialities. For example, it's been said that carrying a shopping bag from an exclusive store is something of an urban status symbol, and New Yorkers joke about buying clothes at Alexander's and then going across the street to Bloomingdale's and getting a Bloomingdale's bag to put them in.

But this kind of status display is a bit empty. Whom do you impress? Strangers on the street who couldn't care less, and whom you'll never see again.

Exercise 8

Social Stratification Using a Single-Item Index

OBJECTIVE: To demonstrate the use of occupation as a proxy indicator of social classes.

For the occupations listed place a 1 next to the occupation that you perceive to have the most prestige, a 2 next to the occupation that you perceive to have the second most prestige, etc. When you have finished, compare your rankings with those of a national survey, which are given in the following table.

_____ Share cropper—one who owns no livestock or equipment and does not manage farm
_____ Garbage collector
_____ Street sweeper
_____ Shoe shiner
_____ Undertaker
_____ Welfare worker for a city government
_____ Newspaper columnist
_____ Policeman
_____ Reporter on daily newspaper
_____ Radio announcer
_____ Bookkeeper
_____ Tenant farmer—one who owns livestock and machinery and manages the farm
_____ Insurance agent
_____ Carpenter
_____ Manager of a small store in a city
_____ Local official of a labor union
_____ Mail carrier
_____ Railroad conductor

_____ Traveling salesman for a wholesale concern
_____ Plumber
_____ Automobile repairman
_____ Playground director
_____ Barber
_____ Machine operator in a factory
_____ Owner-operator of a lunch stand
_____ Corporal in the regular army
_____ Garage mechanic
_____ Truck driver
_____ Fisherman who owns his own boat
_____ Clerk in a store
_____ Milk route man
_____ Streetcar motorman
_____ Lumberjack
_____ Restaurant cook
_____ Singer in a nightclub
_____ Filling station attendant
_____ Dock worker
_____ Railroad station hand
_____ Night watchman
_____ Coal miner

_____ Restaurant waiter
_____ Taxi driver
_____ Farmhand
_____ Janitor
_____ Bartender
_____ Clothes presser in a laundry
_____ Soda fountain clerk
_____ U.S. Supreme Court Justice
_____ Physician
_____ Nuclear physicist
_____ Scientist
_____ Government scientist
_____ State governor
_____ Cabinet member in the federal government
_____ College professor
_____ U.S. representative in Congress
_____ Chemist
_____ Lawyer
_____ Diplomat in the U.S. foreign service
_____ Dentist
_____ Architect
_____ County judge
_____ Psychologist
_____ Minister
_____ Member of the board of directors of a large corporation
_____ Mayor of a large city
_____ Priest
_____ Head of a department in a state government
_____ Civil engineer
_____ Airline pilot
_____ Banker
_____ Biologist
_____ Sociologist
_____ Instructor in public schools
_____ Captain in the regular army
_____ Accountant for a large business
_____ Public school teacher
_____ Owner of a factory that employs about 100 people

_____ Building contractor
_____ Artist who paints pictures that are exhibited in galleries
_____ Musician in a symphony orchestra
_____ Author of novels
_____ Economist
_____ Official in an international labor union
_____ Railroad engineer
_____ Electrician
_____ County agricultural agent
_____ Owner-operator of a printing shop
_____ Trained machinist
_____ Farm owner and operator

Prestige Ratings of Occupations in the United States, 1947 and 1963

Occupation	1947 Rank	1963 Rank
U.S. Supreme Court Justice	1	1
Physician	2.5	2
Nuclear physicist	18	3.5
Scientist	8	3.5
Government scientist	10.5	5.5
State governor	2.5	5.5
Cabinet member in the federal government	4.5	8
College professor	8	8
U.S. representative in Congress	8	8
Chemist	18	11
Lawyer	18	11
Diplomat in the U.S. foreign service	4.5	11
Dentist	18	14
Architect	18	14
County judge	13	14
Psychologist	22	17.5
Minister	13	17.5
Member of the board of directors of a large corporation	18	17.5
Mayor of a large city	6	17.5
Priest	6	21.5
Head of a department in a state government	13	21.5
Civil engineer	23	21.5
Airline pilot	24.5	21.5

Occupation			Occupation		
Banker	10.5	24.5	Mail carrier	57	57
Biologist	29	24.5	Railroad conductor	55	57
Sociologist	26.5	26	Traveling salesman for a wholesale concern	51.5	57
Instructor in public schools	34	27.5	Plumber	59.5	59
Captain in the regular army	31.5	27.5	Automobile repairman	59.5	60
			Playground director	55	62.5
Accountant for a large business	29	29.5	Barber	66	62.5
Public school teacher	36	29.5	Machine operator in a factory	64.5	62.5
Owner of a factory that employs about 100 people	26.5	31.5	Owner-operator of a lunch stand	62	62.5
Building contractor	26.5	31.5	Corporal in the regular army	64.5	65.5
Artist who paints pictures that are exhibited in galleries	24.5	34.5	Garage mechanic	62	65.5
			Truck driver	71	67
Musician in a symphony orchestra	29	34.5	Fisherman who owns his own boat	68	68
Author of novels	29	34.5	Clerk in a store	68	70
Economist	34	34.5	Milk route man	71	70
Official of an international labor union	40.5	37	Streetcar motorman	68	70
			Lumberjack	73	72.5
Railroad engineer	40.5	39	Restaurant cook	71	72.5
Electrician	45	39	Singer in a nightclub	74.5	74
County agricultural agent	37.5	39	Filling-station attendant	74.5	75
Owner-operator of a printing shop	42.5	41.5	Dock worker	81.5	77.5
			Railroad section hand	79.5	77.5
Trained machinist	45	41.5	Night watchman	81.5	77.5
Farm owner and operator	39	44	Coal miner	77.5	77.5
Undertaker	47	44	Restaurant waiter	79.5	80.5
Welfare worker for a city government	45	44	Taxi driver	77.5	80.5
			Farmhand	76	83
Newspaper columnist	42.5	46	Janitor	85.5	83
Policeman	55	47	Bartender	85.5	83
Reporter on a daily newspaper	48	48	Clothes presser in a laundry	83	85
Radio announcer	40.5	49.5	Soda fountain clerk	84	86
Bookkeeper	51.5	49.5	Sharecropper—one who owns no livestock or equipment and does not manage farm	87	87
Tenant farmer—one who owns livestock and machinery and manages the farm	51.5	51.5			
Insurance agent	51.5	51.5	Garbage collector	88	88
Carpenter	58	53	Street sweeper	89	89
Manager of a small store in a city	49	54.5	Shoe shiner	90	90
Local official of a labor union	62	54.5			

Source: "Occupational Prestige in the United States: 1925–1963," Robert W. Hodge, Paul M. Siegel, and Peter H. Rossi, in Reinhard Bendix and Seymour Martin Lipset (eds.), *Class, Status, and Power,* 2nd ed. (New York: Free Press, 1966), pp. 322–334 and pp. 324–325. Reprinted with permission from Free Press, Division of Macmillan Publishing Co., Inc.

Exercise 9

Social Stratification Using a Multiple-Item Index[1]

OBJECTIVE: To provide students with an opportunity to use multiple-item indexes.

Based upon the information provided for the individuals described in paragraphs A and B, determine their social class membership using the Hollingshead Two-Factor Index of Social Class and Warner's Index of Status Characteristic.

There are three steps in securing an index of status characteristics (ISC) for an individual. The first step is to obtain ratings for the head of household on each of the four status characteristics that comprise the Index, usually occupation, source of income, house type, and dwelling area. Each of the four status characteristics is rated on a 7-point scale, which ranges from a rating of 1, very high status value, to 7, very low status value. These rating scales are presented in very brief form in Table 1.

Table 1

Scores and Weights for Warner's Index of Status Characteristics

Occupation (Weight of 4)	Source of Income (Weight of 3)	House type (Weight of 3)	Dwelling Area (Weight of 2)
1. Professionals and proprietors of large businesses	1. Inherited wealth	1. Excellent houses	1. Very high: Gold Coast, North Shore, etc.
2. Semiprofessionals and officials of large businesses	2. Earned wealth	2. Very good houses	2. High: the better suburbs and apartment house areas, houses with spacious yards, etc.
3. Clerks and kindred workers	3. Profits and fees	3. Good houses	3. Above average: areas all residential, larger than average space around houses; apartment areas in good condition; etc.
4. Skilled workers	4. Salary	4. Average houses	4. Average: residential neighborhoods, no deterioration in the area.
5. Proprietors of small businesses	5. Wages	5. Fair houses	5. Below average: area not quite holding its own, beginning to deteriorate, businesses entering, etc.
6. Semiskilled workers	6. Private relief	6. Poor houses	6. Low: considerably deteriorated, rundown, and semi-slum.
7. Unskilled workers	7. Public relief and nonrespectable income	7. Very poor houses	7. Very low: slum.

[1]The author wishes to acknowledge Dr. Louise Kanter of the Sociology Department at California State University, Sacramento, for providing much of the materials for this exercise.

The second step is to assign each rating a weight that expresses the importance of that particular status characteristic in social-class prediction. The ratings should be multiplied by the following weights:

Occupation   4
Source of income   3
House type   3
Dwelling area   2

After multiplying by these weights, the ratings are then totaled.[2] The resultant indexes will range from 12 (very high socioeconomic status) to 84 (very low status) A sample calculation follows:

Status Characteristic	Rating		Weight		Weighted Rating
Occupation	2	×	4	=	8
Source of income	3	×	3	=	9
House type	2	×	3	=	6
Dwelling area	3	×	2	=	6
			Weighted total		29

[2]If the data for any of the four ratings are not available, the proper weights for the other three ratings may be obtained from the following table:

Status Characteristics	Weights If All Available	Occupation Missing	Income Missing	House Type Missing	Dwelling Area Missing
Occupation	4	—	5	5	5
Source of income	3	5	—	4	4
House type	3	4	4	—	3
Dwelling area	2	3	3	3	—

Third, convert the index into social class terms using the scale provided in Table 2 below.

Table 2

Social Class Equivalents for I.S.C.

Weighted Total of Ratings	Social Class Equivalents
12–17	Upper class
18–22	Upper class probably; possibility of upper-middle class
23–24	Intermediate: either upper or upper-middle class
25–33	Upper-middle class
34–37	Intermediate: upper-middle or lower-middle class
38–50	Lower-middle class
51–53	Intermediate: lower-middle or upper-lower class
54–62	Upper-lower class
63–66	Intermediate: upper-lower or lower-lower class
67–69	Lower-lower probably; possibly upper-lower class
70–84	Lower-lower class

Table 3

Hollingshead Two-Factor Index of Social Class[3]

A. Occupation Scale

Description	Score
Higher executives of large concerns, proprietors, and major professionals	1
Business managers, proprietors of medium-sized businesses, and lesser professionals	2
Administrative personnel, owners of small businesses, and minor professionals	3
Clerical and sales workers, technicians, and owners of little businesses	4
Skilled manual employees	5
Machine operators and semiskilled employees	6
Unskilled employees	7

B.   Educational Scale

Description	Score
Professional (M.A., M.S., M.E., M.D., Ph.D., LL.B., and the like)	1
Four-year college graduate (A.B., B.S., B.M.)	2
One to three years college (also business schools)	3
High-school graduate	4
Ten to eleven years of school (part high school)	5
Seven to nine years of school	6
Under seven years of school	7

C. Weighting System

[occupational score × 7] + [educational score × 4] = index score

D. Classification System

Class	Range of Scores
I	11–17
II	18–31
III	32–47
IV	48–63
V	64–77

To calculate the *index of social class* score for an individual, the scale value for *occupation* is multiplied by the factor weight for *occupation* (7), and the scale value for *education* inserts is multiplied by the factor weight for *education* (4). For example, if John Doe was a tool designer (a "minor professional," scale value of 3), with a high school diploma (scale value of 4), we would compute his *index of social class* score as follows:

Factor	Scale Score	Factor Weight	Score × Weight
Occupation	3	7	21
Education	4	4	16
Index of social position score =			37

Source: "Social Class and Mental Illness," A. B. Hollingshead and F. C. Redlick, 1958. Reprinted with permission from John Wiley and Sons, Inc.

A. Michael Lund, a jowl-faced man in his early forties, is a proprietor of a small neighborhood liquor store. He and his wife, Georgia, operate a profitable business netting an average of $40,000 a year. With business doing so well these last eight years, their financial situation has improved noticeably. However, they still choose to live in the same modest, three bedroom, two bath house they have lived in since they were married 25 years ago. Their home is only a ten-minute drive away. The thought of moving never occurred to them. They are comfortable with their neighbors who are mostly blue-collar workers. But they want more for their children and are proud that their two children are both college graduates. For people who did not get past eighth grade, Michael and Georgia feel that life has been kind and generous.

B. From the looks of the guy you would never guess he is a professor at this Ivy League institution. I mean, he looks sorta like a bum. I don't mean he is unclean or anything. He's just a mess—all slovenly, wrinkled, and unkempt. But he has this brilliant mind and I guess that's why they let him stay. On his salary, you'd expect him to live in some kinda really nice house, wouldn't you? But he doesn't. I mean this guy lives in a hotel room and gets his meals from the local greasy spoon. You'd have to be nuts to live there! I mean, I wouldn't ever drive my car through that neighborhood at night. Oh, but don't get me wrong. I don't mean to bad mouth the guy. He's cool. I mean he's nice and sociable and all that. But I mean, this guy's kinda crazy. I mean I just can't figure him out.

1. Discuss any differences made in the assignment of individuals to social classes with the Hollingshead and Warner indexes. What are the implications of any discrepancies to marketing decision making?
2. Compare your classification with those of your classmates. Are there any discrepancies? What are the marketing implications of any discrepancies?
3. After you have identified these consumers' social class, discuss the consumer behavior of these individuals based upon your knowledge of the relationship between social class and consumer behavior.

6

Social Groups

What consumers buy, where they buy, how they buy, and what they do with what they buy are dependent upon their conceptualizations of what others will think of their purchases and their behavior. The article in this section shows how consumers influence each other's consumption behavior.

Whether or not a "superstar's" endorsement will help the sale of a product depends upon the consumers' perception of the superstar as an expert, credible individual. The risks and potential benefits of using superstars as spokespersons for products are discussed in the article "Playing the Endorsement Game."

PLAYING THE ENDORSEMENT GAME

When advertising agency Ted Bates & Co. was looking for a way to help people remember Hertz Rent A Car's new slogan, "superstar in rent-a-car," it didn't take too long to settle on O. J. Simpson. In six years with professional football's Buffalo Bills, Simpson had set so many ball-carrying records that many fans considered him the best running back of all time.

Simpson signed on with Hertz for an endorsement fee widely believed to be $250,000 a year. That was two years ago, and the rest, as they say, is advertising history. Since the fall of 1975, tens of millions of television viewers have watched Simpson dash through airports and leap over baggage in pursuit of his rental car. Public awareness of the company has risen

Reprinted with the special permission of *Dunn's Review*, August 1977, Copyright 1977, Dunn & Bradstreet Publications Corporation.

by two-fifths. Hertz says it has broadened its market share lead over rival Avis to 14 percentage points in major airports. For his efforts, Simpson was recently named Presenter of the Year by *Advertising Age*, and he was able to renegotiate his endorsement fee a year before his original contract expired.

Success stories like that have made many other advertisers envious and anxious to duplicate the performance—so much so that the 1970s have been called the decade of the athlete in marketing because of the number of companies that have used sports to sell everything from toothpaste to air conditioning. Goods and services moved with the help of athletic promotions run into the hundreds of millions of dollars annually, and endorsement fees alone may cost corporations $10 million or more.

A CAUTIOUS NOTE

Yet the use of sports superstars to peddle goods and services is a tricky business, and those who traffic in athlete's names detect a note of caution these days among companies that use them. Advertisers whose pursuit of sports tie-ins made the endorsement game one of the most lucrative around for a number of athletes in 1972 and 1973 have lost some of their old enthusiasm. A number of them, particularly those who sell to men, still use athletes heavily. But they do so advisedly, taking care for the most part to stick with the superstars who not only have performed consistently well on the field, but who have demonstrated mass appeal and selling power.

Part of the disenchantment may trace back to Olympic swimmer Mark Spitz. Arriving home from the 1972 summer Olympics with seven gold medals, Spitz was besieged by companies that wanted his endorsement for their products. He happily obliged, collecting by one reckoning $5 million worth of endorsements and related contracts before falling precipitously from public favor and public view. "Spitz had no personality," shrugs one recruiter of athletes for Madison Avenue. Another bristles at any mention of the affair. "It was the biggest fiasco in the history of sports," he says.

But the main reason for the new caution is the realization that most sports promotions don't work because of poor planning. A soap maker who hires a famous baseball player to stand up and recite the benefits of that brand is asking for trouble, says Bert Randolph Sugar, a New York advertising executive who is writing a book about the history of sports in promotions. The sports star may command attention, but his very presence may overpower the basic purpose of the ad if there isn't a strong sales pitch. Yet that is precisely the trap many advertisers fall into. "Marketers still haven't gained much sophistication," Sugar contends. "They think that if they get one guy to go on TV and say, 'I do it,' it will work." Mark Morris, a vice president on the Hertz account at Ted Bates & Co., agrees. "The public," he says, "is becoming much more astute in terms of what it will accept."

The result has been painful for those athletes who rank somewhere between better-than-average and superstar. David Burns, who formed Chicago's Burns Sports Celebrity Service seven years ago to help companies find athletes for their promotions, observes that the consequent softening of demand has halved the price that most athletes can now get for a television commercial. "It's a buyer's market," he says. "If one athlete wants a lot of money, say $50,000 for a commercial, you can pick up the phone and recruit another for twenty. And you might find someone who wants to get on the tube and build up his popularity, and he'll do it for ten."

Athletes who turned pro in recent years with visions of lucrative endorsement contracts are going begging. Lloyd Kolmer, a former William Morris agent who now recruits celebrities for ad agencies, got a call not long ago from the business manager for Mike Thomas, a Washington Redskin running back who was named Rookie of the Year in 1975 by several news agencies. The manager thought it would be nice to get Thomas into television commercials. "Rookie of the Year," Kolmer grumbled. "Nobody would even know his name." David Burns gets at least one call a day from agents who want to know the chances of their clients' landing some fat endorsement contracts. Lately Burns has been telling them: "Almost zero."

The truth is, the chances were never as good as newspaper headlines and the frequent repetition of commercials led people to believe. At the peak of the endorsement boom in 1973, the research firm of Gallup & Robinson kept track of how many television commercials featured celebrities. The answer, it found, was 15%. And of those, many featured film and television personalities, not athletes. Then, as now, the great majority of athletes—including most baseball, football, basketball and hockey players—have found their off-field promotional income pretty much limited to accompanying salesmen on goodwill calls or appearing in an occasional newspaper ad with a group of players. Two or three dozen athletes will get $5,000-to-$10,000 for lending their names to manufacturers of bats, gloves and hockey sticks. And if their sport happens to be baseball, they will get an average of $600 for posing for Topp's baseball trading cards.

Ever since the days that Ty Cobb let the old American Tobacco Trust name a cigarette after him and Babe Ruth lent his name to Quaker Oats, the big money has gone to those durable few whose reputations transcend their particular sport, making them celebrities in their own right. Today, the collection of superstars who can routinely command more than $100,000 for a TV commercial numbers perhaps thirty, or less than 1% of the professional athletes in the United States. "The key word is consistency," says Lloyd Kolmer, who married Joe Namath, a popcorn fanatic and endorser supreme, to a Hamilton Beach popper.

Advertisers, in short, don't want to tie their marketing efforts to athletes like Mark Spitz, whose career may take a nosedive before the next commercial gets on the air. Yet there seems to be no limit to the lengths an advertiser will go to associate itself with an authentic superstar when it thinks the image of the athlete meshes nicely with its own ambitions. Fabergé thinks little of paying Joe Namath $250,000 a year on an eight-to-twenty-year contract to promote its Brut line of toiletries because it figures Namath will be around forever.

A CANDY BAR

Sears, Roebuck & Co. has no trouble justifying the six-figure commission and fee it pays established golf pro Johnny Miller for the same reason. Officials at Standard Brands no doubt thought long and hard before deciding to name a new candy bar after New York Yankees star Reggie Jackson, a deal that may net Jackson millions. There was reason for caution; after all, Jackson has only been around for a decade. But a spokesman is confident: "We know that Reggie is no flash in the pan."

Choosing a superstar is not always as easy as it may seem. For one thing, it is not always clear who can make it as an advertising pitchman. Magnavox thought Hank Aaron would when it agreed in 1974 to pay him $200,000 a year for five years for television commercials, promotional appearances and dealer sales meetings. Aaron was about to break Babe Ruth's lifetime home-run record of 715, and Magnavox expected Aaron to be an exciting and attention-getting advertising spokesman. He was, but his success was short-lived. Those in the trade say Aaron now goes for less than $100,000 on the open market.

On the other hand, Clairol gambled and won when it tied the identity of a new brand of hair conditioner, Short & Sassy, to the fortunes of a young skater, Dorothy Hamill, who had captured the public eye during the 1976 winter Olympics. During her brief Olympic career, she became known as much for her hair style as for her skating style, and hundreds of thousands of women and girls copied it. Clairol, which had just gone on the market with the conditioner, quickly signed her up and changed its advertising campaign accordingly. Rather than fading, as the careers of so many Olympic stars do, Hamill's career soared. Sales of Short & Sassy soared right along with it, and the company has used her to launch another new product, Short & Sassy shampoo. "It was just luck and timing," marvels an executive at Clairol's ad agency, Young & Rubicam. "When she spins, her hair goes out and falls right back in place. She is able to demonstrate how the product works."

A VITAL HOOK

The Hamill tie-in worked, says Y&R, because it has what is known in the trade as a hook, or a logical connection, between a product and its endorser. When a race driver promotes a motor oil, there's a hook, just as there is when a well-known hitter puts his name on a baseball bat. A hook may be a demonstrable quality, such as ruggedness, as when "Mean Joe" Green, defensive lineman for the Pittsburgh Steelers, tried unsuccessfully to crush an Ideal toy truck on-screen. Or it may be a more intangible quality, like wholesomeness, which General Mills hopes Olympic decathlon champion Bruce Jenner will communicate about Wheaties. So confident is General Mills that the two are com-

patible that it redesigned the Wheaties box to put Jenner's picture on the front.

The best-known connection of that sort is Hertz Corp.'s use of O. J. Simpson. Research the company commissioned in 1974 revealed that businessmen, who are the heaviest users of rented cars, perceived little difference between Hertz and its scrappy competitor, Avis. Other research indicated that what businessmen looked for most in a car rental company was speed of service. Hertz instructed the Bates agency to produce a commercial that would appeal to businessmen and emphasize speed. Bates came up with the slogan, "superstar in rent-a-car," and then went out looking for a superstar.

The Bates agency attributes the success of that campaign not only to a superb hook, but also to a certain flamboyance and credibility that Simpson brought to the job. Those qualities, as much as athletic prowess, mean the difference between a department store commercial in Hoboken and a six-figure national advertising contract.

It's widely agreed, for example, that while Simpson has such charisma, Walter Payton, the Chicago Bear running back who nearly outran Simpson for the NFL rushing title last year, doesn't. Payton has received few offers to endorse anything, and he has done no commercials except a radio spot for Nutrament, a food supplement for athletes, and a television spot for Chicago Buick dealers. Mark McCormick, the super-agent who runs International Management Group, the sports promotion conglomerate in Cleveland, spotted the quality several years ago in Laura Baugh, a teenage golfer in California. He signed her up, and though she has never won a major tournament, she pulls down close to $300,000 a year from endorsements, including one for Ultra Brite toothpaste.

"How's your love life?" she is asked on screen. "Uh," she responds. "What's a love life?" How does one set a value on these things? "Who knows?" says Marty Blackman, a New York sports promoter. "You get a feel for it."

It is tradition on Madison Avenue that if a problem exists, someone will design a research project to solve it. Thus it was in 1973 that a New York market researcher named Alan Nelson persuaded twenty national advertisers to chip in about $6,000 each to help discover what American men thought about TV sports in general and about individual athletes in particular. He surveyed 2,500 men across the country, using a questionnaire designed to measure how well athletes are known, respected, liked and trusted. The results, presumably, would free the sports-minded advertiser from the need for seat-of-the-pants judgments.

TRUST AND RESPECT

The athlete most widely trusted and liked, it turned out was Stan Musial, the all-time great first baseman for the St. Louis Cardinals who had retired ten years earlier. The best-known was Willie Mays, whose long career as a baseball player fizzled to an end sometime during the 1973 season. Yet these sterling qualities don't seem to be sufficient in themselves to make a really outstanding advertising pitchman—and, in fact, neither Musial nor Mays has had a very successful career in TV endorsements. On the other hand, flamboyant quarterback Joe Namath—who shows up in the surveys as one of the least admired, least liked and least trusted of the top athletes—happens to be one of the most effective and sought-after spokesmen.

In the face of these real-life inconsistencies, Nelson has revised his study to measure other qualities as well, and he will publish his findings this fall. In the meantime, he offers a rule of thumb: "If you're dealing with a mundane product, often the only way you can draw attention to it is to get some flamboyant athlete spokesman who doesn't necessarily have trust."

Exercise 10

Social Power in Marketing

OBJECTIVE: To recognize the use of social power in marketing.

Social power is the ability of an agent to influence the behavior of another or others. An agent can be a person, an organization, a value, a norm, and so on. Five types of social power have been suggested.[1]

[1]John R. P. French, and Betram Raven, "The Bases of Social Power," in D. Cartwright, ed., *Studies in Social Power,* Ann Arbor, Michigan, the University of Michigan's Institute for Social Research, 1959, pp. 150–167. Copyright 1959 by the Institute for Social Research.

1. *Reward power* is the ability to give rewards.
2. *Coercive power* is the ability to administer punishment.
3. *Expert power* is based upon a recognition of the agent's possession of expertise.
4. *Referent power* rests with the desire of others to identify with the agent.
5. *Legitimate power* is related to social and cultural norms and values of should's and should not's.

Identify the type of social power you think is used in the following marketing situations.

Reprinted with permission from Omega Watch Corporation.

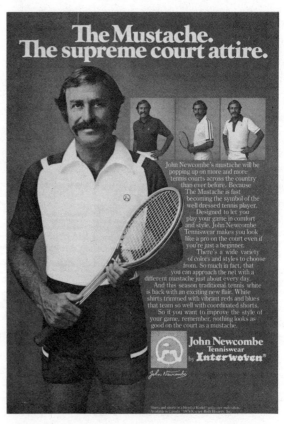

Reprinted with permission from Kayser Roth Hosiery, Inc.

Why Sally Struthers helps support someone else's child.

There are so many children in this world whose parents are too poor, too ill to give them the basic needs of life.

Innocent children with little hope of a better tomorrow.

Unless someone else, outside the family, can help.

Sally Struthers did. She became a sponsor through Christian Children's Fund.

Four years ago, Marites was an eight-year-old little girl who had to go to work just to survive.

Now, because Sally helped, Marites is going to school.

And she has hope.

For just $15 a month, you can become a sponsor through Christian Children's Fund.

You can help give a child like Marites nourishing meals, decent clothing, or a chance to go to school.

Without taking her away from the family she dearly loves.

You needn't send any money right away.

Just send the coupon.

We'll send you a child's picture and background information.

We'll tell you the child's age, how the child lives, what the child wears, and how your 50¢ a day—your $15 a month—can help make a world of difference in this poor child's life.

We'll also tell you how the child will be helped, and explain how you can write to the child and receive very special letters in return.

After you find out about the child and Christian Children's Fund, then you can decide if you want to become a sponsor.

Simply send in your first monthly check or money order for $15 within 10 days.

Or return the photo and other materials so we can ask someone else to help.

Take this opportunity to open your heart to a child who needs you.

And receive something very special in return.

Love.

Reprinted with permission from the Children's Christian Fund, Inc.

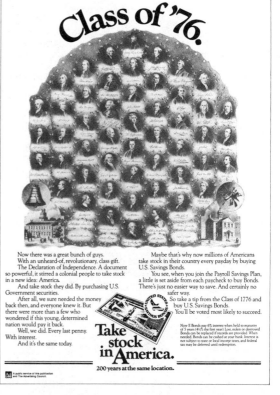
Reprinted with permission from the Advertising Council, Inc.

7

Family Influence

As an earning, consuming, decision-making unit, the family is an important social group that has a major impact on consumer behavior. The articles included in this section discuss the nature and role structure of the family as a consuming, decision-making unit.

The increasing trend for women to enter the work force leads to the conclusion that the "Lady of the House" isn't home any more and she will not be found in the home in the future. According to Maxine Margolis in the article "In Hartford, Hannibal, and (New) Hampshire, Heloise Is Hardly Helpful," the full-time housewife's reaction to this trend is to work "overtime." That may be why today's full-time housewives, with modern time-saving conveniences at their disposal, spend more time doing housework than their predecessors did fifty years ago when such time-saving devices had not been invented.

Patrick E. Murphy and William A. Staples, in the article "A Modernized Family Life Cycle," offer an update on the traditional conceptualization of the family life cycle that incorporates current environmental changes of decrease in fertility rate, delay of time for first marriages, and increase in divorce rates. They propose a modernized family life cycle consisting of five major stages and thirteen subcategories that uses the age of the household head, marital status, and to a lesser extent children's ages to determine the lengths of the stages. The relevance of the financial characteristics and life-style of each stage to the family consumption, decision-making process and purchasing patterns is discussed.

IN HARTFORD, HANNIBAL, AND (NEW) HAMPSHIRE, HELOISE IS HARDLY HELPFUL

Over the past 50 years, "labor-saving" products and appliances have significantly reduced the time spent on domestic chores. However, this "progress" has also left the full-time housewife/mother in the following quandary: her role demands that she devote her days to domestic activities, but these domestic activities are not sufficient to fill her time. Her dilemma is often resolved by C. Northcote Parkinson's Law, which states that "work expands so as to fill the time available for completion." According to Parkinson, the lack of real work does not necessarily result in leisure. Instead, whatever work there is to be done increases in complexity and importance in direct proportion to the time available for doing it.

In truth, despite the presence of myriad labor-saving devices in their homes, today's middle-class housewives spend as much time doing housework as did the women of 50 years ago who entirely lacked these conveniences. In her excellent article in a recent issue of *Scientific American*, Joann Vanek presents the striking statistic that in 1966 the average full-time housewife spent about 55 hours per week at household tasks, while in 1924 her counterpart averaged 52 hours.

This is all the more remarkable when you remember that the typical housewife of 50 years ago had far fewer options in terms of manufactured goods or available services. She washed by hand and ironed; she spent many hours preparing meals, baking, and canning, since few conve-

nience foods or electrical appliances exist-
ed at that time. Of course, dishes were
washed by hand, floors were polished and
rugs were cleaned without mechanical
aids, and without the assistance of the
many detergents, cleaners, and cleansers
that are staples in any contemporary
American middle-class home.

How, then, despite these modern conveniences, can we account for the fact that
in five decades there has actually been a
slight *increase* in hours devoted to housework? One factor is that the time appor-
tioned to various household tasks has
changed. In 1926 about 23 hours a week
were devoted to food preparation and meal
cleanup, but by 1968 this figure had declined to about 18 hours per week. On the
other hand during the same 50 years, general home care increased from about 9 and
a half to 12 hours per week, and time spent
doing laundry increased from about 5 and
a half to 6 and a half hours per week (an
incredible statistic given the ubiquitous
washer and dryer in the modern home).
There is also good evidence that despite
supermarkets and one-stop shopping centers, contemporary housewives spend far
more time shopping than did their counterparts in the 1920s. In one study, 84 percent of the current housewives sampled
entered a store at least once a week, and 25
percent shopped daily or at least three
times a week. Vanek estimates that non-
employed women today spend an average
of one full day a week in stores and en
route compared to less than two hours for
women in the 1920s.

Though modern appliances are supposed to save time, taking care of modern
appliances is actually time-*consuming*.
Anyone who has waited for hours to have a
phone installed or a dishwasher repaired
will appreciate the time required for the

upkeep of such "labor-saving" devices. Pa-
renthetically, sociologist Philip Slater
seeks a link between the failure of repair-
people to make specific appointments and
the general devaluation of the housewife's
role:

> Housewives are expected to operate with-
> out schedules. Repairmen . . . delivery-
> men, and so on, have been successful in
> refusing to constrict their own convenience
> by making scheduled appointments with
> housewives, who are expected to wait at
> home until the workman arrives. Nothing
> could convey more powerfully the low es-
> teem in which the role of housewife is held
> than this disregard of daily scheduling
> needs.

Rising standards of cleanliness also
contribute to sustaining the large number
of hours devoted to housework. Today,
housewives are told that their homes must
be "cleaner than clean" and their laundry
"whiter than white," ideals which far ex-
ceed the requirements of good hygiene.
While these media pressures undoubtedly
help sell more detergents and cleansers for
the advertiser, they also contribute to the
domestic application of Parkinson's Law
and the make-work syndrome. Lacking
sufficient domestic chores to fully occupy
her time, the housewife is urged to find
new crevices to clean and higher standards of innovation and creativity against
which to measure her domestic abilities.

Further evidence for the operation of
Parkinson's Law in the middle-class home
is the amount of time spent on household
tasks by women in the labor force. In 1966,
women with full-time jobs devoted an
average of 26 hours per week to housework, slightly less than half the time spent
on similar activities by full-time housewives. Vanek cites studies which show

that this 50 percent difference is not the result of employed women hiring household help or demanding family members' cooperation in the domestic workload; nor do workingwomen seem to have more labor-saving appliances in their homes or less concern for order and cleanliness than do their home-bound sisters.

The housewife who stays home receives constant television messages encouraging make-work domestic tasks. Many women's magazines and "family" newspaper pages also contribute to this phenomenon. The syndicated King Features column "Hints from Heloise" by Heloise Cruse is a case in point. It is written, to quote the column, "for you the housewife and homemaker," and in it, Heloise passes along her own tidbits and readers' suggestions. It sometimes seems to me to almost be a caricature of Parkinson's Law applied to the domestic sphere. Although offering hints to save housewives both time and money, it, in fact, urges on them an array of time-consuming domestic activities.

My analysis of the hints offered over a two-and-a-half month period from January through mid-March, 1975, indicated that of the 200 hints in the 70 columns sampled, 37.5 percent were needlessly time-consuming, 7.5 percent were time-saving, 40 percent were neutral in time expenditure, 11.2 percent were economy measures, and 2 percent dealt with home safety. Not all the hints were mutually exclusive, that is, a few that were either classified as time-consuming or time-saving also were categorized as economy measures. However, only a handful of the time-consuming suggestions could be justified on the basis of the money saved by doing them. Some hints which consume an inordinate amount of time would result in

a saving of a few pennies at most. Most are make-work exercises. For example, making mailing labels by using gummed wrapping tape, and writing one's name and address over and over the length of the tape, hardly warrants the amount of time spent at the task; such labels are available commercially at very low cost.

How about wrapping Christmas packages by sewing pieces of fabric together and decorating them with sequins, beads, and rickrack? Or learning an elaborate method for preparing homemade dog food; or making a shower curtain and tissue-box cover ensemble by patching together old towels?

Some of the column's hints don't involve much time expenditure, but are mindless superfluous tasks which have an aura of creativity. For example, there is a suggestion that old throw pillows can be made like new again by covering them with a shower cap or hairdo protector or, as another reader suggests, by stuffing them with lint from the clothes dryer. Another column item suggests converting old floor lamps into clothes racks by painting them and decorating the light sockets. Still another tells how to make a planter out of a dish drainer by hanging it backward on the wall and entwining it with artificial flowers.

These examples of the domestic Parkinson's Law in action also reflect a common attitude toward the full-time housewife: her time is of no value. A middle-class American aphorism states that "time is money," and since the housewife receives no wages for her work, her time must be worthless. What does it matter, then, if she spends endless hours sewing dishrags together to make a mop, or waits in vain for days for the appearance of one repairperson or another?

Housewives are supposed to feel fulfilled by their role since they are the only ones in their families who are able to (1) fill the sugar bowl, (2) replace toilet paper, (3) find lost keys, shoes, and socks, and (4) manipulate the washing machine. Finally, and I quote from a letter to Heloise:

> there's absolutely no thrill
> you're really deep in clover
> like when you take out a load of wash
> and don't have a sock left over!

Men are also stereotyped, although not always negatively. They are unable to help dress their children since they have no sense of color. But still they're clever when it suits them. One man wrote to Heloise suggesting the use of red napkins so that lipstick stains would not be so visible, and Heloise replied, "Leave it to a man to figure out a shorter, easier way." Another man, a bachelor, wrote to ask what to do about plastic stuck on pots and pans and was told to "get married and let your wife worry about it." Even small children do not escape sexist casting. One hint suggested that little girls could keep busy and learn coordination by putting the small rods in their mothers' hair rollers.

What is the function of the domestic Parkinson's Law and the make-work syndrome for the society at large? Economist John Kenneth Galbraith says the housewife's job as an unpaid manager of domestic goods and services makes "an indefinitely increasing consumption possible." So keeping women in the home serves the needs of American business and industry. And if women don't have enough to do there to keep busy, "Hints from Heloise," advertisers, and other representatives of the media can easily take care of that.

But why are women willing to go along with these superfluous make-work suggestions? This answer seems to lie in the nature of housework itself. Not only is it unpaid, but it lacks widely accepted standards for measuring job performance. The same tasks must be done over and over again, and most of them make no *permanent visible change* in the home. How can other family members appreciate the long hours spent on housework if its results are not readily apparent and are taken for granted? At least some recognition is achieved by following Heloise-type suggestions for "creative" make-work tasks that, unlike most household chores, have the advantage of visibility. In most homes, a dish drainer entwined with artificial flowers hanging on the wall would be difficult to miss!

A MODERNIZED FAMILY LIFE CYCLE

The family has been one of the hallmarks of American society. However, events in recent years, including rising divorce rates, falling fertility figures, and widespread use of contraceptives, have begun to bring about changes in family structure. It might be argued that the revolution of the 70's is occurring within the home rather than on college campuses or in central cities.

Certain writers (Bernard 1975; Cooper 1970; Davids 1971; Keller 1971; Toffler 1970) have conjectured that families today, and especially those of the future will not resemble those of the past. Others (Bane 1976; Kerchoff 1976; Olson 1972) believe that family formation and

"A Modernized Family Life Cycle," Patrick E. Murphy and William A. Staples, *Journal of Consumer Research,* June 1979, Vol. 6, pp. 12–22, published by the *Journal of Consumer Research.* Reprinted with permission.

dissolution is much the same today as it was in the past. The position taken in this paper falls between those extremes. It appears that certain changes have occurred that affect family life and consumption behavior, but the institution of the family will undoubtedly survive.

One aspect of the family that has been studied by sociologists and consumer and marketing researchers is the "family life cycle" (FLC). It has been shown to be a valuable concept for these three groups of researchers (Lansing and Kish 1957; Rich and Jain 1968; Spanier, Lewis, and Cole 1975). Unfortunately, the life cycle has not been examined in light of current demographic trends. The purpose of this paper is to review the family life cycle concept, discuss prior research concerning its impact on consumer behavior, and suggest a new, more appropriate FLC with research implications.

THE TRADITIONAL FAMILY LIFE CYCLE

Approach and Eras

The family life cycle is derived from the "developmental" approach to studying the family (Hill and Rodgers 1964; Hill 1970; Rodgers 1964; Rodgers 1973), an inter-disciplinary approach drawing from rural and urban sociology, child psychology, and human development. Consequently, alternative views have been expressed about the number, as well as the determinants, of the "stages" in the FLC.

Before examining these viewpoints, other points need to be clarified. A few researchers have argued that the terms "cycle" and "stage" are not appropriate. Specifically, Rodgers (1962) proposed sub-stituting "career" for cycle and "category" for stage. Applying this conceptualization, Feldman and Feldman (1975) suggested four subcareers of a lifetime family career: (1) sexual experience, (2) marital, (3) parental, and (4) adult-parent. Although these ideas have generally not been adopted, it is important to recognize that the FLC terminology has not received universal support.

Family life cycles can be characterized as ranging from simple to complex. Table 1 shows three distinct eras of FLC development.[1] The first one is called the "foundation era" because the concept began to be seriously studied by several writers simultaneously. Although Rowntree (1903) is credited with originating the FLC notion as a method to study poverty patterns in England, it was not until the 30's that family researchers began systematic evaluation of it. In one of the ear-

liest FLC articles, Sorokin, Zimmerman, and Galpin (1931) identified four stages based on the changing family member constellation. Another four-stage FLC developed by Kirkpatrick and others (1934) viewed FLC in terms of the children's position in the educational system, i.e., pre-school, grade school, high school, and adult. In examining the differences between rural and urban families, Loomis (1936) also delineated a four-stage cycle using the children's age as the criterion variable.

During the "expansion era" of FLC research depicted in Table 1, the number of stages identified tended to increase. Bigelow (1942) utilized school placement in a cycle he demarked into seven stages. Similarly, Glick (1947) postulated a seven-stage FLC determined by the birth and marriage of the first and last child, and the husband or wife's death. For the National Conference on Family Life in 1948, another seven-stage FLC was developed using multiple factors to separate stages (Duvall and Hill 1948).

In recent years, further refinements in FLC stages have occurred. Consequently, this period is labeled the "refinement era" (Table 1). The most complex breakdown to date was a twenty-four stage FLC proposed by Rodgers (1960). Although suggested outside the family literature, Wells and Gubar's (1966) nine-stage FLC, based on the ages of parents and children and employment status, has been accepted by family and consumer researchers. Duvall (1971) identified eight FLC stages using both children's and parents' ages to determine the stages.

This review of the chronological eras of the FLC reveals its strong foundation in the sociological literature. Despite the differences in number of stages and the factors causing movement through them,

---

[1]The labels applied to the family life cycle development eras are generic. In other words, they could be used to describe the evolution of most major concepts.

Table 1

Alternative Views of the Family Life Cycle

Author(s)/Stages	Author(s)/Stages	Author(s)/Stages

Foundation era

Sorokin, Zimmerman, and Galpin (1931)	Kirkpatrick, Cowles, and Tough (1934)	Loomis (1936)
1. Married couples just starting their independent economic existence 2. Couples with one or more children 3. Couples with one or more adult self-supporting children 4. Couples growing old	1. Preschool family 2. Grade school family 3. High school family 4. All adult family	1. Childless couples of childbearing age 2. Families with children (eldest under 14) 3. Families with oldest child over 14 and under 36 4. Old families

Expansion era

Bigelow (1942)	Glick (1947)	Duvall and Hill (1948)
1. Establishment 2. Childbearing and preschool period 3. Elementary school period 4. High school period 5. College 6. Period of recovery 7. Period of retirement	1. First marriage 2. Birth of first child 3. Birth of last child 4. Marriage of first child 5. Marriage of last child 6. Death of husband or wife 7. Death of spouse	1. Childless 2. Expanding (birth of first to last child) 3. School age 4. Stable (birth of last child to launching) 5. Contracting (first launched to last launched) 6. Aging companions (no children at home) 7. One partner deceased

Refinement era

Rodgers (1962)	Rodgers (1962) cont.	

1. Beginning families (defined as childless couples)
2. Families with infants (all children less than 36 months old)
3. Preschool families
 a. With infants (oldest child, 3–6 years; youngest child, birth to 36 months)
 b. All children 3–6 years
4. School-age families
 a. With infants (oldest child, 6–13 years; youngest child, birth to 36 months)
 b. With preschoolers (oldest, 6-13 years; youngest, 3–6 years)
 c. All children 6–13 years
5. Teen-age families
 a. With infants (oldest, 13–20; youngest, birth to 36 months)
	b. With preschoolers (oldest, 13–20; youngest, 3–6)
	  c. With school-agers (oldest, 13–20; youngest, 6–13)
	  d. All children 13–20 years
	6. Young adult families
	  a. With infants (oldest, over 20; youngest, birth to 36 months)
	  b. With preschoolers (oldest, over 20; youngest, 3–6)
	  c. With school-agers (oldest, 13–20; youngest, 6–13)
	  d. With teen-agers (oldest, over 20; youngest, 6–13)
	  e. All over 20
	7. Launching families
	  a. With infants (first child launched; youngest, birth to 36 months)
	  b. With preschoolers (first child launched; youngest, 3–6)
		c. With school-agers (first child launched; youngest, 6–13)
		  d. With teen-agers (first child launched; youngest, 13–20)
		  e. With young adults (first child launched; youngest, over 20)
		8. Middle years (all children launched to retirement of breadwinner)
		9. Aging couple (retirement to death of one spouse)
		10. Widowhood (death of first spouse to death of survivor)

Table 1 (*Continued*)

Alternative Views of the Family Life Cycle

Author(s)/Stages	Author(s)/Stages
Wells and Gubar (1966)	Duvall (1971)
1. Bachelor stage (young single people not living at home)	1. Married couples (without children)
2. Newly married couples (no children)	2. Childbearing families (oldest child under 30 months)
3. Full nest I (youngest child under 6)	3. Families with preschool children (oldest, 2½–6)
4. Full nest II (youngest child 6 or over)	4. Families with school children (oldest, 6–13)
5. Full nest III (older married couples with dependent children)	5. Families with teen-agers (oldest, 13–20)
6. Empty nest I (no children living at home, head in labor force)	6. Families as launching centers (first child gone to last child's leaving home)
7. Empty nest II (head retired)	7. Middle-aged parents (empty nest to retirement)
8. Solitary survivor (in labor force)	8. Aging family members (retirement to death of both spouses)
9. Solitary survivor (retired)	

agreement exists on one central idea— each family progresses through a number of distinct phases from point of formation to death of both spouses.

Research over Stages

Considerable attention has been devoted to consumer behavior over the various FLC stages. The first such concerted effort was undertaken in 1954 in a conference entitled "The Life Cycle and Consumer Behavior." Several papers investigated the topic from different perspectives (Clark 1955). Lansing and Morgan (1955) analyzed the family financial situation across the FLC stages, including its relationship to the purchase of durable goods. In another paper at the same conference, Barton (1955) studied the consumption of nondurable goods. Further, Miller (1955) examined the impact of advertising over

the FLC and found stage inversely related to advertising effectiveness. In addition, Fisher (1955) exhorted consumer researchers to conduct more longitudinal family studies and to identify social and psychological factors influencing the FLC stages.

The most comprehensive research relating to the FLC stages was presented by Wells and Gubar (1966). They discussed several of the aforementioned conference papers in detail and supplemented them with data from a then recent *Survey of Consumer Finances* and a *Life* magazine study. In this manner, they were able to develop a thorough profile of financial and consumption behavior across the FLC stages they identified (Table 1).

Several other researchers have concentrated on individual stages of the FLC. Wortzel (1977) studied the "young singles," and concluded that their activities are increasingly oriented toward personal growth and enriching personal experience rather than mate searching and marriage preparation. Specifically, he found purchases decreasingly sex-related and a greater tendency toward buying household durables as an expression of a person's individuality and accomplishments. In an analysis of a "newly forming families" stage, Wattenberg (1974) discussed the demographic make-up of married couples of recent years, contrasted them with married couples of previous times, and indicated their importance as consumers. Earlier studies (Berey and Polley 1968; Ward and Wackman 1972) determined that children have varying influence on family decision making. Finally, Ward (1974) analyzed "consumer socialization" and the family's pervasive effect on it, especially in the childhood and adolescent ages.

The manner in which decisions are made over the FLC stages has also been treated in the literature. Kenkel (1961) found that joint involvement in decision making decreases with the presence of children. Furthermore, the fact that joint spouse involvement decreases over the family life cycle is well documented (Blood and Wolfe 1960; Granbois 1963; and Wolgast 1958).

The applicability of the FLC concept to consumer research is evident from these studies. In fact, a recent text (Reynolds and Wells 1977) adopted a developmental level (i.e., early, middle, and later adulthood), or life cycle approach, to the study of consumer behavior.

Criticisms of the Family Life Cycle

Critics of the FLC, to date, have been few in number. Glick and Parke (1965) attempted to revise and update the lengths of the various stages, using the most recent census data. They examined family social and economic characteristics at each stage, but did not posit any new stages. In discussing marriage and family trends, the same two authors (Parke and Glick 1967) suggested that men and women are now being married at closer ages, teen-age marriages are on the decline, and there are more young women than men living in the U.S. However, their speculations that the frequency of divorce would decline because of reductions in poverty and general improvements in the population's socioeconomic status have not proven accurate. They also did not foresee the declining birth rate.

In two other recent articles with almost identical titles, Norton (1974) and Glick (1977) stipulated that the FLC needed to be "updated." Both stated that the length of time within the stages is changing because women are beginning and completing childbearing sooner and the number of children per family is declining. Specifically, Glick said that a couple now entering marriage has the prospect of jointly surviving for 13 years after the last child's departure. Norton mentioned that rising divorce rates could have profound effects on future FLC studies.

Trost (1974) was more adamant in his criticism of the FLC. After reviewing several of the more popular FLC formulations, he listed their major weaknesses. He pointedly stated that they exclude those couples who never have children, do not account for one parent families, place undue emphasis on the ages of the children, and place stress on the importance of the changing role of the father/husband but not that of the mother/wife.

These criticisms in themselves probably are not sufficient to warrant a revision of the concept. However, when they are considered in light of significant events in recent years, the need for a modernized version of the FLC is more compelling. The following trends suggest that the traditional FLC conceptualization has diminished applicability.

CHANGES IN FAMILY COMPOSITION AND LIFE STYLE

A number of recent demographic shifts have altered the composition of the "typical" American family and, in some cases, changed its life style significantly. One of the most influential factors is the overall decline in the average family size. The fertility rate by 1976 had decreased to 1.8 children per woman.[2] With the number of children in the family declining and likely born within a few years of one another, the middle FLC stages (i.e., those with children present) will tend to last fewer years. Therefore, the time with children living at home may no longer be the predominant portion of the FLC.

A related trend is the tendency for delay of time of first marriage. The annual rate of first marriages has declined almost continuously for two decades. Postponement of marriage has been especially prominent among women in their early 20's. The proportion of women still single at ages 20 to 24 has increased by nearly one-half since 1960, from 28 percent to 43 percent. Continuation of this trend would indicate an increase in the amount of time women and, as a result, men spend in the single FLC stage.

A third important demographic de-

[2]The statistics reported in this section were taken or derived from Glick and Norton (1977).

velopment affecting the FLC is increasing incidence of divorce in the United States. From 1965 to 1976 the divorce rate doubled, from 2.5 to 5.0 per 1,000 poulation. Also, initial divorces are occurring about six months to one year earlier than they did ten years ago, and those who remarry are doing so sooner. Clearly, marital events are being compressed into a shorter span of years.

Although in 1975 four of every five divorced persons remarried by middle age, the decrease in remarriages since 1972 suggests that this proportion may decline in the near future. For example, for persons 35 to 54 years old, the proportion of persons currently divorced increased by one-third between 1970 and 1975. It appears, then, that the middle and older age segments of the family life cycle may be increasingly composed of divorced individuals who are living alone or with children. Divorce projections indicate further increases in the divorce rate. Among women in their 20's today, 40 percent can expect their first marriage to end in divorce. Although it cannot be stated with certainty that this high rate of divorce will proceed unabated, these statistics emphasize the current necessity of recognizing "divorce" as an option within the FLC.

A MODERNIZED FAMILY LIFE CYCLE

Before delineating the steps of the proposed family life cycle, a few exceptions that will not be taken into account in this revised concept need recognition. Although cohabitation as an alternative to marriage is becoming increasingly popular with some segments of society and is beginning to draw research attention

Table 2

Comparison of Population Distributions across the Stages of Two Family Life Cycles, 1970[a]

	Murphy and Staples			Wells and Gubar	
Stage	No. Individuals or Families (000's)	% Total U.S. Population[b]	Stage	No. Individuals or Families (000's)	% Total U.S. Population[b]
1. Young single	16,626	8.2	1. Bachelor	16,626	8.2
2. Young married without children	2,958	2.9	2. Newly married couples	2,958	2.9
3. Other young					
a. Young divorced without children	277	0.1			
b. Young married with children	8,082	17.1	3. Full nest I	11,433	24.2
Infant[c]					
Young (4–12 years old)[c]					
Adolescent[c]					
c. Young divorced with children	1,144	1.9	4. Full nest II	6,547	13.2
Infant					
Young (4–12 years old)					
Adolescent					
4. Middle aged					
a. Middle-aged married without children	4,815	4.7			
b. Middle-aged divorced without children	593	0.3			
c. Middle-aged married with children	15,574	33.0	5. Full nest III	6,955	14.7
Young					
Adolescent					
d. Middle-aged divorced with children	1,080	1.8			
Young					
Adolescent					

(Danzier and Greenwald 1977; Satow 1977), less than one percent of all couples are living together and maintaining a quasi-familial relationship out of marriage (Carter and Glick 1976).

In addition, women who have never been married but are raising a family are also excluded. Individuals who remain single throughout their life are by definition not included in forming a family. Furthermore, married couples who are separated are not explicitly dealt with in this revised FLC. It appears, however, that most persons who separate eventually divorce because it is now easier to afford, and the social stigma of divorce is rapidly lifting (Glick and Norton 1977, p. 15). Finally, young and middle-aged widowed husbands and wives and their families are not taken into account.

Table 2 presents the modernized (i.e., revised) family life cycle; it contains five major stages with 13 subcategories. To provide a sense of continuity for the follow-

Table 2 (*Continued*)

Comparison of Population Distributions across the Stages of Two Family Life Cycles, 1970[a]

	Murphy and Staples			Wells and Gubar		
Stage	No. Individuals or Families (000's)	% Total U.S. Population[b]		Stage	No. Individuals or Families (000's)	% Total U.S. Population[b]
e. Middle-aged married without dependent children	5,627	5.5		6. Empty nest I	5,627	5.5
f. Middle-aged divorced without dependent children	284	0.1				
5. Older						
a. Older married	5,318	5.2		7. Empty nest II	5,318	5.2
b. Older unmarried	3,510	2.0		8. Solitary survivor in labor force	428	0.2
Divorced						
Widowed				9. Solitary survivor retired	3,510	2.0
All other[d]	34,952	17.2		All other[d]	46,738	23.3
	203,210[e]				203,210[e]	

[a]Figures for this Table were taken or derived from U.S. Bureau of the Census 1973, Tables 2 and 9.

[b]As there are single and divorced individuals in some of the stages, the numbers were calculated as a percentage of the entire population, not just the number of families. Also, the percentages of the total for families were determined by multiplying the number of families by 2.3 (average number of children per family in 1970) and adding the parents (or parent, in divorced instances) to the number. For example, the 17.1 percent in the young married with children was computed as follows:

$$\frac{8,082 \ (2.3 \ \text{children}) + 16,164 \ (\text{parents})}{203,210} = 17.1\%.$$

[c]As many families have children at more than one of these age levels, it is not meaningful to compute the numbers for each of these ages independently.

[d]Includes all adults and children not accounted for by the family life cycle stages.

[e]Source: U.S. Bureau of the Census 1970. The numbers do not add up to this total because of the calculations explained in Footnote *b*.

ing elaboration, Figure 1 depicts the flow of families through the revised FLC stages. The viability of this FLC conceptualization is supported by comparison of the number of American families in each of these stages with those in Wells and Gubar's FLC (Table 2). Specifically, 11.8 million more people are accounted for by the inclusion of the divorced and middle-aged married without children stages in the modernized FLC version. As the figures in Table 2 were derived from 1970 census data, the growing percentage of divorced persons (4.3 percent in 1970 to 6.6 percent in 1975, U.S. Bureau of the Census 1975) and the declining family size would tend to magnify the differences between these two FLCs today.

Further support for the proposed FLC is provided by Uhlenberg (1974). He compared the number of females in different age groups who followed the "preferred" or traditional FLC path with those who deviated from it because of early death, remaining childless or single, or experiencing a broken marriage. Although

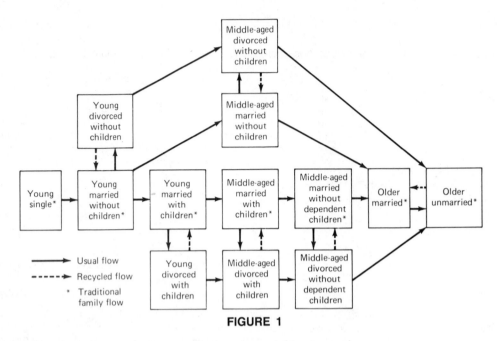

FIGURE 1

Family Life Cycle Flows

he detected a trend toward the preferred life cycle course for women born in the early 1900's, census data utilized in his study revealed that this pattern is not continuing. He stated that for both white and non-white women:

Upon reaching the age category 25–29, the 1940–44 cohort, compared to the earlier one, had a larger percent still single and, among those who were ever-married, a larger percent childless and a smaller percent with their first marriage intact. The movement toward later marriage, delayed childbearing, and increased marital instability initiated by the 1940–44 cohort is continuing among more recent cohorts. These recent cohort changes have been reflected in the highly publicized decreasing annual birth rates and increasing divorce rates during the 1960's and early 1970's. If continued, these changes will reduce the number of women in younger cohorts who follow a preferred life cycle course (p. 288).

The efficacy of this revised family life cycle should not be judged exclusively by the absolute numbers of people that it accounts for, but rather by its ability to reflect changing demographic trends. Wells and Gubar (1966) and other traditional FLC formulations do not take into account the divorced or childless families and, therefore, are not reflective of recent major demographic shifts. Even if the divorce rate subsides somewhat and family size increases in the future, the modernized FLC sufficiently covers these potential changes.

Young Stages

Although "young single" is not technically a family stage, almost everyone passes through it before beginning a family. For most individuals, this stage would begin at about 18 years of age or the time they graduate from high school. Those who marry at 18 or before will skip this stage, but the number of teen-age marriages has been declining (Glick 1977). One study (Bomball, Primeaux, and Pursell 1975) found that as the number of college graduates increases, marriage is temporarily postponed. College enrollments, especially on the part of women, are continuing to grow (VanDusen and Sheldon 1976). Therefore, with the postponement of marriage until the mid-twenties by more individuals, young singles will establish some amount of financial independence and may experience several life styles, e.g., student, employee, dropout.

The second FLC stage is the young (under 35) marrieds without children. Research generally indicates that spouses tend to be alike in age, religion, ethnic group, social origin, and educational level (Kerckhoff 1976). This period of establishment, or "honeymoon" stage, was traditionally rather short, lasting less than two years before the first child was born (Glick and Park 1965, p. 190). Currently, because of the widespread use of contraception, changing attitudes toward parenthood, and more working wives for financial or career reasons, this stage may be extended for several years. This decision usually allows the young married to establish a degree of financial security.

In addition to those who consciously decide not to have children, there are two options for the next stage of the revised FLC. One option is "young divorced." According to recent statistics, one of every three marriages will end in divorce, and, as mentioned previously, divorces are occurring at earlier points in the marriage (Glick and Norton 1977, pp. 25–6). Histor-

ically, blacks (United States Bureau of Census 1972) and lower socioeconomic status couples (Udry 1966) have experienced higher divorce rates than more affluent whites. Life styles of divorced individuals may revert back to the single stage, but sometimes they are psychologically unprepared to begin the "mating game" again. Both are usually financially worse off, unless the wife receives a large alimony settlement or has a career of her own. As most men and women remarry after an early divorce, they would then "recycle" through the young married stage again.

The stage that traditionally follows young married without children is young married with children (Table 1). As shown in Table 2, the subsections of this stage are infant, young (4–12 years old), and adolescent children. The existence of children usually alters drastically the life style and financial situation within the family. Commitment to child rearing in terms of years will probably not be as extensive as in earlier generations.

Divorce within the young-married-with-children FLC stage, although traumatic, is becoming more prevalent. In fact, over 60 percent of divorces in 1976 occurred when the woman was under age 30, and in about two-thirds of these cases children were present (Glick and Norton 1977). Whether the divorce happens when the children are in the infant, young, or adolescent subcategory, both life style and financial implications are significant. Almost always the wife retains custody of the children and, although child support is usually required of the husband, it is frequently inadequate. The wife must then look for employment—sometimes several years after being out of the labor force. The cost of maintaining a separate household leaves many men without much discretionary income.

Middle-Aged Stages

As shown in Table 2, the middle-aged stages contain six possibilities. The range for this category is approximately 35–64 years of age for the family head.[3] One possibility within the middle-aged group is marriage without children. Although this group has historically been a very small segment, it will likely increase in the future because more couples are making a conscious decision not to have children. Urban highly-educated women (Kerckhoff 1976), who are presently growing in number, show the greatest tendency to remain childless. The life style of middle-aged couples without children will probably not be as hectic as when they were younger, but the freedom will remain. If the couple is healthy and financially comfortable, these families could be characterized as occupying the "carefree stage."[4]

The middle-aged divorced situation without children (stage 4b in Table 2) may occur at this time in the family development, or as a continuation of those in young divorced stage not remarrying. A divorce in this stage is less common (Kerckhoff 1976), and when it occurs may present a major life style adjustment for both the spouses. The financial condition of the divorced individual is likely dependent on occupation and socioeconomic status. For some it may be quite comfortable,

[3]The U.S. Bureau of the Census divides ages ending in the digit five according to ten-year intervals (i.e., 25–34, 35–44, etc.). Therefore, the lower limit of middle-age was set at 35 to correspond with these data. Reasons for the upper limit are provided in the "older stages" section.

[4]Of course, race, socioeconomic status, and occupation may affect the degree to which this stage may be characterized as carefree.

but for others financially strained. These persons may remarry (Figure 1), but the likelihood that they would ever have children is small.

The more traditional middle-aged group (stage 4c in Table 2) comprises those with young and adolescent children. The number of families in this stage is large and will continue to be significant. The predominant family life style is one that revolves around the children and their school activities. However, the father's and/or mother's career and its concomitant social and time obligations may alter this life style. Today's family in this stage is better off financially because a larger percentage of the wives are working. Sometimes, it is necessary for the wife to work to meet family financial needs (Oppenheimer 1974).

Middle-aged divorced with children (4d in Table 2) can be arrived at either by a divorce occurring at this time or an extension of the young-divorced-with-children stage. If divorce takes place at this time, life style changes are significant. Both parents and children must adapt. This may mean that the wife and often the children have to take on additional responsibilities for the family's livelihood. On the other hand, families that have experienced a divorce at an earlier stage have likely undergone the adaptive process and are settled in this life style. The procedure for getting to this stage makes little difference in financial terms, however. The divorced father has financial constraints as long as the children are still eligible for child support. Likewise, the mother with children present is saddled with financial burdens.

The final two categories within the middle-aged group are married without dependent children (4e in Table 2) and divorced without dependent children (4f). These represent what Wells and Gubar (1966) and others have described as the "empty nest" stage. Since the age at which children are born is lower for nonwhites and those of lesser education, income, and job status (United States Census 1974), these families or divorced individuals would probably experience a longer empty nest period. The trend toward smaller families in all socioeconomic levels may mean more time in this stage for middle and upper socioeconomic classes in the future, also (Glick 1977). In any event, once the children are on their own the married couple or the divorced man and woman not only experience financial relief, but also many life style options become available.

Older Stages

The final FLC stages (Table 2) are simply labeled "older." The family head's age is about 65 years old, and this category begins at retirement. It might happen at age 60, 62, 65, or possibly later. The recent legislation postponing mandatory retirement may defer this category for some. As retirement represents a major life style and financial change for most, it seems logical that the older stages would start here.

The two major distinctions within the older category are married or unmarried, i.e., divorced or widowed. Older retired couples have few time commitments, but also may have to reduce their standard of living. Those with past savings and good health may have an active retirement, e.g., travel and recreation; others less financially solvent or with infirmities will probably experience an unpleasant final stage.

The "solitary survivor" stage (5b in Table 2), like the young single, is not tech-nically part of the "family" life cycle, but is included to complete the process. For the previously divorced individual, this stage represents only an occupational and possibly a life style change, but not an emotional one. However, the person who was married for most of his/her lifetime may experience emotional as well as physical and financial hardships when losing his/her spouse. Of course, it is possible that an older widowed or divorced person will remarry (Figure 1).

The major stages and their subsections shown in Table 2 attempt to depict a more thorough conceptualization of the modern American family's life cycle. It is possible to follow the flow through the stages as shown in Figure 1. For instance, the "typical" family would progress through stages 1, 2, 3b, 4c and 4e, and 5a and 5b (see Table 2). On the other hand, a woman divorced at age 30 with one child and not remarried would follow the sequence 1, 2, 3b, 3c, 4d, and later 4f and 5b. Those divorced individuals who remarry may recycle through one or more stages, depicted by the dotted lines in Figure 1.

RESEARCH IMPLICATIONS

The objective of this section is to specify areas that may be studied by family sociologists and consumer and marketing researchers. For each of these groups, topics that may be researched, as suggested by recent demographic trends, are examined—e.g., postponement of marriage and declining family size. These might be analyzed by either the traditional or modernized FLC. More significantly, two important areas (divorced persons and childless couples) can be studied using only the revised FLC categories.

Family Sociologists

Although these researchers have extensively investigated family behavior as it relates to the traditional FLC, one issue that needs further analysis is the life cycle squeeze. According to the literature (Estes and Wilensky 1978; Gove, Grimm, Motz, and Thompson 1973; Oppenheimer 1974), the life cycle squeeze occurs in the stages where children are present and family income does not adequately meet family needs. The current trend toward smaller families may reduce the amount of time this squeeze is operable.

Two other topics that deserve attention are marital satisfaction and marital dissolution. Marital satisfaction, according to the traditional FLC stages, has been widely studied (Bossard and Ball 1955; Paris and Luckey 1966; Rollins and Feldman 1970). However, satisfaction within the various "divorced" stages should be measured and compared to the corresponding married stages over time. The modernized FLC would also provide a new context for applying the conceptual framework of marital dissolution developed by Levinger (1976). Moreover, the study of marital dissolution is a subject that could be related to the new FLC.[5] Also, marital satisfaction and dissolution in the revised stages need to be related to social class membership, racial background, and other relevant social factors.

Consumer Researchers

Family decision-making patterns have been extensively analyzed by consumer researchers using the decision process (i.e., problem recognition, search, evaluation, purchase, and postpurchase behavior) and family role structure (i.e., initiator, decider, buyer, etc.) approaches (Davis 1976; Davis and Rigaux 1974; Ferber and Lee 1974). These approaches can be applied in both the traditional and modernized FLC context. In examining the age of family members, the earlier findings (Blood and Wolfe 1960; Granbois 1963; Wolgast 1958) that joint involvement in decision making decreases over the stages of life cycle might be reexamined. For example, those not marrying until the middle or late twenties could have already established strong decision-making patterns or time constraints that may preclude young husbands and wives from extensive joint decision making. Furthermore, those couples spending an extended time in the empty nest stage might become more oriented to joint decision making again.

Another important research area that can be best analyzed by employing the revised FLC concerns family size. For instance, the differences in husband and wife influence in families with children may no longer follow Kenkel's (1961) findings that joint decision-making involvement decreases with the presence of children. Young, middle-aged, or older married couples *without* children might currently differ substantially from families with children, with respect to husband and wife influence in the decision process stages and/or the extent of role specialization. Joint decision making of couples never having children could be analyzed over the revised FLC stages.

The area of future FLC research most obvious from the modernized family life cycle, and most absent in the literature, is a comparison between the decision-mak-

---

[5]For a thorough discussion of this topic, see *Journal of Social Issues,* Winter 1976 (Vol. 32, No. 1), which is devoted to research on divorce and separation.

ing patterns of traditional and nontraditional (those headed by a divorced parent) households. Specifically, does the divorced person engage in more or less external search than married couples? Possible role structure differences in families of married verus divorced parents with one or more children deserve attention. In addition, the role children play in household decision making in divorced families appears to be an important research topic. For example, is the teen-age daughter the primary supermarket products decisionmaker? The degree of husband, wife, or child dominance could vary widely depending on the family composition or the stage in the revised family life cycle. Also, the "gatekeeper" effect for information acquisition and purchase deliberation may not be operable in divorced families.

Marketing Researchers

Those engaged in marketing products and services will be interested in how consumption is affected by the FLC. In fact, Cox (1975) found the traditional FLC stage superior to "length of marriage" in determining consistency between husbands' and wives' attitudes toward automobiles. Hisrich and Peters (1974) also determined that life cycle stage was more significantly correlated with the use or nonuse of several entertainment activities than age or social class.

The changing family size and age profile of the United States population implies that researchers using either the traditional or modernized FLC should investigate the marketing implications of these trends. For example, declining family size affects marketers who sell products appealing to large families, such as station wagons, several-bedroom homes and large size packages. In addition, the quantities of products purchased by families in stages containing children will likely decline. The extended "empty nest" stage identified by Glick (1977) may also be a segment for marketers to study and cultivate. Even if the family is not wealthy, the length of this stage may allow couples to save for vacations, better furniture, and possibly a different home.

The young divorced stage might be a promising segment for marketers of small appliances rather than large ones, because the individual may view this stage as temporary. Within the service area, personal enhancement services, such as health spas and tennis clubs, would seem to be in demand by the more affluent in this group. Also, life insurance marketers may find the divorced woman interested in buying insurance for herself and possibly the children. Moreover, most divorced women with children from middle and lower social classes would probably be seeking inexpensive clothing for herself and the children.

In the middle-aged categories of the revised FLC, those who remain childless may represent a good market for luxury goods, e.g., expensive restaurants, extended vacation packages, high quality furniture. Divorced individuals who hold good jobs and have no dependents may also be classified as part of this same market. Middle-aged divorced parents, on the other hand, would seem to be seeking more low-priced and functional products, such as used cars, inexpensive furniture, and fast food restaurants.

CONCLUDING COMMENT

Although the traditional family life cycle has proven to be a valuable tool for researchers, recent changes in family composition and life style suggest that a revision of the concept is needed. The modernized FLC proposed in this paper utilizes the age of household head, marital status, and, to a less extent, children's ages to determine the length of the stages. Recognition of divorce and remaining childless as options (Table 2) are its major distinguishing features. An explanation of life style and financial characteristics for each stage is given to clarify this conceptualization, and research implications are drawn for family sociologists and consumer and marketing researchers.

References

Bane, Mary Jo (1976), *Here To Stay,* New York: Basic Books, Inc.

Barton, S. G. (1955), "The Life Cycle and Buying Patterns," in *Consumer Behavior,* Vol. 2, ed. Lincoln H. Clark, New York: New York University Press, 53–7.

Berey, Lewis A., and Pollay, Richard W. (1968), "The Influencing Role of the Child in Family Decision-Making," *Journal of Marketing Research,* 5, 70–2.

Bernard, Jessie (1975), "Notes on Changing Life Styles, 1970–1974," *Journal of Marriage and the Family,* 37, 582–600.

Bigelow, Howard F. (1942), "Money and Marriage," in *Marriage and the Family,* eds. Howard Becker and Reuben Hill, Boston: Heath and Company, 382–6.

Blood, Robert O., Jr., and Wolfe, Donald M. (1960), *Husbands and Wives: The Dynamics of Married Living,* New York: The Free Press, pp. 41–4.

Bomball, Mark R., Primeaux, Walter J., and Pursell, Donald E. (1975), "Forecasting Stage 2 of the Family Life Cycle," *Journal of Business,* 48, 65–73.

Bossard, James H. S., and Boll, Eleanor S. (1955), "Marital Unhappiness in the Life Cycle of Marriage," *Marriage and Family Living,* 17, 10–4.

Carter, Hugh, and Glick, Paul C. (1976), *Marriage and Divorce: A Social and Economic Study,* 2nd ed., Cambridge, MA.: Harvard University Press.

Clark, Lincoln H. (1955), ed., *Consumer Behavior,* Vol. 2, New York: New York University Press.

Cooper, David (1970), *The Death of the Family,* New York: Pantheon Books.

Cox, Eli P. III (1975), "Family Purchase Decision Making and the Process of Adjustment," *Journal of Marketing Research,* 12, 189–95.

Danziger, Carl, and Greenwald, Mathew (1977), "An Overview of Unmarried Heterosexual Cohabitation and Suggested Marketing Implications," in *Advances in Consumer Research,* Vol. 4, ed. William D. Perreault, Jr., Atlanta: Association for Consumer Research, pp. 330–4.

Davids, Leo (1971), "North American Marriage: 1990," *The Futurist,* 5, October, 190–4.

Davis, Harry L. (1976), "Decision Making Within The Household," *Journal of Consumer Research,* 2, 241–60.

———, and Rigaux, Benney P. (1974), "Perception of Marital Roles in Decision Processes," *Journal of Consumer Research,* 1, 51–62.

Duvall, Evelyn M. (1971), *Family Development,* 4th ed., Philadelphia: J. B. Lippincott Company, pp. 106–32.

———, and Hill, Reuben (1948), "Report of the Committee on the Dynamics of Family Interaction," Washington, D.C.: National Conference on Family Life, mimeographed.

Estes, Richard J., and Wilensky, Harold L. (1978), "Life Cycle Squeeze and the Morale Curve," *Social Problems,* 25, 277–92.

Feldman, Harold, and Feldman, Margaret (1975), "The Family Life Cycle: Some Suggestions for Recycling," *Journal of Marriage and the Family,* 37, 277–84.

Ferber, Robert, and Lee, Lucy C. (1974), "Husband-Wife Influence in Family Purchasing Behavior," *Journal of Consumer Research,* 1, 43–50.

Fisher, Janet A. (1955), "Family Life Cycle Analysis in Research On Consumer Behavior," in *Consumer Behavior,* Vol. 2., ed. Lincoln H. Clark, New York: New York University Press, pp. 28–35.

Glick, Paul C. (1947), "The Family Cycle," *American Sociological Review,* 12, 164–74.

———, (1977), "Updating the Life Cycle of the Family," *Journal of Marriage and the Family,* 39, 5–13.

———, and Norton, Arthur J. (1977), "Marrying, Divorcing, and Living Together in the U.S. Today," *Population Bulletin,* 32, Washington, D.C.: Population Reference Bureau, Inc.

———, and Parke, Robert, Jr. (1965), "New Approaches in Studying the Life Cycle of the Family," *Demography,* 2, 187–202.

Gove, Walter R., Grimm, James W., Motz, Susan C., and Thompson, James D. (1973), "The Family Life Cycle: Internal Dynamics and Social Consequences," *Sociology and Social Research,* 57, 182–95.

Granbois, Donald H. (1963), "The Role of Communication in the Family Decision-Making Process," in *Proceedings,* ed. S. Greyser, Chicago: American Marketing Association, pp. 44–57.

Hill, Reuben (1970), *Family Development in Three Generations,* Cambridge, MA: Schenkman Publishing Company, Inc.

———, and Rodgers, Roy H. (1964), "The Developmental Approach," in *Handbook of Marriage and the Family,* ed. Harold T. Christensen, Chicago: Rand McNally and Company, pp. 171–211.

Hisrich, Robert D., and Peters, Michael P. (1974), "Selecting the Superior Segmentation Correlate," *Journal of Marketing,* 38, July, 60–3.

Keller, Suzanne (1971), "Does the Family Have a Future?" *Journal of Comparative Family Studies,* 2, 1–14.

Kenkel, William F. (1961), "Family Interaction in Decision Making on Spending," in *Household Decision-Making,* ed. Nelson N. Foote, New York: New York University Press, pp. 140–64.

Kerckhoff, Alan C. (1976), "Patterns of Marriage and Family Formation and Dissolution," *Journal of Consumer Research,* 2, 261–75.

Kirkpatrick, Ellis L., Cowles, Mary, and Tough, Roselyn (1934), "The Life Cycle of the Farm Family in Relation to Its Standard of Living," *Research Bulletin No. 121,* Madison, WI: University of Wisconsin Agricultural Experiment Station.

Lansing, John B., and Kish, Leslie (1957), "Family Life Cycle As An Independent Variable," *American Sociological Review,* 22, 512–9.

———, and Morgan, James N. (1955), "Consumer Finances Over the Life Cycle," in *Consumer Behavior,* Vol. 2, ed. Lincoln H. Clark, New York: New York University Press, pp. 36–51.

Levinger, George (1976), "A Social Psychological Perspective on Marital Dissolution," *Journal of Social Issues,* 32, 21–47.

Loomis, Charles P. (1936), "The Study of the Life Cycle of Families," *Rural Sociology,* 1, 180–99.

Miller, Donald L. (1955), "The Life Cycle and The Impact of Advertising," in *Consumer Behavior,* Vol. 2, ed. Lincoln H. Clark, New York: New York University Press.

Norton, Arthur J. (1974), "The Family-Life Cycle Updated: Components and Uses," in *Selected Studies in Marriage and the Family,* eds. Robert F. Winch and Graham B. Spanier, New York: Holt, Rinehart and Winston, pp. 162–7.

Olson, Daniel H. (1972), "Marriage of the Future: Revolutionary or Evolutionary Change?" *The Family Coordinator,* 21, 383–93.

Oppenheimer, Valerie K. (1974), "The Life Cycle Squeeze: The Interaction of Men's Occupational and Family Life Cycles," *Demography,* 11, 227–45.

Paris, Bethel L., and Luckey, Eleanore B. (1966), "A Longitudinal Study of Marital Satisfaction," *Sociology and Social Research,* 50, January, 212–23.

Parke, Robert, Jr., and Glick, Paul C. (1967), "Prospective Changes in Marriage and the Family," *Journal of Marriage and the Family,* 29, 249–56.

Rainwater, Lee (1974), *What Money Buys: Inequality and the Social Meanings of Income,* New York: Basic Books, Inc.

Reynolds, Fred D., and Wells, William D.

(1977), *Consumer Behavior,* New York: McGraw-Hill Book Company.

Rich, Stuart U., and Jain, Subhash C. (1968), "Social Class and Life Cycle as Predictors of Shopping Behavior," *Journal of Marketing Research,* 5, 41–9.

Rodgers, Roy H. (1962), "Improvements in the Construction and Analysis of Family Life Cycle Categories," unpublished Ph.D. thesis, University of Minnesota.

———, (1960), "Proposed Modification of Duvall Family Life Cycle Stages," paper presented at the American Sociological Association meetings, New York City.

———, (1973), "The Family Life Cycle Concept—Past, Present, and Future," paper presented at Thirteenth International Family Research Seminar, Committee on Family Research, International Sociological Association, Paris, France.

———, (1964), "Towards a Theory of Family Development," *Journal of Marriage and the Family,* 26, 262–70.

Rollins, Boyd C., and Feldman, Harold (1970), "Marital Satisfaction Over the Family Life Cycle," *Journal of Marriage and the Family,* 32, February, 20–8.

Rowntree, Benjamin S. (1903), *Poverty: A Study of Town Life,* London: Macmillan.

Satow, Kay (1977), "Some Comments on Changing Life Styles Among Single Young Adults," in *Advances in Consumer Research,* Vol. 4, ed. William D. Perreault, Jr., Atlanta: Association for Consumer Research, pp. 335–6.

Sorokin, Pitirim A., Zimmerman, Carle C., and Galpin, Charles J. (1931), *A Systematic Sourcebook in Rural Sociology,* Vol. 2, Minneapolis: University of Minnesota Press.

Spanier, Graham B., Lewis, Robert A., and Cole, Charles L. (1975), "Marital Adjustment Over the Family Life Cycle: The Issue of Curvilinearity," *Journal of Marriage and the Family,* 37, 263–75.

Toffler, Alvin (1970), "The Fractured Family," in *Future Shock,* New York: Random House, pp. 211–30.

Trost, Jan (1974), "This Family Life Cycle—An Impossible Concept?" *International Journal of Sociology of the Family,* Spring, 37–47.

Udry, J. Richard (1966), "Marital Instability by Race, Sex, Education, and Occupation Using 1960 Census Data," *American Journal of Sociology,* 22, September, 203–9.

Uhlenberg, Peter (1974), "Cohort Variations in Family Life Cycle Experiences of U.S. Females," *Journal of Marriage and the Family,* 36, 284–92.

U.S. Bureau of the Census (1970), *Census of the Population,* Washington, D.C.: U.S. Government Printing Office.

———, (1973), *Family Composition,* Subject

Report of 1970 Census, Washington, D.C.: U.S. Government Printing Office.

_____, (1974), *Fertility Histories and Birth Expectations of American Women: June 1971.* Current Population Reports, Population Characteristics, Series P-20, No. 263, Washington, D.C.: U.S. Government Printing Office.

_____, (1975), *Marital Status and Living Arrangements,* Current Population Reports, Population Characteristics, Washington, D.C.: U.S. Government Printing Office.

_____, (1972), *Marriage, Divorce, and Remarriage by Year of Birth: June 1971,* Current Population Reports, Population Characteristics, Series P-20, No. 239, Washington, D.C.: U.S. Government Printing Office.

Van Dusen, Roxann A., and Sheldon, Eleanor B. (1976), "The Changing Status of American Women: A Life Cycle Perspective," *American Psychologist,* February, 106–16.

Ward, Scott (1974), "Consumer Socialization," *Journal of Consumer Research,* 1, 1–14.

_____, and Wackman, Daniel B. (1972), "Children's Purchase Influence Attempts and Parental Yielding," *Journal of Marketing Research,* 9, 316–9.

Wattenberg, Ben J. (1975), "The Forming-Families: The Spark in the Tinder, 1975–1985," in *1974 Combined Proceedings,* ed. Ronald C. Curhan, Chicago: American Marketing Association, pp. 51–62.

Wells, William C., and Gubar, George (1966), "Life Cycle Concept in Marketing Research," *Journal of Marketing Research,* 3, 355–63.

Wolgast, Elizabeth H. (1958), "Do Husbands or Wives Make the Purchasing Decisions?" *Journal of Marketing,* 23, 151–8.

Wortzel, Lawrence H. (1977), "Young Adults: Single People and Single Person Households," in *Advances in Consumer Research,* Vol. 4, ed. William D. Perreault, Jr., Atlanta: Association for Consumer Research, pp. 321–9.

Exercise 11

Family Consumption Roles

OBJECTIVES: To underscore the importance of the family as a decision-making and consuming unit. This is accomplished by an analysis of advertisements to determine the decision-making roles of family members for the product in the advertisement.

The family is a consuming and decision-making unit. Analyze the marketing strategy guiding the advertisements of the products. Determine the family consumption roles[1] for the products revealed by the advertisements.

1. *Influencers:* those family members who provide information and advice and thereby affect the selection of a product or service.
2. *Gatekeepers:* those family members who control the flow of information about a product or service into the family, thereby influencing the decisions of other family members.
3. *Deciders:* those family members who have the power to unilaterally or jointly determine whether or not to purchase a specific product or service.

[1]Leon G. Schiffman and Leslie Lazar Kanuk, *Consumer Behavior,* Prentice-Hall, Inc., Englewood Cliffs, N.J., 1978, p. 238.

4. *Buyers:* those family members who actually make the purchase of a particular product or service.
5. *Preparers:* those family members who transform the product into a form in which it will be consumed by other family members.
6. *Users:* those family members who use or consume a particular product or service.

Reprinted with permission from Levi Strauss & Company.

Reprinted with permission of Chevrolet Motor Division, General Motors Corporation.

Reprinted with permission by General Electric Company.

Exercise 12

Stages in the Family Life Cycle

OBJECTIVE: To recognize the implementation of the family life cycle concept in marketing strategy by an analysis of advertisements to assess the stage in the family life cycle of the product's target market.

For each of the advertisements that follow, determine the stage in the family life cycle of the target market. Your instructor will provide you with the family life cycle to use in this exercise.

Reprinted with permission of the Levi Strauss Company.

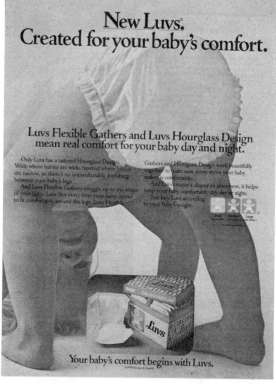

Courtesy of the Procter & Gamble Company.

George, Jr., Mrs. Lang, Maryelizabeth, Mr. Lang.

"A working mother's best friend is her Maytag," writes Mrs. Lang.

Between her family and her job, who has the time to wait around for repairmen?

"Thank you for making a washer a working housewife and mother can count on," writes Mrs. Nancy Lang, Hampton Bays, New York.

"11 years ago, I purchased a Maytag. It wasn't till just this past spring that it needed its first repair."

Mrs. Lang knows from experience that Maytag Washers are

built to last longer and save you money with fewer repairs. She also knows that they can save you the hassle of waiting around for repairmen.

Mrs. Lang adds that she is also delighted with her Maytag Dryer. "As for my Maytag Dishwasher, I would be lost without it," she concludes.

Of course, we don't say all Maytags will equal that record. But long life with few repairs is what we try to build into every Maytag product.

See our washers, dryers, dishwashers and disposers.

MAYTAG
THE DEPENDABILITY PEOPLE

The Maytag Company. Newton. Iowa 50208

Reprinted with permission of Maytag Company.

DUET /TOGETHER.

With a Yamaha organ it's simple. Every Yamaha organ comes with easy-play features like the exclusive Yamaha A-B-C Fun Blocks that give you automatic bass, rhythm, and chord accompaniment the first time you sit down to play. Plus, Yamaha delivers quality and dependability at a very affordable price.

See your Yamaha dealer. Do it today. He's listed in the Yellow Pages under "organs". And ask about the Yamaha Music School for children 4-8 years or the Yamaha Electone Course for everyone.

 YAMAHA

Reprinted with permission of Yamaha International Corporation.

8

Life-Style Research

Life-style research goes beyond demographic portraits of the consumers to include sociological and psychological factors and media and buying habits and preferences. The following articles discuss the concept of psychographics, its application to marketing, and the controversy surrounding its appropriateness and use.

In the article, "Psychographics: Mind over Matter," Alfred S. Boote discusses the contribution of psychographics in deepening the marketers' understanding of the consumer behavior of the target market. Boote emphasizes that psychographics complements but does not replace demographics as a market tool, noting that, whereas demographics describes states of being—age, sex, marital status, income, occupation, location, education—and is useful in determining market potential, psychographics concerns states of mind—life-style, interests, opinions, needs, values, attitudes, personality traits—and are, thus, useful in predicting brand choice.

At Colgate, psychographic segmentation was used in combination with traditional marketing tools to successfully identify and reach a market segment that was not fully satisfied with deodorant soaps available on the market. The article, "How Colgate Brand Manager Applied Psychos to Market and Media for Irish Spring," provides a case history of the successful application of life-style segmentation.

In the article, "Lifestyle Research Inappropriate for Some Categories of Products," Rudolph W. Struse III, of the Oscar Mayer and Company, describes the characteristics of product categories that make them appropriate or inappropriate to life-style research.

PSYCHOGRAPHICS: MIND OVER MATTER

The marketing director of a national restaurant chain proudly reported that sales had jumped by 25 percent since the launch of a new marketing program. Moreover, market research indicated that the sales of the major competitor during the same period had declined by 10 percent.

Both firms' campaigns appealed to the same demographic segment of the population in their area—white-collar, middle-class families who own their homes and have an average of two young children. But the successful firm added another dimension: a psychographic analysis of the market.

The company's research revealed that people who patronize such restaurants value cleanliness and frugality as well as good quality food. So the firm modified its advertising to stress good value and hygienic preparation of food as well as quality. The competitor continued to emphasize only quality, and some patrons switched restaurants.

Interest in psychographics stems from the fact that consumers who share demographic characteristics may differ in purchasing behavior. "Demographic analysis, as a market segmentation tool, may be helpful for identifying market potential, but it appears too insensitive for predicting specific brand choice," Norman L. Barnett wrote in the *Harvard Busines Review* a decade ago.

Although demographics are broadly available, reliable, and widely used, additional information about differences in consumer values and attitudes can help a

"Psychographics: Mind over Matter," Alfred S. Boote, *American Demographic Magazine,* April 1980. Copyright © 1980 American Demographics, Inc. Reprinted with permission.

firm adapt its advertising, promotion, and product design to attract the heaviest users of a class of product to a specific brand. It can also help define special markets that might otherwise be ignored.

Marketers and advertisers create profiles of consumers—the chic suburbanite, the contented housewife, the devoted family man, the frustrated factory worker.[1] These terms reflect shared attitudes, like life-styles, and common purchasing habits as well as similar demographic characteristics. They are based on private surveys, of course, since there is no psychographic equivalent of Census Bureau demographic statistics.

Manufacturers before World War II relied solely on demographics for their consumer marketing strategies (or what passed for them at that time). A product might be intended for consumption by women between the ages of 21 and 30; this segment of the population was assumed to be completely homogeneous with respect to its need for the product. But, if this assumption were true, why didn't all young women buy the product? It seldom occurred to manufacturers that not all young women shared the need the product was designed to meet.

After the war, marketing became more attuned to the needs of prospective customers, creating a demand for better information with which to refine marketing plans and strategies. The "marketing concept," intended to reduce risks associated with introducing new products or new brands of existing products, continued to rely upon the use of demographic descriptors, but their application became considerably more sophisticated.

[1] These examples come from the work of Sunil Mehrotra and William D. Wells. See further information at the end of the article.

A marketer in the late 1940s or early 1950s would probably have divided females 21 to 30 years old into various demographic components: Some would be students, others single and employed full-time, still others divorced, and so forth. This kind of analysis led marketers to conclude that, depending on where they resided or their family status, young women of the same age quite probably differed in their need for products.

This revelation encouraged manufacturers to market several variants of a product, each designed to satisfy the presumed needs of a specific subgroup. This approach, however, resulted in only a marginal improvement in the ratio of success to failure for new product introductions. Some crucial elements were still missing.

PSYCHOGRAPHICS VERSUS DEMOGRAPHICS

Some marketers argue that psychographics have replaced demographics for planning and marketing consumer products. This is nonsense, of course. It is virtually impossible for a company whose market embraces a cross section of the population to ignore demographics. The true basis of the controversy is that marketers have become dissatisfied with demographics as a means of predicting the purchasing behavior of consumers, so they have sought other ways of describing and gauging the market population.

In recent years psychographics have offered help to marketing managers, but the results have been spotty. Since its introduction in the late 1960s, psychographic analysis has passed through a fad stage, as have many marketing research techniques.

To be effective, knowledge about the way people are likely to behave in the marketplace must become part of a systematic plan for a product, from its conception through introduction into the market and maturity. In modern marketing such a plan has become the framework for a marketing strategy. Bringing the matter full circle, an effective strategy must be based on information that is predictive.

Whereas demographics describe states of physical being—age, sex, marital status, income, occupation, location, education-psychographics concern states of mind—lifestyle, interests, opinions, needs, values, attitudes, personality traits, beliefs, intentions. Because a person is seldom able to define these traits directly, they must be measured indirectly. Psychographics, therefore, are subject to ambiguous definition, which means that there is considerable disagreement over the way they should be measured. They are "soft" statistics. By contrast, most demographic statistics have unambiguous definitions that cut across population segments and cultures.

Psychographic analysis has yet to fulfill its early promise of improved predictive power for several reasons. Behavioral scientists say that marketers misuse the standard inventory tests, which were constructed by clinical psychologists for the diagnosis of mental illness. These include the well-known MMPI (Minnesota Multiphasic Personality Inventory) and the Edwards Personal Preference Inventory. Their application by marketers has led to low levels of prediction at best.

Moreover, these predictive associations often have little or no utility. For example, if a market analyst found that buyers of Brand A were more likely than buyers of other brands to be manic-depressive, the information would not help to sell Brand A—except perhaps to patients at a mental institution. Most standardized psychological tests are not appropriate for analyzing market response.

The second source of psychographics' weak predictive capability flows from the first: There is no solid underlying relationship between psychographic characteristics and the choice of a specific product or brand, any more than there is between demographic data and consumer behavior. Without being able to specify how and why different variables combine to describe behavior in the marketplace, it is just a matter of luck that a certain set of variables will have any predictive power.

BUILDING A MODEL

Building an effective marketing strategy depends on being able, in effect, to build a model of consumer behavior. The two simple models for predicting brand choice that are presented here illustrate the essential differences between demographics and psychographics in marketing and also how they are complementary.

The model implies that certain demographic characteristics determine brand choice. For example, it is fairly routine for a soft-drink manufacturer to identify adolescents as the primary market. However, there is no theoretical framework to guide the selection of other demographic descriptors that will predict the choice of the manufacturer's brand over other brands. This model has no predictive power beyond the choice of product class. Moreover, even if a certain combination of demographic descriptors could be associated with brand preferences, the model would have limited strategic value, because it cannot explain why one brand is preferred to another.

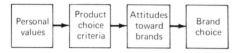

The second model, by contrast, has a theoretical foundation provided by social psychology—particularly in its emphasis on personal values and attitudes. According to theory, values are instrumental in determining people's attitudes toward objects. Research has shown that favorable attitudes toward a product, and toward a specific brand of that product, will lead to its purchase, other things being equal. The "product choice criteria" in the model are those attributes of the product that are critical to the consumer's choice among alternative brands. They are the link between values and attitudes.

This simple model poses two hypotheses that have strategic implications for marketers: First, the more a brand satisfies the product choice criteria associated with a consumer's values, the more likely the consumer will have a favorable attitude toward that brand; second, the more favorable the individual's attitude toward a brand, the more likely the individual will purchase that brand. A recent research study has demonstrated that knowledge of a prospective purchaser's values and choice criteria can help to predict his or her choice of brand.

A decision was made, somewhat arbitrarily, to conduct the study with a demographically homogeneous sample of middle-class women in a Connecticut suburb. They ranged in age from 25 to 40, all of them lived in single-family dwelling units which they (and their husbands) owned, and none of them worked full-time outside the home. All had at least one young child living at home.

Each respondent qualified for participation in the study by saying she planned to buy one or more of the following eight household durables within the three months following the interview: a television set, sewing machine, clothes washer, dryer, dishwasher, vacuum cleaner, food freezer, or a refrigerator. Instrumental values, defined as those which influence attitudes, were derived from a factor analysis of a set of "social orientations," each of which had been rated by the respondents according to their feelings of its importance.[2] Interpretation of the resulting factors defined for the group the following underlying values:

- *Rationality:* A sense of planning, using information to make decisions, and making everyday events routine.
- *Appearance:* Appearance for the sake of impressing others with one's possessions or lifestyle.
- *Independence:* Unconcerned about approval of others with respect to purchases.
- *Novelty:* Responsive to new and modern things; enjoyed the unexpected.
- *Traditionality:* Lived by traditional social norms.
- *Practicality:* Pragmatic with respect to purchases; concerned about value for the money, saving, and realistic expectations.

[2]Factor analysis is a statistical technique used to make data clearer by combining different but related variables.

Since the interview questions were not restricted to a single product class, the product-choice criteria had to be sufficiently general to be applicable to all of the eight products. These product-choice criteria were: reputation for dependability; good style and appearance; good value for the money; and reputation for up-to-date features.

Every respondent rated how important each of these criteria was to her final choice of brand of the product. Then she rated each brand she was considering on the basis of the extent to which she felt the brand satisfied the particular criterion. All of the links between the different parts of the model were therefore established statistically from the survey data, save one—brand choice.

Respondents were called back about four months after the first interview to determine whether they had acted on their expressed intentions to purchase, and if so, which brand was selected. Only about half of the respondents had actually purchased the product for which they were interviewed. These respondents became the source of the data for the final test, which established the statistically significant link between values and brand choice.

EXPLAINING BRAND CHOICE

The research yielded three major benefits: It explained brand preference within an important demographic segment of the market population; it provided the foundation for predicting brand choice based on knowledge of values; and, most important, it produced the kinds of information needed by marketing planners to develop a marketing strategy. The research findings guided the "positioning" of the brand so that advertising could tell prospective customers the important ways in which the marketer's brand was superior to its competition.

If this survey had been done with a large random sample of the entire population, it would have been possible to estimate the psychographic dimensions of the total market; for example, the number of women within a specific demographic classification whose major value orientation is rationality, practicality, or another cluster of values. From this information, the business planner could segment the market for his company's branded products along both psychographic and demographic lines. This information in turn would be useful for forecasting.

BEHAVIORAL DEMOGRAPHICS?

It would be easy to forecast the future if things did not change. We could merely extrapolate from past trends, instead of having to identify the factors that cause change. For example, despite some imaginative attempts, demographers and economists have been unable to explain why the fertility rate fluctuates. Psychographics might provide some help.

A model similar to the marketing model discussed above could be created and tested against a random sample of the entire population of women in the child-bearing age range. If it worked as well as it did for the marketing application, it should become possible to predict shifts in the fertility rate from knowledge of young women's values linked with how those values affect lifestyle.

George Katona and his associates at the University of Michigan, developers of a field of applied research that they call behavioral economics, have found the performance of econometric forecasting models has been improved by incorporating such attitudinal constructs as "buying intentions" and "economic expectations." A reasonable analogy would be behavior demographics—the application of psychographics to population forecasting models.

However, there are many obstacles to be overcome. For one thing, expectations are not always met. For example, Census Bureau surveys have asked young women how many children they expect to bear. In general, women have said they wanted few children, and fertility recently has followed the answers to their questions. On the other hand, women during the baby-boom years often had more children than they said they planned to have. We do not yet understand the underlying values, and much more study is needed before we are able to.

While behavioral demographics may not be with us today, they may be somewhere over the horizon. Just as automobile manufacturers want to know why some people drive Buicks while others choose Olds, politicians want to know why some people vote for Tweedledum instead of Tweedledee, and public planners want to know why some people will ride the bus and others refuse to leave their cars. Why do some people read the newspaper, while others watch television? The list of questions is endless.

Successful marketing will continue to use demographic and geographic data as the essential elements in identifying potential customers. But as we come to learn more about them, psychographics can be expected to deepen our understanding of those we seek to serve.

Further Information

Norman L. Barnett, "Beyond Market Segmentation," *Harvard Business Review,* Jan.–Feb., 1969.

John A. Howard, *Consumer Behavior: Application of Theory,* McGraw-Hill, N.Y. 1977.

Harold H. Kassarjian, "Personality and Consumer Behavior: A Review," *Journal of Marketing Research,* Vol. 8, Nov. 1971, pp. 409–419.

Sunil Mehrotra and William D. Wells, "Psychographics and Buyer Behavior: Theory and Recent Empirical Findings," in Arch G. Woodside, Jagdish N. Sheth, and Peter D. Bennet (eds.), *Consumer and Industrial Buying Behavior,* Elsevier North-Holland, 1977.

William D. Wells, ed., *Life Style and Psychographics.* American Marketing Association, 1974.

HOW COLGATE BRAND MANAGER APPLIED PSYCHOS TO MARKET AND MEDIA FOR IRISH SPRING

Can psychographic segmentation be used to help create and market a new consumer product? The skeptics and cynics still scoff at the idea, certain that psychographic segmentation studies are nothing more than marketing doubletalk. One marketing man of note calls the psychographers "glib manipulators of statistics and sociological jargon."

But at least one major advertiser, Colgate, is crediting the success of a major product, Irish Spring deodorant bar soap, to the application of psychographic segmentation research.

To learn how Colgate developed this successful toilet product, we talked to Doug Wright, group product manager,

"How Colgate Brand Manager Applied Psychos to Market and Media for Irish Spring," *Media Decisions,* December 1976, pp. 70–71. Copyright Decision Publication, Inc. Reprinted with permission.

household products. He set into perspective how psychographics were integrated into the traditional marketing approach. He explained how psychographic segmentation helped develop a product targeted to a group that was not fully persuaded by existing brands. And Wright and media director Harry Way described how segmentation studies interrelated with media selection.

The story begins in 1970 when the overall bar soap market was engulfed by inertia. Colgate's own long-term entry, Palmolive, was in a market share decline.

The situation in the marketplace before Irish Spring was described a couple of years ago by Colgate's board chairman David Foster. He told a marketing seminar at the University of Tennessee, "Bar soaps historically have been a murderously competitive category, and the most difficult in which to introduce a successful new product. From 1958 to 1970, 30 new bar soaps were introduced into test market by competitors within the industry.

"Only three of these expanded nationally: Palmolive Gold, Safeguard and Phase III, all deodorant soaps.

"Interestingly, these brands accounted for only 12% of total bar soap sales. That left 88% of the bar soap market in the hands of brands at least 14 years old at that time. That's almost unheard of in any other category of our business.

"We at Colgate were determined to find a fresh new approach to reach the objective of improving the company's below-par performance in the bar soap field. That fresh approach was psychological segmentation."

Between 1958 and 1970, Colgate put 11 bar soap entries into test market (about one a year). Not one of them went national.

It was then, Wright told us, that Colgate began thinking another approach to new product development was needed. The traditional areas of segmentation (geographic, demographic, and functional or benefit segmentation) had been applied and found wanting. Colgate then began its studies in psychographic segmentation.

Again, in Foster's words, "Psychological segmentation advances the hypothesis that consumers are even more complex than previous segmentation methods had determined—that they may be differentiated along lines of life-style—along lines of personality analysis. Their expectations about the ways in which particular personal products will affect their physical, social, and career lives are central to their choice of brands."

The key question was how to apply that concept and the relevant data to the bar soap field.

In Colgate's approach to the bar soap market before that time, users were neatly pigeonholed into two basic functional segments—the complexion segment and the deodorant segment.

According to Wright, this scheme had failed as a marketing tool for developing new product entries. It gave no clear indication as to *why* persons buy a particular bar of soap. Previous research showed people buying Palmolive as a complexion soap and this stemmed from advertising campaigns stressing that benefit.

Others were buying it for its then-current economy positioning. Some feared "dry skin" and were responding to the now unadvertised lanolin ingredient.

Additionally, functional segmentation had never satisfactorily explained how the same home will use several brands of soap from apparently different functional categories, interchangeably—a usage pattern revealed in probe after probe.

"In essence," Wright said, "what we

Irish Spring Media Expenditures—1972 to 1975

Year	Total	Magazines	Network TV	Spot TV	Network Radio	Spot Radio
1972	$4,856,400	$147,200	$2,647,700	$1,330,300	$250,900	$490,000
1973	3,401,000	81,800	2,183,300	757,700	174,400	262,800
1974	3,795,500	54,500	2,443,800	934,200	251,100	101,900
1975	3,904,400	424,900	2,528,900	472,500	257,600	184,500

Source: Leading National Advertisers: BAR; RER.

attempted to do was take a traditional functional segmentation approach, and combine it with psychographic segmentation. For the first time our research enabled us to go beyond consumer categorizing on the basis of only inherent product use benefits. We could now understand their mental impressions of how a toilet soap influences their roles in life as well as their expectations of physical benefits."

Colgate's segmentation study described three clearly defined consumer types: Rejuvenators, Compensators, and Independents.

It was the Independents who research showed were a psychological group ready for something new and fresh in bar soap benefits. They were defined this way:

The Independent category included an unusual number of leaders, forceful and concerned on getting ahead in the world. Confident, self-assured, calm and unflappable, observant of human failings in others, practical, realistic thinkers, rugged and physically self-reliant, cold shower people who do not pamper themselves. They're geared to the basic function of a toilet soap, cleaning, and not with soothing the skin, but very much concerned with refreshment.

By contrast, the Rejuvenators were shown to be outward directed, basically insecure, needing the support of people around them, a sort of social reassurance.

At the other end of the psychological spectrum was the Compensator group, people whose feelings, it turned out, are directed inward, who are passive and withdrawn by nature and are attracted to images of luxury and comfort in the bath.

What the Independents want from a toilet soap is that it keep them clean, fresh and odor-free. They like a hard soap that lasts a long time. And they like a soap that fits the whole family's needs in a family of like personalities.

Once Colgate had these findings in hand, the company turned full force and full speed to develop the bar soap that would be positioned against the newly discovered vacant position in the deodorant soap market.

From the data disclosed by the psychographic segmentation study, Colgate developed the name and packaging as well as copy tonality and direction in selection of media.

By February 1970, after months of exploration of the many possibilities for concept, name, shape, perfume options and bar color and striations, agreement was reached on the best product fulfilling the core of the psychological product concept: "A deodorant soap for men that is mild enough for the whole family."

From this concept, followed Irish Spring's initial selling phrase, "Manly, yes, but the ladies like it too." Other conclusions from the psychological segmentation study helped guide and keep on track the product development thinking and decisions. Deodorant efficiency, for instance, was shown to be essential as a convincing reason-why for purchasing the product.

"In the Independents segment, we discovered there was a disproportionate number of men, so the copy appeal was to men. That was why we chose the male spokesman, Sean, a rugged looking guy who is self-assured. We brought in the woman in the commercial to show that ladies like it too, in an effort to broaden the appeal to the household purchasing agent," Wright said.

Female reassurance was needed to complement the claim that the soap was effective enough for a man. The synchronization of product appearance, green and white striations, with product promise, "double deodorant system," provided further proof of product efficacy.

As for the Irish image, hardly another country could match the Irish setting for creating a mood of outdoors and freshness, the qualities most associated with cleanliness and deodorancy by consumers. The use of black in the package design, also grew from the psychological data.

NATIONAL ROLL-OUT IN '71

In November, 1970, three TV commercials representing alternate campaign expressions were on-air tested. By early 1971, Irish Spring was in national roll-out.

The major competitors in the deodorant bar soap category then were Dial (from Armour), Zest and Safeguard (from P&G), and Lever's Lifebuoy.

Colgate jumped into the market with a $4,376,000 media budget in 1972, as measured by Leading National Advertisers. By comparison, in that year Dial was spending $6,067,500; Zest $5,118,100; Safeguard, $3,908,100.

Most of the Irish Spring dollars went into television, $2,647,700 into network and $1,330,200 into spot. Network radio accounted for $250,900, and magazines for $147,200.

The competition was banking on television then, neglected network radio and spent little in magazines.

Colgate's introduction was successful enough to secure fourth place in the deodorant category by the end of 1972. By 1973, Irish Spring had a 15% share of the deodorant category as compared with Dial's 33%, Zest's 22%, Safeguard's 12% and Lever's Phase III with 4%.

Only Dial showed a market share decline from 1972 to 1973. Apparently, Irish Spring opened and captured its audience niche without cannibalizing existing brands.

By 1974, the market had settled down, with Irish Spring declining from a 15% share to a 12.5% share, solidly third, just behind P&G's Zest, which slipped from a 22% to a 20% share.

Presently, Irish Spring holds a 13% share of the deodorant category, with its market position established.

Last year, Colgate spent $3,259,000 in LNA measured media, $2,528,900 in network television, $472,500 in spot TV, and $257,600 in network radio for the Irish Spring brand.

The radio campaign essentially made use of the television strategy, Wright told us. It extended the same theme and the same sounds to the additional large audience available via radio.

Colgate is still translating the psychographic profiles it gets for Irish Spring and competitive brands into demographic profiles. The demographics, in turn, become the tool used to select specific media vehicles because the media are still describing their audiences in terms of the demos. Psychographic data is also being applied by Colgate in a similar manner for its detergent products.

Colgate is sold on the value of psychographics as an input in media planning as well as new product positioning. But it is still using the psychographic input as supporting information for the demographic detail that pours out of the usual syndicated media research machines.

Colgate media director Harry Way told us the psychographic segmentation study "provided a confirmation of the direction in which our media plans were already headed, and that is a nice thing to find out.

"In terms of actual vehicle selection, it played a relatively minor role thus far. It came in as after-the-fact information in selection of specific media vehicles.

"The information gleaned from the study has since been taken into account and acted on."

"You're always looking for whatever will give you that extra 10% that puts the odds in your favor. Psychographics gave us that additional 10%," Wright added.

Colgate does not go as far with psychographic factoring of media selection as does Art Boudin, president of The Commercial Analysts, which has been advising Colgate in this area for several years.

Like any other approach to marketing, it must be sold to top management, and when accepted, must be used effectively.

But Colgate's successful application of the concepts and data demonstrate what can be achieved when psychographic data is used by willing hands.

LIFESTYLE RESEARCH INAPPROPRIATE FOR SOME CATEGORIES OF PRODUCTS

Lifestyle research is not useful to all manufacturers, according to Rudolph W. Struse III of Oscar Mayer & Co.

Its most productive uses, he said, are in determining the content and style of communications, in developing new products, positioning them, or developing new packaging.

Lifestyle research, said Struse, is appropriate for products whose function is psychological gratification, or whose performance cannot be evaluated objectively, products with high involvement, or those that are designed for a minority, relatively expensive, or symbolic.

Lifestyle research is likely to pay off, he said, if advertising is a major tool in the

"Lifestyle Research Inappropriate for Some Categories of Products," *Marketing News,* June 17, 1979, published by the American Marketing Association. Reprinted with permission from *Marketing News.*

product's marketing mix, consumers are willing to switch brands because they are not completely satisfied, and the category is not dominated by one or two brands.

Lifestyle research is probably inappropriate for commodities (salt, for instance), products that are purchased on the basis of price or always purchased by an expert, low-involvement products, and those purchased by specifications.

The payoff from such research is likely to be low, Struse said, if ads are a minor element in the marketing mix, consumers are either indifferent or completely loyal to brands, one company totally dominates the category, or consumers find no problems with existing brands.

Before deciding whether to use lifestyle research, he said, a manufacturer must decide how the results will be used. Will results be one more "interesting" input, fodder for the creative group, a framework for creative strategies, a springboard for new product development, or an integral part of the marketing plan?

When considering lifestyle research, the manufacturer must ask if he can focus on a segment, afford multiple segments, develop and test ads and new products with his target, and discipline and segment his market efforts, Struse said.

He must ask whether he can predict consumer behavior from perceptions, descriptive studies, or ad hoc studies.

He must consider whether the research is based on a compulsion to explain and justify behavior, Struse said, and whether behavior really can be explained.

Methods of evaluation are important, he said. Can the efficacy of the results of lifestyle research be measured and can the effectiveness of the actions taken be assessed?

My personal assessment, Struse said, is that lifestyle research is over-promised and overpromoted, used inappropriately and whimsically, subjected to abuse by charlatans, and still an emerging technique with problems to solve.

Exercise 13

Life-Style and Consumer Behavior

OBJECTIVE: To demonstrate to you the relationship between your consumer behavior and your life-style.

Directions to the Writer

Fill in a three-digit number for the writer's identification.
Writer's Identification Number _____

Make a list of some of your possessions.

Make a list of some things you would like to own in the future.

Your instructor will collect your papers when you have completed the list and will randomly distribute them to other students in class.

Directions to the Interpreter

Fill in your three-digit identification number.
Interpreter's Identification Number _____

Describe the person who owns the materials listed.

Describe the person who made a list of things he would like to own in the future.

Your instructor will collect these papers and return them to the writer.

Exercise 14

The Appropriateness of Life-Style Research

OBJECTIVE: To arrive at an understanding of the characteristics of products that make them appropriate or inappropriate to life-style research and segmentation.

The following product characteristics have been offered as guidelines to determine the appropriateness of the application of the life-style concept. Products with the following characteristics would most likely be appropriate for life-style research and segmentation: (1) function is psychological gratification, (2) performance cannot be evaluated objectively, (3) products with high involvement, (4) symbolic, (5) relatively expensive, (6) designed for a minority. Products with the following characteristics would most likely be inappropriate for life-style research and segmentation: (1) commodities, (2) purchased on the basis of price, (3) purchased by an expert, (4) low-involvement products, (5) purchased by specification.

Decide the appropriateness of applying the concept of life-style for the products that follow.

Reprinted with permission of North American Watch.

Reprinted with permission of California and Hawaiian Sugar Company.

Reprinted with permission of Revlon, Inc.

Reprinted with permission of General Mills, Inc.

9

Motivation

Motivation, the force that energizes and directs consumer behavior, is employed by marketers in determining the appropriate appeal for their products and advertisements. Ever since Freud, marketers have used the motivating force of sex to sell their products. As the following article, "King Leer: Sexual Pitches in Ads Become More Explicit and More Persuasive," by Gail Bronson, illustrates, the use of sex to sell products is becoming more explicit. So explicit that it may be a "turnoff" rather than a "turnon."

In the article "Psychological Blocks in Marketing," Alfred Gross discusses the necessity of recognizing and overcoming the antimotivational forces—fear, confusion, and inertia—at work in the marketplace before designing and implementing marketing plans.

Consumers are motivated by curiosity. In the article "Traces of a Treasure and a Harried Hare Beguile Book Buyers," June Kronholz describes how author Kit Williams used curiosity to motivate enough consumers to buy his book *Masquerade* to launch it onto the *New York Times*'s fiction best-seller list.

KING LEER: SEXUAL PITCHES IN ADS BECOME MORE EXPLICIT AND MORE PERVASIVE

Scene: An artist's skylit studio. A young man lies nude, the bedsheets in disarray. He awakens to find a tender note on his pillow. The phone rings and he gets up to answer it.

Woman's voice: "You snore."

Artist (smiling): "And you always steal the covers."

More cozy patter between the two. Then a husky-voiced announcer intones: "Paco Rabanne. A cologne for men. What is remembered is up to you."

For the past month or so, this 30-second commercial has been beamed into America's living rooms courtesy of fragrance maker Puig of Barcelona. Fernando Aleu, a New York neurologist and co-

partner in a Puig unit, readily concedes: "We wouldn't have done this even five years ago."

But as the Paco Rabanne commercial suggests, this has become the Year of the Leer on Madison Avenue. Though sex has always moved merchandise, it has never before been so explicit. Advertisers were once content merely to whisper, hint or suggest. Now the veil on the innuendo is being lifted, and sales pitches are downright steamy. Jeans designers, by turning prime time into a sea of undulating posteriors, led the way. But other advertisers quickly fell in step, using sex to push everything from traveler's checks to tea.

"THE LAST TABOO"

The aim, of course, is to jolt benumbed viewers out of their Barcaloungers. "People are looking for a new stimulant on the subconscious level, and sex is the last taboo," says Arthur R. Ross, creative director of the advertising agency Weiss & Geller Inc. He and other marketers say the newly explicit ads are targeted to reach what they perceive as a jaded, turned-off populace. "Society feels very dead and very pessimistic about the future," Mr. Ross says. Shock value, marketers say, is also useful in penetrating the current "clutter" of competing messages bombarding TV screens. (By one estimate, each one of us is exposed to 500 radio and TV commercials a week.)

Suggestive advertising creates headaches for TV networks, whose censors decide whether a commercial oversteps the boundaries of good taste. Often, getting even mildly provocative material by the censors involves considerable ingenuity—or, at the very least, delicate negotiations.

So far, however, there appears to be little backlash against the new ads. "Our commercial isn't horrendously sensual, just keeping up with the times," says Dr. Aleu, who introduced Paco Rabanne in 1975 with what he terms "very plain" print ads. Now, he says, "our TV and print ads have created a lot of noise in a month's time. But it's only the people in Oregon who write that our ads are too sexy."

MORE EXPLICIT IN PRINT

The Paco Rabanne print campaign is more explicit than its TV commercials. In such publications as New York magazine, Vogue and Esquire, the woman tells her artist-lover: "I'm going to take some (Paco Rabanne cologne) and rub it on my body when I go to bed tonight. And then I'm going to remember every little thing about

you . . . and last night." Another magazine ad for the cologne has a woman calling up a handsome young photographer to invite him over to her place. She introduces herself: "We met last week. At the Wexlers'. You were looking down my dress." (The New York Times Sunday Magazine rejected the artist ad but ran the photographer one.)

While soft-focus sensuality has always been a big factor in cosmetics marketing, today it is even creeping into food advertising. The California Avocado Commission supplements its "Love Food From California" recipe ads with a new campaign featuring Angie Dickinson. The leggy actress will sprawl across two pages of some 18 national magazines next month to promote the avocado's nutritional value. The copy line reads: "Would this body lie to you?"

Dannon Yogurt, in an ad featuring a bikini-clad lovely, touts a new yogurt diet under this headline: "More nonsense is written on dieting than any other subject—except possibly sex." And in Lipton Tea commercials, alluring women urge viewers to spice up their lives with the company's line of flavored brews.

Though Dannon Co. and Thomas J. Lipton Inc. stoutly deny any attempt to titillate, Jacob Jacoby, a Purdue University psychologist and marketing consultant, believes otherwise. "Tea is boring as hell," he says, "and the yogurt maker merely chose a provocative value to grab attention."

SYMBOLISM IN ACTION

In any case, he contends, marketers—like everyone else—carry around sexual symbols in their subconscious that, intentionally or not, they use in ads. He cites the Newport cigaret "Alive With Pleasure" campaign. One such ad features a woman riding the handlebars of a bicycle driven by a man. The main strut of the bike wheel stands up vertically beneath her body, symbolism that Mr. Jacoby says needs no interpretation.

Mr. Jacoby notwithstanding, advertisers suggest that TV-network censors win the prize for turning up sexual connotation where none exists. And, they contend, such primness smacks of a double standard.

"Incest, rape and homosexuality go into programming because the networks realize the pulling power of sex," Weiss & Geller's Mr. Ross says. Jay Jasper, who handles the Paco Rabanne account at the ad agency Ogilvy & Mather Inc., agrees. "By network soap-opera and hit-show standards," he says, "we're pretty tame."

But Mary Lou Jennerjahn, a CBS censor and attorney, argues that while a TV program appears once or twice, often with an advance warning about racy content, "a commercial comes into the home unannounced, over and over again." She neglects to mention, however, the many hit sit-coms that have leaped to the top of the ratings mainly on the strength of their salacious content.

Nonetheless, the censors have the last word, and advertising executives must live with their subjective judgments. To minimize risk, most will show censors an illustrated "story board" of a commercial before it is filmed. "It's the unwise ones who don't," says Julie Hoover, an ABC censor.

Noxell Corp. recently ran afoul of the censors with commercials for Noxzema shave cream. One that showed a man resting his head on a well-endowed showgirl's bosom was turned down. "It was too much for us," says the rejecting censor, who prefers to go unidentified. Another Noxzema commercial that wasn't aired on networks featured Farrah Fawcett helping a lonely woodsman shave. After she murmurs things like "So manly . . ." he remarks: "I haven't seen a woman in nine years." Then, with a nod to Freud, the shave-cream can bursts through the earth's crust, rising like a skyscraper into the forest. (Noxell Corp. officials declined to be interviewed for this article.)

Sometimes, network objections are negotiable. When Ogilvy's Mr. Jasper showed censors the story board for the Paco Rabanne commercial, they insisted that the artists be filmed wearing a wedding ring. Mr. Jasper agreed, but balked at another suggestion. "They wanted to show him wearing pajama bottoms, but we said it wasn't germane," Mr. Jasper says, explaining that the model is shown only from the waist up.

A Citicorp subsidiary squeaked by with a humorous commercial for its traveler's checks that shows a vacationing couple using the public baths in Japan. (The wife cringes in embarrassment as a Japanese man edges closer to strike up a polite conversation with them.) Before approving it, one network censor needed reassurance from the ad agency that in Japan it's customery for men and women to bathe together *au naturel,* as shown on the air. "Still," says the censor, "it was a close call." The Citicorp unit, which previously featured bank tellers in its commercials, has seen its market share "grow substantially" since the campaign began, officials say.

What passes without so much as a blink at one network may be rejected at another. CBS's Miss Jennerjahn concedes that censor decisions are subjective. "I go with my gut," she says. She turned down the Paco Rabanne commercial for network airing because "people beyond the HudsonRiver might feel it shows promiscuity." Local CBS and ABC stations in New York and other selected markets accepted it for late-night viewing.

In creating the first TV commercial for shoe designer Charles Jourdan Boutique Inc., the ad agency Case & McGrath Inc. "made an end-run around the censors," according to Eugene Case, one of the partners. In the commercial, a female shopper cavorts in a lush country garden with a nearly nude Greek statue, who scoops her up and swings her about.

"It's an elegant and sensual way to promote our image," says Terry Pandel, Charles Jourdan's advertising director. "When the statue moves, he's so strong and overwhelming." (The unspoken assumption is that a statue can take liberties that a male model wouldn't be permitted.)

The new sexy ads reflect another change: Women, as often as not, are shown taking the lead in encounters with men. Heublein Inc.'s Harveys Bristol Cream sherry commercials have young, alluringly clad women confiding to friends on the phone: "A few years ago, it wasn't considered respectable for a woman to ask a man over for a drink. But I figure when I'm serving Harveys Bristol Cream, it's more than just respectable, it's downright upright." A parting line, as a man enters the room: "Nancy, I have to go." Previous commercials for the sherry featured stuffed shirts chatting about yachts in paneled studies.

(Interestingly enough, the two-year-old sex-oriented ad campaign hasn't increased Harveys' sales. But the company blames the advent of imitator sherries that cost about $3 a bottle, competing with the $8 Harveys, and it says it is "very committed" to continuing the commercial campaign.)

"Women like it when they're portrayed as taking charge of a situation," says Rena Bartos, a vice president of JWT Group Inc., formerly J. Walter Thompson Co. "It implies power." Mrs. Bartos compares two fragrance ads (neither created by Thompson) that her agency tested last year. One that drew lukewarm—and even negative—response from women was for Aviance. It shows a homemaker stripping off apron and rubber gloves suggestively, as she sings: "I've been sweet and I've been good . . . I've had a whole full day of motherhood, but I'm gonna have an Aviance night." A commercial for Enjoli ("The 8-Hour Perfume for the 24-Hour Woman") drew raves: "I can bring home the bacon, fry it up in a pan," belts the career woman. "I can work till five o'clock . . . and (as she emerges in evening dress) if it's loving you want, I can kiss you and give ya the shiverin' fits!"

The gains women have made in the workplace have actually made them more receptive to overtly suggestive advertising, marketers say. Brenda Harburger, vice president of Charles of the Ritz Group Ltd.'s fragrance division, says the company's Enjoli ad would have been rejected by women 10 years ago "because they were still battling to feel equal to men at work." With one out of two women now working, "people are comfortably recognizing that sex exists, and that it's healthy to desire it," says Sanford D. Buchsbaum, executive vice president for Revlon Inc.'s U.S. cosmetics.

Though barriers are tumbling fast, advertisers still complain they toil under unreasonable restrictions. In TV commercials, for example, live models can be shown in underwear only if it's worn over other clothing.

Hanes Corp. circumvented this rule with what one censor calls a "very tongue-in-cheek commercial" for Underalls pantyhose. In 1976, Underalls made its television debut, with cameras focused on the models' fully—if tightly—clothed backsides. One model exclaims: "I feel like I'm not wearing nothin'!" In recently updated commercials, the announcer commands models to "Show us your Underalls." Viewers again see their backsides, and are invited to search out tell-tale panty-lines.

Formfit Rogers Inc. must rely on magazine support for its television advertising in order to "tell our whole story," says Dorothy Tivi Pollack, the lingerie maker's advertising director. In March, Formfit will begin a $4.6 million TV campaign to introduce a panty fashioned from a new polypropylene fabric. The fabric has absorbency and stain-resistant properties that censors generally won't allow to be mentioned on TV, she says.

And if nudity is common in European commercials, it is still anathema in the U.S. market. "We've okayed party scenes where cleavage was visible," ABC's Miss Hoover says. "But we don't want to titillate the audience, and have them oohing over seeing a nipple."

Some advertisers see a pragmatic reason for such reserve. "When the sexual content of a message is very potent, it can overpower the brand name and be very counterproductive," observes Joan S. Holbrook, a creative vice president at the McCann-Erickson ad agency. McCann, which has the Coca-Cola and Tab accounts, uses wholesomely attractive—but never sexy—models. In Mrs. Holbrook's words: "We don't invite America to have a Coke and a smirk."

PSYCHOLOGICAL BLOCKS IN MARKETING

Consumer motivation is so vital a topic to marketers that it is central to all thinking and planning of marketing campaigns. Consumer behavior, a broader view of the problem, has commanded the attention of behavioral technicians over many years and the exploration of this subject continues unabated. However, most of the study is centered around buying behavior rather than around the general market attitudes of the consumer. In this respect such study tends to concentrate on the consumer as an active purchaser, particularly when he is in the market for some product. It is concerned with how he goes about buying.

But suppose he is turned off? What if

"Psychological Blocks in Marketing," Alfred Gross, *MSU Business Topics,* Winter 1974, pp. 61–72. Reprinted by permission of the publisher, Division of Research, Graduate School of Business Administration, Michigan State University.

he is not in the market even though, by most of the rules of marketing men, he should be? How do we turn him on? (We are alluding to prospects, that is, people who normally would need and want the product, and who would have the money to pay for it.)

There are forces at work which can negate the best marketing intentions. People do have negative thoughts and attitudes about various products and marketing techniques. It is important to understand the range and depths of these negative feelings before designing or implementing marketing campaigns. Otherwise, we can dream up the most creative promotions and then find, to our dismay, that they fail.

It is the purpose of this article to explore various negative attitudes which disturb people, then to offer some approaches to resolving these difficulties. We shall call these negative influences psychological blocks. They are the antitheses of motivational forces (possibly antimotivational forces) and surely warrant careful study by the marketer.

For the purposes of study the blocks have been grouped in three broad categories: those that emanate from fear, those that arise from confusion, and those that result from inertia.

The sequence of topics should not be considered as an indication of their order or importance. Each or any combination may be applicable to a particular product. The array of negative forces involved will vary. These will depend upon the individual, the product under consideration, and the marketing techniques brought into play. The range of negative forces at play in any specific instance may vary from none to virtually the entire gamut. In some instances, even one negative response may kill a sale, whereas in others, a number of such responses may be overcome.

Many negative feelings and potentially negative reactions to products and promotions seem to lie deep within the psyche of the individual. These are independent of the marketing situation. They precede any contact and only come to the fore when a prospect is confronted with the possibility of purchasing.

FEAR AS AN INHIBITING FORCE

Some negative responses are obviously learned and can easily be explained, but others cause us more trouble. These might be called instinctive negative reactions. For example, people fear air flight. Many studies have shown that a large segment of the public is more than a little frightened at the thought of flying. That is certainly true of first flights—but how about second, third, and fourth flights? Most people seem to accept flying with minimal concern after having experienced flight, but we know that large numbers, possibly most air travellers, are somewhat uncomfortable from takeoff to landing. This group even includes many of the ones who have adjusted to flying. They are sensitive to every bump, every change in motor noise, and to every banking turn. Most people are somewhat tense on takeoff and especially at landing. Notice how often, especially on long flights, the travellers break out in spontaneous applause at touchdown.

Why do people fear flying, but do not fear auto driving—even though the latter is far more dangerous in terms of accidents and deaths per passenger mile travelled? For that matter, passengers in both airplanes and autos involuntarily "assist" the pilot or driver in his operations of the vehicle. Every time the pilot banks, some of the passengers mentally help the pilot straighten out: similarly, back seat drivers brake to avoid accidents. How do we sell air flight when people react as they do?

Another interesting example is the problem of marketing contact lenses. These sell slowly despite their obvious advantages. Quite simply, many people cannot stand the thought of putting something in their eyes. It even disturbs them to see other people putting things in their eyes—or worse, taking something out.

An appliance which suffers from some indefinable fear is the electric blanket. This product was expected to sell in large quantities when it was introduced. Its advantages are many, and its cost is reasonable when compared with a quality blanket. When asked why they do not buy an electric blanket, the same response is repeated again and again. "It is dangerous. I wouldn't think of going to sleep under an electric appliance. I might be electrocuted." When it is pointed out that the power consumption of the electric blanket is extremely low, that maximum protection is built into the product virtually excluding any danger, the response is still the same. They fear the product.

These same people do not question having a television set in the home with its 25,000 volt chassis. Nor do they think twice before inserting an arm into the chassis area to check a tube. This, despite the fact that there is often enough voltage stored up, even when turned off, to cause injury—even death. No doubt they want the television set very badly, and are ready to rationalize away any danger possibly emanating from it.

Reactions to different foods are also hard to understand. Why does a child dislike spinach? Probably because he has been taught by others that "spinach tastes bad." Evidently, children are not supposed to like spinach—unless they have had contact with unprejudiced teachers.

Limburger cheese is in a similar category. Ask a roomful of people whether any of them dislikes limburger cheese, and a sea of hands goes up. Then, ask those who have responded how many have tasted limburger cheese: most of the hands will go down. One might ask how so many people can dislike a product which they have never tasted. They know mostly from hearsay that it smells bad, and that it does not taste good.

To take another tack: People know that servicemen are "thieves." Owners quake when the television serviceman shakes his head. They get a queasy feeling in the pit of the stomach when he says the set will have to come out and go to the repair shop. The auto owner, looking at his bill for a tune-up is sure he is being taken. Why is his bill double that of the advertised special price for a tune-up with "parts extra?" The person bringing in a watch or an electric appliance for repair feels similarly disturbed. Is he being overcharged? Were the parts actually replaced? Will the device work right now? Why should he feel disturbed? Are all repairmen really dishonest? Not to hear their side of the story.

Salesmen have been maligned since time immemorial. Insurance salesmen, book salesmen, and house-to-house salesmen have been the butt of nasty stories for generations. People are taught from childhood to beware of the tricky salesman. Is it any wonder that people are skeptical when an unsolicited salesman approaches?

The underlying point in all these examples is that potential buyers are turned off before really evaluating the product or meeting the salesman. In advance, something has happened which has conditioned them against the product. Obviously, unless something can be done to soften the negative reaction or to assuage fear, sales are going to suffer.

With some products there are no easy answers. What can the marketing man do about innate fear—whether of air flight, or of inserting something into the eyes? Psychologists can help the air traveler by providing him with attractive surroundings, pretty hostesses (note the successful "Fly Me" campaign by National Airlines), and personnel who seem confident in their every action—despite the buffeting of the plane. They can feed him liquor and plenty of food (people eat and drink much more while in air flight than normally) and entertain him with movies, music, and reading material. It all helps, but the basic fear remains.

With the electric blanket and products with similar marketing problems, it is important to build confidence. The Underwriter's Laboratory Seal of Approval conveys a feeling of protection. Long life warranties imply quality construction. Descriptive matter may point up low wattage not as a safety matter but to suggest how little energy is needed to keep the user comfortable. Add testimonials about use in hospitals and nursing homes and we are on the way to bypassing the unspoken concern of the consumer.

Foods which evoke negative responses are best promoted by diverting attention through the use of newer, different, and attractive packaging. Take limburger cheese: repackage it in pretty glass containers, and re-name it "luncheon spread." Offer it to people and a surprisingly large percentage of them will say that they like it. Sampling, also, is most helpful. There is no substitute for getting the product into the mouths of people so they can judge for themselves whether or not they like it.

How about the service problem? Guarantees help, but more important is the attitude of personnel handling the customer. Since it is not unusual for a mechanic to find that additional parts or repairs are necessary after he opens up the defective areas, a successful automobile agency insists on telephoning the owners and getting approval before going ahead with repairs beyond those originally agreed upon. The same procedure is followed by a quality high fidelity component

repair service. The owner is put on notice and can decide whether he wants to invest the additional sum or not. He invariably says, "Yes."

The automobile agency goes further. It returns all defective parts to the owner. He usually asks that they be thrown away, but at least the shop gives the impression of being scrupulously honest. The same practice is followed by some leading electronic repair services. The owner is right to be quizzical when the repair man takes along the used tubes or parts.

Solving preconditioned negative responses to salesmen is not easy. They will always have trouble getting in to see prospects. However, careful preparation helps.

Fuller Brush is well aware that women fear strange men at their doors. One answer: teach the salesmen to smile and step backward as the woman opens the door or looks through the peephole. To facilitate matters even more, the salesman is advised to distribute notice one day in advance of his intended visit, stating that he will be coming with a free gift. These tactics will improve his success ratio amazingly.

Of course, more can be done to make certain that improper selling is minimized. To control this danger, leading land development companies have contracted with shopping service organizations to check up on their salesmen periodically. And when salesmen overstep the bounds, they are either reprimanded, corrected, or in serious cases, dismissed. Major retailers have followed this practice for many years.

More recently, an ombudsman has been introduced by most automobile manufacturers to help alleviate customer forebodings. At least the purchaser is given an outlet for his irritations. That alone is enough to relieve many a disgruntled owner. And if he can really get help, he may think less worriedly about buying.

A caution is in order, however. Unless the ombudsman is given adequate stature and the power which is implied in his title, little is likely to be accomplished. What is called for is an independent ombudsman, at least one who is not subservient to sales. If he is able to report directly to a higher echelon with the power to effectuate corrective action he will gain respect and truly build up customer confidence. The latter should not be minimized as a potent ally for future business.

Despite all our efforts some negative preconditioning will remain. It may lie dormant only to rise again when least expected. Unfortunately, much of the consumer movement—which is excellent in its overall objectives—tends to increase consumer fear. It focuses on the troublesome aspects of marketing and tends to spread a blanket of doubt over all. This is all the more reason for the marketer to be conscious of consumer negativism and to work even harder to overcome this problem.

FEAR OF SOMETHING NEW

Many people have a strong tendency to find fault with virtually all new concepts and new products. They will object to their introduction, fight them, and often will try to kill them.

It is amazing how rapidly badmouthing of new products develops. Sometimes the denigration is based on fact, perhaps on some deficiency in the new product. But, even if such findings do not exist, the reaction takes place. Perhaps the most exciting invention in modern times has been the electronic computer. It was certain to replace old fashioned equipment and methods, yet large numbers of people who should have known better—such as accountants, controllers, and professionals in many fields—belittled them. The public quickly picked up the cry, and few people have not heard at least one story ridiculing the computer. But, all in vain. Progress of this giant has been astonishing, sweeping away those who fought its entry into science and business, affecting the lives of every man, woman, and child.

On the consumer level there are many examples. Teflon-coated greaseless cooking utensils were disbelieved and then avoided as dangerous. ("Did you know that at high temperatures the Teflon coating would melt and then be ingested with dire results?") Over the years, their tendency to scratch has been improved and Teflon utensils now are an important addition to the family watching its cholesterol and calorie intake. Fortunately, this product is admirably suited to in-store demonstration. It is difficult indeed for a homemaker not to be excited by a pan in which she can fry sticky foods, such as eggs and cheese, and then see them slide right out although the utensil has not been greased.

It is true that slight radiation was found emanating from early color television sets—hardly enough to be dangerous, but enough to give the industry a black eye. Similarly, the microwave electronic oven has been frowned upon—despite its ability to cook food in a fraction of the time required with conventional ranges. Although they now are widely used in restaurants and institutions where speed and convenience count, many people fear them. After all, if they can cook so quickly are they not dangerous? Official Certification Seals of Safety are highly recommended for such items. In addition, free radiation checking may assuage the fears of those customers who raise this issue.

Servicemen are a major cause of product failure rumors. When tubeless tires were introduced as standard equipment on automobiles (lower operating heat, much less danger of blowouts, longer life) gas station operators and even some tire supply stores recommended that auto owners install tubes for their protection. It need not be said that intensive education before the product is released is mandatory with such products. If service personnel can be provided with the product for their own use and convince themselves of the merits of the new item, it is much more likely to be favorably received when finally marketed to the consumer.

However, we wish to distinguish between general negative reactions to new products, such as the examples just noted, and those of a segment of the populace who tend to be negative about new things. Just as there are people who wish to be first, who are always ready to experiment, there are sizable numbers who will not buy until a product is well established; and there is still another significant segment who will never buy the new item, or, if confronted with it (perhaps when receiving it as a gift), will feel ill at ease with its use.

Marketing men have evolved a number of tools to overcome fear and doubts surrounding new products; one of the most effective is the free sample. When an item can be touched, tasted, smelled, and operated it is sound practice to offer the potential user an opportunity to try the product. Then, he can tell, by personal test, whether he likes it or not.

Large, expensive items as well as inexpensive ones can be offered on a trial basis, or with a money-back guarantee. Assuming that the new product is sound, getting it into the home or business for experimentation under normal conditions will convince many people of the product's merits. In recent years expensive items such as television sets, automobiles, electric typewriters, and steel-belted radial tires have been offered on a free trial or money-back guarantee basis.

Lincoln automobile dealers, for example, selectively have offered "a new car with full tank of gas, free for a weekend" so that prospects could prove to themselves how fine the autos really were and (hopefully) switch from their present models. In order to make headway against difficult opposition, Royal Typewriter offered its new electrics in quantity on a free trial basis to businesses willing to try them. Firestone has offered to equip autos with a full set of new tires on a money-back guarantee.

Perhaps most interesting in this regard was the campaign by Leavitt Builders to sell their houses on a trial basis. Would-be owners were asked to rent a new house for a year. If they decided to keep it, the rental payments became the down payment. If not, the rentals were just that and they could move out. Needless to say, very few moved at the end of the year.

Once a follow-the-leader pattern develops, the product is on its way. How many large firms were able to resist the installation of electronic computers once the leaders put them in? Clothing styles move from the young to the old. Entertainment patterns flow from the wealthy to middle class to low income people, and so forth. The problem is to get a product moving; then, if it is sound, acceptance and momentum will build up.

WORRY ABOUT LARGE EXPENDITURES

Fear commonly arises when large dollar purchases are contemplated. Interestingly, the question of what is a large purchase is hard to answer. "Large" depends upon the shopper. But speaking psychologically, it is a large purchase when the shopper feels it is one. For example, to the woman accustomed to paying $20 for a dress, a $50 garment will seem like a large purchase. The man accustomed to buying a $3,000 car may become fretful when thinking of stepping up to one costing $4,000.

Certain products give consumers a feeling that they are large purchases although they really are not—in light of the family's typical expenditure pattern. Men's suits, for example, are considered large purchases by many who would not hesitate about going out and spending at least as much for an ephemeral evening. Jewelry "signals" large purchase even though many items, such as watches, have dropped down in price, relatively, and often cost less than some popular toys. If it is a large purchase in the mind of the shopper, then it is to the marketing man in terms of how he must present the product and treat the prospect.

In any case, a serious block arises when a big purchase is contemplated. Such purchases call for careful consideration, often by the entire family. It becomes important to shop around, to check all sources of helpful, dependable information. It calls for being careful in the store, in not committing oneself too readily to the salesman, and in moving slowly before making a decision.

This pattern is normal and proper. Certainly, a man contemplating the purchase of a new car should be far more circumspect than the same individual buying gasoline for the car.

The family is well advised to tread carefully and explore fully before making the down payment on a house. The woman buying furniture, especially expensive custom-made pieces, had better be careful before placing the order. The security investor is well advised to check out his information carefully before committing himself.

What can we do to help? Translate price into value. That quality $100 mattress actually costs less than three cents per night when figured over a lifetime guarantee of ten years. (Simmons Beautyrest or similar quality mattresses offer such long life warranties. Some guarantee twenty years of satisfactory wear.) That extra $200 for automatic transmission in the automobile actually may not cost anything if it increases the trade-in value as much two or three years hence. A diamond or other fine piece of jewelry is likely to appreciate in value over time. A number of leading jewelers offer to take in trade, at the full original price, any piece of jewelry purchased from them. Quite simply, the value must be made clear to the buyer; then the sale is likely to take place.

CONFUSION AS AN INHIBITING FORCE

It would seem logical to assume that shoppers would prefer the greatest possible variety when selecting merchandise. After all, if it costs no more, why not go to a dealer with the broadest range of goods. A choice then can be made that most exactingly fits the needs and desires of the customer, ensuring the least danger of his having missed an opportunity. Conversely, the smaller the display, the less chance the customer has of getting exactly what he wants. On this premise, the manufacturer's line should be as extensive as possible, and the retailer should strive to offer the greatest possible range of merchandise.

Unfortunately, logic does not jibe with reality. As any experienced marketing man knows, it is very easy to swamp the shopper with too wide an array and lose the sale. The problem applies in situations ranging from comparatively simple goods to those which are very complex. The result is the same. If the shopper becomes confused, he or she will not buy. Let it be understood that we are talking about situations where the shopper wishes to purchase, the dealer certainly wishes to sell, the merchandise is available in the desired quality and price, and yet a purchase is inordinately delayed, or worse, never takes place.

At the elementary end of the scale we may observe a woman shopping for perfume. It is customary for the customer to smell various scents before buying one. The sales clerk proceeds by spraying on the arm of the customer first once scent, another, and then another. At this point, if a selection has not been made, the trained perfume sales clerk is in a quandary. Because of the nature of perfume, by the time the customer has tested three or four scents the olfactory senses become confused, and additional samples can only increase the confusion. Consequently, unless the customer seems to know exactly what she wants, the sales clerk is well advised first to discuss with the customer her interests, her perfume experience, and possibly, price range. Only after focusing on the kind of perfume which probably will be selected should she offer samples.

This procedure benefits both customer and store. If the purpose of the shopper is to buy perfume, it is to her advantage to explain her problem, so that the sales clerk can help her without causing uncertainty. Then a few properly selected samples should resolve the choice intelligently. A poor clerk will spray the perfumes at random, offering anything in which the shopper shows interest, probably confusing the shopper and losing the sale.

The problem becomes far more serious as the selection of merchandise becomes more complex. The shopper for a camera is faced with the dilemma of a seemingly never ending series of improvements. Regardless of whether he is in the market for motion picture equipment or a still camera, change is the norm. Selecting one type of equipment over another is enough of a problem, but let us assume he is interested in a still camera; a large distributor estimates that there are literally thousands of models on the market. In any one price bracket—for example, quality cameras in the $100 to $200 range—hundreds of models are available. And any quality camera brand can be purchased with different lenses, various body options, attachments, and other extras, enough to make the novice blanch. Even the "old hand" may feel he has made a mistake in the particular combination he ordered some time after he has used it.

With high fidelity sound equipment the choice range is astronomical. Let us say a man has decided he wants quality equipment and is ready to spend between $700 to $1000 for a good system. He then probably goes to one of the better component stores and is ushered into a hi-fi display audio room. Equipment of all types lines the shelves and a switchboard mixer makes it possible to listen to any combination of components in the room. It is possible to listen to a particular combination with one set of speakers, then another combination of speakers, and so on. Any combination is available at a touch. The firm not only offers the merchandise on display, but anything in its extensive catalog. Everything in the field is available. All the individual has to do is make the choice of the combination he wishes. But he has to make a choice from at least: twenty-five speakers on display (over 100 in the catalog); twenty amplifiers, stereo or four channel, definitely not mono (over fifty in the catalog); five pre-amplifiers (for the sophisticated audio bug); twenty-five record players or turntables, plus arm, plus cartridge (scores of combinations available in catalog); twenty-five cartridges (over fifty in the catalog); twenty-five radio receivers; or ten tape player attachments, and so on and on.

Actually, the shopper is faced with a problem in mathematical combinations. Since each component is available with any other combination of components, we are asking the customer to select any combination from the total number of combinations available—which, mathematically, amounts to a minimum of four billion.

By the time the shopper has listened to six or eight combinations, he is hopelessly confused. He then tells the clerk, quite honestly, that he is not sure, wants to think about it, and then he walks out. He will repeat the exercise (perhaps three or four times) and then probably select some reasonably good sounding system; he never will feel quite certain that he bought the best combination for his purposes. The problem can become unbelievably complex even though we find manufacturer and dealer working closely together to give the devotee what he wants—a personalized quality music reproducing system.

The logical solution? Simplify the selection. Coordinate the components into matched combinations. Offer the audiophile an opportunity to individualize his system—but within a minimal range of options (for example, a choice of cartridges). Furthermore, it is feasible to offer the combination at a better price than if the components were purchased independently, thereby giving the shopper an added inducement to buy the completely assembled system.

In home furnishings the situation is replicated—perhaps it is even more complex. Consider what a woman is faced with when she tries to decorate a quality home. She probably will start with the living room. First, she must decide on the kind of atmosphere or feeling her home should have, the furniture pieces and sizes suitable for the particular members of her family, then the best color schemes, and so forth. She must choose among the various period styles—and variations within each style—for furniture frames; probably each piece selected will be somewhat different from the other pieces, and yet they must blend together. Then she must select a fabric for each piece, considering colors, textures, patterns, and not forget about the price. Literally tens of thousands of choices are foisted upon her. (In any quality decorating showroom or furniture store large numbers of fabric sample books are opened to her, then, if she is not satisfied, trips to special fabric showrooms follow, each of which can show thousands of varieties.) She also must choose among various frame finishes, upholstery constructions, cushion fillings, and so forth.

She must blend in carpeting to go with the furniture, then consider draperies to carry the colors and fabric tone of the pieces already selected. Next she must pick wallpaper or she may decide on paint, which is easier to match or blend into the decorating scheme. Now the woman must add suitable occasional furniture, lamps and lighting fixtures, accessories, and possibly paintings—all to blend into a cohesive whole. This is a monumental task: truly a fine art. Again, we are calling for unified choices among an unbelievable number of possible combinations. And we have just decorated one room. The others, hopefully, should fit in with the feeling developed in the living room.

Is it any wonder that the typical woman considers decorating a home to be a highly traumatic affair? Not only must she please her family—physically and esthetically—while keeping within budget limits—but she also wishes to please her friends, and even her mother-in-law. That is why most women decorate so slowly, and then feel frustrated with the result. The complexity of the process which slows down selection often extends over years and means so much less consumption and less dollars in the till. Again, we must reiterate, this constraining force exists despite a strong desire on the part of the shopper to buy; she has been given the money and go-ahead signal, and merchandise which dealers are anxious to sell is available in the marketplace.

The answer here is to show groupings. For many years decorating shops have stressed their model rooms. Coordinated ensembles show how the units may be used. It is not surprising that many women buy the entire package—furniture, floor covering, draperies, and so forth, exactly as shown in the model room.

In recent years manufacturers have concentrated on bringing out broad groupings of a wide range of pieces which blend together. A still newer development by the manufacturer is the expansion of the line to make feasible a complete franchise operation. Baumritter's Ethan Allen Early American line, for example, is franchised selectively to dealers who will sell only that firm's line. As a result, both primary and secondary selection are greatly facilitated.

Clearly, many industries suffer from the aggravating problem of shopper confusion which slows down or kills sales. We can add to the list: clothing (trying to buy a matched ensemble), buying a home, investing in stocks or even in mutual funds, selecting from various vacation alternatives (tour packages), and so forth. Whenever the choice is broad, there is danger of confusion.

BLURRED IMAGES

Again, we begin with a person who wishes to buy something. He needs new tires, or shoes, or wishes to buy a wristwatch. She wants a new coat or dress. The family wishes to buy a new toaster or a television set. The shopper is ready to pay for good quality, but is faced with a serious problem. To a considerable degree, every item just mentioned is available in a wide range of prices and qualities, yet all items look alike.

The man shopping for a suit sees illustrations in advertisements for identical-looking suits with a wide range of prices. The copy hardly enlightens him: the emphasis is on current styling and quality. It is naive to expect the lower priced lines to apologize for poorer fabrics or tailoring, much less styling. They all claim that their suits are well made. In the store, the uncertainty regarding style or quality is unrelieved. Why is one suit selling for $95 and a similar looking suit selling for $135? or one for $165 and another for $250? Is it the cut or the fit? Is it the fabric? Possibly. Will the higher priced one last longer? No, possibly it will wear out more quickly. The higher priced suit may be made of a distinctive or imported fabric or it may have more hand tailoring. But you cannot see it. You just have to trust the dealer. Is it surprising if the customer hesitates, is confused, or buys the lower priced garment?

To overcome these disturbing questions, an effective tactic has been to promote the names of leading designers: Oleg Cassini, Pierre Cardin, Bill Blass, and many others. Once the reputation of the designer is established it is expected that the customer will assume the quality characteristics to be expected in the price line he is buying.

Consider wristwatches: even the trained eye will have difficulty telling from a short distance whether a watch is worth $25, or $50, or $100. This certainly is true if one tries to tell quality from the advertisements (excluding prices or brands). New processes make it possible for cases of base metals to resemble precious metals. Anodized aluminum looks like gold, and gold plate looks like fourteen karats. Furthermore, even relatively inexpensive watches properly may advertise that they have seventeen jewel movements, include a day-date, or are automatic. Why pay ten times as much for a watch when your friends can tell only by reading the name that it is a better watch?

The simple answer is heavy brand advertising coupled with quality of product. People know that Omega, Longines, and Piaget are quality watches. Similarly,

they know that Timex offers attractive looking inexpensive watches. The choice is up to the customer. With jewelry, dealer reputation is the sine qua non. While few people would question Tiffany's or Cartier's there can be doubt and trouble in the typical shop.

How does one evaluate automobile tires? They all look alike. This is especially true when they are mounted. Can the buyer test them by the ancient ritual of kicking them? Ridiculous! They all seem strong. Tread patterns may be identical, or one variation may be as good as another.

The Goodrich Rubber Company offers the shopper a free tire selector device. First, it is pointed out that tires come in more or less standard grades, and that each grade serves a distinct purpose. Next, the shopper must ask himself what is his primary use of the automobile, such as high speed, long-distance driving, or local, relatively slow speed runs. He uses the selector to determine the quality level he needs, then he is ready to buy.

A common problem the shopper encounters is the tendency toward homogeneity in product design. This is hardly surprising; better selling designs rapidly drive out slow moving numbers. Competing manufacturers carefully watch the market and quickly adapt their lines to successful selling items. But are the products all the same? Are all electric toasters alike, or all steam irons, all washing machines, or all television sets? Definitely not! They may look alike, yet have significantly different operating and quality characteristics. The consumer is faced with a serious problem. One of his major rules of thumb for gauging value has withered. Once upon a time, bigger was better—whether one was buying fountain pens or furniture, radios, or automobiles.

Once, he knew that gold was better than steel and he could see the difference. He still expects to see differences in quality commensurate with price differentials, but in all too many cases this determinant has disappeared.

By no means do we wish to imply that people will buy only price. Nothing is further from the truth. People often want quality; but unless they can be given good reason for paying a higher price, they will buy the lower priced item—if they buy at all. The solution, then, is clear, even if it is not easy. It is vital to stress the quality features and especially the advantages of the better product. Does the higher priced television set have solid state circuitry? Then stress advanced design, better reception, and relatively trouble free operation. Does the higher priced iron have a stainless steel sole for easier ironing, a pressure spray, a water level indicator? Then make sure the customer knows about it. Is the quality suit made of imported fabric, with quality interlining for longer and better shape retention? Is it hand tailored throughout? Then be sure these points come across. Are the better pearls carefully matched, with deep pearl coating, fourteen karat gold clasp, nylon strung and double knotted for long, troublefree wear? Then stress these points in the presentation. The customer must be educated to the finer points of the products. She undoubtedly wants the better product and is willing to pay for it, but it is up to the marketing fraternity to make sure that she sees the differences even though the products may seem to look alike. We know that after the purchase the satisfied customer often becomes the product's best salesman. She makes sure that those who see her new possession understand its special qualities.

Theoretically, the salesman should be the one to convey the requisite information and to point up product benefits. But, for a variety of reasons this font of information often fails. He may be too busy, or he may not have studied the line carefully, or he may be more interested in pushing a competitive line, or simply, he may be so inured to the line that he takes it for granted that the customer knows all he knows about it. One answer: attach a "tell all tag" to all merchandise. The tag clearly (if necessary, discretely) can point up the unique advantages of the item. The tag can be read by the customer without a salesmen, or used by the salesman to refresh his memory. In any case, it is likely to make certain that the shopper has the requisite information needed to select the item intelligently.

INABILITY TO GAUGE VALUE

When shoppers are uncertain they do not buy. A shopper likes to feel that he is getting good value, or at least fair value for his money. If for any reason he is doubtful that such is the case, he is very likely to hold off, to shop further, or never to buy at all.

Examples of cases where it is difficult for the buyer to gauge value abound—diamonds and other precious jewels, a used automobile, or an older house. But help is sometimes available.

For the skeptical home buyer, in some areas there are services such as Home Inspection Consultants (a franchised service with about sixteen operating units in the Northeast) which will check out a house for a fee and submit an engineer's value analysis. Automobiles may be checked out by the new Diagnostic

Service organizations which promise to give the car a physical exam and report condition in detail. Also there are many dealers who fully warrant their products for a reasonable post-sale period.

Many consumers decry advertising, but let them try to gauge value when names and brands are removed. How do you evaluate that watch, the shirts on a counter, a dress or a suit, or canned foods? We depend heavily on a variety of hallmarks. Familiar brands convey certain standards and qualities to consumers. From experience, or from the secondary experience of fellow shoppers, the consumer can judge branded lines fairly well—at least enough for his satisfaction.

The reputation of the dealer or manufacturer is helpful to the shopper. So are warranties and guarantees, and again, samples and free trial offers help.

Everything possible must be done to relieve this uncertainty or the deal won't be consummated.

INERTIA AS AN INHIBITING FORCE

If you should dare to suggest to the average person that he is a stick-in-the-mud, you can expect a strong argument. With few exceptions, people like to feel and believe that they are alert and up-to-date. This is true of the old as well as young. They like to think that they do what they want, and not what the crowd wants—that they think what they think, and not what they are told to think. But this hardly is the case. Psychologists know that we are creatures of habit. We continue doing something we like, with little or no change, unless something shocks us into a new direction.

This factor is serious for the firm

marketing a new product or service. When new concepts are greeted skeptically, negatively, or even with derision, sales are hurt. Many products have had to fight an uphill battle all the way: "Hire a horse" greeted the early automobile owner. "If God wanted man to fly, he would have given him wings" was the reaction to the airplane.

We still have sizable numbers of people who won't have a television set in the home (a few won't have telephones, either); there are many who object to synthetic fiber in clothing, those who question frozen foods, and there are some who keep their savings in the mattress. Many people never change, despite their protestations to the contrary.

The problem becomes serious for the marketing man who expects reasonable open-mindness to the new. There are restaurant owners who go out of their way to add new items to their menus, but most people go on eating the same foods every day, complaining that "there is nothing on the menu." It is true that many people eat the same breakfast year after year although hundreds of new and interesting products have become available.

Furniture men expect people to redecorate after five or ten years, then find that most families decorate only twice in a lifetime: once when they get married, and again when the children have fully grown or after they have left home. As a result, two buying cycles (not four or five) in the family lifetime hold down home furnishing sales.

Silverware is sold to "last a lifetime," but then people are expected to discard the old pattern for the new. Similarly, quality watches are sold as potential heirlooms, and are so treated by older generations.

This problem pervades all facets of

life: the way people entertain, the way they vacation, their attitudes toward medical service, clothing styles, and so on. Quite simply, people tend to continue doing what they have been doing, to use what they have been using, to buy what they have been buying. To the degree that they cannot be diverted to new concepts and new products, sales tend to be held back—because the furniture can be made to last and last. The television set, clothing, and so forth, all can have their lives extended indefinitely—with sales suffering.

We are not suggesting that people change their habits and go out and buy new things just because the marketing man wants them to do so, but we do believe that significant advances have been made in many fields and that the consumer would benefit if he broke out of his mold periodically.

The color television set is superior to the black and white set, and the solid state set has many advantages over the older tube set. Today's automobile has a wide array of safety features which yesterday's car did not have. Today's refrigerator has many important improvements and conveniences which were unknown yesterday. As clothing styles change, few people wish to look "seedy." While one need not buy every new fashion, refusing to keep up-to-date hardly is acceptable to most people. Home furnishings do become worn. The old vacation haunt goes flat. Newer foods are worth trying. Synthetic fibers, plastic furniture, and such things are superior in many respects. It is untenable that yesterday was better in all respects; much is to be gained by experimenting with the new.

Quite naturally, significant advances in engineering or styling activate change. Some industries are particularly fortunate because their products are amenable to trade-in and resale. The automobile is the obvious example. But the technique also is common in other fields such as housing, machinery, high fidelity equipment, and cameras. Of course, resale is feasible only with items which retain a significant portion of their value after periods of use.

For most products the problem is more serious. For whatever the reason, inertia is predominant. How can the marketing fraternity handle this problem? Gently! People who are resistant to change cannot be pushed hard or fast. They will fight back. But people are amenable to reasonable suggestions, to logical change. The salesman must be careful and gentle. First, he might sympathize with the old. Yes, it is good. It served its purpose very well. But, then, he can introduce the new version—preferably not an extreme variation of the new—and explain carefully why it is superior, why people seem to like it. He then may recommend the new product, if possible with a return privilege.

Quite naturally, strong sales effort is often necessary to overcome customer inertia. Such effort commonly is referred to as high pressure. By implication, people dislike high pressure. What is high pressure? The simple answer is that when people "feel" it, it is pressure. Some people need help, want help, and react favorably to suggestions by the salesman. It helps them to make up their minds. Others react exactly the opposite way. They think they know their minds or are fearful of being misled. Such people are likely to avoid salesmen until they are ready to buy. Then, they will approach him. It does little good to try to discourage such a prospect, for such action can only make him suspicious. Normally, he must be left alone or be assisted minimally until he convinces himself that the deal is right. Then he will buy.

SOME RECOMMENDATIONS

The negative motivational forces at work in the marketplace are many and varied. It is untenable to develop marketing campaigns without taking these factors into consideration; they are strong enough to impede or even ruin the best laid sales plans.

Careful study of the product should include an analysis of the negative forces likely to be encountered as well as the positive benefits which will accrue to the buyer. Then a balanced campaign can be designed which will minimize the possibly latent negative forces.

Many suggestions have already been offered for meeting particular negative motivating forces. Of course, these are generalizations, and each particular product requires its unique combination of tactics. Not the least among these should be consideration of a follow-up program, where feasible, to enhance customer satisfaction. Consumers need assistance in product use and care as well as in proper selection. User dissatisfaction often can be corrected by the expert. It is impotant to reinforce satisfaction and gain the confidence of the purchaser, who then is almost certain to become a loyal customer as well as a font of goodwill for the future.

TRACES OF A TREASURE AND A HARRIED HARE BEGUILE BOOK BUYERS

Here is a synopsis of the book that has just climbed to ninth place on the *New York Times* fiction best-seller list:

The moon is in love with the sun, but the sun remains distant and remote. So the moon commands our hero Jack, who is a hare, to deliver a token of her love: a necklace of gold and gems.

There follow 12 action-packed pages of text in which Jack cavorts with a dandelion that is out looking for lost dreams, chats with a violinist who is sitting on a sow, is almost barbecued by a Henry Kissinger look-alike, is saved from the spit by Sir Isaac Newton and—just when you think everyone will live happily ever after—realizes he has lost the jewel.

The book—*Masquerade*—ends there, but the mystery of the missing amulet doesn't. The author, Kit Williams, has buried it somewhere in the British Isles. Dig it up, he says, and the jewel—which his publisher claims is worth $36,000—is yours.

It obviously isn't the plot that has pushed *Masquerade* above Eudora Welty, Sidney Sheldon and Michael Crichton on the best-seller list. No, it's something more basic: greed.

SOLVE THE RIDDLE

The difficulty in finding the treasure is that clues to its whereabouts are concealed in an elaborate riddle. *Masquerade* is, in fact, crammed with puzzles: Find the hidden hare in each of the 15 magnificent color illustrations (in a bowl of Jell-O on one page); count the animals corralling the sun (12 if you include the ham, a cross between a hare and a ram); and solve this riddle to see what happened when the moon strayed too near her love:

I am the beginning of eternity,
Followed by half a circle, close on by
half a square,
Through my fourth my fifth is seen,
To be the first in every pair,
My sixth begins my seventh,
The end of time and space,
Now put my parts together to see what's
taken place.

But none of this (all right already, the answer is "eclipse") helps you find the treasure—seven ounces of gold beaten into a filigree rabbit several inches long with a ruby eye and turquoise spots. To find that, you have to scour the 15 illustrations that Mr. Williams has crammed with hares, frogs and field mice, old men and odd ladies, English landscapes, country villages and wildflowers, all painted in nit-picking detail.

"If I have a spare hour or two, I sit down and study those pictures," says Graham Geary, a London accountant who is determined to find the golden hare at the end of the tale.

Why? For the treasure itself, of course, but also, explains Gavyn Davies, a London economist who was an adviser to former Prime Minister James Callaghan, "to dig the thing up and bury it yourself. Do the same thing to Kit Williams."

ON THE TRACES

In pursuit of the treasure, other readers have tried to dredge a lake on the grounds of a stately home in Derbyshire, dig up a lady's topiary in Tewkesbury and burgle a fire station in Somerset. They have dug so many holes in a Gloucestershire parkland called Harefield Beacon—which is covered in harebell blooms in spring—that Mr. Williams has erected a sign swearing the jewel is elsewhere.

And not incidentally, the treasure hunters have bought the book—well over 100,000 copies in the U.S. since it appeared in September and 350,000 in Europe over the past 17 months. It's in 10 languages. The Japanese have snapped up 20,000 copies, and in Italy the publishers have buried their own treasure—they won't tell Mr. Williams where.

Suppose someone from a faraway land figures out where the necklace is? No problem; the book jacket promises that Mr. Williams will send a plane ticket to England to whoever solves the riddle.

The man who dreamed up the puzzle is a red-bearded former British Royal Navy electronics engineer who decided one day to become a painter. After he had done all right at that, he decided to become a writer, too. This was after a publisher, who had spotted a puzzle Mr. Williams had carved to look like a book, offered him a $4,800 advance to create a book that was actually a puzzle.

Even in England, a country famous for its eccentrics, Mr. Williams stands out as odd—"one off," he says. All sorts of things take on voices and personalities in his presence. "You aren't going to leave me, are you?" he claims his house asked when he was thinking of moving. When the idea for the puzzle book appeared in his kitchen one morning, he says, he ordered it, "Go away, you." But it wouldn't; it moved in.

So in his back garden in Gloucestershire, a rural county well west of London, Mr. Williams built a tent from a sheet of plastic. He settled in with his paints and a paraffin lamp. "With the fumes, I was pleasantly going around the bend," he recalls.

First, he made the jewel, the hare of gold and gems. Next, he decided where to bury it. He thought for a time of hanging it in a young oak tree, but the prospect of the oak's falling—and revealing the treasure—in a mere 500 years or so dissuaded him. Then, without knowing the plot, he started painting the illustrations.

A year later, Mr. Williams had painted Sir Isaac Newton, the violin man and the Henry Kissinger look-alike ("a malevolent little man," he says, apparently not referring to Mr. Kissinger). But still he didn't have a plot or the lead characters.

BY THE LIGHT OF THE MOON

By the seventh painting—a year and a half into the project—"I was getting a bit worried," Mr. Williams says. "How on earth could I pull them into one story?" When the idea did come, he spent 2½ weeks writing the book, put in another two weeks pondering a title, and finally—with only one witness, a British television personality—buried the treasure in a ceramic container by the light of a full moon.

Mr. Williams, who is 34 years old, cheerfully admits he has hit upon an 18-karat-gold gimmick. "It's a way to make people want to look at my paintings—and look for a long, long time," he says. It's a way to make them read his charming text. And as if that weren't enough for the readers, there's real gold at the end of this treasure hunt.

There's real gold in it for Mr. Williams, too—a $1.50 royalty on every $9.95 book. The only indication of Mr.

Williams's current affluence, though, is a new workshop at the back of the four-room stone cottage he shares with his wife, E-leyne, a weaver. There's no furnace in the house, no electric stove, no hot water in the kitchen and, because Mr. Williams is a writer who doesn't read, no books. He thought for a time of buying a Porsche to celebrate his wealth, but then wondered, "Where would I carry the firewood?" So he stuck with his Ford station wagon.

BEES AND A LION

Mr. Williams has largely spurned the potentially lucrative market in *Masquerade* spinoffs because he says they would diminish the "uniqueness" of his book. He did authorize a *Masquerade* calendar that notes his birthday—April 28—and he has sold the rights to a *Masquerade* musical comedy scheduled to open in London in March. But he retained the rights to a *Masquerade* opera he plans to write someday—something so unusual "that it's never been done before," he promises. Ditto a *Masquerade* ballet.

These days, though, Mr. Williams spends his time on a second book, this one about bees and a lion that acquires its fearsome roar by swallowing the London Symphony Orchestra. There will be treasure in this book too, but it will be found quickly; Mr. Williams insists that finding the treasure in this case will heighten interest.

That probably won't be the case with *Masquerade*. When the treasure is found, interest in the book will plummet, Mr. Williams realizes, so he is tight with the clues. He *will* say that the golden hare doesn't lie on private land, that its location isn't marked by map coordinates and that it won't be found with the aid of computers or sextants or surveyors' equipment. A child—all right, a bright child—has as much chance of finding it as the Oxford don, he says.

But Mr. Williams's hope is that the treasure won't be found—that the treasure hunt will continue and the masquerade will go on and on. He intends to will the solution to a stranger, he says, and leave it to the stranger to choose between recovering the jewel and leaving it where it is while continuing to collect the royalties.

Now *that* would be a quandary—a real puzzle.

Exercise 15

Motivational Conflicts

OBJECTIVES: 1. To arrive at an appreciation of the marketing strategy of positioning products to solve motivational conflicts.

2. To underscore the importance of marketing's role in providing solutions to consumers' needs.

Because of time and money limitations, consumers may find that they cannot simultaneously satisfy all their motivational needs. Thus, when two or more motives have been activated, consumers may find themselves in an uncomfortable state of motivational conflict. Marketing solutions to these motivational conflicts can be marketing opportunities.

Types of Motivational Conflicts

1. *Approach–approach:* Consumers must make a decision between two desirable alternatives. The marketing opportunity is to solve the consumers' conflict by providing them with products that incorporate the positive features of both desirable alternatives.
2. *Approach–avoidance:* Consumers must choose from available alternatives that possess both positive and negative features. In this situation, the marketing solution is to provide consumers with products that offer the positive features while simultaneously nullifying the negative features.
3. *Avoidance–avoidance:* Consumers must make a decision but all the choices available to them are negative. The situation the consumers find themselves in is to choose between two evils. The marketing opportunity in this situation is to solve the consumers conflict by providing them with a product to alleviate the negative aspects of one or both of the alternatives.

Describe the conflict and determine the type of motivational conflicts the following products are attempting to solve.

Reprinted with permission of General Motors Corporation.

Reprinted with permission of Toyota Motor Sales, U.S.A. Inc.

Reprinted with permission of the J.M. Smucker Company.

Reprinted with permission of General Foods Corporation.

AND ANTI-PERSPIRANTS THAT DON'T CLASH

Introducing 3 fabulous Babe anti-perspirants. All with a fresh, quiet scent that won't fight your fragrance. Choose new Babe solid that goes on silky smooth and very dry. Or the roll-on or super-dry spray. You'll get hours of long-lasting protection that won't clash with your splash.

And that's fabulous news, Babe.

Reprinted with permission of Hunter J. Freeman and Nadler & Larimer, Inc.

1. Uninsulated house is exposed to cold, heat. Insulate attic first.

2. In severe climates, add up to a foot (R-38) of Fiberglas* insulation.

3. Insulate all exterior walls. Also, floors above garages, crawl spaces.

4. Now house is in the pink—with Owens-Corning Fiberglas insulation.

Owens-Corning built this glass house to show you all the places Fiberglas insulation can save you money

The pictures above show *where* the insulation goes.

To decide *how much* you need in each place, check with your Owens-Corning dealer or contractor. He has our guidelines on insulation "R-values" (insulating power) for your part of the country.

People who advertise with glass houses aren't about to throw stones at competitors. But we urge you to insist on insulation with R-values plainly marked, and with an NAHB Research

Foundation label verifying that samples have been tested and actually *deliver* the R-value promised.

You won't go wrong if you put

It's cheaper than oil

your house in the *pink* with Owens-Corning Fiberglas insulation, America's leading brand.

Do it soon. The cost to insulate an average attic (30'x45') is only a few hundred dollars—and you'll get a bit of a tax break, too. Then just sit back and watch the savings add up, year after year after year.

OWENS-CORNING
FIBERGLAS

*T.M. Reg. O.-C.F. Corp. © 1979 O.-C.F. Corp.

Reprinted with permission of Owens-Corning Fiberglas Corporation.

Exercise 16

Motivational Needs

OBJECTIVE: To arrive at an understanding of the motivational needs that the products are attempting to satisfy.

Analyze the products shown in the advertisements that follow to determine the motivational needs on Maslow's Need Hierarchy that they are attempting to satisfy. Maslow's Need Hierarchy Theory classifies motives into five basic categories and structures motives in a hierarchy of prepotency. Maslow believed that all preceding lower-order motivation levels had to be satisfied before the next higher-order motivation level demanded satisfaction, and that it is possible for a behavior to satisfy several needs simultaneously. In ascending order, Maslow's Need Hierarchy is as follows:

1. *Physiological:* motives concerned with basic body requirements such as food, water, and oxygen.
2. *Safety:* motives which seek security, protection, and stability in life.
3. *Love:* needs for affection and affiliation with others.
4. *Esteem:* motives oriented toward recognition, achievement, prestige, status.
5. *Self-actualization:* motives for self-fulfillment and maximizing one's potential.

Reprinted with permission of the 3M Company.

Reprinted with permission of the Mutual Life Insurance Company of New York.

Reprinted with permission Seagram Distillers Company.

10

Perception

Marketers concern themselves not with objective reality but with the consumers' perception of it. Brand images and product positioning are marketing creations based upon an understanding of consumer perception. The articles in this section illustrate the marketing application of the consumer perception process.

Permanent media are "all things the public sees which relate to a product and have a visual, cumulative effect on the public's impression of the product and the corporation." In the article "Marketer Designs Permanent Media to Position Firms," Bernard F. Whalen describes the use of permanent media as a marketing tool to position products.

To Northeasterners, a succulent quality chicken is yellow-skinned. The old, familiar, hard-to-pour from the bottle packaging for ketchup reinforces consumer preferences for thick, viscous ketchup. William Copulsky and Katherin Marton, in the article "Sensory Cues: You've Got to Put Them Together," tell us how product characteristics are used by consumers as cues to determine the quality and nature of products.

In the article "The Marketing Importance of the 'Just Noticeable Difference'," Steuart-Henderson Britt and Victoria M. Nelson discuss the usefulness of a 100-year-old psychophysical law, Weber's law, to marketing today.

Are there hidden messages in advertisements? In the article "Secret Voices," some current uses of subliminal techniques to curtail shoplifting, train atheletes, and motivate weight loss are discussed.

MARKETER DESIGNS PERMANENT MEDIA TO POSITION FIRMS

"You don't pull the mask off the old Lone Ranger," the late pop singer Jim Croce insisted in one of his hit tunes.

But recently a judge in California ruled that Clayton Moore, TV's Lone Ranger, could no longer wear the mask in public because a motion picture firm had purchased all rights to the Lone Ranger character, including the mask.

That decision meant Moore had to appear in public wearing dark sunglasses which, needless to say, virtually destroyed his livelihood. Moore is no longer very convincing, saying "Hi Ho Silver, Away" while wearing sunglasses.

Non-verbal communication (in that case a mask) is important, as Moore found out. The National Broadcasting Co. and the Radio Corp. of America also found out. After negative experiences with their stark new logos "N" and "RCA" the firms returned to the popular symbols of the past, the colorful peacock and "Nipper" the dog who "listens to his master's voice."

John Diefenbach, 42, president of Landor Associates Inc., San Francisco, is a specialist when it comes to non-verbal communication. His vocabulary includes such terms as "permanent media, visual pollution, corporate identity resource management, nomenclature systems, prisms of change, visible retail segments, communications mix, aggregate perceptions analysis, appropriate selling environments, integrated product concepts, and symbology."

To the average person, that may seem like a bunch of mumbo jumbo, but to Diefenbach it means $10 million a year. He and his staff, 1975 designers and re-

"Marketer Designs Permanent Media to Positions Firms," Bernard F. Whalen, *Marketing News*, November 2, 1979, Reprinted from *Marketing News*, published by the American Marketing Association.

searchers stationed in 11 offices through-out the world, earn a living by performing corporate facelifts, by repositioning com-panies, by designing new images.

Landor's client list is long, impres-sive, and diverse. It includes hundreds of companies, from Coca-Cola to Colgate-Palmolive, from small Wisconsin banks to multibillion dollar retail chains in Japan.

But they all have one thing in com-mon—they were suffering from corporate identity crises—and called on Landor to help. (The help costs from $50,000 to $250,000 and is well worth it, according to the clients.)

"Throughout history," Diefenbach said, "companies weren't terribly con-cerned about their identities. They were more concerned about stock shares and profit margins.

"Then about 1970, the emphasis shifted to one of social responsibility. Now we're in a stage when a corporation must take a position to be visible and reflect its personality to society."

This need for an acceptable corporate image came about because of what Diefen-bach calls "the age of overcommunica-tions." There are currently more than 300,000 brand names in circulation—a montage of logos creating "visual pollu-tion." Therefore it has become very impor-tant for companies to stand out.

"The need for identity, be it for a product or corporation, is imperative in our visually oriented world," Diefenbach explains. "We all recognize that standing out and being an individual is not only part of our heritage, but must be our very survival in an overcommunicated-to world where various publics are both cautious and concerned.

"Today, the commitment to person-ality is not only a right, but a business necessity. It would therefore seem right to use your corporate identity as a marketing tool to position your products. Use the equities you have built into your corpo-rate image over the years. Use your unique personality, for every corporation has one."

Landor's business of non-verbal com-munication takes many routes. A simple logotype design may cost $50,000, mod-ernizing of product line packaging may take $150,000, and a total repositioning of a corporation may hit $250,000.

One of Landor's repositioning efforts is currently being reviewed in the mass media. The client is Allegheny Airlines, which had grown to become the sixth largest U.S. carrier in terms of passengers served. Yet the company suffered from a "rinky-dink" image, Diefenbach said.

Research showed that when it comes to airlines the consumer feels that "big is better," so Landor set out to reposition Al-legheny as a big carrier. The name of the airline was changed to "USAir," the jets and ground vehicles repainted in bright modern colors, terminal stations refur-bished, employee uniforms redesigned. The new ad campaign stressed the slogan, "It takes a *big* airline to fly more flights than TWA . . ."

The results of Landor's facelift have been fantastic, according to Jack King, the airline's vice president of public affairs. He said USAir has benefited from in-creased passenger traffic and improved employee morale.

Another Landor success story in-volved the introduction of "Lite" beer, which the Miller Brewing Co. inherited when it bought Meisterbrau Breweries. Lite was positioned and packaged as a low-calorie feminine product, a category tainted by failure.

In an effort to successfully market Lite, Landor decided to package it as an independent brand capable of standing on its own strengths. The new concept for Lite would project a premium brand image and broad appeal.

To overcome the low-calorie, feminine product stigma, Landor created a new logotype letterstyle and graphics for Lite. They had a traditional Germanic feeling which evoked the country's heritage of masterful brewing.

"The inherent excellence of Lite was further reinforced by the package's strong bulls-eye design, emphasizing natural ingredients by focusing attention on the prominent hops illustration," Diefenbach said.

The introduction of Lite turned out to be one of the most successful marketing stories in history, and Miller credits the work of Landor.

"Positioning is the single most important element in successful marketing today." Diefenbach insists, "You don't redesign an airplane, or anything else, simply for the sake of esthetics.

"The ultimate goal has to be to create an image that will place the company at its proper position within the market it serves."

Diefenbach believes that repositioning and designing of corporate identities is necessary not only to overcome "visual pollution" but also to combat a negative social factor.

"In most of the world's developed societies, there is a distrust of business, a distrust that is likely to continue, if not intensify," he explains. "It is not uncommon for a chief executive in the U.S. today to spend at least 25% of his time on issues of public and corporate responsibility.

"In a business environment of distrust and visual pollution, the difficulty of managing communications in a corpora-

tion seeking growth is readily apparent."

Diefenbach said that Landor's clients are usually on a "positive growth trend" and have products or services that are perceived to be good by their publics. The clients seek to use every tool available to them to get their message across in an overcommunicated-to society. They have reached a level of success, but desire to pass up their competitors.

"When the profits or market shares are fairly even for several companies in an industry," Diefenbach said, "the subjective things (like packaging, images, and logos) can swing interest to a particular firm in the group.

"Companies can no longer afford a low profile because the general public isn't happy with business anyway. To be successful a company has to build a reputation of responsibility, not adopt a manipulative public relations program.

"Instead, it should be taking account of its positive aspects and unique characteristics and stressing them."

One reason the demand for Landor's service has increased is the high cost of TV advertising. Diefenbach said his firm is working with many small companies now because they have been priced out of the video ad market.

"Small or regional companies know they can't outspend their national competition on advertising," he said. "Once you could have a major ad campaign on TV for $3 million. That has now swollen to $30 million. If you don't have that much to spend on TV, you don't have a chance. That's why we urge firms with product identity to use everything about the product to sell it."

If a firm doesn't have $30 million to spend on TV advertising, Landor recommends it take stock of its identities and use "permanent media," which Diefenbach describes as "all things the public sees which relate to a product and have a visual cumulative effect on the public's impression of the product and the corporation."

Permanent media are a corporation's logos, stationery, brochures, signs, business forms, call cards, rolling stock (vehicles), buildings, retail environments, etc.

Landor recently redesigned the "permanent media" of Allied Van Lines, Broadview, Ill., which wanted to spur growth but didn't have $30 million to spend on a comprehensive TV ad campaign.

Research indicated that each of Allied's 12,000 trucks was a "moving billboard," and each promoted 24.2 million impressions a year. But the Allied logo on its trucks was considered stale and old. The lettering was of the script variety and the wording, "Allied Van Lines—World's Largest Mover," didn't seem to excite anyone.

The orange color of the trucks completely dominated the Allied name and research showed that the public identified the orange color as signifying a moving van, and not Allied.

In creating the new graphic design, Landor maintained the orange color, but changed everything else. A diagonal, three-dimensional drawing of a superhighway was painted across the sides of each truck. The highway sort of disappears into the horizon.

A bold italic type face was chosen for the word Allied and underneath it was painted the company's new slogan, "The Careful Movers." All of Allied's trucks are scheduled to be redesigned by 1982 at regular intervals so no extra painting cost is incurred.

Allied reportedly paid Landor about $80,000 for the new corporate facelift. But since Allied now has 12,000 "moving billboards" tied into its regular TV commercials by repeating the slogan "The Careful Mover," the cost of a comparable TV ad blitz has been avoided.

In terms of marketing, Diefenbach said, permanent media are extremely important for the following reasons:

- The cost of advertising media space is rising steadily.
- All companies are not created equal in their ability to communicate to their publics. An industrial product may not have direct exposure to the public, and the corporation must use every available visual tool to create the corporate image.
- The message delivered by permanent media can be measured. (For example, the 24.2 million advertising impressions a year delivered by each Allied truck)
- Many regional companies are using corporate identity programs as part of the marketing strategy by which they go national, or by which large companies go international. The names and symbols have a lot to do with the success or failure of a product expanding into a new market.
- The visual symbols that affect opinions of paying customers also influence other important publics, such as employees and investors. If the company's visual signs are not friendly and progressive, attitudes of these publics will be affected in a negative way.
- If a company's visual messages express something different from its promotional messages,

like advertising, there is confusion in the minds of the publics, and marketing efforts are dissipated.

In the late 1960s and early 1970s, Diefenbach said, many corporations began to realize the value of their logos and permanent media in the overall marketing mix. In an effort to be in vogue, he said, some of these firms deserted their traditional images in favor of abstract, stark symbols. They felt this would make the companies appear more modern and technologically aware.

However, research by Frank Delano, a Los Angeles marketing consultant, shows that these stark symbols are perceived to be cold and dehumanizing by the public. As examples he points to Chrysler's pentastar logo and Chase Manhattan Bank's octagon symbol.

Delano said such stark logos are perceived by the public as being transitory, ambiguous, impersonal, and sterile. He said friendly, picturesque, real-life symbols, like NBC's peacock and RCA's Nipper the dog, "engender positive feelings among millions of Americans." And this is why NBC and RCA returned to their time-honored symbols.

In the case of NBC, the abandonment of the peacock was not only harmful from a public relations standpoint, but from a financial one as well. The TV network reportedly paid thousands of dollars for the design of the "N" logo. And, when it was learned the "N" was also the logo of a small TV station in Nebraska and a bank in Kentucky, copyright concerns appeared. NBC actually settled out of court with the Nebraska station for $550,000, rather than give up its geometric "N."

Today, Diefenbach said, corporations are adopting a more professional approach when deciding to change symbols or images. He feels that the proliferation of abstract logos in the late 60s and early 70s resulted in "corporate sameness," and that progressive firms now favor "word marks" that are human and connote the personality of the product or corporation.

"The importance of non-verbal communication cannot be stressed enough," Diefenbach said. "Research shows that 70% of human learning is through visual perception. What people see is usually what they base their action on. We often make buying decisions based on a quick impression of how a firm looks."

Although the redesigning of logos is important, Diefenbach said, it is only "the tip of the iceberg" in terms of a total corporate repositioning. He said when Landor goes to work for a new client it spends months conducting marketing, demographic, and psychological research before recommending any creative changes.

Brand names, company names, divisional subsidiary names, and system organizing names, are studied. Product packaging and styling is reviewed, as is the firm's advertising, sales promotion, publicity, and permanent media. A company's personnel is even researched, Diefenbach said. (Landor once found that a client's major problem consisted of discourteous telephone receptionists.)

Environmental and social factors are also weighted, Diefenbach said, as are the positionings of the company's competitors. When all of these factors are put together, Landor develops a variety of plans and executions. The entire identity resource management program is presented to the client and a final decision is made.

The keystones to a successful design program, Diefenbach said, are "personality, permanence, honesty, believability, and appeal."

Landor Associates also practices what it preaches. The firm's headquarters aren't located on the top floor of a highrise office building. That is too devoid of personality. No, Landor wants to stand out in a crowd. Its central office is located in the moored ferryboat Klamath in San Francisco harbor.

SENSORY CUES: YOU'VE GOT TO PUT THEM TOGETHER

Those grains of color in the traditionally white detergents are an important part of the product: They probably could just as well be white from a performance standpoint, but they visually reinforce the marketers' claim of "extra, added ingredients."

Those strips of color in new toothpastes are pretty. More importantly, they communicate the claim of "new and improved."

And would a cold remedy like Contac be as successful in promoting its time-release capsule idea if the grains were all laboratory white, instead of varied colors?

More and more, marketers are using the senses—all the senses—to tell consumers about their products. Of course,

"Sensory Cues: You've Got to Put Them Together," William Copulsky and Katherin Marton, *Product Marketing*, January 1977, pp. 31–34. Copyright © 1977, Product Marketing/Cosmetic & Fragrance Retailing. Reprinted with permission.

flavors, real and imitation, have long been first-rate sellers of products. And in the past decade, the skillful use of fragrances has even helped build subcategories of products, notably shampoos.

Other sensory cues—using color, texture, shape, form—are in a relatively developmental stage in marketing. But already there are cases where messages from these sensory stimuli have been used successfully—and unsuccessfully.

Frank Perdue, for example, uses color to signify health and fresh-killed qualities in his chickens. Northeasterners associate a yellow-skinned chicken with a succulent chicken. Perdue's golden yellow chickens are produced by using plenty of marigold petals and corn in their feed. The yellow Perdue chicken stands out from other chickens. This is one of the reasons for Perdue increasing his New York City market share from less than 1 per cent in

1968 to almost 20 per cent currently—and, in addition, selling half his total output outside the city.

Just how influential sensory cues can be is shown in research conducted by Stephan Jellinek, a fragrance consultant. He took standard facial tissue and added to it two fragrances, then tested the two sets of tissue on consumers.

The consumers perceived one set of facial tissue as "elegant," "expensive," and "high quality." The same tissue with a different scent scored relatively low in these three qualities. It was seen as a product to use in the kitchen. Less than half the respondents perceived the "high quality" tissue as a kitchen product.

Taste is another signal which communicates psychological and physical properties to the consumer. But beware. Taste is elusive, and its influence on sales is still elusive, in some cases often illusionary.

Alcoholic beverage drinkers often claim they select on a basis of taste. But take beer—Americans drink it very cold, so how much can taste count?

David A. Kendall, who heads up Arthur D. Little's flavor science unit, has been taste-testing beer for many years. He claims the public is split equally in three groups: (a) those who can't tell taste differences, (b) those who can differentiate taste, but buy beer on a price basis, or for other reasons than taste, (c) those who really discriminate taste and buy what tastes best to them.

Another study shows that 40 percent to 50 percent of beer drinkers can reliably tell the difference in taste between beers. Heavy drinkers do better than light drinkers. But beer drinkers, even when they discriminate taste, do not closely agree on what tastes better. A leading consultant on beers, Dr. Kurt Konigsbacher, sums it up by saying: "It is extremely difficult to separate the actual taste stimulation from the marketing and psychology of the beer and what a consumer feels he or she should like."

There are taste differences, but their effect on beer sales is not known as yet. Quality is what the consumer believes it to be, and his perception will depend on his conditioning. This is shown in vodka consumption. Heublein does about one-third of the vodka business with its Smirnoff brand. Smirnoff is the No. 1 vodka and the most expensive vodka brand. Yet Consumer's Union says: "Buy any brand, at the lowest price—they are all very much alike. . . . " The trade literature describes vodka as alcohol—plain alcohol, treated so it has no distinctive character, aroma, or taste.

Are "natural" flavors the key to future food sales, borrowing the natural idea from the success of natural fragrances and other natural trends? Again beware.

According to a U.S. Department of Agriculture report, foods fresh from the farm have a peculiar taste to many consumers brought up on canned and factory-processed products. Many consumers have become so accustomed to the slightly metallic flavors of canned pineapple juice that they reject freshly squeezed juice as not "real." A ketchup which duplicated the natural tomato taste flopped in supermarkets because the consumers preferred the overcooked scorched taste they were accustomed to in existing brands.

The flavor signal has to be appropriate. Candy-like fruit flavors are very pleasant and acceptable, but not in toothpaste because consumers feel that candy is not good for the teeth.

Physical form is also a signal. The form could be that of the product or its package.

Most consumers like their ketchup thick and viscous, and the package shape should reinforce the form of the contents. Heinz ketchup still sells in the old, familiar, hard-to-pour-from bottle. The narrow-neck bottle was originally necessary because when ketchup was exposed to air, a black deposit formed at the top. The narrow-neck minimized exposure to air, and a label around the neck concealed the unsightly deposit. When this problem was solved, a wide-mouth bottle was tried, but sales dropped. Market tests show that buyers think of good ketchup as one with many tomatoes, and this essence of "tomatoness" is conveyed by a "hard-to-pour" quality.

Commercials for ketchup on television show many tomatoes being forced into a bottle, or a slowness "race" to see which ketchup is hardest to pour. "Hard-to-pour" is essential to good ketchup image, and an easy-to-pour package is a move in the wrong direction, even though it appears to be a very "natural" move in the direction of consumer desires.

Stanely Sacharow, a package designer, has described how the Tetra-Pak tetrahedron milk package when introduced into Switzerland was carefully designed to convey a desirable market image through color and design, using research which indicated how people reacted to certain visuals. To achieve the desired perception of cleanliness and purity, light but strong colors against a white background were selected. To convey a non-fattening quality, "heavy" colors (orange and brown) were avoided. Various shades of blue connoted thirst quenching characteristics, and vivid contrasts a pleasant taste. Modern design and close detail in printing suggested high quality while linear, angular design and the strong colors

indicated this was an adult's drink, not a child's.

The result was a modern looking package in red, white, and blue colors.

In 1975, General Foods' Maxim, the pioneer freeze-dried instant coffee, had a 5.5 per cent market share. Nestle's Taster's Choice, a later entry, had an 11.7 per cent share. One marketing expert has attributed a considerable part of Nestle's lead to selection of a package shape which communicates the right signal. Much coffee is purchased to please a man. The Maxim jar is a sexless truncated cone. The Taster's Choice jar is a broad masculine shape with concave sides. This supposedly transmits a "this-is-for-your male" signal.

False signals or cues can be disastrous to product success. If a "signal" causes the consumer to perceive an attribute which the product does not possess, there will be confusion, and trouble with initial or repeat sales. The consumer does not understand the product properties or will not be happy when a "signaled" benefit does not result.

In February, 1971, Brown-Forman Distillers unveiled a new product, Frost 8/80, a "dry-white" whisky. After less than two years, the product was withdrawn. Sales were 100,000 cases, one-third of that projected. Costs were $6.5 million and losses $2 million, according to the *Wall Street Journal*.

About $500,000 was spent with eight outside research and packaging firms. The research indicated that brand rated very high on "uniqueness." William Carroll, who directed sales of Frost 8/80, believed the research was misread. "Uniqueness" was interpreted to mean people would be anxious to try it; instead "uniqueness" was the biggest problem. The product looked like vodka but tasted like whisky.

It upset people. "They didn't know what to make of it," Carroll concluded.

Physical form of the product itself must give only the correct signal in context. A General Foods marketing executive involved in developing Maxim's freeze-dried coffee tells how their researchers came up with two ways of making Maxim. One end product with a granular appearance looked very much like ground coffee, but the other could only be described as large "lumps." They didn't look like anything anyone had seen in coffee.

In consumer home-testing, the granules were greatly preferred. After all, shouldn't a product which is meant to taste like ground coffee look like ground coffee? But the lumpy product gave better market test results and eventually a large market share to General Foods. Why? Consumers were more likely to accept Maxim as a new form of coffee—different from conventional instants—when it looked unlike anything else they had seen before.

A General Foods executive said: "No amount of panel testing can beat the real world when it comes to actual consumer acceptance of a product. Had we not challenged the results of the home-use tests with actual market experience, we might have made a serious mistake on a very basic product characteristic."

A case in point comes from the liquor industry. While Brown-Forman's dry-white whisky presented the consumer with conflicting cues (a whisky taste with a vodka look), Heublein has introduced an offbeat product which signals to the consumer exactly what it is—a "soft drink" laced with liquor.

The drink is called Malcolm Hereford's Cows. This is a 30 proof flavored liquor aimed at a vast audience, mostly women presumably, who don't like the taste of liquor but see some social benefits in drinking it. It may have been inspired by the soda pop wines some young adults have adopted in weaning from soft drinks. Whatever, Cows was "unique."

Heublein tells its audience what it is buying—a milky concoction flavored in strawberry, banana, chocolate mint, mocha, coconut, and French vanilla. Flavor is important, but Heublein has supported this sensory appeal with complementary stimuli in color and texture. The liquid is more viscous than usual liquor, reinforcing the "milk" idea. The color of the liquid matches the flavor—strawberry Cows looks strawberry. And the label and graphics continues to project the image of a milky substance with pleasant, dessert flavor added.

Are Cows successful in winning over new consumers for liquor? Well, a year after Cows' debut, Heublein has introduced Kickers, a light liquor in strawberry, coconut, mocha, and banana. Seemingly, only the name is significantly different, carrying a more liquor-oriented note.

Obviously, then, sensory cues built into your product can help sell the product, if the cues are appropriate. Now comes the "but." But one of the dangers in being caught up in cue-building is to focus in on sensory cues as individual entities. They are not; they must be integrated as a team and should be tested as such.

Let's say you decide to reposition your household product with a new fragrance. It has actually happened that various fragrances are tested in themselves: the focus of all attention is on one sense. A fragrance is chosen overwhelmingly by panel or market tests. Placed in the product, however, it fails to tell the consumer what it should—that the product is "new" or "different." The reason: it does not team up with the other sensory messages in the product. It has been tested as if it were the product—not just part of the product.

Critic Dale Harris makes a pertinent comment in an article on recordings. "Hearing a recording of Alice Faye's 'Now It Can Be Told' from Irving Berlin's 'Alexander's Ragtime Band' makes you realize," says Harris, "that an Alice Faye came over effectively on the screen because she had more to offer than a voice." As Harris points out, for many a movie star singing was the extension of a likeable personality. Both the visual image and the sound were required to make the star come to life as a singer. An Alice Faye had to be seen to be believed. With only the pictureless voice, Alice Faye was much less a successful entertainment product.

THE MARKETING IMPORTANCE OF THE "JUST NOTICEABLE DIFFERENCE"

In today's avalanche of closely competing products, a brand with a clearly perceptible difference stands a much better chance for success than another "me-too" product. And, after a time, even a very successful product needs the restaging boost of a perceptible improvement in the product itself, in its name, in its container, in its price, or in the methods of distribution, merchandising, sales or advertising. The key to product improvement is the word *perceptible*. This means perceptible to the consumer, who must perceive the improvement as truly better or different than before.

WEBER'S LAW

Most marketers do not know that two German physiologists of the nineteenth century discovered a guideline, called Weber's Law, that can be applied to product improvements in the last half of the twentieth century. It has already been demonstrated how this law can be applied to marketing.[1] Weber's Law states that the stronger the initial stimulus, the greater is the change in intensity required for the resulting stimulus to be perceived as different.

For example, anyone can perceive readily that a 10-inch line is longer than a 7-inch line, but the addition of 3 inches to a line measuring 25 feet may not be enough

[1] Steuart-Henderson Britt, "How Weber's Law Can Be Applied to Marketing," *Business Horizons* (February 1975), pp. 21–29.

for the resulting 25 feet and 3 inches to be perceived as longer than the 25-foot line. As much as 2 feet in additional length might be required for the majority of people to perceive that the second line is longer than the first.

According to Weber's Law, an additional level of stimuli—known as the *just noticeable difference* or j.n.d.—is necessary for the majority of people to perceive that there is a difference between the resulting stimulus and the initial stimulus. This j.n.d. is not an absolute amount, but rather is relative to the intensity of the initial stimulus. Gustav Fechner, a colleague of Ernst Weber for whom the law is named, expressed this relationship in the mathematical ratio

$$\frac{\Delta I}{I} = k$$

where "k" is the constant ratio, "I" is the initial stimulus and "ΔI" is the j.n.d.

Happily, Weber's Law holds for all the senses and for almost all intensities. Although it is not quite accurate or precise at extreme intensities, it does hold remarkably true in the middle range of intensities; and these are the ones to which consumers are most often exposed. The j.n.d. varies with the type of stimuli tested, but there is a j.n.d. for every type of stimulus that is sufficiently intense for the majority of individuals to perceive a noticeable difference.

THE CONSTANT STIMULI METHOD

Weber's principle can be applied to product improvement by using a research technique to find the correct j.n.d. This technique is the *constant stimuli method*. In this method, an individual is asked to compare increasingly intense stimuli with a standard set of stimuli until he reports that he perceives a difference between the current set of stimuli and the standard set of stimuli. The degree of difference between the standard stimuli and the final set of stimuli, then, is the just noticeable difference.

Applications to Product Improvement

How can this technique be applied to product improvement? Suppose that a luggage manufacturer wants to produce a suitcase that is perceived as lighter than his leading competitor's suitcase by the majority of women who travel.

The competitor's suitcase weights 5 pounds. Women travelers individually and separately first pick up the 5-pound suitcase and then a case of identical appearance, but weighing 4 pounds 15 ounces, and each woman reports which is lighter.

Next, each woman picks up the 5-pound case, and then one weighing 4 pounds 14 ounces, and reports which is lighter, and so on. The order in which each woman lifts the cases is varied, of course, but the 5-pound case always represents the standard, that is, the constant stimuli.

This paired-comparison technique is continued until the majority of the women actually perceive the lighter case as being lighter. Let us suppose that at a weight of 4 pounds, over 50% of the women correctly identify it as the lighter case. Using Weber's Law we see that:

$$\frac{\Delta I}{I} = \frac{5 \text{ pounds} - 4 \text{ pounds}}{5 \text{ pounds}} = \frac{1}{5}$$

Thus, for this particular situation, the weight of the suitcase must be decreased by one-fifth of the original weight before the majority of women can perceive the change. If the suitcase manufacturer had decreased the weight by only one-half pound, his improvement would have gone undetected. If he had selected a 2-pound weight reduction, he probably would have sacrificed the durability and desirability of a heavier material.

Because Weber's Law holds true for most intensities, the manufacturer now knows what weight reduction will be required for his full line of luggage in order for the majority of women to perceive the lightness of his suitcases. For example, he must produce an 8-pound suitcase for the majority of women to perceive it as lighter than his competitor's 10-pound model.

$$\frac{\Delta I}{I} = \frac{10 \text{ pounds} - 8 \text{ pounds}}{10 \text{ pounds}} = \frac{2}{10} = \frac{1}{5}$$

As another example, a company has decided to manufacture a soap that is more economical than soaps of competitors, and will use the theme "lasts longer" to represent the product improvement. The marketing executive in charge of developing the new brand wants at least 50% of the consumers to perceive this new bar of soap as one that will last longer.

He finds that for an average family the company's present regular-sized bar lasts about 20 days. Using slightly harder mills, he has his company produce what are perceptibly the same kinds of bars, but ones that will last 21 days, 22 days, 23 days, 24 days and 25 days respectively.

In a series of experiments, he has individuals first use his regular-sized 20-day bar, then the 21-day bar, and report which lasts longer. Each person then compares the 20-day bar and the 22-day bar and reports which bar lasts longer. This process is continued until all the bars have been tested against the constant stimuli, that is, the 20-day bar of soap.

Suppose that only 25% of the individuals perceive the 23-day bar as lasting longer than the original bar, but that 35% of them perceive that the 25-day bar lasts longer.

$$\frac{\Delta I}{I} = \frac{25 \text{ days} - 20 \text{ days}}{20 \text{ days}} = \frac{5}{20} = \frac{1}{4}$$

The marketing executive now knows that the improved bar must last at least one-fourth of the time longer than the present bar for it to be perceived by the majority of users as improved. By finding this j.n.d. of 5 days, the soap company has isolated the minimum amount of time necessary to make its claim believable to the majority of consumers.

If the decision instead had been to make the bar last 30 days, a good deal of purchase frequency would have been sacrificed. Had the decision been that 3 extra days of product life would be sufficient, the improvement claim of "lasts longer" would not have been perceived as true by most consumers, thus possibly resulting in a loss of sales.

Similarly, the company now knows that the product life of its big 40-day bath-sized bar must be extended to 50 days in order for the improvement claim to be perceived by most consumers as true.

$$\frac{\Delta I}{I} = \frac{50 \text{ days} - 40 \text{ days}}{40 \text{ days}} = \frac{10}{40} = \frac{1}{4}$$

The ratios for Weber's Law vary, of course, among different individuals, in different stimuli ranges, and among different kinds of stimuli. But the fact remains that equal changes in stimuli intensity are not necessarily perceived as equal. By using the constant stimuli method, a marketer can ensure that his product improvement will be perceived as just noticeably different by the majority of his consumers or customers.

SECRET VOICES

A shopper in a department store picks up a scarf, glances furtively about, crumples it up and shoves it into her pocket. Then come second thoughts. She fishes out the scarf, smooths it again and returns it to the counter. Another victory for honesty? Not quite. Credit for the would-be shoplifter's change of heart really belongs to what the store's managers call their "little black box," a kind of electronic conscience.

Basically a sound mixer like those used by disco deejays, the box mingles bland music with subliminal anti-theft messages ("I am honest. I will not steal"). Repeated rapidly—9,000 times an hour—and at very low volume, the words are barely audible to shoppers and employees. But they do register in some deep recess of the brain and apparently influence behavior.

About 50 department stores in the U.S. and Canada have installed the device to reduce shoplifting and employee theft. One undisclosed East Coast chain is said to have cut the number of thefts by 37%, for a saving of $600,000, during a nine-month trial. The device also seems to be catching on with other businesses. In Toronto, a real estate office uses a black box to inspire sales personnel ("I love real estate. I will prospect for new listings for clients each and every day"). Says black box Inventor Hal C. Becker: "I see no reason why there won't be audio-conditioning the same way we now have air conditioning."

Becker, founder and head of his own little company in Metairie, La., Behavioral Engineering Center, may be a little premature in his Orwellian zeal. But the idea of subliminal communication has long intrigued behavioral scientists. In the mid-1950s a marketing researcher named James Vicary broke ground of sorts by inserting rapidly flashing words between the frames of a film to stimulate refreshment sales ("Hungry? Eat popcorn") in a Fort Lee, N.J., moviehouse. Pictures of a skull and the word blood were also added to two horror movies. But this practice soon fell out of favor after it was exposed in Vance Packard's alarming bestseller, *The Hidden Persuaders*.

Now the persuaders seem to be making a comeback. A television commercial for children's toys included the subliminal message "Get it!" until the Federal Communications Commission issued a warning against further TV or radio subliminations. In the movie *"The Exorcist"* the image of a death mask was flashed before audiences to give them an extra scare. The tactic may have worked. Warner Bros. is being sued by an Indiana teenager who fainted during the movie, breaking his jawbone and several teeth. His lawyer contends that the fleeting death mask is "one of the major issues" in the case.

Becker and his former partner, Louis Romberg, who has established his own operation in Toronto, think that black boxes are especially useful in sports. Romberg says that he is providing subliminal pep talks to hockey's Montreal Canadiens, and Becker is working with an unidentified National Football League team. The box is also being used by psychologists to help people lose weight, stop smoking and overcome phobias like the fear of flying. If subliminals were put on TV, explains Becker, they could be directed specifically at such killers as obesity, drugs and bad driving. Says he: "We could eliminate weight problems in one generation, reduce auto insurance by 50%."

Becker is not worried about abuses. He says that he has already turned down politicians and advertisers who wanted to hire him, and explains that his black boxes include a "fail safe" mechanism that prevents clients from playing anything but the message he has programmed into them. Still, many Americans would undoubtedly be outraged by any secret attempts to influence their behavior for better or worse. As Aryeh Neier, former executive director of the American Civil Liberties Union, puts it, "People have a right to go about their business without being subjected to manipulation they don't even know about."

Exercise 17

Hidden Messages

OBJECTIVES: 1. To illustrate the concept of subliminal perception.
2. To stimulate discussion of the use of and effectiveness of subliminal perception in advertising.

Subliminal perception by definition is perception below threshold or limen. Subliminal advertisement incorporates the use of embeds, incongruities, and suggestiveness.

1. *Embeds:* Pictures and/or words are hidden or camouflaged in the advertisement.
2. *Incongruities:* There is an inconsistency in the advertisement. Something does not fit. In other words, there is something wrong with this picture that is not evident upon first glance.
3. *Suggestiveness:* The advertisement implies more than the explicit copy would indicate.

Analyze the advertisements that follow for subliminal elements. Then turn to page 183 to compare your analyses with those of the author's.

FIGURE 1

From *Media Sexploitation,* Wilson Bryan Key, New American Library, New York, 1976. Reprinted with permission of Dr. Wilson Bryan Key.

FIGURE 2

FIGURE 3

NEW...
FIRST SKIN CREAM
THAT EVEN PROTECTS
YOUR HANDS IN WATER

FIGURE 4

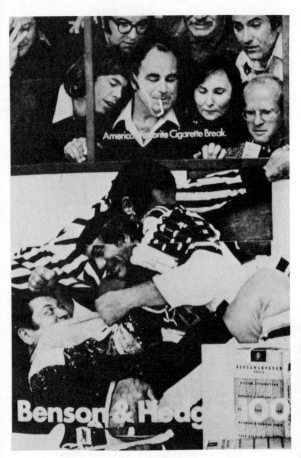

FIGURE 5

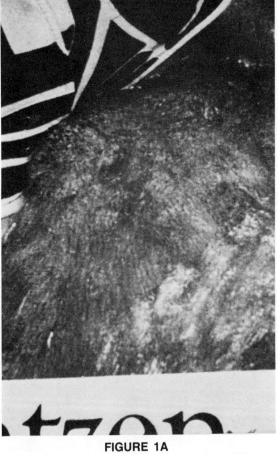

FIGURE 1A

Figure #1, an advertisement for Jantzen swimsuits that appeared in the Canadian edition of the April 1972 *Reader's Digest,* contains elements of incongruity and the use of embeds. "The ad portrays two suntanned models posed crotch-deep in boiling surf, wearing red and blue swimsuits designed on a Union Jack motif. . . . There appear to be several details in the photography which do not make sense. First, the female model's trunks do not fit. Notice the wrinkles and sagging front. . . . The female model's trunks also have a zipper fly—a highly functional device in men's clothing, but not really necessary in women's. On the other hand, the male model's trunks fit quite snugly. And in addition, his suit design matches the female's brassiere. In short, she is wearing his and he is wearing hers. . . . Another somewhat disconcerting question involves the female hand gently resting upon the female model's hip. With the wrist at that angle, there is no way it can belong to the female model—unless her arm is six feet long. The hand, resting on this erogenous zone, suggests subliminally the possibility of a ménage à trois relationship—two women and a man. There is a third model standing beside the two models."[3]

The embed can be seen when Figure #1 is held upside down as shown in Figure 1A. The embed is a face "reminiscent of the old Farmer's Almanac drawing of the weatherman, cheeks distended, his puckered mouth blowing the cold north winds down across the nation. The old weatherman in the surf is. . . . blowing on a delicate portion of the model's anatomy."[4]

Figure #2 shows an ad from the January 1973 edition of *Oui* magazine published by the Playboy organization and contains elements of suggestiveness. The beautiful blonde model dressed in a silver brassiere and miniskirt is not a woman but a man in drag. "The model's wrists, shoulders, neck, fingernails, and breasts are strongly and clearly male. In addition, the blond hair is a wig. Some curious changes were airbrushed into the photograph, suggesting that the artists and editors knew precisely what they were doing. Male navels, for example, appear to be horizontal and the female appear vertical due to a layer of fatty tissue women usually carry just below their navel. Microscopic examination of the photograph revealed the navel had been carefully airbrushed into a vertical appearance."[5]

The embed in Figure #3 is shown below in Figure 3A. This advertisement for *Playgirl* magazine shows "a young woman posed with sunglasses, dressed in a sleeveless blouse and simple skirt. The caption reads simply, 'What kind of girl reads *Playgirl?*' Though attractive, she did not appear as sexually provocative as other females portrayed in the magazine. Her dress was quite commonplace, hardly an appropriate, exotic, sexually provocative costume for the erotic fantasies of a young American male. The reader, however, cannot see what she is thinking as her eyes remain obscured behind the sunglasses, suggesting she may have had a secret. . . . embedded lightly on the model's blue skirt is a very large, erect penis."[6]

In Figure #4, the advertisement for Vaseline Intensive Care Cream appeared in the *Ladies' Home Journal.* The nature of the advertisement in Figure #4 is suggestive and embeds are used to enhance the suggestiveness. In this ad a jar of Vaseline Intensive Care Cream "is held suspended between a woman's thumb and middle fingers—highly significant parts of the female hand in many ad illustrations. . . . Every woman who has ever lived knows, at both conscious and unconscious levels, how these fingers are used in

FIGURE 2A

FIGURE 3A

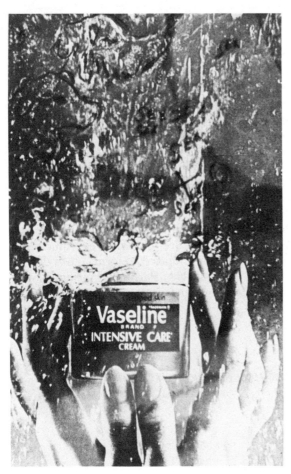

FIGURE 4A

FIGURE 5A

masturbation. . . . To assure the message does not become confused or remain ambiguous within the reader's unconscious, the hands, jar, and blue background are covered with mosaics of embedded SEXes."[7] The embeds are shown in the figure 4A.

Figure #5, a "two-page, four-color B & H advertisement, which appeared in the January 14, 1972, issue of *Life*, in *Look*, and a score of other national publications, portrayed spectators presumably watching a fight while two players crush a referee against the railing."[8] This ad contains elements of incongruity and suggestiveness. The protruding right hand (by the words "Benson & Hedges") does not belong to the referee or to the two hockey players. "There is no possible way in which the right hand could belong to any of the three bodies, unless the referee's arm was severed and the hand pulled through the bodies. The effect was created by the artist gluing a hand on the photograph and the rephotographing after he had retouched the layout."[9] On the top hockey player's padding appears the word COOPER, a widely known manufacturer of hockey equipment. On the glove, however, the letters have been carefully manipulated to form, quite distinctly, the word CANCER as shown in the closeup in Figure 5A. Perhaps this suggests that people who smoke defy death or that they are self-destructive.

References

[1-2]Figures 1–5 and Figures 1A–5A are from *Media Sexploitation,* Wilson Bryan Key, Prentice-Hall, 1976. Reprinted by permission of Wilson Bryan Key.

[3-9]The explanatory materials for Figures 1–5 are from *Media Sexploitation,* Wilson Bryan Key, Prentice-Hall, 1976.

Exercise 18

Consumer Use of Surrogate Indicators of Quality

OBJECTIVES: 1. To demonstrate the strength of intangible product attributes such as brand name on the consumers' evaluation of the product quality.
2. To provide you with some experience with behavioral research.

Consumers use certain characteristics of products as surrogate indicators of product quality. Brand name and its underlying brand image are common surrogate indicators of quality. In this exercise, you will conduct an experiment to assess the impact of brand name on consumer perception of the quality of beer.

MATERIALS
  Prestigious beer (e.g., Michelob, Lowenbrau, Grolsch)
  Popular beer (e.g., Budweiser, Coors)

Unprestigious beer (e.g., generic beer)

Sampling containers

PROCEDURE

Present consumers with three samples of beer. One will be labeled with the prestigious beer name, one will be labeled with the popular beer name, and the third will be labeled with the unprestigious beer name. All three beer samples that consumers will taste will in reality be the unprestigious beer. Ask consumers to taste the beer samples and state their preference.

RESULTS

Tabulate the results from the data sheet and interpret your findings. What are the marketing implications of your results?

DATA SHEET FOR EXERCISE 18

Talley of Consumer Preferences

First Sample_____
(Brand Name)

Total: _____

Second Sample_____
(Brand Name)

Total: _____

Third Sample_____
(Brand Name)

Total: _____

Exercise 19

The Shrinking Candy Bars

OBJECTIVES: 1. To provide an experiential understanding of the just noticeable difference concept of Weber's law.
2. To provide an opportunity to apply Weber's law to marketing.

Weber's law, $K = \Delta I/I$, states that the amount of change necessary to bring about an awareness of the change is a ratio rather than an absolute amount. In the formula, K is the ratio, ΔI is the change in intensity necessary to bring about an awareness of a change, and I is the original intensity. The just noticeable difference (j.n.d.) is the minimum amount of change necessary to bring about an awareness of a change.

Marketers can incorporate the use of Weber's Law in their strategy formulation. In some cases, it may be advantageous to the marketer to ensure that the target population is aware of a change such as in the case of a price reduction for a sale. In other cases, it may be to the marketers' advantage if the target population is not aware of a change. For example, to cover increasing expenses in the cost of producing goods, marketers can either increase the cost of the product or maintain the price of the product but decrease the amount of the product. In the latter case, marketers would want the decrease in the amount of product to be below the consumers' awareness or below the j.n.d.

In this exercise, you are asked to apply Weber's law for the situation where you want to cover cost by decreasing the quantity of the product and maintaining the present price of a product.

MATERIALS

1. Plain chocolate candy bars (6)
2. Scissors
3. Scale
4. Glue
5. Cardboard
6. Paper

PROCEDURE

1. Unwrap all six of the chocolate bars. Shave increasingly larger amounts of chocolate off of five of the candy bars. Place an equal size, equal weight piece of cardboard underneath each candy bar. Rewrap them so that they appear identical. Inconspicuously label the candy bars with numbers 1 through 6. Candy bars 1 to 5 are the experimental candy bars. Candy bar 6 is the original candy bar. No chocolate is to be shaved off of candy bar 6.
2. Weigh and record the weight of each candy bar.
    1 _____
    2 _____
    3 _____
    4 _____
    5 _____
    6 _____
3. Have twenty consumers compare the original candy bar to the five experimental candy bars one at a time. Starting with candy bar 1, have them place the experimental candy bar in one hand and the original candy bar in the other. Ask each consumer if they notice a difference in weight between the two candy bars. Stop when the consumer notices a difference in weight. This is the consumer's just noticeable difference.

RESULTS

1. Record the point at which consumers can perceive a difference in weight.
2. Plot the results on the following graph.

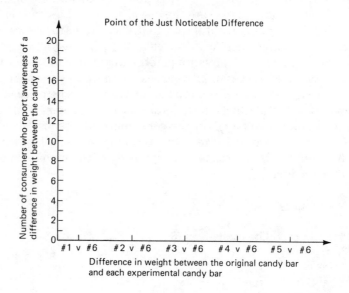

Point of the Just Noticeable Difference

INTERPRETATION
Discuss the marketing application of the results.

11

Learning

The articles included in this section illustrate the implementation of learning principles in marketing.

In the article "Snap, Crackle, Pop . . . and the Rustle of Greenbacks," Christopher Lanier tells us that the consumers' learned behavior of eating popcorn and drinking soft drinks at movies is essential to the survival of movie theaters and movies.

In the article "Exploiting Proven Brand Names Can Cut Risk of New Products," Bill Abrams discusses the application of franchise extension, "a method for a company to enter a new business through the leverage of its most valuable asset—the consumer awareness, goodwill and impressions conveyed by its brand name." The learning principle, generalization, underlies the marketing practice of franchise extension.

SNAP, CRACKLE, POP . . . AND THE RUSTLE OF GREENBACKS

The sounds are familiar: the slurp of Coca-Cola, the crunch of popcorn. The place is the darkened interior of any cinema in the country. The product is the only thing more American than apple pie—movie-theater-concession food. And the business keeps the entire motion picture industry alive.

Ordinary people consider movie eats either a convenience (what would *Superman* be without popcorn?) or a nuisance (oh God, my shoes are sticking to the floor *again*). But to theaters, concessions are simply income. Enormous income. About $5 million a year's worth.

The first key to candy-counter success rests in the words "per capita." Divide

concession sales for the day by the number of patrons and you arrive at a per capita sales figure. The larger the per capita, the larger the income.

While per capita in a first-run movie house in Los Angeles averages 30 cents, different pictures generate vastly different per capita figures. A serious film such as *Interiors* won't gross 25 cents a head. Lighter entertainment flicks do considerably better: *The Great Train Robbery* threw off a 40 cent per capita, and a James Bond picture will hit 50 cents.

To go beyond the half-dollar mark in first run, a motion picture has to pull an "eating audience." Films appealing to ethnic minorities do very well. Last year's *Blue Collar* topped 60 cents per capita. An *Up in Smoke* will reach 55 cents per capita because munchies-crazed dopers buy an awful lot of food. Kids are the really big spenders, and Disney pictures are the all-time per capita heavyweights.

The second key to making a fortune at the snack bar is the huge profit margin involved. Theaters buy low, sell high, pass Go and collect millions.

A 46-ounce cup of buttered popcorn selling from 75 cents to 85 cents in Los Angeles has a per-unit cost of 27 cents. Crank the numbers through a pocket calculator and they turn into a markup ranging from 178 percent to 215 percent. A 14-ounce soft drink costs 8 cents, sells for 60 cents, and shows a 650 percent markup. Candy supports a 100 percent-to-200 percent markup.

Be generous—figure popcorn at 175 percent, sodas at 600 percent, candy at 100 percent. Snack-bar sales distribute fairly evenly between the three items; overall markup works out to 198 percent. When the data are massaged a little more, the profit margin appears: 66.45 percent. Over 66 cents out of every *dollar* is profit.

At this point exhibitors usually start screaming about gross rather than net profit. "We have to take out labor costs, rent, corporate overhead. . . ."

Yes and no. Neighborhood cinemas do pay part of their fixed expenses with concession revenues. However, a method of accurately allocating such costs as interest, amortization and executive salary between box office and concessions doesn't exist. As a result, the amount of candy-counter profits eaten up by overhead remains a matter of conjecture, rhetoric and accounting practice.

First-run houses book films on the basis of what is called "90/10 over nut" deals. Translated into English, this means that the theaters subtract operating costs (the nut) from the box-office gross, then give the film distributor 90 percent of what's left. Unless a picture drops dead at the box office, no fixed costs remain to be covered by snack-bar receipts.

Due to the existence of 90/10 deals, it's easy to estimate the amount of earnings derived from the candy counter of a first-run cinema. The theater can turn a profit in three areas: from concessions, from the 10 percent over nut, and from the nut itself. (Theater nuts, as negotiated between exhibitor and distributor, invariably contain considerable net profit.)

Financial model building is now in order. Assume that the No-Name Theater, showing a major hit in the range of a *Deer Hunter,* takes in a weekly box office of $45,000. Per capita is only slightly above normal—say 40 cents. Admission is the first-run standard of $4.50 per person, and the house nut, a typical $6,000 per week, includes both theater costs and $2,000 pure profit.

No-Name makes $8,540 in profit during the week. Two thousand dollars comes from the nut, $3,900 from the 10 percent over nut, and $2,640 from the candy counter with the 66 percent profit margin. Despite the socko box-office returns, concessions contribute close to a third of the theater's total profit.

In the real world of Los Angeles, a first-run theater averages about $1,500 a week at the snack bar. In a year concessions make more than $50,000 in profits.

However, snack bars are much more important in neighborhood houses, which screen four-hour double bills, than in first-run cinemas. Many local theater owners claim that concession sales make up 90 percent to 100 percent of their profits.

In the neighborhoods, per capita figures average 50 cents to 60 cents, while ticket prices run considerably less than $4.50. Second-run cinemas book pictures on the basis of a flat percentage of box-office earnings and don't realize house nut profits. Concession prices keep pace with inflation while admission prices do not.

These are walk-in theaters; drive-ins depend even more on food sales. Hawking pizzas, hamburgers, hot dogs and tacos, "ozoners" are essentially restaurants that show movies as a loss leader. Most drive-ins would let people in free if they could get distributors to agree.

How important is the snack bar, overall? With an interest in more than 700 screens, United Artists Theatre Circuit is one of the few major exhibitors in the country to publish data on concessions sales. As set forth in the company's 10-K Form for the fiscal year ending August 31, 1978, on file with the Securities and Exchange Commission, candy counters contributed no less than 15.3 percent of consolidated revenues during the fiscal years ending 1975 through 1978. Net income before taxes never rose above 6.1 percent of revenues. Assume a net-profit margin on snack-bar sales of only 30 percent to 50 percent; concession profits still account for 75 percent to 125 percent of corporate profits before taxes annually.

No soft drinks or popcorn, no movie theaters. No movie theaters, no movies. It's as simple as that.

EXPLOITING PROVEN BRAND NAMES CAN CUT RISK OF NEW PRODUCTS

Building new brands is tougher than ever. Advertising costs are growing rapidly, as is rivalry for consumers' attention. Technological breakthroughs are harder to find. Top executives are queasier about spending large sums on products that history warns are likely to fail. Says a marketing executive: "Financial people are putting the squeeze on us."

One way to cope with these pressures is to make better use of brands that already have been created. "Names like Armour, Maxwell House and Del Monte represent a huge investment over years," says John Diefenbach, president of Landor Associates, a San Francisco design concern. "The incredible cost of introducing new brands points out the need to hitchhike on what already exists."

That technique is called "franchise extension" by Edward Tauber, a University of Southern California marketing professor. "It's a method for a company to enter a new business," he says, "through the leverage on its most valuable asset—the consumer awareness, good will and impressions conveyed by its brand name."

Some examples: Sunkist orange soda, Minolta copiers, Levi shirts and shoes, Del Monte Mexican food, Woolite rug shampoo, Easy-Off window cleaner, Gerber insurance and Vaseline Intensive Care skin lotion, bath oil and baby powder.

Ten years ago Bic Pen's sole U.S. business was making ballpoint pens. Today Bic also puts its name on shavers, lighters and two other types of pens. Bic's reputation as a manufacturer of inexpensive, disposable products "is a very big plus for us, especially with new products," says Bruno Bich, vice president for sales and marketing.

Bic is spending $11 million to advertise its new Bic Roller pen. Under a different name, says Mr. Bich, the cost would have been higher. In addition, he says, the Roller campaign "helps all Bic products, especially other writing instruments."

Although hitchhiking on established brands isn't a new idea, Mr. Diefenbach maintains it's an underappreciated one. "We anticipate a world of 100 to 200 superbrands that have found ways to capitalize on their existing reputations," he says.

General Foods is following that approach for its Jell-O Pudding Pops, a frozen dessert on a stick. It borrows the name from the General Foods pudding mix and uses entertainer Bill Cosby, who stars in Jell-O Pudding commercials, for its ads. Another sign that General Foods is paying more attention to its existing name: the company recently began test-marketing Maxwell House freeze-dried coffee after its Maxim freeze-dried coffee fizzled.

A stroll down any supermarket aisle reveals many names that may have untapped value. Among them, marketers cite R.T. French, Kraft, Fleischmann's, Planter's, Popsicle, Best Foods, Lipton, Hunt, Wesson, Green Giant and Weight Watchers. Even American Telephone & Telegraph is studying products that could carry the Bell name.

Many companies already have tried to leapfrog into new categories without success. Among products that have been flops: Arm & Hammer antiperspirant, Certs gum, Life Savers gum, Sara Lee Chicken & Noodles Au Gratin and Listerol, a household cleaner from the maker of Listerine.

Many of these have been "me-too" products, those without any significant benefit different from their competitors; a familiar name alone rarely is enough to ensure prosperity. Welch Foods, known for grape-flavored products, found that out when it tried to sell prune juice.

Marketers need to do some homework before applying their names to new product areas. The first step is "looking at the strengths, weaknesses and image of the brand," says Richard Tongberg, marketing research manager at Miles Laboratories, the maker of Alka-Seltzer, One-A-Day vitamins, S.O.S. scouring pads and other consumer products. "Most companies haven't even done that."

Next, "assess the boundaries of the brand's franchise," Mr. Tongberg says. "What is its ability to be stretched to different product categories?"

The third step, he says, is to "identify creative ways of communicating the parent brand's image in a new category but in a way that is relevant."

Several obstacles await marketers who try to extend franchises. One is the risk of unexpected problems harming other related brands. The association of Rely tampons with toxic shock syndrome last year might have harmed Procter & Gamble's image even more if the company hadn't followed its tradition of making each of its brands stand alone.

If you're going to have your name on all your products," says Bic's Mr. Bich, "you should never produce a bad product. If you make a mistake, you'll hurt your whole company."

Spinoffs can hurt parent brands in other ways. Mr. Tauber criticizes Coca-Cola's decision to bring out a line of diet soda flavors, such as root beer and ginger ale, under its Tab name, which has become nearly synonymous with diet cola. "To the extent the line of flavors is a success," he says, "you can't go in and ask for a Tab anymore."

Brands stretched too far could lose their individuality. "The housewife could write 'Charmin, Kleenex, Bounty and Pampers' on her shopping list and we'd know exactly what she was going to get," ad executives Al Ries and Jack Trout note in *Positioning: The Battle for Your Mind,* their recent book. "'Scott' on a shopping list has no meaning."

The key to finding new places for old names is to find product categories that are compatible with their parents. Welch Foods frequently has been advised to enter the wine business; the company says it won't. "You can't be the No. 1 name in peanut butter and jelly sandwiches," says Theodore Wolfe, executive vice president, "and the number one name in wine. You have to decide which horse you're going to ride."

Exercise 20

Low-Involvement Learning

OBJECTIVE: To bridge the abstract principles of low-involvement learning with their concrete operations in your everyday life.

Low-involvement learning is a type of learning based upon association and repetition. Logos, packages, and jingles through repetition and association are classically conditioned to have certain meanings. How many of the following logos, packages, and jingles do you know?

With what brand do you associate the following jingles?

1. "When it rains, it pours."   1. _____
2. "We're No. 2, we try harder."   2. _____
3. "Good to the last drop."   3. _____
4. "Finger-lickin' good."   4. _____
5. "Have it your way."   5. _____
6. "Don't leave home without it."   6. _____
7. "Our legs fit your legs."   7. _____
8. "M'm, M'm good."   8. _____

  9. "For iron-poor blood."   9. _____
10. "Builds bodies twelve ways."   10. _____
11. "Does she or doesn't she?"   11. _____
12. "You deserve a break today."   12. _____
13. "The wine remembers."   13. _____

Test your memory and identify the companies behind the logos.

14. _____

15. _____

16. _____

17. _____

18. _____

19. _____

20. _____

21. _____

22. _____

The logos on the previous page are used with the permission of the following companies.

Exercise 21

Principles of Learning

OBJECTIVE To provide concrete examples of the marketing applications of the abstract principles of learning theories.

For each of the marketing communications that follows, determine the principle(s) of learning that is/are being applied. Some learning principles can be described as follows:

1. *Generalization* emphasizes the similarity in objects/situations and refers to the same response to similar but different objects/situations.
2. *Discrimination* emphasizes the differences in objects/situations and refers to different responses to a different but similar objects/situations.
3. *Association* refers to the pairing of items to establish linkages among them.
4. *Mental completion* refers to the human tendency to remember incomplete patterns better than those that are complete.
5. *Covert involvement* refers to the mental or emotional feelings that are evoked by stimuli.
6. *Semantic generalization* refers to the process of establishing meaning for words that essentially have no meaning.
7. *Visual imagery* refers to the visual image that is associated with verbal material.

Reprinted with permission of MEM Co., Inc.

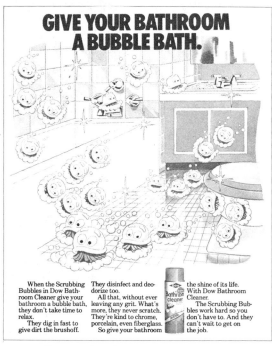

Reprinted with permission of Dow Chemical U.S.A.

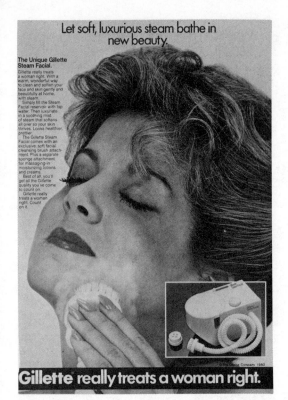

Let soft, luxurious steam bathe in new beauty.

The Unique Gillette Steam Facial.

Gillette really treats a woman right. With a warm, wonderful way to clean and soften your face and skin gently and beautifully at home, with steam.

Simply fill the Steam Facial reservoir with tap water. Then luxuriate in a soothing mist of steam that softens all over so your skin thrives. Looks healthier, prettier.

The Gillette Steam Facial comes with an exclusive, soft facial cleansing brush attachment. Plus a separate sponge attachment for massaging-in moisturizing lotions and creams.

Best of all, you'll get all the Gillette quality you've come to count on.

Gillette really treats a woman right. Count on it.

Gillette really treats a woman right.

Reprinted with the permission of The Gillette Company.

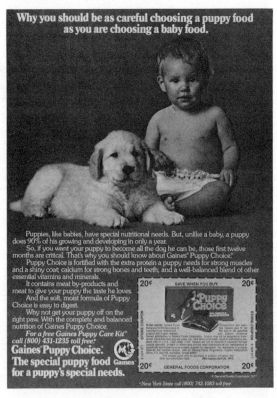

Why you should be as careful choosing a puppy food as you are choosing a baby food.

Puppies, like babies, have special nutritional needs. But, unlike a baby, a puppy does 90% of his growing and developing in only a year.

So, if you want your puppy to become all the dog he can be, those first twelve months are critical. That's why you should know about Gaines® Puppy Choice®

Puppy Choice is fortified with the extra protein a puppy needs for strong muscles and a shiny coat; calcium for strong bones and teeth; and a well-balanced blend of other essential vitamins and minerals.

It contains meat by-products and meat to give your puppy the taste he loves.

And the soft, moist formula of Puppy Choice is easy to digest.

Why not get your puppy off on the right paw. With the complete and balanced nutrition of Gaines Puppy Choice.

For a free Gaines Puppy Care Kit call (800) 431-1235 toll free.*

Gaines® Puppy Choice. The special puppy food for a puppy's special needs.

New York State call (800) 742-1083 toll free.

Reprinted with permission from General Foods Corporation.

Disappears rather quickly, doesn't it.

Reprinted with the permission of General Wine & Spirits Company.

If you want to lock in freshness, Tupperware really locks it in.

Reprinted with permission of Tupperware.

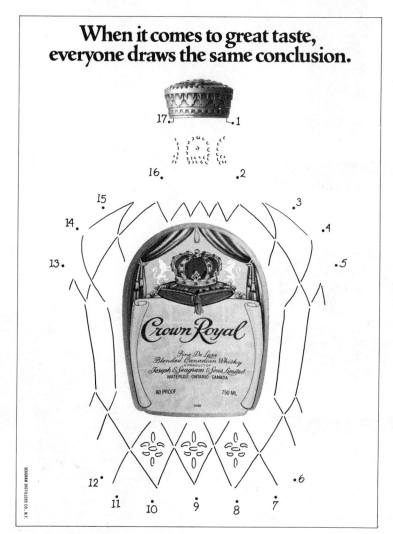

Reprinted with permission from Seagram Distillers Company.

12

Personality and Consumer Behavior

Marketers and scholars of consumer behavior have borrowed the concept of personality from psychology and have applied it with varying degrees of satisfaction to the practice of marketing. The article included in this section demonstrate the influence of personality theories on the practice of marketing and discuss the predictive and explanatory usefulness of personality to consumer behavior.

In the article "Personality and Consumer Behavior: One More Time," Harold H. Kassarjian and Mary Jane Sheffet describe the elusive nature of the relationship between personality and consumer behavior. Their review of the research in the field of personality and consumer behavior leads them to conclude that, rather than approach the study of personality and consumer behavior unidimensionally, a holistic approach may bring more positive results.

PERSONALITY AND CONSUMER BEHAVIOR: ONE MORE TIME

By late 1969 some one hundred studies were available in the marketing literature relating personality variables to consumer behavior. A review of these studies (41, 43, 89) can be summarized by the single word, "equivocal." The purpose of this paper is to enumerate what has happened to the field in the ensuing half decade. The previous quarter century had produced some one hundred studies. The outpouring of recent research has accumulated an additional one hundred studies in the last five years, not including working papers, privately distributed pre-prints and unpublished proprietary studies.

No major obvious changes have been

"Personality and Consumer Behavior: One More Time," Harold H. Kassarjian and Mary Jane Sheffet, *1975 Combined Proceedings of the American Marketing Association,* Chicago, pp. 197–201, published by the American Marketing Association. Reprinted by permission.

discernible although some new fads in researchable variables have emerged. For example, one no longer finds the topic of motivation research from a psychoanalytic point of view in the literature. The only true attempt to use a projective technique to be found in the published literature is a replication of the classic Mason Haire Shopping List study by Webster and Von Pechman (85) which, interestingly, yielded significantly different results from the original paper. Instant coffee users are no longer perceived as psychologically different from drip grind users. The only other attempts at the use of projective techniques are studies by David Gardner (29) and Hughes (38) in which McClelland's TAT type pictures were used to measure need for achievement. Landon (52) measured the same variable but by using Merabian's paper and pencil test avoided the interpretation problems of a projective tool.

The use of the traditionally available paper and pencil psychological inventories is still quite popular. The Edwards Personal Preference Schedule, originally used by Evans in his landmark Ford-Chevrolet study, was used in studies by Alpert (3, 4), Peterson (73) and Bither and Dolich (12). Horton (36), in a penetrating article, attacked the use of this and similar paper-and-pencil tools on procedural grounds. The Thurstone Temperament Schedule appears in a study by Wiseman (94) using linear discriminant analysis while the Gordon instrument was utilized in two studies (33, 78). Cohen's CAD test of Horney's classification scheme is reported in three papers. One by Kernan (45) concerning message advocacy, group influence, fashions, brand loyalty, and new product information produced significant results with the conclusion that the instrument "works." The second by Cohen and Goldberg (19) again produced positive results and a third by Nicely (64) found correlations between CAD, Eysenck's introversion-extroversion variable and Kassarjian's inner-and-other-direction variables. Donnelly and Ivancevich (24) in turn found a weak but positive relationship between inner-other-direction and innovator characteristics. Perry (69) tied in anxiety, the Eysenck variables, and heredity to product choice concluding that consumption was genetically influenced. He claimed that this genetic relationship has application to primary demand but not product choice.

Rokeach's dogmatism as a variable appeared in some half a dozen studies (7, 14, 21, 42, 60, 72) correlating the variable to risk, innovation and adoption, generally with weak but significant results.

Openmindedness seems to be positively related to risk taking and willingness to innovate.

Several new instruments appeared for the first time in consumer type studies. Morris and Cundiff (6) and Vavra and Winn (83) turned their attention to anxiety and the Taylor Manifest Anxiety Scale, and Hawkins (35) used the State-Trait Anxiety Inventory. The mixed results generally indicate that low anxiety is related to acceptance of more threatening material such as males' acceptance of feminine products. Peters and Ford (72) used the California Test of Personality and could find no personality difference between women who buy and do not buy from door-to-door salesmen. Hughes (38) compared the CPI and Rotter's Locus of Control to bargaining behavior. Webster (85) aimed the CPI at social responsibility concluding that the better socially and psychologically integrated consumer displays greater social consciousness.

The most widely used instrument new to consumer behavior is the Jackson Personality Research Form. Wilson et al. (91) correlated these scores with segmentation variables, Fry and Ahmed (1, 28) with cigarette smoking, Kinnear and Taylor (49, 50) with ecological products, Worthing et al. (96, 97) with a variety of consumer products, and Matthews et al. (57) with perceived risk.

Studies using intolerance of ambiguity (15, 58) and Rotter's internal and external control (38, 58) have appeared using available instruments. Additional new instruments appeared in the literature as Paul and Enis (68), Goldberg (31), Kirchner (51), Kegerreis and Engle (45), Baumgarten (11), and Feldman and Armstrong (25) developed their own tools to measure venturesomeness, Murray's needs, ordinal birth position, personal competence and so on.

Self-confidence had been heavily examined prior to 1969. Its fascination to researchers has not diminished. Studies by Bither and Wright (13), Barach (8, 9) and Ostlund (65, 66, 67) have since appeared. Work in self-concept continues to appear in some eleven studies (5, 23, 27, 32, 34, 37, 42, 53, 55, 56, 77) in the struggle to explain purchase behavior by measuring the ideal self and actual self-concept.

Perhaps the most dramatic change in the field has been the influence of studies using life style, AIO, or psychographics as they are alternatively termed. These factor analyzed scales have been applied to media exposure (47, 59), credit card usage (75), advertising (74), creativity (93), opinion leadership and innovation (81), and market segmentation (17, 39, 40, 98). Discussion articles of The Methodology (76, 87, 92, 99) as well as reliability and validity studies (16, 80) are now available among many others. These two dozen articles, however, merely scratch the surface. The book by King and Tigert (48), *Life Style and Psychographics* by Bill Wells (88) and the AMA Attitude Research Proceedings (6) contribute still more papers to this field. In addition, no topic in our memory has produced as many unpublished papers, university working papers, and private pre-prints as has life style research. Interestingly, the impact has not been as great as the sheer weight of publications might suggest, although psychographics certainly has become a buzz word in industry.

On overview, the conclusions from published research studies over the past five years remain quite similar to those drawn in 1969. The additional studies have generally made little contribution to the depth of our knowledge, although its breadth has certainly been expanded. The correlation or relationship between personality test scores and consumer behavior variables such as product choice, media exposure, innovation, segmentation, etc., are weak at best and thus of little value in prediction. The reasons for such poor predictions have been discussed by Jacoby (41), Wells and Beard (89) and Kassarjian (43), and all agree that personality is a critical variable in the explanation of the purchasing process. The critical question is why do we insist on considering personality, by itself, a salient variable when the data are at best equivocal?

Nakanishi, in a most insightful paper (63) presented at the 1972 meetings of the Association for Consumer Research, has suggested that the low explanatory power of personality characteristics may have stemmed, in part, from naive conceptualizations of the relationship between personality and consumer behavior often held by researchers in the field. It is obvious that simple linear statistics such as variance analysis, chi square and t-tests are insufficient. For example, canonical correlations have been used by Sparks and Tucker (78), Bither and Dolich (12), Alpert (3) and Darden and Reynolds (22) with more complex results and somewhat more variance statistically explained. Unfortunately, this adding of additional variables still involves a static view of the consumer. Personality is perhaps better conceived of as a dynamic concept which is not constant over a variety of situations. Rather, personality is a consistency in the manner the individual adjusts to change over time and over situations. Nakanishi writes it is perhaps "more correct to conceive of personality as a moderator variable whose function is to moderate the effects of environmental change in the individual's behavior. This dynamic concept of personality has not been taken seriously in personality research."

Nakanishi seems to be suggesting that what we need is data somewhat analogous to a combination of cross-sectional and times series analysis. The studies conducted to date are of the cross-sectional variety correlating test inventory variables with consumption variables over subjects. And yet, as Wells (89) points out, a single personality trait may lead to a variety of behaviors. For instance compulsiveness can lead to extremely orderly behavior or expulsive disorderly behavior depending on the situation. On the other hand, several personality traits may lead to a single response, again depending on the situation. Correlating a single trait with a single behavior is bound to be frustrating.

Hence, according to Nakanishi, the relevant variables include personality traits, response and behavior patterns, moderator variables, situations and individuals. Furthermore, for some of these variables it is essential that measurements be taken over time. That is, we sample individuals, traits and responses, we should also take samplings of situations over time.

If one turns to other concepts in consumer research, an overview of the results again appears to be frustrating at times. For example, static research and linear statistics on the relationship between attitudes, values, or beliefs and the behavior of the individual are weak at best. Research on repetition and learning, perceived risk, motivation, level of involvement, group influence, reference groups, personal influence, class, and cultural influences have produced similar conclu-

sions. The data indicate sufficient relationships between the concept and behavior to be enticing and to encourage even further research, but quite insufficient to satisfy a statistician attempting to validate a simple mathematical model or the marketer seeking explanations of the variance in consumer behavior that are not so small as to be meaningless.

If one can generalize from Nakanishi, the low explanatory power of each of these variables stems from naive conceptualizations of the relationships between the variable and the actions of the consumer in the marketplace.

Trained as we have been, by psychoanalytic logic, simplistic beliefs emerging from stimulus-response psychology, and basic Aristotelian modes of thought, we insist on retaining the belief that, "The stimulus possesses an adhesion with certain reactions (54)." This adhesion is regarded as the cause of the event, and somehow, there are mechanically rigid connections or associations between a stimulus and a response. The purchase of canned peas is somehow related to a specific personality variable, a specific type of perceived risk, or to a set of attributions. The belief is that once the mathematical relationship of this mechanically rigid connection is uncovered, the variance will be accounted for and a statistical error term will no longer exist. Hence, if the Edwards schedule does not account for the variance, perhaps the Jackson Inventory will, and if not, there are still Fishbein attitude models, reference groups, and measures of the level of involvement upon which to fall back.

The conception that the individual must be perceived as a dynamic whole has not yet been internalized by the modern-day consumer researcher. We ought not to be concerned with rigid connections, but rather with temporally extended whole individuals. In short, further traditional research attempting to connect the purchase of canned peas with a personality variable using cross sectional data is bound to fail. What is missing are the interaction effects of that personality variable with other personality characteristics as well as the interaction effects accounted for by needs, motives, moods, memories, attitudes, beliefs, opinions, perceptions, values, etc. in addition to the situation or field. As Tucker (82) has already suggested, our theories must begin with the study of the whole individual in a purchase act, at a point in time. In short, every specific instance of behavior must be viewed as the result of the interaction and integration of a variety of influences or forces impinging upon the person. The description of behavior cannot concentrate exclusively on one or another of the variables involved. Only after the analysis examines the situation as a whole is it possible to turn to the specific elements and the interactions among the elements (44). Unfortunately a simple methodology for research of this sort has not yet emerged. We do not necessarily advocate a return to the extensive study of a single individual such as the psychoanalytic methodology employed by Freud, or the environmental probability of Egon Brunswick. But, greater awareness of views espoused by Tolman, Freud, Brunswick, Lewin, and other great minds in the social sciences and philosophy might help point out the location of the light at the end of the tunnel.

Only when we can explain the behavior of a single individual in a variety of situations over time can we grasp the idea that there are, in fact, interactions between personality, attitudes, perceived risk, and the psychological field or situation. Once the concept of an interaction effect has been internalized, we can turn from an examination of the whole to analyses of the parts. The proper question then would be, "All other things being equal, what is the relationship between a specific personality variable and a specific act?" The problem with the literature as it exists today is that "all other things are not equal" and yet we continue to express dismay, surprise, or pleasure that personality measures, or attitude measures, or what have you, only account for 5% of the variance. As has already been expressed (43), "What is amazing is not that there are many studies that show no correlation between consumer behavior and personality, but rather that there are any studies at all with positive results. That 5% or 10% or any portion of the variance can be accounted for by personality variables (taken out of context and studied independently of other cognitive or physical variables) . . . is most remarkable, indeed!"

References

1. Ahmed, S. A. "Prediction of Cigarette Consumption Level with Personality and Socioeconomic Variables," *Journal of Applied Psychology,* 56 (October 1972), 437–438.

2. Alpert, Lewis, and Ronald Gatty. "Product Positioning by Behavioral Life Styles," *Journal of Marketing,* 33 (April 1969), 65–69.

3. Alpert, Mark I. "A Canonical Analysis of Personality and the Determinants of Automobile Choice," *Combined Proceedings,* American Marketing Association, 1971, 312–316.

4. Alpert, Mark I. "Personality and The Determinants of Product Choice," *Journal of Marketing Research,* 5 (February 1972), 89–92.

5. American Market Research Bureau, "Measuring Self-Concept," Unpublished Working Paper, May 1972.

6. American Marketing Association, *Attitude Research Reaches New Heights,* Chicago: American Marketing Association, 1971.

7. Anderson, W. T., and William H. Cunningham, "Gauging Foreign Product Promotion," *Journal of Advertising Research,* 12 (February 1972), 29–44.

8. Barach, Jeffery A. "Self-Confidence, Risk

Handling, and Mass Communications," *Proceedings,* Fall Conference, American Marketing Association, 1969, 323–329.

9. Barach, Jeffrey A. "Self Confidence and Four Types of Persuasive Situations," *Combined Proceedings,* American Marketing Association, 1972, 418–422.

10. Bass, Frank M., Edgar A. Pessemier, and Douglas J. Tigert. "A Taxonomy of Magazine Readership Applied to Problems in Marketing Strategy and Media Selection," *Journal of Business,* 42 (July 1969), 337–363.

11. Baumgarten, Steven A. "The Innovative Communicator in the Diffusion Process," *Journal of Marketing Research,* 12 (February 1975), 12–18.

12. Bither, Stewart W., and Ira J. Dolich. "Personality as a Determinant Factor in Store Choice," *Proceedings,* Association for Consumer Research, 1972, 9–19.

13. Bither, Stewart W., and Peter L. Wright, "The Self Confidence-Advertising Response Relationship a Function of Situational Distraction," *Journal of Marketing Research,* 10 (May 1973), 146–152.

14. Blake, Brian, Robert Perloff, and Richard Heslin. "Dogmatism and Acceptance of New Products," *Journal of Marketing Research,* 7 (November 1970), 483–486.

15. Blake, Brian, Robert Perloff, Robert Zenhausern, and Richard Heslin. "The Effect of Intolerance of Ambiguity upon Product Perceptions," *Journal of Applied Psychology,* 58 (October 1973), 239–243.

16. Bruno, Albert V., and Edgar A. Pessemier. "An Empirical Investigation of the Validity of Selected Attitude and Activity Measures," *Proceedings,* Association for Consumer Research, 1972, 456–473.

17. Bushman, F. Anthony. "Market Segmentation via Attitudes and Life Style," *Combined Proceedings,* American Marketing Association, 1971, 594–599.

18. Carman, James M. "Correlates of Brand Loyalty: Some Positive Results," *Journal of Marketing Research,* 7 (February 1970), 67–76.

19. Cohen, Joel B., and Ellen Golden. "Informational Social Influence and Product Evaluation," *Journal of Applied Psychology,* 50 (February 1972), 54–59.

20. Coney, Kenneth A. "Dogmatism and Innovation: A Replication," *Journal of Marketing Research,* 9 (November 1972), 453–455.

21. Darden, William R., and Fred D. Reynolds. "Predicting Opinion Leadership for Men's Apparel Fashions," *Journal of Marketing Research,* 9 (August 1972), 324–328.

22. Darden, William R., and Fred D. Reynolds. "Backward Profiling of Male Innovators," *Journal of Marketing Research,* 11 (February 1974), 79–85.

23. Dolich, Ira J., and Ned Shilling. "A Criti-cal Evaluation of 'The Problem of Self-Concept in Store Image Studies,'" *Journal of Marketing,* 35 (January 1971), 71–73.

24. Donnelly, James H., Jr., and John M. Ivancevich. "A Methodology for Identifying Innovator Characteristics of New Brand Purchasers," *Journal of Marketing Research,* 11 (August 1974), 331–334.

25. Engel, James F., David T. Kollat, and Roger D. Blackwell. "Personality Measures and Market Segmentation," *Business Horizons,* 12 (June 1969), 61–70.

26. Feldman, Laurence P., and Gary M. Armstrong. "Identifying Buyers of a Major Automobile Innovation," *Journal of Marketing,* 39 (January 1975), 47–53.

27. French, Warren A., and Alan B. Flaschner. "Levels of Actualization as Matched against Life Style Evaluation of Products," *Combined Proceedings,* American Marketing Association, 1971, 358–362.

28. Fry, Joseph N. "Personality Variables and Cigarette Brand Choice," *Journal of Marketing Research,* 8 (August 1971), 298–304.

29. Gardner, David M. "An Exploratory Investigation of Achievement Motivation Effects on Consumer Behavior," *Proceedings,* Association for Consumer Research, 1972, 20–33.

30. Goble, Ross Lawrence. "New Psychometric Measurements for Consumer Credit Behavior," *Proceedings,* Fall Conference, American Marketing Association, 1969, 368–376.

31. Goldberg, Marvin E. "A Cognitive Model of Innovative Behavior: The Interaction of Product and Self-Attitudes," *Proceedings,* Association for Consumer Research, 1971, 313–330.

32. Green, Paul E., Arun Maheshwari and V. R. Rao. "Self Concept and Brand Preference: An Empirical Application of Multidimensional Scaling," *Journal of the Marketing Research Society,* 11 (1969), 343–360.

33. Greeno, Daniel W., Montrose S. Sommers, and Jerome B. Kernan. "Personality and Implicit Behavior Batterns," *Journal of Marketing Research,* 10 (February 1973), 63–69.

34. Grubb, Edward L., and Bruce L. Stern. "Self-Concept and Significant Others," *Journal of Marketing Research,* 8 (August 1971), 382–385.

35. Hawkins, Del I. "Reported Cognitive Dissonance and Anxiety: Some Additional Findings," *Journal of Marketing,* 36 (July 1972), 63–66.

36. Horton, Raymond L. "The Edwards Personal Preference Schedule and Consumer Personality Research," *Journal of Marketing Research* 11 (August 1974), 333–337.

37. Hughes, G. David, and Jose L. Guerrero, "Automobile Self-Congruity Models Reexamined," *Journal of Marketing Research,* 8 (February 1971), 125–127.

38. Hughes, G. David, Joseph B. Juhasz, and

Bruno Contino. "The Influence of Personality on the Bargaining Process," *Journal of Business of the University of Chicago*, 46 (October 1973), 593–603.

39. Hustad, Thomas P., and Edgar A. Pessemier. "Industry's Use of Life Style Analysis: Segmenting Consumer Market with Activity and Attitude Measures," *Combined Proceedings*, American Marketing Association, 1971a, 296–301.

40. Hustad, Thomas P., and Edgar A. Pessemier. "Segmenting Consumer Markets with Activity and Attitude Measures," Unpublished Working Paper, Purdue University, 1971.

41. Jacoby, Jacob. "Multiple-Indicant Approach for Studying New Product Adopters," *Journal of Applied Psychology*, 55 (1971), 384–388.

42. Joyce, Timothy. "Personality Classification of Consumers," Unpublished paper presented at 1972 Annual Meetings, American Psychological Association.

43. Kassarjian, Harold H. "Personality and Consumer Behavior: A Review," *Journal of Marketing Research*, 8 (November 1971), 409–418.

44. Kassarjian, Harold H. "Field Theory in Consumer Behavior," in Scott Ward and Thomas S. Robertson (eds.), *Consumer Behavior: Theoretical Sources*, Englewood Cliffs, N.J.: Prentice-Hall, 1973, 118–140.

45. Kegerreis, Robert J., and James F. Engel. "The Innovative Consumer: Characteristics of the Earliest Adopters of a New Automotive Service" *Proceedings*, American Marketing Association, 1969, 357–361.

46. Kernan, Jerome B. "The CAD Instrument in Behavioral Diagnosis," *Proceedings*, Association for Consumer Research, 1971, 301–312.

47. King, Charles W., and Douglas J. Tigert (eds.), *Attitude Research Reaches New Heights*, Chicago: American Marketing Association, 1971.

48. Kinnear, Thomas C., James R. Taylor, and Sadrudin A. Ahmed. "Socioeconomic and Personality Characteristics as They Relate to Ecologically Constructive Purchasing Behavior," *Proceedings*, Association for Consumer Research, 1972, 34–60.

49. Kinnear, Thomas C., James R. Taylor, and Sadrudin A. Ahmed. "Ecologically Concerned Consumers: Who Are They?," *Journal of Marketing*, 38 (April 1974), 20–24.

50. Kirchner, Donald F. "Personal Influence, Ordinal Position and Purchasing Behavior," *Proceedings*, Association for Consumer Research, 1971, 82–98.

51. Landon, E. Laird, Jr. "A Sex-Role Explanation of Purchase Intention Differences of Consumers Who Are High and Low in Need Achievement," *Proceedings*, Association for Consumer Research, 1972, 1–8.

52. Landon, E. Laird, Jr. "Self-Concept, Ideal Self Concept, and Consumer Purchase Intentions," *Journal of Consumer Research*, 1 (September 1974), 44–51.

53. Lewin, Kurt. *A Dynamic Theory of Personality*, New York: McGraw-Hill, 1935, 43–65.

54. Martin, Warren S. *Personality and Product Symbolism*. Austin, Texas: Bureau of Business Research, Graduate School of Business, University of Texas, 1973.

55. Mason, Joseph Barry, and Morris L. Mayer. "The Problem of the Self-Concept in Store Image Studies," *Journal of Marketing*, 34 (April 1970), 67–69.

56. Mathews, H. Lee, John W. Slocum, Jr., and Arch G. Woodside. "Perceived Risk, Individual Differences, and Shopping Orientations," *Proceedings*, Association for Consumer Research, 1971, 299–306.

57. Mazis, Michael B., and Timothy W. Sweeney. "Novelty and Personality with Risk as a Moderating Variable," *Combined Proceedings*, American Marketing Association, 1972, 406–411.

58. Michaels, Peter W. "Life Style and Magazine Exposure," *Combined Proceedings*, American Marketing Association, 1972, 324–331.

59. Michman, Ronald D. "Market Segmentation Strategies: Pitfalls and Potentials," *Combined Proceedings*, American Marketing Association, 1971, 322–326.

60. Morris, George P., and Edward W. Cundiff. "Acceptance by Males of Feminine Products," *Journal of Marketing Research*, 8 (August 1971), 372–374.

61. Morrison, Bruce John, and Richard C. Sherman. "Who Responds to Sex in Advertising," *Journal of Advertising Research*, 12 (April 1972), 15–19.

62. Nakanishi, Masao. "Personality and Consumer Behavior: Extentions," *Proceedings*, Association for Consumer Research, 1972, 61–65.

63. Nicely, Roy E. "E, I-O and CAD Correlations," Unpublished Working Paper, Virginia Polytechnic Institute & State University, 1972.

64. Ostlund, Lyman E. "The Role of Product Perceptions in Innovative Behavior," *Proceedings*, Fall Conference, American Marketing Association, 1969, 259–266.

65. Ostlund, Lyman E. "The Interaction of Self Confidence Variables in the Context of Innovative Behavior," *Proceedings*, Association for Consumer Research, 1971, 351–357.

66. Ostlund, Lyman E. "Identifying Early Buyers," *Journal of Advertising Research*, 12 (April 1972), 25–30.

67. Paul, Gordon W., and Ben M. Enis. "Psychological and Socioeconomic Atypicality of Consumer Panel Members," *Proceedings*, Fall Conference, American Marketing Association, 1969, 387–391.

68. Perry, Arnon. "Heredity, Personality Traits, Product Attitude and Product Consumption—An Exploratory Study," *Journal of Marketing Research*, 10 (November 1973), 376–379.

69. Pessemier, Edgar A., and T. P. Hustad. "Segmenting Consumer Markets with Activity and Attitude Measures," Unpublished Paper, Marketing Science Institute, 1971.

70. Peters, Michael P., and M. Venkatesan. "Exploration of Variables Inherent in Adopting an Industrial Product," *Journal of Marketing Research,* 10 (August 1973), 312–315.

71. Peters, William H., and Neil M. Ford. "A Profile of Urban Inhome Shoppers: The Other Half," *Journal of Marketing,* 36 (January 1972), 62–64.

72. Peterson, Robert A. "Psychographics and Media Exposure," *Journal of Advertising Research,"* 12 (June 1972), 17–20.

73. Plummer, Joseph T. "Life Style and Advertising: Case Studies," *Combined Proceedings,* American Marketing Association, 1971a, 290–295.

74. Plummer, Joseph T. "Life Style Patterns and Commercial Bank Credit Card Usage," *Journal of Marketing,* 35 (April 1971b), 35–41.

75. Reynolds, Fred D., and William R. Darden, "An Operational Construction of Life Style," *Proceedings,* Association for Consumer Research, 1972, 475–489.

76. Ross, Ivan, "Self Concept and Brand Preference," *Journal of Business of the University of Chicago,* 44 (January 1971), 38–50.

77. Sparks, Davis L., and W. T. Tucker. "A Multivariate Analysis of Personality and Product Use," *Journal of Marketing Research,* 8 (February 1971), 67–70.

78. Swan, John E., and Frederick E. May. "Comments on Personality and Persuasibility in Consumer Decision Making," *Journal of Advertising Research,* 10 (June 1970), 1–27.

79. Tigert, Douglas J. "Psychographics: A Test-Retest Reliability Analysis," *Proceedings,* Fall Conference, American Marketing Association, 1969, 310–315.

80. Tigert, Douglas J., and Stephen J. Arnold. "Profiling Self-Designated Opinion Leaders and Self-Designated Innovators Through Life and Style Research," *Proceedings.* Association for Consumer Research, 1971, 425–445.

81. Tucker, William T. *Foundations for a Theory of Consumer Behavior.* New York: Holt, Rinehart and Winston, Inc., 1967.

82. Vavra, Terry G., and Paul R. Winn. "Fear Appeals in Advertising: An Investigation of the Influence of Order, Anxiety and Involvement," *Combined Proceedings,* American Marketing Association, 1971, 444–449.

83. Venkatesan, M. "Personality and Persuasibility in Consumer Decision Making: A Reply," *Journal of Advertising Research,* 10 (June 1970), 1–12.

84. Webster, Frederick E., Jr., and Fredrick Von Pechmann. "A Replication of the 'Shopping List'

Study," *Journal of Marketing,* 34 (April 1970), 61–63.

85. Webster, Frederick E. "Determining the Characteristics of the Socially Conscious Consumer," Unpublished Paper, 1975.

86. Wells, William D. "Seven Questions about Lifestyle and Psychographics," *Combined Proceedings,* American Marketing Association, 1972, 462–465.

87. Wells, William D. (ed.). *Life Style and Psychographics.* Chicago: American Marketing Association, 1974.

88. Wells, William D., and Arthur D. Beard. "Personality and Consumer Behavior," in Scott Ward and Thomas S. Robertson (eds.), *Consumer Behavior: Theoretical Sources.* Englewood Cliffs, N.J.: Prentice-Hall, 1973, 141–199.

89. Wheatley, J. J. and S. Oshikawa. "The Relationship Between Anxiety and Positive and Negative Advertising Appeals," *Journal of Marketing Research,* 7 (1970), 85–89.

90. Wilson, David T., H. Lee Mathews, and Timothy W. Sweeney. "Industrial Buyer Segmentation: A Psychographic Approach," *Combined Proceedings,* American Marketing Association, 1971, 327–331.

91. Wind, Jerry. "Life Style Analysis: A New Approach," *Combined Proceedings,* American Marketing Association, 1971, 302–305.

92. Winter, Edward, and John T. Russell. "Psychographics and Creativity," *Journal of Advertising,* 2 (1973), 32–35.

93. Wiseman, Frederick. "A Segmentation Analysis on Automobile Buyers During the New Model Year Transition Period," *Journal of Marketing,* 35 (April 1971), 42–49.

94. Woodside, Arch G. "Effects of Prior Decision Making, Demographics and Psychographics on Marital Roles for Purchasing Durables," *Proceedings,* Association for Consumer Research, 1974, 81–91.

95. Worthing, Parker M., M. Venkatesan, and Steve Smith. "A Modified Approach to the Exploration of Personality and Product Use," *Combined Proceedings,* American Marketing Association, 363–367.

96. Worthing, Parker M., M. Venkatesan, and Steve Smith. "Personality and Product Use Revisited: An Exploration with the Personality Research Form," *Journal of Applied Psychology,* 57 (April 1973), 179–183.

97. Ziff, Ruth. "Psychographics for Market Segmentation," *Journal of Advertising Research,* 11 (April 1971), 3–9.

98. Ziff, Ruth. "Closing the Consumer-Advertising Gap Through Psychographics," *Combined Proceedings,* American Marketing Association, 1972, 457–461.

Exercise 22

Do Self-image and Brand Image Match?

OBJECTIVE: To demonstrate a method to empirically test the relationship between self-image and brand image in consumer behavior.

Do consumers purchase products that match their self-concept? In this exercise you are asked to empirically determine the answer to this question. First, measure your self-image using the form on the following page. Second, measure your perception of the image of the car you presently drive, using the Form 1 Questionnaire. Third, measure your perception of the image of the car you would one day like to own, using the Form 2 Questionnaire. Fourth, measure your perception of the image of a car you would not like to own, using the Form 3 Questionnaire. Finally, use the following distance formula to determine the distance between your self-image and your perception of each of the brand images.

Distance formula: $D_{ij} = \sqrt{\Sigma\, d_{ij}{}^2}$ where D_{ij} is the linear distance between the self-image and the brand images, and d_{ij} is the numerical difference between the brand image rating and the self-image rating of a characteristic.

Does the relationship between brand image and self-image predict your preference? Discuss the marketing implications of your findings.

Questionnaire

Please rate yourself as you see yourself on the following scales.

Sexy	____	____	____	____	____	Reserved
Innocent	____	____	____	____	____	Flirty
Venturesome	____	____	____	____	____	Shy
Free-spirited	____	____	____	____	____	Practical
Fun loving	____	____	____	____	____	Serious
Fashionably stylish	____	____	____	____	____	Classically stylish

Form 1 Questionnaire

Please rate your perception of the car you presently own on the following scales.

Name of the car you presently own: _____

Sexy	____	____	____	____	____	Reserved
Innocent	____	____	____	____	____	Flirty
Venturesome	____	____	____	____	____	Shy
Free-spirited	____	____	____	____	____	Practical
Fun loving	____	____	____	____	____	Serious
Fashionably stylish	____	____	____	____	____	Classically stylish

Form 2 Questionnaire

Please rate your perception of the car you would one day like to own on the following scales.

Name of the car you would one day like to own: _____

Sexy	____	____	____	____	____	Reserved
Innocent	____	____	____	____	____	Flirty
Venturesome	____	____	____	____	____	Shy
Free-spirited	____	____	____	____	____	Practical
Fun loving	____	____	____	____	____	Serious
Fashionably stylish	____	____	____	____	____	Classically stylish

Form 3 Questionnaire

Please rate your perception of the car you would not like to own on the following scales.

Name of the car you would not like to own: _____

Sexy	____	____	____	____	____	Reserved
Innocent	____	____	____	____	____	Flirty
Venturesome	____	____	____	____	____	Shy
Free-spirited	____	____	____	____	____	Practical
Fun loving	____	____	____	____	____	Serious
Fashionably stylish	____	____	____	____	____	Classically stylish

Exercise 23

Marketing According to Freud

OBJECTIVE: To demonstrate the influence of Freud's personality theory in marketing.

Freudian personality theory has had a tremendous impact on marketing and consumer behavior. The products selected for this exercise demonstrate this influence. Marketing applies the following elements from Freudian personality theory: (1) primary process thinking (fantasy), (2) appeals to the id (hedonism), (3) appeals to the ego (rationality), (4) appeals to the superego (forgiveness, should's and should not's), (5) eros (sex), and (6) thanatos (death, aggression). Determine the elements from Freudian personality theory that are being applied in the following advertisements.

Reprinted with permission of DANA Perfumes Corporation.

Reprinted with permission of Negril Beach Village, Jamaica Resort Hotels, Inc.

216

Reprinted with permission of Jovan, Inc.

Reprinted with permission of Rust-Oleum Corporation.

Reprinted with permission of Max Factor & Company.

Reprinted with permission from the Children's Christian Fund, Inc.

Indulge yourself. You deserve it.

Glocamora. For your country side, wherever you live. Hats, scarves, and gloves with the look of the Irish in every stitch. Glocamora isn't just another knit. It's a totally coordinated mood, mode and motif. Misty tweeds colorfully topped by a primitive Gaelic pattern that'll get your Irish up. And the rest of you, too. How are things in Glocamora? Looking lovely.

Hansen® Knits, A Division of Zwicker Knitting Mills.
Appleton, Wisconsin 54913 **Hansen**

Indulge yourself at these fine stores. **Alabama:** Gaylers, Ira Watsons • **Arizona:** Diamond's, Phoenix • **California:** Capwells, Oakland, Emporium, San Francisco, Macy's, San Francisco, May Co., Los Angeles, Weinstocks, Sacramento • **Colorado:** May D & F, Denver • **Florida:** Gaylers • **Georgia:** Rich's (Jr. Dept.), Atlanta • **Idaho:** Blocks • **Illinois:** Joseph Spiess, Elgin, Marshall Fields, Chicago & Suburbs, Weises, Rockford • **Kentucky:** Ira Watsons • **Michigan:** J.L. Hudson • **Minnesota:** Daytons, Minneapolis • **Missouri:** Famous Barr, St. Louis • **Montana:** Hart Albin, Billings & Missoula • **Nevada:** Macy's, Reno, Weinstocks, Reno • **New Jersey:** Bambergers, All Stores, Hahne & Co., Newark • **New York:** Abraham & Straus, All Stores, Gertz, Jamaica & L.I., Gimbels, All Stores • **Ohio:** J.L. Hudson • **Tennessee:** Castner Knott, All Stores, Ira Watsons • **Utah:** Blocks, ZCMI • **Virginia:** Ira Watsons • **Washington:** Elvins, Puyallup • **West Virginia:** Ira Watsons • **Wisconsin:** Pranges, All Stores, Zahn's, Racine.

Reprinted with permission of Hansen Knits.

219

13

Attitude and Attitude Change

The concept of attitude occupies a central position in marketing. Products are developed and positioned based upon the results of attitude research. Marketers spend millions of dollars to develop, change, and reinforce attitudes toward their products and services. It is vital to marketers to understand the predictive ability of attitudes, their process of formation, and change. The articles in this section discuss this important concept.

In the article "Cognitive Dissonance and Consumer Behavior: A Review of the Evidence," William H. Cummings and M. Venkatesan critique the research investigating the application of cognitive dissonance theory to consumer behavior. They conclude that, overall, research supports the applicability of cognitive dissonance theory to explain consumer attitude change and repurchase behavior, but that the generalizability of cognitive dissonance theory to explain postpurchase information-seeking behavior has not been substantiated. They offer directions for further research in this area.

H. Keith Hunt discusses the FTC's use of attitude research in its regulatory activities in the article, "FTC Now Conducts Attitude Research before Entering Costly Legal Battles." Hunt reports that the FTC's emphasis on restorative actions is based upon attitude research rather than punitive actions based upon litigation.

COGNITIVE DISSONANCE AND CONSUMER BEHAVIOR: A REVIEW OF THE EVIDENCE

INTRODUCTION

In the last 10 years substantial research has been applied to a number of topics in consumer behavior. Most of the studies have involved concepts and propositions formulated on the basis of social psychological theories. One such theory which has been found to have applications to consumer behavior is the theory of cognitive dissonance [7, 20].

Several articles have provided critical reviews of the theory and have described how the theory relates to consumer behavior [8, 19, 25, 45]. Many of these earlier summaries of the theory gave much

promise for an increased understanding and applications for consumer behavior. There are now 23 studies which have examined empirically the arousal and reduction of cognitive dissonance in the context of consumer behavior.[1] Therefore, it would be valuable to examine critically all of the empirical studies that have investigated the applicability of cognitive dissonance theory to the consumer behavior context.[2] For clarity, the findings of studies critiqued in this review are organized in two

"Cognitive Dissonance and Consumer Behavior: A Review of the Evidence," William H. Cummings and M. Venkatesan, *Journal of Marketing Research*, Vol. XIII, August 1976, 303–308, printed by the American Marketing Association. Reprinted by permission.

[1]Three studies [4, 32, 35] are not included in this review as they do not fit in any one of the three categories because of their dependent measures. More important, the studies by Bell [4] and Reizenstein [35] are peripheral to dissonance: Oshikawa's study [32] is an attempt at experimental refutation of a basic prediction from dissonance theory and the context in which it was tested does not relate to consumer behavior.

[2]Oshikawa critiqued some studies, primarily on the grounds of "ceiling effect" [30, 31, 33].

categories: (1) effects of dissonance arousal on attitude change and tendency to repurchase, and (2) effects of dissonance arousal on selective information seeking by consumers.

By far the greatest amount of dissonance-related research in consumer behavior has used attitude change as the dependent measure. Brehm's study [5] was the first to observe the predicted effect of magnitude of dissonance (relative desirability of the alternatives) on reranking of the chosen and unchosen alternatives. Several studies [1, 9, 12, 23, 27, 28, 37, 38] have replicated and extended Brehm's initial findings with different products and settings. Only a single study [11] reported no effects of magnitude of dissonance on measures of brand preference, intention to purchase, or brand loyalty. Also the two studies [16, 25] that investigated "real life consumer situations" generally obtained findings consistent with the theory. A somewhat different approach was taken in three studies [15, 24, 43] which used postpurchase reinforcement techniques to reduce purchasers' dissonance after the purchase of major products. In general, the studies which have examined the effects of dissonance arousal on attitude change and tendency to repurchase have supported the predictions from the theory (although there are some obvious exceptions).

After reviewing all the available evidence within social psychology, Freedman and Sears [21] and Sears [36] concluded that the empirical findings have not supported either a general preference for supportive over nonsupportive information or a greater information seeking/avoidance tendency by high dissonance subjects. Similarly, studies [17, 18, 27] of the effects of dissonance arousal on selective information seeking by the consumer have not strongly supported the predictions from the theory. Thus, the evidence from the consumer behavior literature on this question is (like the evidence from social psychology) most equivocal. It cannot be concluded at this time that dissonance arousal factors are relevant to postpurchase information-seeking variables in the marketing situation.

CRITIQUE

Any conclusions to be drawn from the studies reviewed must be made in light of the methodological and conceptual limitations of these studies. Such an examination should be of use both to the researcher and to the practitioner. Chapanis and Chapanis [10] critiqued the earlier research on cognitive dissonance. They criticized the studies by Brehm [5] and by Ehrlich et al. [17] for rejection of large numbers of subjects (both studies) and failure to include a proper control condition [Ehrlich et al.). For the most part, however, the studies which investigated the application of dissonance theory to consumer behavior have presented a different set of problems, not previously cataloged.

Measurement of Magnitude of Dissonance

Some researchers have attempted to assess magnitude of dissonance by questioning the subject about his (her) level of conflict or worry about the "rightness" of his (her) decision [4, 11, 24]. It is not clear that these measures were tapping magnitude of dissonance. In fact, as Oshikawa

[34] and Hawkins [22] demonstrated, these measures probably were tapping a good deal other than dissonance arousal. These investigators demonstrated that such measures are correlated with measures of general confidence and anxiety. Thus, unless a theoretically relevant and unambiguous measure of magnitude of dissonance aroused is used, the results are of questionable relevance to dissonance theory.

Regression Artifacts

Four studies [1, 5, 27, 38] employed the free choice paradigm in which the high-dissonance situation consisted of a choice between two products of similar desirability, and the low-dissonance situation consisted of a choice between two products of disparate desirability. By chance alone, after a period of time has elapsed, there should be greater spread in the desirability of the "high-dissonance" products than of the "low-dissonance" products. This is precisely the effect predicted by the theory. Thus, any study employing this paradigm must include the appropriate correction for regression (as in [5]) or a no-choice control condition (as in [27]). Without such a correction, it is impossible to assess that portion of the overall effect which is due to statistical regression and that portion which is due to dissonance reduction.

Oshikawa's criticisms [30, 31, 33] of the studies using this paradigm appear to be somewhat overstated. As noted, [5] and [27] included appropriate corrections for ceiling effects or regression artifacts. Similarly, there are certain aspects of Sheth's [38] data which cannot be explained by recourse to a regression artifact argument

(see [39]). In general, it seems that the studies which have employed this paradigm have supported the predictions from the theory, despite the possibility of regression artifacts.

Failure to Meet Prerequisite Conditions for Producing Dissonance

Accumulated evidence has demonstrated that certain prerequisite conditions are necessary in order for dissonance effects to occur. Brehm and Cohen [7] emphasized that *volition* and *irrevocable commitment to the decision* (product choice) are necessary. It is not clear, for example, in some studies [3, 9] whether subjects were given any choice as to whether or not to perform the task which was instrumental to obtaining the product. Certainly this choice was not made salient to the subjects. Aronson [3] emphasized that the dissonance-producing decision must be an *important choice;* it must to some degree bear on the individual's self-concept. Again the situation provided in the studies is questionable: even if a decision were made by the subject, would a decision concerning a rather inexpensive item be an important one? Maybe, but maybe not. A clear test of the theory is not provided. Similarly, the obviously role-playing situations in some studies [23, 28] necessarily reduce the importance of the decision for the subjects. Subjects in these role-playing situations are probably making decisions of minimal importance to themselves. To the extent that the experimental situation fails to meet the prerequisite conditions of volition, irrevocability of the commitment, and importance of the decision, it is doubted that dissonance was aroused. Although the studies may obtain effects in line with the theory, these effects may be due to causes other than dissonance arousal.

Failure to Shield Against Alternative Modes of Dissonance Reduction

Several modes of dissonance reduction are open to the individual who has made a decision, and it is difficult to predict which mode the individual will use. It is likely that more than one or perhaps all modes are used at different times. Unless the investigator allows only one mode of reduction to vary while holding all other modes constant, it is likely that many different modes will be used by different subjects. This variation will necessarily weaken the dissonance-produced effect.

The failure to shield against alternative modes of dissonance reduction has been particularly salient in investigations of dissonance theory in the consumer behavior area [17, 18]. For example, Straits [42] criticized Engel's [18] study on a number of points which indicate a failure to shield against alternative modes. Ehrlich et al. [17] likewise permitted subjects ample opportunity to reduce dissonance by various means prior to the study.

The failure to shield against alternative modes sometimes appears in more subtle forms. For example, LoSciuto and Perloff [27] followed a product-reference reranking task with a recognition task. Significant effects of magnitude of dissonance were obtained with the reranking task but not with the recognition task. These results are in line with the theory: once dissonance has been reduced by means of product re-evaluation, there should be little or no subsequent effect of magnitude of dissonance on information-seeking behaviors.

Accepting Null Differences as Support of the Theory

Chapanis and Chapanis [10] applied this criticism ("straining for significance") to the earlier tests of dissonance theory. This criticism applies as well to some of the studies in the consumer behavior area. Experimental differences which appear to support predictions from dissonance theory, which appear to qualify the theory, or which appear to specify the conditions under which dissonance theory should or should not be applied, must be interpreted as *no* difference between experimental conditions unless a predetermined level of statistical significance is reached.

Questionable Relevance to Dissonance Theory

A number of studies which have cited dissonance theory as a source of hypotheses do not, in fact, appear to be relevant to dissonance theory. For example, three studies examined the effect of prior expectations on subsequent evaluations of the product [2, 9, 29]. Though this is certainly an important question, it is not, as these investigators claimed, a question relevant to dissonance theory. There is no decision, no initial commitment, and no postdecisional phase involved in any of these studies. Likewise, some studies [e.g. 41] have manipulated varibles that are not clearly relevant to the theory. The effects of such manipulations cannot be taken either to support or not to support the theory.

Correlational Evidence Taken as Causal

Correlational evidence is certainly valuable in demonstrating potential relationships and suggesting new and fruitful lines of research. However, such evidence is not nearly conclusive. Correlation studies which have been cited in support of dissonance theory may be considered to be *consistent with* the theory but not actually *supportive of* the theory. However, these studies made stronger conclusions than are warranted. One study [11] presented correlational evidence of a different sort. The investigators divided the subjects into a high-dissonance group and a low-dissonance group on the basis of the subjects' postdecisional ratings of predecisional conflict. The investigators observed no significant effects of "dissonance" on a number of measures. These findings were interpreted as a disconfirmation of dissonance theory. What the results *do* demonstrate is that there is little if any correlation between this initial measure of conflict and the subsequent measures. Because there was no manipulation of magnitude of dissonance, these findings cannot really be taken as a disconfirmation of the theory.

Compelling Alternative Explanations

The presence of compelling alternative explanations is certainly not a flaw in any study. However, such alternative explanations make it difficult to use a set of findings as compelling proof of the theory. Doob et al. [16] demonstrated that introducing a product at a special low price decreases later sales, as predicted by the theory. However, this effect may be due either to buyers' "stockpiling" goods at the time of the sale or to "frustration" on the part of the buyers who are suddenly faced with a more expensive item. Reinforcement notions provide a simple and compelling alternative explanation to the findings reported by Van Dyke [43] and Donnelly and Ivancevich [15]. Both studies employed postpurchase contact as a means of improving buyers' attitudes toward the product [43] or decreasing backout rates [15]. One simply can view the contacts as postpurchase social reinforcements, rather than attempts to assist the purchaser in reducing dissonance, which should have similar effects on postpurchase satisfaction.

OVERALL EVALUATION

Because of the methodological and conceptual limitations of the studies, it is difficult to make a definite statement of the applicability of dissonance theory to consumer behavior. Certainly none of the findings in this literature have presented a major challenge to the validity of the theory, because of the methodological problems involved. However, no single study has provided evidence which conclusively supports the application of dissonance theory to consumer behavior. In brief, the evidence is far from definite. But it should be noted that the evidence in favor of the applicability of dissonance theory is more voluminous and somewhat more substantial than the evidence against. This conclusion should, in turn, be properly qualified: as noted, it appears questionable that magnitude of dissonance has any effect on the consumer's information-seeking behavior. The evidence with respect to attitude change and tendency to repurchase is, however, more substantial. Studies have demonstrated the predicted effects with a wide range of products, a number of dependent measures, a range of settings, and a number of operationalizations of the conceptual variable, "cognitive dissonance." *There is no other single explanation—other than cognitive dissonance theory—that can account fully for the results of these studies.* Though several important and intriguing problems and alternative explanations have been presented, none can account adequately for all the findings in this area. The empirical realization of "cognitive dissonance" and the generalizability of this phenomenon to consumer behavior—excluding information-seeking behavior—has been substantiated.

DIRECTIONS FOR RESEARCH AND APPLICATION

Application of Dissonance Theory in Consumer Behavior

Because of the limitations in the existing research, it is difficult to draw conclusions with respect to the proper application of the theory to marketing situations. However, it was noted heretofore that predictions from the theory can be applied most accurately when there is high perceived volition concerning the choice or purchase, when there is an irrevocable commitment to the choice or purchase, and when the choice or purchase is an important (ego-involving) one for the buyer. Similarly, it was noted that the manipulation of magnitude of dissonance can be expected to influence postpurchase attitude or behavior change, but not postpurchase information seeking. Finally, a clear prediction can be made from the theory only when one mode of dissonance reduction is allowed to vary while all other modes are held constant. It is not possible to offer further guidelines for the application of the theory in the marketing situation at this time. The

studies to date have not examined the conditions under which dissonance theory will and will not work. Certainly more research is needed on this point. Until more evidence is available, careful pilot testing must be undertaken for each new situation.

One reason that so little is known about the conditions under which the theory is or is not applicable in the marketing situation is that most of the research has been done in the laboratory rather than in the field. Of the 23 studies reviewed here, only five [15, 16, 24, 38, 43] have examined the effects of magnitude of dissonance, as a manipulated variable, on subsequent attitude or behavior change in the field. The problems associated with field research are compounded in dissonance research, in which the investigator must have careful control over both the antecedent conditions and the various alternative modes of dissonance reduction. However, certain studies [15, 16, 43] apparently have overcome this obstacle successfully.

Experimental research in this area has concentrated primarily on the *free choice paradigm.* However, there are other paradigms which seem to be relevant to consumer behavior. Because the objective of this review is to examine critically the empirical findings from the cognitive dissonance concepts in consumer behavior, this review is not the place to point out in detail how these paradigms might apply to consumer behavior or to provide compelling arguments as to why consumer behavior researchers should explore these paradigms. However, because recent investigations in social psychology have been focused on two paradigms, *the forced compliance paradigm and the fait accompli paradigm,* a brief discussion of them is provided to encourage consumer behavior researchers to use these two dissonance-related approaches.

FORCED COMPLIANCE PARADIGM

Can the forced compliance paradigm—in which the subject is persuaded to behave in a manner that is inconsistent with his prior beliefs—be used in the marketing situation? Oshikawa [32] has replied with a definite "No!" However, it appears that there are some situations in which the forced compliance paradigm can be applied. Oshikawa argued that "the applicability of the theory to consumer behavior is considerably limited," because "in the natural market setting, consumers do not comply with such requests as buying the second-best brand when the best brand is available" [40, p. 134]. However, Darley and Cooper [14] negated this criticism by demonstrating that the forced-choice type of prediction can be made from dissonance theory even when individuals are induced *not* to engage in discrepant behaviors. Moreover, Varela [44] suggested some imaginative applications of the forced compliance paradigm. Likewise, Doob et al. [16] made use of the "crucial theoretical statement" of the forced compliance situation: *"the less the pressure . . . put upon the person to perform the act, the greater the dissonance* [italics added] . . . the greatest attitude change will occur theoretically when the pressure is the minimal amount necessary to induce the subject to perform the act" [26, p. 206]. This principle should be of great applicability in the consumer context.

FAIT ACCOMPLI PARADIGM

Brehm [6] introduced the *fait accompli* paradigm with a demonstration that a negative event following a "bad decision" would increase the dissonance produced by that decision. The *fait accompli* paradigm certainly appears to be applicable to the marketing situation. Investigations with this paradigm should suggest the situations and techniques by which buyer dissatisfaction can be minimized. Recent investigations in social psychology [13, 40] have attempted to specify the conditions under which the *fait accompli* effect will occur.

CONCLUSIONS

Chapanis and Chapanis [10] reviewed the evidence regarding dissonance theory in 1964 and concluded that dissonance theory was "NOT PROVEN." Reviewing the evidence to date on the application of dissonance theory to consumer behavior, the writers also must conclude that such applicability is "not proven." (But then, is any theory in the behavioral sciences ever really proved?) We must conclude, however, that the evidence in favor of dissonance theory in the consumer behavior literature looks good. To be sure, although the supportive evidence is restricted by certain methodological and conceptual limitations, dissonance theory provides the best single explanation which can account for all the results across these studies. Moreover, there are no conclusive negative findings in the areas of postpurchase attitude change and tendency to repurchase. The evidence has not supported the applicability of dissonance theory to selective exposure and similar behaviors.

At this point, research would be directed best toward specifying the marketing conditions under which dissonance theory would be most applicable. Furthermore, the applicability of two dissonance paradigms which have not been studied in consumer behavior should be investigated further. Dissonance theory already has provided new ideas and spawned much new research in consumer behavior. Additional insights into postpurchase behavior are promised by dissonance theory and related approaches.

References

1. Anderson, L. K., J. R. Taylor, and R. J. Holloway. "The Consumer and His Alternatives: An Experimental Approach," *Journal of Marketing Research*, 3 (February 1966), 62–7.

2. Anderson, R. E. "Consumer Dissatisfaction: The Effect of Disconfirmed Expectancy on Perceived Product Performance," *Journal of Marketing Research*, 10 (February 1973), 38–44.

3. Aronson, E. "Dissonance Theory: Progress and Problems," in R. P. Abelson, E. Aronson, W. J. McGuire, T. M. Newcomb, M. J. Rosenberg, and P. H. Tannenbaum, eds., *Theories of Cognitive Consistency: A Sourcebook*. Chicago: Rand McNally, 1968.

4. Bell, G. D. "The Automobile Buyer After the Purchase," *Journal of Marketing*, 31 (July 1967), 12–6.

5. Brehm, J. W. "Post-Decision Changes in the Desirability of Alternatives," *Journal of Abnormal and Social Psychology*, 52 (May 1956), 384–9.

6. _____. "Increasing Cognitive Dissonance by a Fait Accompli," *Journal of Abnormal and Social Psychology*, 58 (May 1959), 379–82.

7. _____ and A. R. Cohen. *Explorations in Cognitive Dissonance*. New York: John Wiley and Sons, Inc., 1962.

8. Calder, B. J. "Cognitive Consistency and Consumer Behavior," in H. H. Kassarjian and T. S. Robertson, *Perspectives in Consumer Behavior*. Glenview, Illinois: Scott, Foresman and Co., 1973.

9. Cardozo, R. N. "An Experimental Study of Customer Effort, Expectation, and Satisfaction," *Journal of Marketing Research*, 2 (August 1965), 244–9.

10. Chapanis, N., and A. Chapanis. "Cognitive Dissonance Five Years Later," *Psychological Bulletin*, 61 (January 1964), 1–22.

11. Cohen, J. B., and M. E. Goldberg. "The Dissonance Model in Post-Decision Product Evaluation," *Journal of Marketing Research*, 7 (August 1970), 315–21.

12. _____ and M. J. Houston. "Cognitive Consequences of Brand Loyalty," *Journal of Marketing Research*, 9 (February 1972), 97–9.

13. Cooper, J. "Personal Responsibility and Dissonance: The Role of Foreseen Consequences," *Journal of Personality and Social Psychology*, 18 (June 1971), 354–63.

14. Darley, S. A., and J. Cooper. "Cognitive Consequences of Forced Noncompliance," *Journal of Personality and Social Psychology*, 24 (December 1972), 321–6.

15. Donnelly, J. H., and J. M. Ivancevich. "Post-Purchase Reinforcement and Back-Out Behavior," *Journal of Marketing Research*, 7 (August 1970), 399–400.

16. Doob, A. N., J. M. Carlsmith, J. Freedman, T. K. Landauer, and S. Tom. "Effect of Initial Selling Price on Subsequent Sales," *Journal of Personality and Social Psychology*, 11 (April 1969), 354–50.

17. Ehrlich, D., I. Guttman, P. Schonbach, and J. Mills. "Post-decision Exposure to Relevant Information," *Journal of Abnormal and Social Psychology*, 54 (January 1957), 98–102.

18. Engel, J. F. "Are Automobile Purchasers Dissonant Consumers?" *Journal of Marketing*, 27 (April 1963), 55–8.

19. _____ and M. L. Light. "The Role of Psychological Commitment in Consumer Behavior: An Evaluation of the Theory of Cognitive Dissonance," in F. M. Bass, C. W. King, and E. A. Pessemier, *Applications of the Sciences in Marketing Management*. New York: John Wiley and Sons, Inc., 1968.

20. Festinger, L. *A Theory of Cognitive Dissonance*. Stanford: Stanford University Press, 1957.

21. Freedman, J. L., and D. O. Sears. "Selective Exposure," in L. Berkowitz, *Advances in Experimental Social Psychology*, Vol. 2. New York: Academic Press, 1965.

22. Hawkins, D. I. "Reported Cognitive Dissonance and Anxiety: Some Additional Findings." *Journal of Marketing*, 36 (July 1972), 63–6.

23. Holloway, R. J. "An Experiment on Consumer Dissonance," *Journal of Marketing*, 31 (January 1967), 39–43.

24. Hunt, S. D. "Post-Transaction Communications and Dissonance Reduction," *Journal of Marketing*, 34 (July 1970), 46–51.

25. Kassarjian, H. H., and J. B. Cohen. "Cognitive Dissonance and Consumer Behavior," *California Management Review*, 8 (Fall 1965), 55–64.

26. Kiesler, C. A., B. E. Collins, and N. Miller. *Attitude Change: A Critical Analysis of Theoretical Approaches*. New York: John Wiley and Sons, Inc., 1969.

27. LoSciuto, L., and R. Perloff. "Influence of Product Preference on Dissonance Reduction," *Journal of Marketing Research*, 4 (August 1967), 286–90.

28. Mittelstaedt, R. "A Dissonance Approach to Repeat Purchasing Behavior," *Journal of Marketing Research*, 6 (November 1969), 444–6.

29. Olshavsky, R. W., and J. A. Miller. "Consumer Expectations, Product Performance, and Perceived Product Quality," *Journal of Marketing Research*, 9 (February 1972), 19–21.

30. Oshikawa, S. "The Theory of Cognitive

Dissonance and Experimental Research," *Journal of Marketing Research,* 5 (November 1968), 429–30.

31. _____. "Can Cognitive Dissonance Theory Explain Consumer Behavior?" *Journal of Marketing,* 33 (October 1969), 44–9.

32. _____. "Consumer Pre-Decision Conflict and Post-Decision Dissonance," *Behavioral Science,* 15 (March 1970), 132–40.

33. _____. "Dissonance Reduction or Artifact?" *Journal of Marketing Research,* 8 (November 1971), 514–5.

34. _____. "The Measurement of Cognitive Dissonance: Some Experimental Findings," *Journal of Marketing,* 36 (January 1972), 64–7.

35. Reizenstein, R. C. "A Dissonance Approach to Measuring the Effectiveness of Two Personal Selling Techniques Through Decision Reversal," *Combined Proceedings,* American Marketing Association, Spring and Fall Conferences, 1971, 176–80.

36. Sears, D. O. The Paradox of De Facto Selective Exposure Without Preference for Supportive Information, in R. P. Abelson, E. Aronson, W. J. McGuire, T. M. Newcomb, M. J. Rosenberg, and P. H. Tannenbaum, eds., *Theories of Cognitive Consistency: A Sourcebook.* Chicago: Rand-McNally, 1968.

37. Sheth, J. N. "Cognitive Dissonance, Brand Preference, and Product Familiarity," in J. Arndt, *Insights into Consumer Behavior.* Boston: Allyn and Bacon, 1968.

38. _____. "Are There Differences in Dissonance Reduction Behavior Between Students and Housewives?" *Journal of Marketing Research,* 7 (May 1970), 243–5.

39. _____. "Dissonance Reduction or Artifact? A Reply," *Journal of Marketing Research,* 8 (November 1971), 516–7.

40. Sogin, S. R. "Bad Decisions, Responsibility, and Attitude Change," unpublished master's thesis, University of Iowa, 1973.

41. Stoerzinger, C. A. "The Selectivity of Information After a Consumer Decision," unpublished master's thesis, University of Minnesota, 1965.

42. Straits, B. C. "The Pursuit of the Dissonant Consumer," *Journal of Marketing,* 28 (July 1964), 62–6.

43. Van Dyke, J. E. "A Study of the Arousal and Reduction of Post-Decision Dissonance Following the Purchase of a New Automobile," unpublished master's thesis, University of Iowa, 1966.

44. Varela, J. A. *Psychological Solutions to Social Problems: An Introduction to Social Technology.* New York: Academic Press, 1971.

45. Venkatesan, M. "Cognitive Dissonance," in R. Ferber, *Handbook of Marketing Research,* New York: McGraw-Hill Book Co., 1975.

FTC NOW CONDUCTS ATTITUDE RESEARCH BEFORE ENTERING COSTLY LEGAL BATTLES

In its attempt to monitor unethical advertising and business practices while overcoming its "Big Brother" image, the Federal Trade Commission (FTC) is emphasizing restorative actions based on attitude research rather than punitive actions based on litigation.

"The use of consumer research at the FTC has changed," said H. Keith Hunt, professor of business management, Brigham Young University, Provo, Utah. "I can still remember that when I joined the FTC staff in 1973 it was choking over spending $30,000 for a major piece of consumer research on a critical case. The pre-

"FTC Now Conducts Attitude Research before Entering Costly Legal Battles," *Marketing News,* May 16, 1980. Reprinted from *Marketing News,* published by the American Marketing Association.

vious high was a few hundred dollars on the ill-fated Wonder Bread study.

"Now, in 1980, the FTC will spend more than $1 million on research. Research is being done to find out whether damages in the market are real and substantial before cases are brought. Research on the probable effects of possible remedies is being done before the remedies are prescribed."

Most FTC actions, Hunt said, are based on the cognitive component of the attitude structure, not the affect or action tendency components. The commission's corrective advertising actions are an example of this emphasis on cognition, he said.

"If advertising needs correcting, what we need to correct are the beliefs, essentially the cognitions which are incorrect," Hunt said. "The advertiser's infraction was in creating a false belief and the remedy should be the correction of that false belief."

As an example of a cognition-based FTC action, Hunt mentioned the Listerine mouthwash ads which feature corrective messages. The FTC's affirmative disclosure program is also totally cognition-oriented, Hunt said.

"The Hawaiian Punch-type remedy requires the inclusion of key information (percentage of fruit juice listed on label) until marketer-caused incorrect cognitions have been corrected," he said. Cognition-oriented actions have also been taken by the FTC in the fields of funeral service, used car, and life insurance marketing, he said.

FTC officials are more concerned with cognitions than actions because there is a "cultural value common in the U.S. that individuals should be free to choose for themselves what they will do," Hunt said.

"We abhor Big Brother telling us what to do or exerting undue influence on us to behave in some certain way. We feel individuals should be free to choose except when that choice infringes on someone else's freedom to choose.

"And we somehow have the opinion that we intrude less on individual freedom of choice when we influence cognition than when we influence affect or action tendency.

"Another specific value of those who influence FTC decisions is that FTC activity should be restorative but not punitive. An underlying assumption seems to be that by emphasizing cognition rather than affect or action tendency, the FTC is less likely to be punitive in its programs."

The issue of corrective advertising centers on cognitions or beliefs, not on affect or action tendency, Hunt said. "Deceptive or false advertising has created an incorrect set of cognitions. The problem is how to correct them," he said.

"Just stopping the deceptive or false communications won't necessarily lead to a purging of the deceptive or false cognitions from the cognitive system. Rather, they may be firmly implanted and only information in direct conflict has any possibility of dislodging them."

There are exceptions, Hunt said. The recent corrective ads for STP additive were subject to pre- and post-tests. After the ads appeared the survey noted a statistically significant impact on the public's purchase intentions.

"While it wasn't clear whether the decline in purchase intentions was due to the publicity or the ads, both resulting from the FTC actions, purchase intention was negatively affected," Hunt said.

The public's purchase intentions in regards to Fresh Horizons bread were also negatively affected after the FTC disclosed that the ads touting fiber content failed to mention that the fiber in the bread was wood pulp.

"But it is evident that up to now the FTC has focused its interest on the cognitive component of attitude," Hunt said. "We will see more attention to affect and to action tendencies. Some studies have already shown that cognitive corrections cause negative shifts in affect for the total firm.

"While these have been viewed as side effects up to now, that view will certainly change as more evidence is compiled showing the influence of cognitive corrections on both affect and behavioral intention (toward the brand and the company)."

Copy testing, Hunt said, is one area of attitude research which has grown in acceptance not only among advertising professionals but also within the FTC itself. This has given FTC personnel a greater understanding and appreciation of how ad copy can affect cognitions.

"It used to be that a couple of (FTC) attorneys would sit around looking at ads, usually print ads, and find some that looked like they might be deceptive, and they would decide to take action against those ads," Hunt recalled.

In the Fresh Horizons bread case, he said, the FTC conducted several different ad copy tests before conducting a formal investigation.

"And this use of attitude research is increasingly sophisticated," Hunt said. "As researchers from the business and academic research community enter the FTC and other government agencies, the previous naivete within the agencies has disappeared.

"We now find agency personnel asking the 'right' questions for a change— right from the professional research point of view—rather than the legal questions the attorneys have been asking over the years.

The result is that attitude research is now used by people who are well-schooled in the area rather than by attorneys who learned just enough about attitude research to get them through one case."

Hunt listed four other specific applications of attitude research being used at the FTC:

1. Performance Remedies

In its corrective advertising program, the FTC used to specify the content of the message and the time or dollar volume of advertising which had to be placed.

Now, instead of prescribing a specified amount of corrective advertising, the FTC determines the amount of deception and specifies an acceptable level for that measure and leaves it up to the company to reduce the incorrect perception to the specified level.

The first deceptive ad campaign remedied in this way was Hawaiian Fruit Punch. In a similar case, AMF was required to distribute public service announcements on bicycle safety to a specified number of broadcast stations. The goal is message exposure. Incorrect cognitions caused by AMF's deceptive ads will have to be corrected to a specified level.

2. Problem Documentation

There is increasing use of attitude research to document and examine problems proposed for FTC action *before* the FTC jumps in to launch an investigation or propose a remedy.

The FTC is currently studying housing defects to determine the extent of the problem and what kinds of remedies might clear up the situation.

3. Prospective Studies

Often called "strategy evaluations," these studies attempt to assess the likely outcomes if different remedies are used. Usually there are several alternative remedies which can accomplish the public policy objectives.

These studies are frequently conducted to determine the best remedy for certain products or practices which are a risk to some, but not all, consumers. For instance, a warning or corrective message could lead to misperceptions in people not deceived by the original problem ad.

4. Joint Research

Most FTC attitude research is done in an advocacy setting, with each side trying to find secondary research or do primary research which will support its view.

However, several years ago a case involving Yamaha offered an alternative method. The FTC took objection to a Yamaha ad which stated that with proper instruction a motorcycle could be just as safe as a car.

The key issue was how consumers perceived that statement in the ad. So the FTC and Yamaha jointly commissioned a research study to find out how consumers perceived the message. A nonbinding pilot of the study was tested, and the results were so powerful that the case was settled with a consent decree.

Both sides saved tremendous litigation costs through the simple step of asking the empirical question at the heart of the matter. And it was done jointly, with both parties agreeing on the study design. The research was conducted by a third party.

Exercise 24

Multiattribute Model of Attitude

OBJECTIVES: 1. To introduce you to the use of a multiattribute model of attitude by applying it to your own consumer behavior.
2. To have you determine the applicability of a multiattribute model to marketing strategy formation.

Attitude is an intangible abstract construct that has played an important and significant role in the study of human behavior. Recently, the multiattribute model of attitude has become popular in the study of consumer behavior.

Select one of the following products and determine your own attitude. First, obtain ratings for the product's attributes. Second, use the multiattribute model to determine your attitude toward the various brands of the product. Third, determine whether the multiattribute model predicts your preferred brand and/or the brand you most recently purchased. Fourth, discuss the implications of the results to marketers.

$$\text{Multiattribute model:} \quad A_o = \sum_{i-1}^{n} w_i B_i$$

where A_o = consumer's attitude toward the object

w_i = consumer's assessment of the importance of the ith attribute of the object

B_i = consumer's evaluation of the object in terms of the ith attribute or his belief in the extent to which the object possesses the ith attribute

n = number of attributes the consumer considers to be important regarding this object

TENNIS SHOES

1. Use the following scale to rate the importance of the following characteristics to you in your decision to buy tennis shoes.
   5 = very important; 4 = important; 3 = neutral; 2 = unimportant; 1 = very unimportant
   Price _____
   Status _____
   Durability _____
   Comfort _____
   Color selection _____
   Style _____

2A. Use the following scale to rate the following brands of tennis shoes' possession of the characteristics.
   5 = very satisfactory; 4 = satisfactory; 3 = neutral; 2 = unsatisfactory; 1 = very unsatisfactory

	Nike	Adidas	Brooks	Pumas	Brand currently purchased
Price	_____	_____	_____	_____	_____
Status	_____	_____	_____	_____	_____
Durability	_____	_____	_____	_____	_____
Comfort	_____	_____	_____	_____	_____
Color selection	_____	_____	_____	_____	_____
Style	_____	_____	_____	_____	_____

2B. Use the multiattribute model of attitude to compute the attitude score for each brand: Nike _____ Adidas _____ Brooks _____ Pumas _____ Current brand _____

3A. Which of the brands of tennis shoes do you prefer? _____
3B. Which of the brands of tennis shoes does the model predict you prefer? _____

4. Discuss the marketing implications of your results.

JEANS

1. Use the following scale to rate the importance of the following characteristics to you in your decision to buy jeans.
   5 = very important; 4 = important; 3 = neutral; 2 = unimportant; 1 = very unimportant

Price _____
Status _____
Durability _____
Comfort _____
Color selection _____
Style _____

2A. Use the following scale to rate the following brands of jeans' possession of the characteristics.
5 = very satisfactory; 4 = satisfactory; 3 = neutral; 2 = unsatisfactory; 1 = very unsatisfactory

	Wrangler	Calvin Klein	Levis	Brittania	Brand currently purchased
Price	_____	_____	_____	_____	_____
Status	_____	_____	_____	_____	_____
Durability	_____	_____	_____	_____	_____
Comfort	_____	_____	_____	_____	_____
Style	_____	_____	_____	_____	_____

2B. Use the multiattribute model of attitude to compute the attitude score for each brand: Wrangler _____ Calvin Klein _____ Levis _____ Brittania _____ Brand currently purchased _____

3A. Which of the brands of jeans do you prefer? _____
3B. Which of the brands of jeans does the model predict you prefer? _____
4. Discuss the marketing implications of your results.

Exercise 25

Dissonance

OBJECTIVE: To apply the concept of dissonance to your own consumer behavior.

Dissonance is sometimes the outcome of the consumer's decision process. Describe a purchase that you made that produced postpurchase dissonance and the method that you used to reduce that dissonance. The following information may be helpful in organizing and describing your experience.

The conditions most likely to produce dissonance are as follows:[1]

1. A minimum level of dissonance tolerance is surpassed.
2. The action is irrevocable.
3. Unchosen alternatives have desirable features.
4. A number of desirable alternatives are available.
5. The individual is committed to his decision because of its psychological significance to him or her.
6. Available alternatives are qualitatively dissimilar; that is, each has some desirable unique features.
7. Perception and thought about unchosen alternatives is undertaken as a result of free will with little or no outside applied pressure.

The resolution of dissonance can be accomplished with the following strategies:[2]

1. Reevaluation of alternatives to increase the perceived attractiveness of the chosen alternative and/or to decrease the desirability of those that were not chosen.
2. Reevaluation of alternatives to perceive that all alternatives were nearly identical.
3. Post-decision information search to confirm the wisdom of the choice.

Exercise 26

It Depends upon Who Said It

OBJECTIVE: To demonstrate the influence of source credibility in marketing communications.

Equally as important, and sometimes more important than what is said (the message), is who said it (the source). This exercise demonstrates the importance of the source of the communication.

Create two sets of four advertisements. For both sets of four advertisements, the message of the ad (what is said) will be identical. Only the source of the advertisement (who said it) will differ. One set of advertisements will consist of original magazine ads. You will create the other set of ads by cutting and pasting together different sources for these same messages. (You can obtain different sources from other magazine ads.)

---

[1]James Engel, Robert Blackwell, and David Kollat, *Consumer Behavior,* Third Edition, Dryden Press, Hinsdale, Illinois, 1978, pages 496–498.
    [2]Ibid.

Administer the original set of advertisements to 15 consumers. Administer the created set of advertisements to 15 different consumers. After you have administered the statements, compare the average rating for each statement for the original advertisements with that of the created advertisements. Discuss the source effect.

QUESTIONNAIRE

Indicate the effectiveness of each of the following advertisements. Use this scale:

From *Very Ineffective*   1 2 3 4 5   to *Very Effective*

Advertisement 1 _____
Advertisement 2 _____
Advertisement 3 _____
Advertisement 4 _____

Exercise 27

The ABC's of Attitude

OBJECTIVE: To familiarize you with the components of attitude and to arrive at an understanding of their uses in persuasive communication.

Attitude is conceptualized as consisting of three components: (1) affective or feeling component, (2) behavioral or action component, and (3) cognitive or belief component. Persuasive communication may attempt to change attitude by emphasizing one or more of these components. Analyze each of the following persuasive communications to determine which component of attitude it appeals to.

Courtesy of American Telephone and Telegraph Company, Long Lines Division.

Reprinted with permission of Lever Brothers
Company.

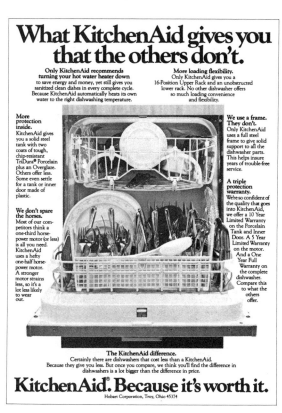

Reprinted with permission of Hobart Corporation.

Reprinted with the permission of Anheuser Busch, Inc. Copyright © 1981.

14

The Decision-Making Process

In the article "The Long Trek to the Perfect Sneaker," Jane Bosveld describes her experiences in attempting to buy a pair of all-purpose tennis shoes. Her description of her experiences takes us through the phases of the consumer decision process: problem identification, the search for solutions to the problem, an evaluation of the alternative solutions available, a choice, and a post-choice evaluation of the solution.

THE LONG TREK TO THE PERFECT SNEAKER

About a year ago, I walked into a shoe store in search of a pair of all-around sneakers. Spread along one huge wall were racks of them—sneakers for running, basketball, tennis, sailing, and squash. There were hundreds of them in every color, shape, and style—bright yellow nylon-topped ones, green and orange ones with elaborate mesh tops, blue leather ones with removable plugs in the soles, and even a boring old pair of white canvas ones. I asked the salesperson for a good all-purpose pair. "They don't make such a thing," he said. I told him I wasn't a professional athlete. I just wanted sneakers I could play a variety of sports in without ruining my feet. He glanced at the

other people waiting for help, huffed over to the display, grabbed a pair of blue-and-white running shoes with waffles the size of boils on the soles, and said, "Try these." I went to another store.

There I was told again that "they" didn't make an all-around shoe. So I sat down and tried on a bunch, settling on a pair of red Nike joggers. (I settled on them mostly because they were red.) Since then, I have played a little basketball in them, some volleyball, countless softball games, a few tennis matches, and walked God knows how many miles. I've done everything but jog in them, which is, of course, what they were made for.

My shoes are just about worn out now, and when I buy a new pair I would like to have something more in mind than just color. So I decided to find out about the anatomy of a sneaker and the way that an average weekend athlete can recognize the right pair for her needs.

The kind of sneakers you should buy depends largely on one question: Are you going to jog in the shoes? If the answer is yes, then you need a pair of running shoes *and* a pair for other sports. That's because the running shoe is designed with an elevated, wedged heel, which makes lateral movement difficult and dangerous. I discovered during several tennis games that when I moved quickly to the side and stopped, I'd roll off the elevated heel and onto my ankle.

"If you wear a running shoe to play a court game," explains Dr. John Waller, chief of the foot service at Lenox Hill Hospital in New York City, "you could get hurt and you will certainly ruin the shoes." The elevated heel, important for joggers as a shock absorber, also keeps the calf muscles from stretching too much during running. Stretched calf muscles cause achilles tendonitis, a problem that particularly plagues women. "The tendon has been shortened from wearing high heels," explains Dr. Joan Ullyot, a sports medicine specialist and author of *Women's Running* (Anderson World) and *Running Free* (Putnam's). "When a women who's used to wearing high heels changes to a flatter shoe," she explains, "her calf muscles may tighten up, often causing her ankle to hurt." Dr. Ullyot calls this problem a "pseudo-running sprain" that will usually clear up as the muscle stretches out during exercise.

For nonjoggers, court shoes, which range from leather-topped Adidas to canvas-covered no-names, may serve best as all-around sneakers. The quality of court shoes varies markedly: no-name courters won't cause physical damage, but brand names tend to be better made. "A ten-dollar court shoe may be put together in the same way as a thirty-dollar one," explains John Fisher, vice-president of sales for Hyde Industries, manufacturer of Saucony shoes, "but the workmanship will differ and generally the quality shoe will have more cushioning and a higher-grade gum rubber used in the sole." Very likely, it will also be lighter, Fisher says: "If you pick a shoe up and think it's heavy, it's too heavy."

The type of material used for the sole generally determines weight. Polyurethane soles are lighter than rubber ones, but polyurethane tends to be slightly hotter and to provide less traction on most surfaces. Five years ago, I purchased tennis shoes that were labeled "the world's lightest shoes"—and probably the ugliest. With polyurethane soles and canvas uppers, they felt as light as cotton. But they had practically no traction properties on grass, clay tennis courts, or anything wet. Dr. E. C. Frederick, director of research for Nike's Sports Research Laboratory, explains that compounds of polyurethane do vary in quality and on some surfaces polyurethanes actually have better traction than rubber. But a number of manufacturers now add a thin layer of rubber as an outsole to compensate for polyurethane's general bad "stick."

If you're really set on something superlight and want polyurethane, make sure the tread design is good. "If all else is equal between two pairs," explains Dr. Frederick, "go with a herringbone zigzag configuration with a circle under the ball of the foot. The circle design allows the foot to rotate easily." If you're looking for a shoe just for walking, it's probably best to stay away from polyurethane since it's murderously slick on wet surfaces.

As for what the upper should be

made of, most experts agree that it's a matter of personal preference. A canvas-topped courter will be lighter and cooler than a leather one, but leather molds itself to the shape of the foot, which is particularly important for those with bunions or other problems.

Flexibility is another important feature. Good flexibility will help keep your foot from tiring. Dr. Peter Cavanagh, associate professor of biomechanics at Pennsylvania State University, suggests a simple method to test a shoe's flexibility: "Put the heel of the shoe in one hand, the toe in the other, and press your hands together. A lot of shoes flex in the middle, which is not where your foot bends. If you divide the shoe into three parts," he explains, "it should flex in the front third."

If you don't play court games and need a shoe for walking, one of the less specialized running shoes may be the best buy. Manufacturers estimate that 40 percent of their running shoes have never been used for running: and, as Dr. Cavanagh says, "There's a reason for that. As a walking shoe, the running shoe is hard to beat."

One reason is the shoe's extensive cushioning. Made to protect the feet from the pounding they take while running, the shoes are constructed with three separate layers of padding: the insole (the socklike liner), the mid-sole (usually made of lightweight forms), and the outsole (usually rubber for durability and traction). Also added to help absorb shock is the elevated heel.

Perhaps the feature to check out most closely in a store is the heel counter, the rigid piece of material at the back that is used to control the rear of the foot while walking or running. The difference between a well-made shoe and a shoddy one

can often be seen by placing the pair on a flat surface and looking at the back. Heel counters should run straight up and down. If they slant to the inside or the outside, they may throw the feet off balance. Obviously, this is particularly important for people who overpronate (have flat feet) or oversupinate (have a high-arched foot, which is generally less flexible and needs more cushioning to absorb the shock). A stiff heel counter will help control the lateral movement of the foot. Dr. Cavanagh thinks that the counter "should be as stiff as possible as long as it's not going to irritate your foot." Unlike most court shoes, many running shoes are made with nylon and nylon-mesh uppers, which tend to be lighter and cooler than leather or suede. But beware of the supercheap versions: a $10 model topped with what looks like nylon may actually be made of vinyl—the microwave oven of uppers.

Of course, if the shoe doesn't fit, it doesn't matter how well made it is, and this is where many women have problems. Although few studies have been done to find out about women's feet and our needs in shoes, it appears that, compared with a man's, woman's heel is proportionately more narrow than the ball of the foot. Some manufacturers make women's styles with a last (the foundation around which the shoe is built) that takes this difference into account. But many simply scale down their men's versions and call them women's. They believe, as Dr. Cavanagh puts it, that "a woman's shoe is rather like a man's shoe, but made in powder blue and blessed with some romantic name. If you know that you can be fitted well for dress or casual shoes, but cannot find a good fit in a particular brand of athletic shoes, you are probably trying on a small man's shoe."

Several modified styles of running shoes are currently being manufactured. These shoes have a slight heel lift, to guard against achilles tendonitis, but not enough to sacrifice good lateral stability. Dr. Frederick believes these "intermediate" models to be good all-arounders for women.

Dr. Cavanagh, in his excellent guide, *The Running Shoe Book* (Anderson World), suggests examining your worn sneakers before buying a new pair; they "hold a lot of secrets about your needs." For instance, if the heel counters turn inward, it indicates excessive pronation and the wearer may want to find stiffer counters, or try a varus wedge. (A varus wedge elevates the inside of the heel more than the outside.) On a pair with leather uppers, if the leather is badly stretched, you should try a wider size. If you've worn a hole above the big toe, look for a shoe with a higher toe box.

As for trying a shoe on, Dr. Waller urges that you kick your heel into the heel counter before lacing up the shoe. Once laced—tightly at the top for support, loosely toward the toe—there should be at least a half inch between the toes and the tip of the shoe, and the sides shouldn't bulge.

The time of day that you try on a shoe makes a difference in fit, too. "The worst thing that you could do," says Dr. Cavanagh, "would be to go in the shoe store in the morning and try the shoe on only while sitting down. Then, your foot will be at its smallest, shortest, and narrowest."

As far as brand names are concerned, Dr. Waller goes with New Balance— "They're good walking shoes, lightweight, with good heel counters, and they come in a variety of widths and lengths." The New Balance shoe doesn't have a high enough toe box for Dr. Ullyot, so she wears Nikes. But she doesn't like to say which brand she prefers because "it may encourage people to go out and buy only that brand without paying enough attention to the fit." Dr. Cavanagh doesn't like to choose, either, since he directs the research team that conducts the lab tests for *Runner's World* magazine surveys.

As for me, now that I know what to look for? I'm going for something lightweight, with rubber soles, stiff heel counters, and plenty of cushioning . . . oh, and *red*.

Exercise 28

Consumer Decision Making

OBJECTIVES: 1. To introduce you to the nature of the consumer decision-making process.
2. To provide a link between the theory and application of the consumer decision-making process.

The consumer decision process for high involvement products is conceptualized as occurring in the following hierarchically ordered sequence: problem recognition, search, alternative evaluation, choice, and outcomes.

In order for the decision process to be meaningful to you personally, apply this process by describing how you arrived at the decision to attend this college. (This is, afterall, a purchase decision in the nonprofit sector.)

1. *Problem recognition:* What happened to initiate the process?
2. *Search.* What sources of information did you use to arrive at a decision? What was the relative influence of each?
3. *Alternative evaluation:* What criteria and other factors did you use to assess alternatives? What factors were most influential in your decision?
4. *Choice:* What selection did you make from the available alternatives?
5. *Outcomes.* Are you satisfied with your choice or do you have doubts that the best decision was made?[1]

Exercise 29

The Role of Evaluative Criteria

OBJECTIVE: To demonstrate the use of evaluative criteria in marketing.

Evaluative criteria are the product characteristic(s) by which consumers judge products and that consumers consider in their purchase decisions. For each of the products depicted in the following advertisements, identify the evaluative criteria that are emphasized.

[1]James Engel, Roger Blackwell, and David Kollat, *Consumer Behavior,* Third Edition, Dryden Press, Hinsdale, Illinois, 1978, p. 27.

Reprinted with permission of Green Giant Company. "Green Giant" and the Giant Figure are registered trademarks of Green Giant Company, Minneapolis, Minnesota. © Green Giant Company.

Courtesy of the Proctor & Gamble Company.

Reprinted with the permission of Bausch & Lomb.

Exercise 30

Decisions, Decisions, Decisions

OBJECTIVE: To illustrate the application of decision rules in your own consumer behavior.

    Consumers use decision rules in their decision making. Decision rules are the procedures by which consumers evaluate and compare alternative brands. Whether or not consumers purchase a brand depends to a considerable extent upon the decision rule they are using.

    Compensatory and noncompensatory decision rules are two types of consumer decision models. When consumers use compensatory decision rules, consumers compensate perceived strengths of an object for the perceived weaknesses of an object. When consumers use noncompensatory decision rules, perceived strengths of an object do not compensate for the perceived weaknesses of an object.

1. Describe a decision that you have made that used a compensatory type of decision rule.
2. Describe a decision that you have made that used a noncompensatory type of decision rule.

15

Consumer Information Search: Mass Media Sources of Consumer Information

For marketers to provide consumers with information, it is first necessary to understand the consumers' information-seeking behavior. Mass media and interpersonal communications serve as complementary sources of information for consumers. The articles selected for this section cover mass media sources and interpersonal sources of information.

In the article "Back from the Twilight Zone," Stephen Farber describes how the consumers' shift from print to television, as a major source of information, has dramatically affected the movie industry. Movies that cannot be easily positioned for television advertising may not be released.

In the article "Time-Compressed TV Commercials," James MacLachlan and Priscilla LaBarbera report on the findings of their experiment that tested the effect of the new technique, time-compressed speech. Time-compressed speech allows advertisers to say more in less time but without any noticeable distortion to the audience. MacLachlan and LaBarbera report that their audience found time-compressed advertisement more interesting than normal-speed advertisement. Moreover, there was no appreciable difference in recall between time-compressed and normal-speed advertisements.

BACK FROM THE TWILIGHT ZONE

Everybody loves an underdog, and that's at least one reason why the press has rallied round *The Stunt Man* and *The Great Santini*—two movies that sat on the shelf for almost a year and then shocked industry pundits by breaking box office and house records when they finally opened. Yet *The Stunt Man* and *The Great Santini* aren't isolated cases; their troubled histories reflect some disturbing trends in film distribution.

Unreleased movies are nothing new, but in the past most of the movies that never hit the theaters were out-and-out catastrophes or bizarre curiosities that had a potential audience of 37 devoted film buffs. In the last year the situation has

"Back from the Twilight Zone," Stephen Farber, *New West,* October 20, 1980. Reprinted with permission from the October 20, 1980 issue of *New West.* Copyright 1980 by *New West.*

changed: The movies that struggled to get released include a surprising number of films by major filmmakers, including Robert Altman, Hal Ashby, Nicolas Roeg and Roman Polanski. Besides, most of these movies have plenty of crowd-pleasing ingredients: well-known actors, spectacular action scenes, emotional confrontations, broad humor, sex and violence. They are ambitious and adventurous *commercial* movies, and the difficulty they have had getting released signals some radical changes in the industry—and a possible crisis for moviegoers.

What has delayed the release of these movies for such a long time? Is the problem with the movies or with the people who sell the movies? Obviously each case is different, but all of these films have one thing in common: They are difficult to pigeonhole—they don't fit a familiar commercial mold. As Richard Rush, director of the *The Stunt Man,* says, "What I kept hearing was that the movie was hard to sell. It wasn't that the studios didn't like the movie but that they couldn't get a handle on it. They kept asking, 'Is it a comedy or an action picture or an exercise in deception? How do you describe it in a phrase?' What they were really asking was, 'What ad campaign that I've already used can I revamp for this movie?' "

Jonas Rosenfield, senior vice president of worldwide marketing for Melvin Simon Productions, which financed *Stunt Man,* elaborates, "The strangeness and uniqueness of the film, which are just what audiences love about it, are the very qualities that baffled the studios." That identical paradox has plagued most of these unreleased movies. They may well have popular appeal, but distributors do not know how to capitalize on it. These films are trapped by changing distribution patterns.

First of all, advertising and distribution costs have skyrocketed—to such an extent that studios have decided that even a film by Altman or Polanski may be cheaper to shelve than to release. Studios estimate that to open a film nationwide costs a minimum of $3 million and sometimes as much as $8 million or $10 million.

The reason for the burgeoning advertising costs is the increasing reliance on TV advertising, as opposed to newspaper advertising, to sell movies. The rates are astronomical: A single 30-second TV spot in prime time costs $60,000 to $100,000. Since TV ads are so ubiquitous today, most people may not realize that this is a very new phenomenon. *Jaws,* made in 1975, was the first blockbuster film to rely primarily on television advertising, and that campaign paid off handsomely.

Why has there been such a dramatic change from print to TV advertising? Lee Beaupre, vice president of advertising and publicity for Lorimar (the company that backed *Carny* and *Second Hand Hearts*), explains, "We get surveys that gauge how the public's awareness of a film is built. Today the awareness of young people comes almost entirely from television. Teenagers rarely look at a newspaper. They don't watch a lot of TV, either, but they watch some, and they listen to the radio. That's how they find out about films. It's frightening in a way. The country is moving toward a kind of illiteracy."

Movies that are hard to describe in a 30-second TV spot face rough going in today's marketplace. Charles Pratt, the producer of *The Great Santini,* pinpoints the problem: "With *The Great Santini* we could not find one 30-second piece of film that would make people jump out of their seats. The whole film gives off an aura people find very affecting, but there's nothing to encapsulate for television."

Along with the changes in how movies are advertised have come equally significant changes in how they are distributed. Not long ago, most movies opened in a single first-run house in each city, then weeks or even months later the picture moved out to more theaters in the suburbs or neighborhoods. Multiple theater openings were reserved for exploitation films. Today, however, the exclusive single-theater opening is an exception; most films open in hundreds of theaters all across the country on the same day. Many films—even successful ones—are played out in a month.

The reason for this change is economic. "It costs almost as much to open a movie in one theater as it does to open in twenty theaters," insists Lorimar's Beaupre. "Whether you open in one theater or twenty, you still have to let people know you're there, which usually means you have to take TV ads. And if you open an exclusive engagement, then move into a wider break several weeks later, you have to pay for TV advertising all over again. There is no way to make a slower opening cost efficient."

Yet the disappointing returns on many of 1980's big summer movies suggest that mass openings are not always the best way to release a movie. This system actually works best for bad films that have some exploitable element and need to be played off quickly. A mass release makes sense for *Cheech and Chong's Next Movie, Smokey and the Bandit II* or *Caddyshack*. On those movies, you don't want to let word of mouth build; you want to take the money and run. But a mass release pattern will never work for a film of more subtle quality, which needs time to find and build an audience.

"After the original openings of *The Great Santini* last fall," comments writer-director Lewis John Carlino, "I realized that we had nothing to sell except the quality of the picture. You can't open the film broadly and expect people to come. It has no stars. It's not a horror movie or a science fiction movie, which have built-in audiences. It's a domestic drama. What makes it different from a TV movie? Only endorsements from the media can suggest that it is different. You have to open in New York, where the media are concentrated. And that's finally how we sold the movie. We used newspaper ads with quotes from the reviews. We didn't use television at all."

Other films could obviously benefit from a similar distribution plan. *Carny* originally opened on Memorial Day in 300 theaters in the Southeast and Midwest, where the distributor spent about $1.2 million on advertising and prints. "*Carny* was sold as a shit-kicker southern movie," Lorimar's Beaupre explains. "If it had starred Peter Fonda and Sally Field, that approach might have made sense. But Robbie Robertson, Jodie Foster and Gary Busey appeal to critics and media people much more than they appeal to southern audiences. The director, Robert Kaylor, also has a critical following in New York as a result of *Derby*. We should have opened it at one theater in New York and gone from there."

On the other hand, it isn't fair to place all the blame on the studios. Part of the problem rests with today's audience, which doesn't seem inclined to support venturesome or challenging films. "Something has changed in the audience," argues Beaupre. "People today seem to want to see prefab films. They aren't into making discoveries." Orion's Gabe Sumner concurs: "I am sick and tired of hearing filmmakers pissing and moaning about marketing people who do not understand their film. When they say marketing and distribution killed their film, that's bullshit. The audience out there just didn't care to buy those films, and the filmmakers won't face that fact."

Carny director Kaylor challenges this view: "The studios are interested in nothing but a fast payoff. A slow payoff film like *Carny* is a pain in the ass for them. As a businessman I can understand that. But they're working in a business that's a little more than a business. They have a responsibility to the artistic side of movies as well. If they finance the film, they should support it—unless it's just irredeemably bad."

Still, most of these completed films

will eventually be released. The real crunch could come in the future, when these directors can't find backing for their next projects.

In analyzing the disappointing performance of many of this summer's movies, studio executives agree on one reason for the slump—the number of movies in the marketplace. About 25 percent more movies opened this summer than opened last summer, and executives feel the market simply cannot absorb so many films. (They overlook the fact that most of the movies were terrible.) Now, as a result of the actors' strike, the studios are all cutting back on their production schedules. If they make 25 percent fewer films this year, which do you think will be the projects they drop? Studios certainly won't cancel *Smokey and the Bandit III* or *Cheech and Chong Light Up Again;* those are movies that fit into the current distribution system. The casualties most certainly will be the idiosyncratic movies like *The Stunt Man, The Great Santini, Carny* and *Bad Timing.*

Then what are the solutions for filmmakers like Richard Rush, Robert Altman, Robert Kaylor and Nicolas Roeg, who want to continue making their kinds of movies for a marketplace that doesn't know how to absorb them? Is it possible that smaller distribution companies—like Analysis, Atlantic and New Line Cinema—are the answer for more specialized films?

Richard Rush has explained that several small distributors expressed intense interest in releasing *The Stunt Man.* "If it had been a very low budget film," he says, "we might well have considered that option. The problem is that *The Stunt Man* cost $7 million, and that means it would have to gross at least $21 million to break even. There is no record of a smaller distributor ever grossing that much." For lower budgeted independent films, however, small distributors should definitely be considered as an alternative.

There is, additionally, a slim possibility that the studios may try to expand or revamp their distribution outlets to accommodate a broader range of movies. Universal has a special-projects division, headed by Mike Ridges, which is handling the national release of *Resurrection,* an offbeat Ellen Burstyn movie about a faith healer.

At Twentieth Century-Fox, two executives—Claire Townsend, a production vice president, and Mike Nolin, who works in distribution—are talking about setting up a separate division within the Fox distribution apparatus to handle specialized films. "We're putting together a prospectus," Townsend explains. "We need to prove that the economics are sound. But the overhead for this division would be minimal. The returns do not have to be great or immediate. There *is* a market for specialized films that can't support massive TV advertising."

Creative financing has blossomed in the last several years; now we need creative distribution. Until a few people jettison the current system, we may continue to wait for months or even years to see the best movies produced today.

TIME-COMPRESSED TV COMMERCIALS

As the cost of television commercials continues to escalate, advertisers are asking with greater urgency: Is the money being well spent? Every second is precious. Advertisers should also be asking: Is every second being utilized effectively? A critical evaluation in response to these questions may reveal that portions of a commercial present material too slowly to hold viewer interest. It might also be found that some sections present information too quickly for the viewer to assimilate.

How can an advertiser determine the most effective rate of information flow? Research by cognitive psychologists pro-

vides some useful guidelines. An experiment dealing with the pace of television commercials is developed based on those guidelines. Experimental results demonstrate that advertising impact can be increased by adjusting the original rate of information flow.

It is now possible to vary the speed of speech with an electronic technique called time compression. Normally, when the speed of a tape recorder is increased, the speed of speech increases but takes on a "Donald Duck" quality—that is, the speech sounds unnaturally high and strident in pitch. To eliminate the "Donald Duck" effect, a computerized time-compression device is connected to the tape recorder. This device restores the pitch of the voice to normal regardless of alterations in the speed of the tape recorder.

Therefore, it is possible to vary the

pace of a tape-recorded speaker simply by turning a knob. The effect sounds quite subtle and natural as long as the speed is not increased by more than about 40 per cent. Using time compression, researchers are able to vary the rate of information flow without changing any other qualities of a tape-recorded communication. Many experiments utilizing this technique have been reported in education and psychology journals (Duker, 1974). The following key findings have emerged:

(1) listeners can assimilate communications at twice the normal rate of speech with virtually no loss in learning (Fairbanks, Guttman, and Miron, 1957);

(2) listeners prefer communications delivered at a pace faster than normal speed (Foulke, 1969; MacLachlan and LaBarbera, 1977);

(3) the sales effect of a persuasive message did not diminish when the speed of the communication was increased (Wheeless, 1971);

(4) faster radio commercials were reported to be more interesting than normal-speed commercials (MacLachlan and LaBarbera, 1977);

(5) faster radio commercials were recalled better than normalpaced commercials (MacLachlan and LaBarbera, 1977).

These findings strongly imply that effectiveness of television commercials might be increased through speeding them up by using time compression. Increased speed could be achieved through use of a variable speed projector in conjunction with a computerized time-com-

pression device. As the speed of the projector is increased, the speed of the motion picture would increase and sound would remain synchronized with the projected image. The computerized time-compression device would maintain the normal pitch of sound. A suitable device for such an application is the Lexicon Varispeech II.

EXPERIMENTAL DESIGN

A major New York-based advertising agency was contacted to supply six television commercials that it felt represented the high quality of the agency's work. Five were 30-second commercials, and one was 60 seconds. Equipment was arranged to permit these commercials to be projected at either normal speed or 25 per cent faster than normal. The Lexicon Varispeech II was used to maintain a normal voice pitch when the faster rate of projection was chosen.

Subjects saw three commercials at normal speed and three commercials at the faster speed according to the rotational design schedule presented in Table 1. Sub-

Table 1

Experimental Design

Commercial	Group 1	Group 2
AT&T	Normal	Fast*
Carrier Air Conditioners	Fast	Normal
DuPont Teflon	Normal	Fast
Sargent's Sentry Flea Collar (60 seconds)	Fast	Normal
Sealtest Yogurt	Normal	Fast
U.S. Army	Fast	Normal

*Fast = 25 per cent faster than normal speed (e.g., a 30-second commercial is shown in 24 seconds).

jects were undergraduate students at a major northeastern university. They were assigned at random to one of two groups. Subjects were given the following instructions:

> We are going to show you six television commercials. After you have seen a commercial we will stop the projector and ask you to rate the commercial according to how interesting you felt it was.

Each subject was asked to indicate his level of interest on a six-point semantic differential scale that ranged from "very dull" to "very interesting."

Two days later, without any advance notice, subjects were asked the following unaided brand recall question:

> We would like to know which brands of products were advertised in the commercials you saw two days ago.

EXPERIMENTAL RESULTS

Table 2 displays the reported level of interest in each of the six commercials by the two groups. It shows that in five of the six cases the faster version was reported as the most interesting. For each commercial t tests were performed to determine the probability that the difference in means was due to chance alone. As Table 2 indicates, three of the results are significant at least at the .01 level.

Table 3 demonstrates that unaided brand recall measured two days after the experiment was not appreciably different for the two conditions. In three situations it was higher for the faster-paced commercials; in two cases it was higher for the normal-speed commercials; the two conditions were tied for one commercial.

To summarize, the faster commercials, which required only 24 seconds rather than the original 30 seconds of broadcast time, resulted in slightly better performance in the aggregate. These results would seem to suggest that an advertiser might be able to save advertising dollars through the use of time compression while maintaining the effectiveness of commercials.

In this experiment the time-compres-

Table 2

Level of Reported Interest in Television Commercials, Normal Speed versus 25 Per Cent Faster

Commercial Number	Group Number	Mean Level of Reported Interest	Standard Error of Sample Mean	One-tailed t-Test Probability
AT&T	1 (Normal)	2.36	.21	.16
	2 (Fast)	2.66	.22	
Carrier Air Conditioners	1 (Fast)	2.42	.18	.24
	2 (Normal)	2.22	.21	
DuPont Teflon	1 (Normal)	4.06	.23	.004
	2 (Fast)	4.86	.17	
Sargent's Sentry Flea Collar	1 (Fast)	4.94	.18	.003
	2 (Normal)	4.14	.22	
Sealtest Yogurt	1 (Normal)	2.50	.22	.11
	2 (Fast)	2.89	.22	
U.S. Army	1 (Fast)	2.64	.24	.01
	2 (Normal)	3.50	.25	

Table 3

Unaided Brand Recall, Normal Speed versus 25 Per Cent Faster

Commercial Number	Group Number	Number Recalling Brand Name*	Per Cent Recalling Brand Name
AT&T	1 (Normal)	14	40
	2 (Fast)	21	60
Carrier Air Conditioners	1 (Fast)	19	54
	2 (Normal)	16	46
DuPont Teflon	1 (Normal)	15	43
	2 (Fast)	11	31
Sargent's Sentry Flea Collar	1 (Fast)	10	29
	2 (Normal)	10	29
Sealtest Yogurt	1 (Normal)	23	66
	2 (Fast)	8	23
U.S. Army	1 (Fast)	20	57
	2 (Normal)	15	43

*There were 35 subjects in each group.

sion technique was used indiscriminately in that every commercial was speeded up by 25 per cent in the treatment condition. In a field setting one would expect that judgment would be exercised and compression applied selectively in appropriate degrees. A commercial might contain certain segments that could be compressed considerably. Other segments might not benefit from compression. Some segments of a commercial might be strengthened if the material were extended. The Lexicon device permits extension as well as compression. Thus, the creative department could adjust information flow over a wide possible range.

There are other methods by which a creative department may alter the rate of information flow. These include

(1) tighter editing;
(2) using faster-paced announcers;
(3) using more frequent changes in pictorial material;
(4) introducing superimposed titles.

Any of these techniques might be used to advantage where research demonstrates that a faster pace of information flow is desirable.

INFORMATION FLOW AND ATTENTION

Why did the subjects prefer the faster commercials? An explanation may be drawn from the literature on cognitive psychology.

The human mind was designed to accommodate two-way communications. As a person is listening to a speaker, he is able concurrently to formulate his own thoughts so that he can articulate them in reply. Thus, in a two-way communication the mind is both receiving information and developing appropriate replies. In a one-way communication, however, the mind is involved simply in receiving a communication.

What happens to the cognitive capacity that might otherwise have been used in developing replies to the communication? Frequently it is channeled into distractive thoughts. Zimbardo and Ebbesen (1970) state:

> It is well to think about the nature of distractions as they occur in real life. If you were listening to an important message, there would rarely be *external* distractions present which could not be easily eliminated. However, what about *internal* distractors, such as states of anxiety, disgust, love, and passion? These are not so easily brushed aside while you are supposed to be attending to the presentation of important information. To the point is a recent study by Cameron, Frank, Lifter, and Morrissey [1968] of student attention during a lecture. It revealed that 60 percent of the time the students were not listening—even though the lecturer was very good. Moreover, they reported that about a fourth of time they were engaged in daydreaming sexual fantasies.

Distraction interferes with attention, and attention is considered to be a prerequisite of memory. In 400 B.C. the written rules of memory contained statements such as "if you pay attention, the judgment will better perceive the things going through it" (Yates, 1966). Exactly what is meant by *attention?* William James (1890) answered that question in this way:

> Everyone knows what attention is. It is the taking possession by the mind, in clear and vivid form, of one out of what seems several simultaneously possible objects or trains of thought. Focalization, concentration of consciousness are its essence. It implies withdrawal from some things in order to deal effectively with others.

James's definition suggests that for the attention level to be high, only a limited number of items can be attended to at one time. Can we pay attention to more than one thing at a time? James answers:

> If, then, by the original question, how many ideas or things can we attend to at once, [is] meant how many entirely disconnected systems or processes of conception can go on simultaneously, the answer is, not *easily* more than *one, unless the processes are very habitual;* but then *two, or even three,* without very much oscillation of the attention. Where, however, the processes are less automatic, as in the story of Julius Caesar dictating four letters whilst he writes a fifth, there must be a rapid oscillation of the mind from one to the next, and no consequent gain of time.

James suggests that there is a severe limitation on the number of ideas the mind can be processing at one time. The mind cannot easily be entertaining both distractive thoughts and a communication simultaneously. Therefore, a communicator should avoid conditions that predispose the mind to distractive thoughts.

Berlyne (1960) suggests that distractive thoughts set in when the pace of information in a communication falls below a satisfying level. For an individual there is an optimum level of information intake that is most satisfying. If the flow of information from a one-way communication is too slow, boredom will set in and attention will shift to distractive thoughts in an effort by the subject to increase his level of mental involvement. On the other hand, if the pace of communication is too fast, subjects may find it difficult and uncomfortable to assimilate the information. The most pleasant kind of communication is one that falls within these two extremes.

If a broadcast advertisement is paced too slow, people may lack interest in the communication and shift their attention away from it. In contrast, if a commercial is too fast, the advertiser's message may not be assimilated.

MANAGERIAL IMPLICATIONS OF TIME COMPRESSION

The findings reported here suggest that time compression could be a potentially useful tool in the following situations:

1. It could provide a means of increasing interest in a commercial where interest is low due to the slow rate of information flow.
2. It could be useful when advertisers wish to tell a more complete story than would otherwise be possible in a 30-second commercial. It would, in fact, be possible to transform a 30-second commercial into a "38-second commercial."
3. It could increase the attention power of commercials. Time compression for this purpose could range from the type of modest adjustment reported here (25 per cent faster) to a rate as much as 100 per cent faster than normal speed. An increase of 25 per cent is subtle, and such an adjustment would not be noticed by viewers. A pace that is 100 per cent faster is still intelligible, but viewers would be aware of the unnatural speed.

This might or might not result in a creative advantage, depending on the particular advertisement.

Rate of information flow is a dimension that has not been explored previously in the advertising literature. Time compression has provided a method for conducting initial experiments in this area. These experiments indicate that the effectiveness and efficiency of advertising could be increased substantially by intelligent adjustment of the rate of information flow.

References

Berlyne, D. E. *Conflict, Arousal, and Curiosity.* New York: McGraw-Hill, 1960.

Cameron, P., et al. Cognitive Functionings of College Students in a General Psychology Class. Paper presented at a meeting of the American Psychological Association, 1968.

Duker, Sam (Ed.). *Time-Compressed Speech: An Anthology and Bibliography.* 3 vols. Metuchen, N.J.: Scarecrow Press, 1974.

Fairbanks, Grant, Newman Guttman, and Murray S. Miron. Effects of Time Compression upon the Comprehension of Connected Speech. *Journal of Speech and Hearing Disorders,* Vol. 22, No. 1, March 1957, pp. 10–19.

Foulke, Emerson. *Comprehension of Rapid Speecy by the Blind: Part III.* Louisville, Ky.: University of Louisville, 1969.

James, William. *The Principles of Psychology.* Vol. 1. New York: Holt, 1890.

MacLachlan, James, and Priscilla LaBarbera. Time Compressed Speech in Radio Advertising. Working paper, New York University, 1977.

Wheeless, Lawrence R. Some Effects of Time-Compressed Speech on Persuasion. *Journal of Broadcasting.* Vol. 15, No. 4, Fall 1971, pp. 415–420.

Yates, Frances A. *The Art of Memory.* Chicago: University of Chicago Press, 1966.

Zimbardo, Philip, and Ebbe B. Ebbesen. *Influencing Attitudes and Changing Behavior.* Menlo Park, Calif.: Addison-Wesley, 1970.

Exercise 31

How Well Do You Read Body Language?

OBJECTIVE To demonstrate the impact of nonverbal communication in communication.

Facial expressions and body gestures are integral to everyday conversations. Yet the important effects of nonverbal communication on the meaning of the communication escapes explicit awareness. This exercise demonstrates the role of nonverbal communication in marketing communications.

The verbal communication for the following advertisements have been removed. Only the nonverbal part of the advertisements remain. Try to match the pictures on page 261 with the statements. Then turn to pages 262 and 263 to see how well you did.

"A 20-minute call anywhere in
the country will cost me only
$3.33. What's the catch?"

"Vassarete just made it easy to
get a 'second glance'."

"Our diamond means we have
the best of both worlds.
Yours and mine."

Picture _____

Picture _____

Picture _____

Picture A

Picture B

Picture C

Courtesy of American Telephone and Telegraph Company, Long Lines.

Reprinted with permission of DeBeers, NW Ayer ABH International.

Reprinted with permission of Munsingwear, Incorporated.

Exercise 32

Let's Make a Deal

OBJECTIVE To investigate the effect of interpersonal perception and communication in "negotiations" in the marketplace.

This exercise centers upon interpersonal perception and communication. The purpose is to investigate the effect of interpersonal perception and communication in "negotiations" in the marketplace. A group of students from the class will carry out this exercise. The other students in the class will participate by offering suggestions and evaluating and analyzing the outcome of the exercise.

Students participating in this project will negotiate for used cars at various dealerships in the surrounding city area. However, the students' background, dress, and behaviors will differ according to a predetermined plan. Class members can help the participating students determine the various roles, dress, backgrounds, and behaviors to assume. The purpose of this exercise is to investigate the effect of interpersonal perception on the cost of the negotiated item. The car, the salesperson, and dealership should remain constant, and only the consumers (the participating students' roles) should vary.

16

Consumer Information Search: Interpersonal Sources of Information and Diffusion of Innovations

How does the diffusion of innovations occur? What is the process by which innovations are diffused and adopted by a society? The following articles address some of the elements involved in the diffusion of innovations.

In the article "As the Word Turns," Curt Suplee of the *Washington Post* discusses how the word-of-mouth communication of Big Mouth opinion leaders helps launch books into best-seller lists.

The trickle-down theory states that innovations diffuse from upper to lower stratas of society. The existence of opinion leaders suggests the validity of the trickle-across theory—innovations spread within social strata. In the "The Status Float Phenomenon," George A. Field offers a third theory—the trickle-up theory—to explain the diffusion of innovations from lower to higher social strata.

AS THE WORD TURNS

In the beginning was the Word of Mouth.

"It was during the Jean Harris trial," says ABC-TV correspondent Lynn Sherr. "We were waiting for the verdict, and spending a lot of time just sitting around— several dozen representatives of the most prestigious news organs in the country, there in a corner of the lobby, all piled on each other."

As the hours passed and the tedium thickened, Sherr remained visibly engrossed in what she was reading, an advance "reader's copy" of a soon-to-be-published espionage thriller by a minor author. When her restless colleagues asked what it was, Sherr recalls, "I must have said three dozen times, 'It's called

"As the Word Turns," Curt Suplee, *Sacramento Bee*, July 1, 1981, p. F1. Copyright © 1981, *The Washington Post*.

Gorky Park and it's published by Random House and it's great.'"

Afterward, Sherr called her friend Carol Schneider, publicity director at Random House, and said, "I think I have done a wonderful thing for you."

A few weeks later, *Gorky Park* topped off the best-seller lists and Martin Cruz Smith was a hard-cover household word.

Before the ad campaign, before the talk shows, even before the printed page, there is Word of Mouth, perhaps the strongest sales organ in the body politic and certainly the least expensive.

It is as integral as ink to the book business. Thousands of titles hit the racks every year, and getting special attention for a single one is like whistling in a hurricane. So publishers with a hot property reach immediately for their Big Mouth lists.

That is: a protean roster of prominent people who put the quo in status and the dicta in obiter, whose luncheon musings or cocktail hour verdicts can change the shape of the season. Three or four months before a book's publication, these literary logrollers receive either paperbound uncorrected galleys or, later, slick-cover "reader's copies," and the big-mouthing begins.

Mailing lists differ from book to book, depending on subject and genre, and range in number from 200 to 2,000 (as for *Gorky Park*), depending on dollar investment and expected popularity. But generally, there is a triad of word-of-mouth weapons in the integrated battlefield of publishing.

The first is getting prepublication quotes from name-brand authors. Among the most desirable: Kurt Vonnegut, Gloria Steinhem, John Updike, Erica Jong, Joan Didion, John Gregory Dunne, Dan Greenberg, John Gardner, Woody Allen, Joseph Heller, Gay Talese and Thomas Pynchon, many of whom are consequently knee-deep in new novels and scarcely know where to begin reading. "I stopped giving quotes," says Nora Ephron, "because the number of books you really want to give quotes to is outnumbered six to one by books like your veterinarian's new volume on how to feed your cat. If you don't give him a quote, then God help you next time your cat is sick." Nonetheless, she is adamantly promouth: "I believe that what makes books sell, more than anything else, is word of mouth."

Phase two involves a number of institutional Big Mouths, leading literary indicators like Barbara Bannon of *Publisher's Weekly* and B. Dalton's Kay Sexton, whose weekly newsletter goes to all 540 stores in the chain and hundreds of people in the industry: columnists such as Hilary Mills and Leonore Fleischer; heads of the major book clubs; book buyers for the large chains; editors empowered to buy excerpts for such supermarket showcases as *Ladies' Home Journal, Redbook, Woman's Day, Playboy, Penthouse, Family Circle* and *McCall's;* talk show hosts and agents of every kind; and scouts for the screen. And then there are opinion-shapers like Steve Rubin of Writers Bloc and Emily Boxer, book coordinator of NBC's "Today" show. Says Stuart Applebaum of Bantam Books, "People use these early warnings as evidence that somebody besides the publisher believes in the book."

Meanwhile, everybody in the business is constantly reading everyone else's material. "When a book comes along that people really love," says Wendy Nicholson, publicist for Summit Books, a division of Simon & Schuster, "lots of things start to happen—for example, people start Xeroxing manuscripts and sending them to friends." The rule is: If you've bought it, flaunt it. Galleys shuttle between publishing houses, and soon a big book has a big following even at competing companies. "Publishing is incestuous," says Rubin, and big-mouthing "has much more clout within the industry."

Finally, each publicist and editor also has a mental list of friends, associates and special-interest readers. For example, Random House's Schneider regularly sends readers' copies to such industry outsiders as Bill Kenly, a public relations officer with Paramount Pictures, and Herb Hellman, who works in corporate public affairs for RCA records. "Herb lunches the way I lunch," she says. "He'll say, 'I just read a terrific book last night.' You also include whoever you know who goes to a lot of parties, who because of business or celebrity sees a lot of people."

And, of course, there are ad-hoc specialty lists: Ralph Lauren was the target of an advance copy of Crown's *How to Make Love to a Man,* which publicity director Nancy Cahan also sent to Calvin Klein and photographers Francesco Scavullo and Richard Avedon. Nicholson bombarded the feminist community with early copies of Summit's *The Women's Room.*

As the word turns, the only cardinal rule is that each big mouth really believe in the book. "You have to have credibility," says Rodney Pelter, book-seller-turned-agent and a notoriously effective Big Mouth. "You never go out on a limb for a friend, an author or a publisher—you only do it for a book."

Right now, the conversational drums are beating for a number of coming summer and fall titles: Colette Dowling's *The Cinderella Complex* (Summit) about why women fear independence; Joyce Carol Oates' Washington thriller called *Angel of Light* and the new John Irving novel, *Hotel New Hampshire,* both from Dutton; Thomas *Black Sunday* Harris' new chiller, *Red Dragon,* from Putnam's; Addison-Wesley's *Theory Z: How American Business Can Meet the Japanese Challenge,* by William Ouchi; Simon & Schuster's *Mr. American,* a novel by George M. Fraser; Colleen *Thorn Birds* McCullough's *An Indecent Obsession* from Harper & Row; *Baby Love,* from Knopf by Joyce Maynard, who caused a stir in the early '70s with *Looking Back;* and Crown's *Traditions,* the big upcoming show-biz novel by Alan Ebert with Janice Rotchstein.

The genteel jawboning doesn't always work. Anne Tolston Wallach's new novel, *Women's Work*—a sort of "Scruples Goes to Madison Avenue" about a female advertising honcha's fight for recognition—looked like a big-mouth bonanza after New American Library paid $850,000 for it at auction, hustled it at this year's ABA and sent out 2,000 galleys to a list that included leading woman executives such as Gloria Vanderbilt. But the August release is already meeting some resistance from the major mouths in New York (despite favorable early notices in the trade press) and the prognosis is uncertain.

Similarly, a few years ago, despite a hard sell on the salon circuit, Random House's *Kramer vs. Kramer* proved a hardcover disappointment. Yet the movie became a national phenomenon. And screen success, too, can be the result of big mouths in motion.

Four years ago, just before William Diehl's Atlanta-based thriller, *Sharkey's Machine,* came out at Delacorte, "I was invited to a dinner as a big mouth," recalls free-lance publicist Betsy Nolan, who had worked on the book and was a personal friend of Diehl's, "I picked up a prepublication copy and sent it to Sidney Sheldon, a client of mine. I am very circumspect about sending works to authors, unless it's something I'm absolutely willing to stake my reputation on." She was and Sheldon (*The Other Side of Midnight*) got the book at his Los Angeles home.

Meanwhile, Diehl's attorney, Irving Kaler, had sent a copy to Edwin Spivia, director of the Georgia film office, who in turn sent it to producer-director-star Burt Reynolds. At the same time, Reynolds' friend Tommy Culla, who reads books for potential film projects, had also sent him a copy. One night after Sheldon and Reynolds had appeared on the same talk show, Reynolds went to Sheldon's house. There on the coffee table was the ubiquitous

Sharkey's Machine. "That's the third time today I've seen that book," Reynolds said. "Somebody's trying to tell me something."

Maybe so: Reynolds just finished shooting the film version of *Sharkey's Machine* in Atlanta.

Depending on the strength of the book and the reputation of its advocate, it can take as few as one or two people to get the town talking. Robert Gottlieb, editor-in-chief at Knopf (and the man who helped get *Catch-22* off the ground in the mid-'60s), didn't have to go the extra mile for Jacobo Timerman's *Prisoner Without a Name, Cell Without a Number.* It was only a few blocks to the *New Yorker* offices, where he gave a manuscript copy to editor William Shawn. The excerpt appeared, and the book was off.

Agent Rodney Pelter, a former owner of the Madison Avenue Bookstore ("the most glittering list of customers any bookstore ever had"), developed big-mouth clout on the strength of his taste and his volume, which sometimes accounted for 10 percent of the hard-cover sales on a single book. He claims to have outpromoted the publishers on more than one occasion. In the case of Hugh Trevor-Roper's *The Hermit of Peking,* he stunned Knopf by single-handedly ordering 700 copies and making the title an East Side shibboleth. That kind of customer charisma, he says, takes years to achieve: "You give a book to a Brooke Astor, a Paul Melion or somebody, and say, 'I want you to buy this book, and if you don't like it, I'll take it back.' And after a while, it's anything you want."

Pelter was also an early and strong supporter of Gael Greene's steamy 1977 novel *Blue Skies, No Candy.* After reading the galleys, he says, "I realized that there wasn't a good, trashy, sexy novel—by a personality who would get out and promote it—on anybody else's list that season.

"I called (an executive) at Morrow and told him, 'You've got a hot book on your list. Do something about it.' I was met with dead silence. So when I went to the American Booksellers Association convention, I told every buyer I knew that there was only one really trashy book of the season. After the book took off, I called Howard Kaminsky (president of Warner Books, the paperback publisher of *Blue Skies*) and he said, 'Glad to know you—you made the Gael Greene book for us.'" Kaminsky does not remember the conversation, but does recall the word-of-mouth impact of the Warner cover. The image of a woman's hand unzipping the fly on a pair of obviously male jeans was a lubricious hit, and Warner used it for display cards on the New York subway. "Then a priest and a couple of his parisioners saw it," Kaminsky says, "and took offense and ripped a few of them down. Finally, they convinced the transit authority to have the cards removed. We got a lot of publicity out of that."

Sometimes it takes an outright oral attack. That's the conclusion Nancy Cahan, publicity director at Crown, came to when faced with promoting *Princess Daisy* by Judith Krantz. "Judy got sick, and I had to think of some way to get people talking about this book, since I knew we weren't going to do terrific in the reviews." She decided "to get it linked up with a charity. I did some investigating, and came up with Lighthouse for the Blind" in New York. After lengthy negotiations with leading socialites ("they have the money to buy books and the time to read"), Cahan got the desired result: Last April at the Plaza, the Lighthouse held a Princess Daisy Ball with all the attendant attention in social columns, the fashion press and television.

Cahan likes "planting items" with columnists and generating news stories about books before they are published. The technique worked well with *The Spike,* by journalists Arnaud de Borchgrave and Robert Moss, although Cahan also sent out almost 2,000 pre-publication copies (no inconsiderable investment—at nearly $4 each, bound galleys or readers' copies cost about twice as much to produce as finished books) and worked the authors themselves pretty hard. "They had a lot of friends in high places, and we had lots of cocktail parties all over the country," especially in Washington, where she invited "Alexander Haig and the top defense and political people, not so much press as opinion-makers."

In a few months, Crown will publish Moss' first solo novel, a thriller called *Death Beam.* The original working title was *Death Star,* and when Cahan managed to get it into *New York Magazine's* intelligent column, representatives of producer George *Star Wars* Lucas wrote to complain that the words *Death Star* were their property. A legal liability, but an asset for Cahan. "I got up a press release about how Robert Moss was ready to take on the KGB, but not Darth Vader. It was picked up in *The Times,* on cable TV, Leonore Fleischer ran part of the letter, and then Shirley Eder did it."

No amount of talk can compensate for genuine literary excitement, however, and no book in the coming months is going to match the liveliest literary lobbying in recent memory, the oral orgy that accompanied John Irving's *The World According to Garp.* When the manuscript came in to Dutton in 1977, jaws started dropping from day one. The excitement over a major book always begins at home. ("You can't fake it," says Kaminsky, "but if you can get people in your own house hot, it radiates out"). With *Garp,* it began when Jan Rosenman, assistant to the late Henry Robbins, wrote a rousing in-house memo. Then Robbins—who enjoyed enormous respect in the literary world—sent a heartfelt endorsement letter accompanying the 1,500 readers' copies. "It worked like it was supposed to," says Lois Shapiro, Dutton's publicity chief.

Even the incorrigible Pelter got a piece of the pre-publication action. "I called Henry (Robbins) and said, 'What have you got? I'm home sick and I need something good.' He said, 'Have I got a book for you!' I read it straight through, called him back and said, 'This is the greatest book I've read since *Catcher in the Rye.*' Pelter's endorsement, which went out with the Dutton salesmen, said, "Booksellers who don't stock *Garp* are going to miss the biggest book of the season."

Those who didn't did.

THE STATUS FLOAT PHENOMENON

Traditional theories of acceptance of new products, fashions, and of social patterns have been under assault for some time, partly because of probable changes in the patterns, partly because of improved observational techniques. The pioneer statistical studies published by Kroeber have been supplemented over the years by more elaborate analysis, such as the well-known work of Nystrom and Young. The armchair commentaries of anthropologist Sapir, an accomplished linguist and passable violinist but not necessarily an empirical authority in this field, are typical of the early writing.[1]

The trickle-down fashion cycle was once a widely accepted model of new product acceptance by persons at different social class or status levels. The basic premise was that the adoption of fashions by people high on the status pyramid is followed by the adoption by people on progressively (or regressively!) lower levels. Whether this model actually represents anything in the real world has not yet been established. It has been subject to occasional attacks on a variety of grounds, and it would appear that the trickle-down theory, under pressure from empirically oriented diffusion theorists and students of fashion, has fallen into disfavor.

"The Status Float Phenomenon," George A. Field, *Business Horizon,* August 1970, pp. 45–52. Copyright 1970, by the Foundation for the School of Business at Indiana University. Reprinted by permission.

[1]A. L. Kroeber, *American Anthropologist* (July–September, 1919); Paul H. Nystrom, *Economics of Fashion* (New York: The Ronald Press, 1928); Agatha Brooks Young, *Recurring Cycles of Fashion, 1760–1937* (New York: Cooper Square Publishers, Inc., 1966); Edward Sapir, "Fashion," *The Encyclopedia of Social Sciences* (New York: The Macmillan Company, 1931), pp. 139–44.

Studies originating in media research led to serendipitous findings applicable to marketing, and eventually the research sparked by Lazarsfeld and his colleagues led to substantial revisions in accepted doctrines concerning the diffusion of innovation, positing the role of innovators and influentials in a lateral small-group interactive process.[2]

Attacks on the trickle-down theory of fashion adoption soon followed. The pertinent research has been conducted in limited areas, but enough evidence has accumulated to suggest that the trickle-down hypothesis is still just a hypothesis, and probably one with rather limited applicability.[3] As a result of these findings, it has been suggested that fashion (and presumably other innovations that, like fashion, have status implications) may be described as trickling across rather than down, and the "trickle across" nomenclature has found its way into some basic marketing texts.

It now appears that some fashions, as well as some analogous nonfashion phenomena, climb the status pyramid from below, trickling up, as it were. If this is true, the process, which we call the Status Float phenomenon, deserves careful study. Our purpose here is simply to call attention to the phenomenon by citing some possible examples.

UP FROM SLAVERY: BLACK IS BEAUTIFUL

The traditional symbolic equation of black with death, evils, and servitude in our cul-

[2]Elihu Katz and Paul Lazarsfeld, *Personal Influence* (Glencoe, Ill.: The Free Press, 1962). Also Everett Rogers, *Diffusion of Innovations* (New York: The Free Press, 1962).

[3]Charles W. King, "Fashion Adoption: a Rebuttal to the 'Trickle Down' Theory," in Stephen A. Greyser (ed.), *Toward Scientific Marketing* (Chicago: American Marketing Association, 1964), pp. 108–25.

ture is yielding to deepening respect for the Negro culture and the Negro race in general. The placement director of Wayne State University states that demand for Negro graduates is now three or four times as great as the demand for whites with comparable degrees. But even before this growing and explicit acceptance of the American Negro, there was a long-term interculturation during which a number of elements from the Negro subculture were gradually assimilated into the dominant white culture. These elements moved inexorably up the status ladder to ever-higher levels. Examples that come readily to mind are in the areas of music, dancing, fashion, and speech patterns.

Negro music has penetrated the national culture through several channels, and its influence has been profound. Jazz, as the name implies, was in its early days associated with brothels and slums. Its rise in stature has been spectacular. Jazz artistry today is acclaimed by intellectuals, critics, and composers, and the technical accomplishments of jazz musicians are remarkable. Jazz artists co-star with symphonic musicians at leading concert halls, and the unorthodox harmonies and syncopations of modern jazz blend with atonality, unusual modes, and the innovative contributions of modern composers like Richard Yardumian to produce new forms of "long-hair" music.

At the same time, pop music (as opposed to jazz) has been profoundly influenced by blues singing of Negro origin and also by Negro church music. It is not unusual for some white rock groups to be mistaken (on radio or records) for the Negro voices they imitate.

The influence of the *Negro dance* on the majority culture was apparent in the more extravagant antics of the jitterbug era. Commenting on dancing in the sixties, Goldman said in part: "What set the '60s apart was the way dance created a whole new milieu in the discotheque, the way the new dances totally supplanted the professional performer with the inventive amateur, and, above all, the way dance movements and body styles worked back year by year, step by step, to the roots of American dance in the rural Southern Negro culture of the turn of the century, a culture rich with residues of the tribal life of Africa."

The take-over by Negro culture is much more than a set of mechanical steps, as Goldman points out: "Following the Dance Decade from its first uptight gyrations in the original twist to its final ecstatic vibration in the African twist was like watching a mass cultural regression-cum-metamorphosis. In 10 years millions of white people danced right out of their skins into new suits of skin and bone that hung much more loosely, bent much more freely (in the oddest places!) and offered a real see-through of their souls."[4] At the same time, African dance stimulated more than a casual interest among esthetic dance groups and performers.

Negro fashions that have moved into higher status groupings seem to have two main channels of diffusion: the jazz culture and the youth culture. From these beachheads they sometimes find lodging in modified form in the middle and upper strata of white adult culture. However, more direct transplants are now possible through the increasing use of Negro television models, actors, and testimonials by Negro celebrities; it is increasingly "in" to promote the black subculture. Designers, clothing manufacturers, and fashion editors also play an important role, stimulating sales of Afro print fabrics and hair styl-

[4]Albert Goldman, "What's Deader Than Discotheques? the Dancing Sixties," *Life* (Feb. 27, 1970).

ings, easily emulated with the wig. Afro boutiques cater to the white seeking something different, or perhaps simply wishing to display his liberal racial attitudes.

Negro speech has also made deep inroads on the American language, a tongue in which the most crudite give slang prestigious acceptance; indeed, it is our language's eclectic ability to integrate foreign words, neologisms, and argot that gives it much of its prized vitality and expressiveness. Negro language seeps into standard American from many directions, beginning with the influence of song lyrics and musical interracial dialogue in jazz, rock, blues, and perhaps combinations, such as folk-rock and folk-blues.

Negroes today are regularly interviewed on radio and TV; they are quoted daily in the national press; and they interact at all social class levels, with the most picturesque and colorful speech probably emanating from the groups with least status and taking root in areas such as the white hippie subculture. Vista volunteers and social workers are another type of contact. The speech patterns are so different that some educators have found it helpful to teach standard American English to disadvantaged Negroes as a second, or foreign, language. Today's integration movement may accelerate the adoption of some Negro speech patterns by upper status levels of the population.

GROWING UP ABSURD: ROLE REVERSAL

The Status Float phenomenon is crystal-clear in today's patterns of fashion dissemination from the youth culture. For a number of years, extremes in fashion have been adopted by the youth market, perhaps to express rejection of the older generation, the Establishment, the conventional, or perhaps out of boredom or the need for self-expression. Now certain youthful fashions have been adopted by the middle-aged; these include hair styling, facial hair (for males), beach attire, casual clothes, pajamas, shoes and socks, hats, necktie styles, and informal as well as formal garments.

Scholars who have devoted their lives to analyzing the history of fashions have pointed out that clean shaving is an attempt to maintain a youthful appearance; the adoption of facial hair by boys may represent an attempt to look more adult. It may also represent a flouting of the clean-shaven Establishment. It is an interesting example of reciprocal age emulation or switching.

The contemporary youth emphasis on facial hair, to some extent imitated by adults, is not a new phenomenon. The hairy face and generally unkempt look were adopted by rebellious youth for similar reasons in the early nineteenth century. The clean-shaven look has been basically a striving for youth, a status float since it is in imitation of a low status segment of the population by those in power, but the symbolism of shaving changes when youth adopts the bearded or adult look. The beard is thus transformed into a youth symbol, at first rejected by adults and then gradually accepted, after the manner of other fashions initially rejected.

In the fifties and early sixties the radical fashion innovations adopted by youth triggered a good deal of criticism from the adult world. Middle-aged men continued to wear long, full-cut, baggy pants with cuffs, short hair, and conservative neckties. But by 1969, even in the ultraconservative world of the automotive

executive, one could find corporate presidents and vice-presidents sporting sideburns, square-toed buckled shoes, short, cuffless pants, wide, flashy polka-dot ties, sport coats, colored shirts, and even a sport shirt on occasion. They were emulating the fashions pioneered by the teen-age crowd and floating up through the collegiate market to attack the citadels of middle-aged resistance to innovation.

The fashion editor of *Playboy* magazine explained the reason for age inversion in patterns of emulation in a radio interview by WJR's J. P. McCarthy. A generation ago, he said, the teen-aged boy looked enviously at the conservatively dressed, middle-aged man. He told himself that with hard work and ambition he might some day wear similar conservative clothes and take his place behind that prestigious desk. Today, the roles are reversed. The teen-ager disdains Establishment goals and values, and flaunts his rejection in deviant fashions. Meanwhile, the aging businessman looks with envy at the new freedom of youth and wishes he could trade places. He expresses this wish, perhaps an unconscious one, in his tardy emulation of youthful dress. By the time he has adopted the style, however, the younger market segments may well have abandoned it.

The Status Float phenomenon in the youth—age symbiosis antedates the spectacle of fashion emulation. Youthful influence on adult expenditure patterns, documented by numerous marketers from the time of Eugene Gilbert, represents an upward programming of taste patterns from below. Children take part in determining the family's choice of automobile make, model, and options; their vacation or recreational expenditures; or (in the case of girls) their mothers' selection of home furnishings. Girls also often exert direct pressure on their mothers to adopt more youthful fashions, an action that sometimes leads to inappropriate stylings in clothing, hair-do, and make-up.

The growing popularity of the guitar among middle-aged adults who grew up to the sound of the big bands with heavy brass and wood-wind instrumentation constitutes still another example of the phenomenon. The oldsters may recoil in horror at the loudness of the amplifier and the strangeness of the sounds, but the very ubiquity of the instrument and the apparent ease with which sounds can be produced on it tend to arouse interest. The increased popularity of classical and folk guitar music among adults is probably due in part to increased exposure to the instrument.

FROM BLUE COLLAR TO WHITE

Marketing scholars have devoted considerable attention to the differing life-styles and their effects on the expenditure patterns of blue- and white-collar workers. They have pointed to a possible melding of the two classes, as the increasingly affluent blue-collar people move to the suburbs and acculturate. We might speculate, however, that this acculturation may, to some extent, be reciprocal. The middle class has tended to live more in the future, postponing immediate gratification. But growing secularization shortens the life-span from eternity to tomorrow, if not today, and emerging hedonism is supported by a shrinking work-week and labor-saving devices. The search today is for more immediate pleasures, and what better place to find them than among the recreational choices of the blue-collar set?

It might be useful to study patterns of diffusion in boat ownership, hunting, fishing, camping, bowling, and similar sports that are typically either blue-collar or blue-collar and upper class, rather than predominantly middle class. Hunting and fishing are popular sports for both upper and lower classes, but upper-class sportsmen seek more exotic locales. Middle-class people have now adopted the camping craze; are they also buying pick-up truck campers, first popular among working-class families who already owned pick-ups? Bowling, too, is apparently more popular among blue-collar and lower level clerical workers, but there seems to be a growing trend for participation by middle-class teens and some adults.

Interculturation may also operate both ways in the spread of taste patterns among classes; the evidence is difficult to obtain. However, the author can remember days when garish male clothing—for example, red or green suits—was worn only by the lower-class male. One cannot be certain whether today's coats of many colors are copying lower-class taste, feminine fashions, or the youth culture; perhaps they are derived from all three sources.

At one time, conservative taste prevailed in colors of automobiles; bright colors were regarded as vulgar. Did the acceptance of brighter colors begin in the large lower-class market segment? Automotive market researchers who have made extensive studies of preferences for car colors feel that a valid answer to this question may be difficult to find. (Some experts on automotive paints suspect that feminine taste also played a significant role in the acceptance of more colorful cars.) Lower-class patterns of manners and speech are also moving up the pyramid—for example, gum chewing in public and such ungrammatical expressions as "go slow," "it works good," "lay low," "who do you trust," "tastes good like a cigarette should," "me and my Winston," and "chaise lounge."

Historically, lower-class influence on fashion made its large-scale debut after the French Revolution of 1789. Members of the upper classes who wanted to keep their heads adopted lower-class dress as a disguise; colorful finery gave way to dull, ragged, and utilitarian garb. The workingman's long pantaloons replaced the gentlemen's culottes or knee-breeches.[5] The pantaloon was gradually adopted by the upper classes in American and England in the face of determined resistance by the Establishment: ". . . students at Oxford and Cambridge in England were at first directed not to wear the new long trouser styles and later were counted absent if they appeared in classes with this style of apparel. The Duke of Wellington was turned away at the door of London's most famous restaurant, Alamack's, when he tried to enter wearing long trousers. The Church opposed members of the clergy adopting this type of apparel even during the 20's (the 1820's), not only in England but in America as well. The long trousers were considered as highly undignified and immodest types of apparel and were greeted with derision and scorn wherever they first appeared."[6]

According to Nystrom, the spread of democracy appears to have involved a long-range emphasis on somber, dull clothing for men, a trend which paralleled the transfer of both political and fashion leadership from monarchs to the masses.

[5]Nystrom, *Economics of Fashion*, pp. 244–49.
[6]Nystrom, *Economics of Fashion*, pp. 306–308.

It seems likely that this democratic stress on unattractive clothing was reinforced by the austere puritanical philosophy of the Protestant ethic and the emphasis on at least outward humility.

The manufacture of ready-to-wear men's clothing began with garments designed for sailors on whaling ships in the 1830's. Clothing for Southern slave laborers was produced during the period from about 1840 until the Civil War, and the California gold rush of 1849 created a demand for miners' ready-to-wear clothing. In addition, settlers were living without women to sew for them, a condition that led to a storage of second-hand clothing, ever in demand since colonial times. The need was met by ready-mades. The ready-made apparel industry prospered during the Civil War and postwar period, supplying soldiers and veteran laborers with cheap clothing. The panic of 1873 forced many men of the upper classes to wear ready-made outfits, and depressions in 1893 and 1907 reinforced the trend toward middle- and upper-class adoption of ready-mades. Concurrently, the status of suppliers of ready-made clothing rose; Brooks Brothers, one of the early manufacturers of coarse, rough clothing for sailors, became a prestige source for ready-to-wear suits.

The fact that ready-to-wear suits and trousers are worn by the vast majority of middle-class males today is an example of the Status Float phenomenon. The practice had its beginnings in the lower classes, but the ready-made garment today competes with the one that is tailor-made. Indeed, it may be that a ready-made suit by one of the top men's suppliers of the more expensive suits outranks a suit hand-crafted by some obscure tailor. Lower-class influence on men's clothing is also apparent in men's casual clothing adapted from work clothes—jackets, Levi's, boots, and, in 1970, a sleeveless undershirt marketed as summer outerwear for men.

Women's fashions have also freely copied lower-class styles. An early example is the milkmaid clothing craze that swept Versailles during the reign of Marie Antoinette; the St. Tropez fisherman's stylings are another example. Women today have adopted the Levi and have followed men in appropriating the working-man's pantaloon. The miniskirt, which made the scene in the latter half of the 1960's, originated with English working-class girls who allegedly cut the skirts short to evade a tax based on skirt length. Although the shortened skirt ran counter to the fashions sponsored by leading designers, it was enthusiastically adopted by middle and upper classes. Attempts in 1970 to lower the skirt at the behest of prestigious fashion houses led to organized opposition—demonstrations and picketing—from organizations such as GAMS (Girls Against More Skirts).

Lower class apparel may affect middle or upper class fashions through the class backlash effect. The adoption of an upper class style by the lower class may cancel, modify, or attenuate its attractiveness in the upper class. This type of feedback reached a comical high in the fashion war between England's Charles II and France's Louis XIV. When Charles II originated a fashion, the French monarch ordered his servants to wear the style, thus making it unfit for gentlemen. According to Nystrom, colors favored by the English court were prescribed for use at French executions, which did nothing to promote the colors' popularity. What happened to the attenuated frou-frou is another example of class backlash. In the last decade of the nineteenth century, women adopted a skirt and petticoat style that produced a rustling sound, or "frou-frou." When this upper-class fashion became available in the cheaper dress lines, the upper classes chose a frou-frou with a more subdued sound.

THE SEXUAL REVOLUTION

Most adoptions of fashions by one sex from fashions worn by the other sex seem to have been made by women. Women borrow quite freely from men's fashions. Some styles, such as the ascot, appear to shift back and forth between the sexes in different eras. However, we can find a few instances where feminine fashions have achieved a limited adoption by men. One example of this phenomenon, which is a form of the status float, are flare pants, adopted first by women in the late 1960's and then by some college men and entertainers in 1969. Some men even began carrying purses.

Young, in a research monograph on fashion cycles, points out that men's fashions tend to change more gradually and imperceptibly then women's. Often the changes will be limited to barely detectable traces, but they do follow the changes in women's fashions: "with the evidence of the cycles in feminine dress as a guide, it can be seen that all the major changes in women's fashions have been followed by contour changes in men's styles. They occur a little later than in women's dress, but they bear this relation to women's dress consistently, and important changes occur only then."[7] The similarity was more pro-

[7]Young, *Recurring Cycles of Fashion, 1760–1937*, p. 178, ff.

nounced until men's fashions became relatively stabilized in the mid-nineteenth century, but subtle resemblances continue during each major contour cycle, with the feminine fashion setting the standard and the masculine following in moderated form. Men's fashions also tend to retain more residual elements from previous cycles.

In a real sense, then, we find the status float operating in major fashion contour cycles. This has not always been true, however; different periods show differing degrees of divergence between male and female fashions, and Young points out that men tended to be fashion leaders rather than followers up until the mid-eighteenth century. In the 1825–45 era, on the other hand, men's fashions became rather effeminate, featuring corsets and a distinct waist-line effect.

We have considered the influence of women's fashions on the male wearer in the context of the upward influence on the status hierarchy. There is sometimes a third stage in this float process, when some feature of masculine clothing is considered passe for ordinary wear, but the style survives on a higher level as formal attire. Young cites as examples the knee-breeches worn in court, the tail coat, the silk hat, and the skirted coat, adding, "The instances are so many that it amounts almost to a characteristic of masculine costume that features of dress pass through the two stages of everyday and formal wear before they die out."

MINORITY SPECIALTIES AND UP THE MORES!

Fashions, music, dance, and speech patterns are only a few examples of the trickle-up or Status Float phenomenon. The dominant majority has always borrowed cultural artifacts from minorities, no matter how low their status; the popularity of Mexican and oriental foods is one example. The acceptance of pizza and Polish sausage preceded the social elevation of the people who brought them to this country. We have adopted moccasins for casual wear and archery as a sport without elevating the status of the American Indian. (The popularity of archery in this country probably owes more to its use by the Indian than to its European antecedents in our cultural heritage.) Smoking tobacco is another example. Indeed, the number of borrowings traceable from lower-status groups is probably only limited by the amount of research devoted to seeking them.

As a final example of the Status Float phenomenon, we will cite the adoption of a number of customs from prostitutes. A notable instance is the high heel, originally adopted by a queen as a corrective measure for her short, dumpy figure. The style, when adopted by Parisian prostitutes, quickly spread to the middle and upper class ladies. Early commentators on the diffusion of our mores have pointed out that prostitutes pioneered in the use of rouge and lipstick. They were also the first women to smoke cigarettes in this country. The current sexual revolution may constitute another example of mores borrowed from prostitution.

Earlier hypotheses that fashions and perhaps innovation spread in a general trickle down the status pyramid were jolted by evidence that fashions, and perhaps most innovations, may trickle *across* in a horizontal pattern of diffusion. We have presented some arguments to indicate that there may also be a significant upward flow of innovative influence from lower to higher status levels, a process which we have called the Status Float phenomenon. More research is needed to document the extent of the phenomenon.

Exercise 33

Diffusion of Innovations

OBJECTIVE To demonstrate the importance of the structure of the communication system to the speed of the diffusion of innovations in a society.

This exercise demonstrates the vital role of communication to the successful diffusion and adoption of innovations. In this exercise, your instructor will assign you to one of the following communication networks. Each member of your network will receive a card. Each card will have five symbols on it. There is one symbol common to every member of your network. The task of your group is to determine the common symbol and communicate this to every member of the group. When every member of the group knows the common symbol, the innovation will have diffused to every member of your society. The only type of communication permissible is written communication and only with individuals designated by the network. Communication Nets: The symbol ○ designates individuals. Each individual may communicate directly *only* with the individual(s) specified by the connecting lines.

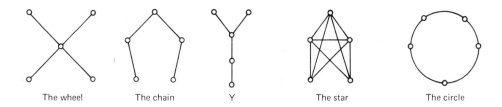

The wheel   The chain   Y   The star   The circle

Exercise 34

What's New?

OBJECTIVE To illustrate the definition of "new" in products.

Marketers are constantly introducing "new" products into the market. These "new" products differ in their degree of innovativeness. The following conceptualization of "new" has been offered to distinguish the varying degrees of innovativeness.

1. *Continuous innovation* has the least disrupting influence on established patterns. Modification of an existing product is characteristic of this type of innovation, rather than the establishment of a totally new product.
2. *Dynamically continuous innovation* has more disrupting effects than a continuous innovation, although it still does not generally alter established patterns of customer buying and product use.
3. *Discontinuous innovation* involves the introduction of an entirely new product that causes buyers to alter significantly their behavior patterns.

Determine the type of "new" that is most appropriate for the products that follow.

Reprinted with permission of RCA Consumer Electronics Division.

Reprinted with permission of General Mills, Inc.

A nice smile should be more than just a memory.

A nice smile should last a lifetime. Unfortunately, many don't. All too often they become just a memory. Because of gum disease—the major cause of tooth loss in persons over 35 —and a common cause of bad breath and that unpleasant taste in the morning.

Gum disease is an infection usually caused by a complex community of bacteria called plaque. Plaque grows and thrives beneath the gumline and in the most difficult to reach areas of the mouth.

The Water Pik® Oral Hygiene appliance is uniquely designed to complement brushing and flossing and to complete the task of plaque control.

Up to 1200 jets of water per minute reach into the deepest and most difficult to reach areas of the mouth, flushing out bacteria and odor causing food residue. This is why the Water Pik appliance is a valuable part of a complete oral hygiene program and why it's recommended by so many dentists.

If you don't like the thought of your smile becoming just a memory, remember Water Pik.

It can help a nice smile last a lifetime.

WaterPik
Oral Hygiene Appliance

Reprinted with permission of Teledyne Water Pik.

The new technology.

Burroughs "900" Series computers give you higher performance and lower cost through advanced technology.

Burroughs B 2900 computers introduce entirely new levels of price-performance and flexibility. For the first-time computer user. And for experienced computer users with requirements for interactive processing, distributed processing and heavy-duty central processing work loads.

These new systems provide up to five times the throughput performance of our entry-level B 2800 in our "800" Series. Their main memory can be expanded to five times the maximum previous capacity. Yet they occupy half as much space. They use 50 percent less power. And the monthly lease price for a B 2900 starts as low as $4,250.

This increased performance and economy comes from the use of Burroughs entirely new "micro-modular concurrent" architecture, and advanced high-density logic and memory circuits.

This architecture is made up of independent elements that process data simultaneously. For optimum efficiency and a consistently high rate of throughput.

The B 2900 is completely software-compatible with earlier Burroughs intermediate systems. No rewriting or recompiling of existing application programs is required.

And remember, every Burroughs system comes with the element that got you thinking about a computer in the first place: Increased productivity. Burroughs has understood this need of business for over 90 years. And we know it's never been more important to you than right now.

That's why we provide not only total capability in hardware, but system software, application programs, training, maintenance, business forms and supplies. We call it Total System Support. And it's there to help you realize your productivity potential.

Find out more. Call your local Burroughs office or write Burroughs Corporation, Dept. FOR-3, Burroughs Place, Detroit, Michigan 48232.

Burroughs

Reprinted with permission of Burroughs Corporation.

281

Reprinted with permission of Minolta Corporation.

Reprinted with permission of Home Box Office, Inc.

Introducing: Solar French Fries.

American fingers pop some 260,000 pounds of frozen french fries into American mouths every day.

Before they're frozen, all those fries have to be cooked in boiling oil.

Keeping that oil hot uses a lot of energy, so a company called TRW and the Department of Energy decided to put the sun to work—french frying potatoes at a potato processing plant in Oregon.

Now with the help of a TRW-designed solar energy system, this plant is cooking up the country's first solar french fries.

water as the heat transfer liquid, yet still provides the high efficiency the process must have.

What we came up with is a solar steam-generating system that's both efficient and safe for food processing.

Everybody always knew the sun could make the sidewalks hot enough to fry eggs on.

Now it's french frying potatoes—by the ton!

Idaho Potatoes. Oregon Sunshine And A TRW System.

Perched on the roof of the plant are solar collectors. Their job is to soak up enough Oregon sunshine to generate 425°F of industrial steam—which is what it takes to heat the 900 gallons of cooking oil needed to fry 20,000 pounds of potatoes every hour.

TRW engineers had to design a system that uses

A COMPANY CALLED TRW

Reprinted with permission of TRW, Inc.

NEW! Sesame RyKrisp
snack crackers
Light 'n' Tasty

Now RyKrisp®—the whole grain rye snack cracker—is lighter than ever and enhanced with the spirited flavor of whole sesame seeds. For an uplifting taste sensation, try New Sesame RyKrisp...the whole sesame seed snack cracker that's light and tasty. Use the coupon on this page... and open sesame!

Sesame
NEW!
Light 'n' Tasty

Whole grain rye snack crackers with sesame seeds

10¢ STORE COUPON **10¢**
SAVE 10¢
on your next purchase of NEW Sesame
RyKrisp

Reprinted with permission of Ralston Purina Co.

283

17

Information Processing

Marketers expose consumers to information. What happens to the information then? Does the consumer attend to the information? Comprehend it? Retain it? Dump it? Act on it? This is an exceedingly difficult question to answer because information is processed in the consumer's mind and this is not directly observable to marketers. In an effort to answer this question, marketers have measured consumers' pupil dilation, sweat levels, brain activities, and recognition speed. The articles in this section discuss the marketers' efforts in this area.

At one time, pupilometrics held the promise that consumer likes and dislikes could be revealed by measuring their pupillary responses. Berkeley Rice, in the article "Rattlesnakes, French Fries, and Pupillometric Oversell," examines the marketer's experiences with pupillometrics.

In the article "Hemispheral Lateralization: Implications for Understanding Consumer Behavior," Flemming Hansen reports on findings that indicate that humans specialize in the usage of the right and left hemispheres of their brain. Hansen discusses the implications of hemispheral lateralization on furthering our understanding of consumer information processing and consumer decision-making behavior.

RATTLESNAKES, FRENCH FRIES, AND PUPILLOMETRIC OVERSELL

The history of psychology can be summed up simply as the attempt to find out why people do what they do. To know that, however, one must first know what people really think and feel, in contrast to what they say they think or feel. Psychology's search for such knowledge over the years has resembled the search for the Holy Grail, or the philosopher's stone. Whoever found it would certainly win fame and fortune, if not tenure. He would win fortune because private industry has been engaged in a similar search for many years, and could be expected to reward the discoverer handsomely. This is the story of "pupillometrics," which seemed for a time to be the psychologists' stone everyone had

"Rattlesnakes, French Fries, and Pupillo-metric Oversell," Berkeley Rice, *Psychology Today,* February 1974. Reprinted from *Psychology Today Magazine.* Copyright © 1974, Ziff-Davis Publishing Company.

been looking for, and how it was used, flaws and all, by the advertising industry.

THE $25-BILLION QUESTION

With annual sales of more than $25 billion in 1973, advertising ranks as one of the biggest industries in the country. To appreciate just how big $25 billion is, one might consider that it equals the total combined 1973 budgets for the Departments of Justice, Commerce, Labor, State, Transportation and HUD. With so much money at stake, advertisers have understandably been curious to know just what they get for it. The question of how to measure the effectiveness of TV commercials and printed ads or even the design of products and packages has plagued industry for years, and remains today, the $25 billion question.

Of course one can always test an ad by watching its supposed effect on sales. But since so many other factors influence consumer behavior, this method can hardly claim scientific precision. Besides, most manufacturers want to know how their products will be received by the public *before* investing the millions of dollars necessary to get them to the marketplace. Another traditional method of measuring public taste has been to pretest ads or products by showing them to a representative sample of people who then answer a questionnaire about their attitudes. The trouble with this method, as most of those who use it freely admit, is that people's verbal responses often don't accurately reveal their true attitudes.

In 1960, when Eckhard Hess claimed that pupillary dilation did just that, the advertising world was immediately intrigued. Hess, a German-born psychologist at the University of Chicago, had not really discovered pupillometrics, as he called it, but he was the first to suggest how it could be used to measure a person's favorable or unfavorable response to a visual stimulus. The beauty of this new technique and what particularly appealed to both psychologists and advertisers, was that unlike verbal response, pupillary dilation is an *involuntary* physiological response, and thus an apparently infallible measure of a person's true feelings. As one of Hess's colleagues put it, "The eye cannot lie."

"EUREKA" IN THE BEDROOM

For those who like to think of the history of science as a series of "Eurekas!," the story of Hess's discovery had just the right touch of drama. According to Hess, whose pre-vious work had involved animal behavior, it all began one evening at home, as he lay in bed looking at a book of animal photographs. While he studied a particularly beautiful picture, his wife happened to look over at him and remarked that his reading light must be bad because his pupils were enlarged.

"The light is perfect," Hess replied. His wife insisted that his pupils were dilated nevertheless, then turned out her own light and went to sleep.

Hess did not. He lay awake, thinking. The next morning he arrived at his lab still thinking about what had happened the night before. He was familiar with a number of studies and observations dating back to the 18th century that suggested a relationship between pupillary response and human emotions. Pursuing his curiosity, Hess assembled a group of pictures of landscapes, added one nude female pin-up, mounted them all on similar cards, and showed them one by one to his lab assistant, James Polt. Sure enough, Polt's pupils dilated noticeably when he came to the pin-up. "Jim and I both agreed then that we might have stumbled on something really significant," Hess recalled years later, "and we immediately started research into the phenomenon."

First they designed a relatively simple "pupillometer," or "pupillograph," consisting of a movie camera that records pupillary dilation while the subject watches a stimulus. All that remained was to measure the changes in pupil size using the successive frames of the developed film. As Hess began experimenting with his new "eye camera," he soon made a number of startling discoveries. Pupillary dilation could apparently be used to measure interest, emotion, attitudes and mental difficulty. "It was as though a portion of the brain were in plain sight for the psychologist to peer at," Hess exulted. "We were both exhilarated and puzzled. It seemed unforgivable that we scientists had overlooked such an obvious conclusion for centuries."

BLACK MAGIC YEARS

The desire to expose and tinker with the brain became popular during World War II and the years that followed. Sociologists, psychologists and other specialists in human behavior had mobilized their knoweldge for the total war against the enemy. They tried to show the Government how to make gas rationing work, how to sell Savings Bonds, how to make Americans hate the Japanese, and how to persuade them to save food and fat. One task force in the Office of Strategic Services, predecessor of the CIA, developed covert tests to identify potentially resourceful intelligence agents. Others designed "black propaganda," the lies that psychological warriors used against the enemy.

Those who performed such work were proud of it, and saw their cause as noble. Their success lured the first big wave of behavioral scientists out of the universities and into postwar Government and industry as part-time consultants or full-time policymakers. Some of their work showed the manipulatory impulse that had been inevitable in their war deeds against a common enemy.

Tentative findings on subliminal perception, for instance, inspired one group to try secret salesmanship. If movie customers would buy more popcorn after a picture of it flashed on the screen—too briefly for conscious recognition—then such tricks might be used in dozens of other ways. Vance Packard's exposé, *The Hidden Persuaders,* was instrumental in stopping the subliminal tricksters before anybody knew for sure the technique would work, but rumors of new attempts continue to boil up every few years.

Sigmund Freud's notion of the unconscious filtered deep into the popular culture of the postwar period. While novelists and screenwriters retailed our hidden sex drives in books and movies, their counterparts in advertising played with the same concepts in marketing. Psychologist Ernest Dichter suggested that a hot car lets the driver "rape Mother Earth" and applied Freud's poetic insight to dozens of homely consumer products. Dichter did not stoop to the rigors of the research as most psychologists would define it, but his Motivation Research, as he called it, gave many advertisers the feeling that they had the consumer on the couch.

By the standards of the day, then, the Hess method of measuring a sample consumer's likes and dislikes was naturally attractive to industry. Within a year of his discovery, Hess had been signed up as a consultant by Marion Harper Jr., then president of Interpublic, one of the giants of the advertising world. Under Hess's direction, Interpublic set up a pupillary-research lab at the Chicago offices of Marplan, Inc., one of its marketing research subsidiaries. Harper also gave Hess a sizable grant to help finance the work at Hess's own laboratory at the University of Chicago.

Until ousted by an office coup in 1968, Harper was one of the most influential and powerful men on Madison Avenue. By using social science, computerized marketing data, and shrewd business sense, he built Interpublic into a worldwide advertising conglomerate. Harper looked on a product and its advertising as a message sent out to a large audience. Their answer, he felt, came back in terms of sales, but only after millions of dollars had been spent on the message. Harper saw in pupillometrics a way to cut the expensive risk of guessing whether consumers would say yes or no.

Within a few years Marplan was using the eye camera to gauge consumer reaction to everything from greeting cards to beer bottles to sterling-silver patterns. By the mid-1960s the company was pre-testing magazine ads, package designs, TV pilot films, and TV commercials. At the peak of the boom, Marplan tested several commercials a week (at a cost of about $2,000 each) at field labs in shopping centers in Los Angeles, Chicago, New Jersey and Texas.

Several other big ad agencies, including J. Walter Thompson, Leo Burnett, and Foote, Cone & Belding, had also begun experimenting with this new technique that promised to revolutionize the industry. But since Interpublic had Hess and his expertise under contract, it pretty much had a monopoly in the field. The monopoly did weaken a bit as Marplan researchers described their work in trade journals, and as former employees of Marplan left to set up rival pupillary-research firms. Hess scoffed at the threat of competition: "What we have that they don't have is more than six years of background in the field."

By the mid-'60s, the field was beginning to open up anyway, at least academically. Hess and his colleagues had published some of their findings in academic journals, as well as in *Science* and *Scientific American*. Feature articles on Hess and his discovery appeared in *The Saturday Evening Post* ("Your Eye Can't Lie"),

Life ("The Not So Private Eye"), and *Business Week* ("Admen try 'eye-spy' to read buyer's mind").

CRACKS IN THE WINDOW ON THE BRAIN

As more psychologists became intrigued by the new area, pupil-research labs sprang up at dozens of universities, including Michigan, Ohio State, Kentucky, Colorado, UCLA and Harvard. While these late-comers lacked Hess's background, they did bring fresh approaches and critical attitudes to pupillary research. They soon began having difficulty in replicating a number of Hess's basic experiments, particularly those that supposedly demonstrated how pupillary dilation and constriction indicated approval and disapproval.

At about the same time, many researchers in the advertising industry began having second thoughts about how well pupillary response indicated like and dislike, or even whether it offered a more accurate measure than verbal response. Although they willingly sold pupillary research during the boom years, several former Marplan executives now say they never had all that much confidence in the technique. Elliot Young, a former Marplan project manager who now presides over a New Jersey firm called Perception Research Services, recalls: "It was never really accepted by people in industry because of the dilation-constriction problem. We know something is there; it's real, it does happen, and it could have great application. But it's a very highly controversial measure.

"Suppose a guy tells you he can't stand that ad," says Young. "And suppose, contrary to his verbal response, he has tremendous pupil dilation. Which one do you believe? If you present those results to top management as proof of the approval of their ad, they'll tell you you're a nut.

RATTLESNAKES VS. BUNNIES

"The problem of like or dislike is really the crux of the whole issue," says Young, "and personally I just don't believe pupil response measures that. Let's say you show a picture of a rattlesnake to some people, and you get a constriction. Or let's say you show a *Playboy* centerfold to some men and you get a dilation. Sure, you can assume these reactions indicate like and dislike. But suppose I'm testing a TV commercial, or a magazine ad, and I get a certain pupil response. Does that indicate like or dislike? I don't think so. I think it really measures the degree of interest, of attention, and that's what I use pupillary response for now.

"Isn't that what's really important anyway? Let's face it. Without attention, like or dislike is irrelevant. I'm not so concerned about whether he dilates or constricts. I'm looking for a significant pupil response either way. What I worry about is the guy who shows no pupil response. Then your ad really has a problem. Suppose you show a pretty girl just before you mention or show the product, and the pupils dilate. It may not tell anything about the opinion of the product, but it's certainly better than falling asleep."

Another factor that cast doubt on the usefulness of pupillary research as a measure of like and dislike was that the pupil also varies in size according to the degree of difficulty or mental concentration required. The conflict between the two measures didn't cause much concern in the ad-

vertising community during most of the 1960s, but it does now. Wallace Wallace, who runs a Philadelphia advertising and marketing research firm called Associates for Research in Behavior, did a good deal of pupillary work at one time, but no longer. "We pushed it for a while," says Wallace, a Ph.D. in psychology, "but we stopped using it around 1970 because it simply didn't predict what it had been claimed to predict. It was supposed to measure both like and dislike, and degree of interest or difficulty. But if you dilate, does that mean you like the ad, or that it's tough to understand? Pupillary research is still potentially a valuable tool, but it gives ambiguous results."

By the late 1960s, the ambiguities of pupillary research caused most of those in the advertising industry to lose faith in its ability to measure like and dislike, although many still feel it can be useful in measuring arousal. But even this limited application raises problems. For example, the eye may not even be looking at the advertiser's product when the pupil dilates. In one test of an ad for frozen French fries, the advertisers were pleased at the amount of pupillary dilation until they learned that the subjects were generally looking at the steak in the picture, rather than the French fries.

MACHINERY TO MEASURE THE PUPIL

Attempts to deal with this and other problems in the field of pupillary research have led to the development of equipment far more sophisticated than Hess's simple eye camera. Today, you can buy a TV pupillometer which projects the pupil's dilations and constrictions, and provides a precise and continuous record of its diameter. Whittaker Corporation's Space Sciences Division, in Waltham, Massachusetts, sells a variety of pupillometers at prices ranging from $7,600 to $10,000. It also makes a combined TV pupillometer and "eye-view monitor" that not only measures and records pupillary dilation, but also projects on a separate screen the scene the viewer is watching and the exact point of his gaze. This combined system runs about $13,600 stripped, and more than $20,000 with such extras as a three-channel computer-compatible recorder for the pupillometer, and a video-tape recorder for the eye-view monitor. One of these systems is now being used to test the layouts in Sears catalogues.

In its promotional brochures, Whittaker carefully describes pupil diameter "as an indicator of arousal or interest," and omits any reference to its relationship to like or dislike. But even this latest bit of gadgetry doesn't solve all the problems. Harding Bush, Whittaker's product manager for this equipment, raises another issue: the nature of the product being tested, and the degree of arousal. "Just how excited can you get about French-fried potatoes or detergents?" asks Bush. "Now you take the average male and show him pictures of nude women, and you probably would get a much more significant response than you would with potatoes."

With all these ambiguities and problems to contend with, pupillary researchers face a far more complex task than anyone realized back in 1960. Hess still believes firmly in the value of his invention; other psychologists push forward with pupillary research, although at a less frenzied pace; Whittaker Corp. and a few other makers of pupillometers and eye-movement monitors still manage to find customers in a variety of fields of research. But in the advertising industry, the boom is over. Many of the firms that bought a lot of expensive pupillary-response equipment or invested serious money in the field now feel badly burned.

OVERSELLING EXPERTISE

Considering the immense sums of money involved, the advertising industry's eagerness to apply promising research should not be surprising. If you were paying a million dollars a minute for a commercial during the Superbowl, you too might be a little nervous about its effectiveness, a bit curious to know what you're getting for your money, and somewhat overeager to underwrite any research discovery that promised to tell you.

Howard Anderson, a marketing consultant to Biometrics in Cambridge, Massachusetts, and a graduate of Harvard Business School, has watched this process occur with pupillary research and earlier discoveries. "Advertising is a trendy kind of business," he explains, "partly because they spend such a phenomenal amount of money on it, and yet no one really knows if it's spent wisely. So they occasionally follow a Pied Piper who turns out to be right, but more often wrong. Take subliminal advertising, for example, or the whole field of motivational research. You don't hear much about them any more. Yet the whole advertising world went crazy over them until further research showed them to be ineffective.

"The ad agencies are always trying to convince the advertisers that all their money is being well spent, but the companies always wonder if it's really worth it. You take those great Alka-Seltzer ads, you know, 'I can't believe I ate the whole thing,' and 'Try it, you'll like it.' They were really creative, and won all the awards, but they weren't effective in terms of sales, so Alka Seltzer changed agencies. Whereas the Anacin ads, the terrible ones showing the hammer hitting the head, were very effective in terms of sales."

Since sales, rather than creativity is the name of the multibillion-dollar game of advertising, those who play it will undoubtedly continue to grab at any new discoveries from the psychology labs that promise to reveal some key to human behavior. The trouble is everyone seems to oversell the promise of the research. The professors need grants, consultancies and affirmation to keep their research going; the advertising and marketing-research firms need expertise to offer their clients; the agencies make money only when they come up with some way to talk the companies into spending some; and the companies can't afford to pass up any potentially valuable knowledge that could help them or their competitors.

But sooner or later, those in search of the psychologist's stone must recognize that no single technique will accurately predict human behavior. Fortunately for us all, the human psyche always proves too complex, too stubborn to submit to a single measuring device. The best we can hope for is that by checking and balancing each other, the thousands of psychologists now at work in universities, business, and Government can slowly extend our limited insight into why people do what they do.

HEMISPHERAL LATERALIZATION: IMPLICATIONS FOR UNDERSTANDING CONSUMER BEHAVIOR

Interest in hemispheral lateralization is increasing among psychologists (Lindzay and Norman 1977), brain researchers (Wittrock 1977), and psychiatrists (Wexler 1980). It has been found that humans specialize in the use of the right and left hemispheres of their brain. Whereas the left hemisphere is primarily responsible for traditional cognitive activities relying on verbal information, symbolic representation, sequential analysis, and the ability to be conscious and report what is going on, the right brain—without the individual being able to report verbally about it—is more concerned with pictorial, geometric, timeless, and nonverbal information.

"Hemispheral Lateralization: Implications for Understanding Consumer Behavior," Flemming Hansen, *Journal of Consumer Research*, June 1981, Vol. 8, pp. 23–37, published by the Journal of Consumer Research, Inc. Reprinted by permission.

Students of consumer behavior are beginning to speculate about the implications of the specialized functioning of the brain. For instance, it is proposed that even when attention—in the sense it is normally referred to in advertising research—is not present, it is still possible for the individual to receive and store information. Moreover, it is proposed that this process is particularly efficient with pictorial material, and that the information is stored in a holistic, unedited, nonverbal fashion very different from the way we normally store verbal and similar information (Krugman 1977).

Likewise, the provocative findings by Zajonc (1968) regarding the effects of "mere exposure" are interesting. It is possible that the increased liking he observes resulting from repeated exposures could be explained as a result of predominantly right brain information processing. In the discussion of the effects of advertising on society, it is claimed that advertising has unfortunate long-run effects in addition to the more immediate effects that can be identified (Ottesen 1980; Packard 1957).

It is, however, hard to see how such secondary effects can be explained by means of the conceptual framework underlying existing advertising research, and it is even more difficult to imagine how such effects could be identified with the measurement tools used by the advertising researcher. Here, also, contemporary brain research may contribute. The growing understanding of hemispheral lateralization suggests that individuals may be able to receive and to store information in ways very different from those normally assumed to be at work.

Before these and other implications are covered in more detail, parts of the research on left/right brain functioning are reviewed. This is done by describing a few properties of the human brain, which are necessary prerequisites for understanding this type of research. Following this, some of the more important research findings are presented. Research methodologies are then described, and, implications of hemispheral lateralization for selected areas within consumer behavior are considered. The implications for understanding long-run effects of advertising and other types of mass communication are evaluated, and, finally, research needs in the area are discussed.

SOME PROPERTIES OF THE HUMAN BRAIN

Hemispheral lateralization has been known for many years. It is well established (Wittrock 1977) that impressions from the left field of view, left ear, and left side of the body are transmitted to sensory areas in the right side of the brain, and vice versa. However, that the left and right half of the brain may treat information very differently is a more recent observation. In spite of the fact that fundamentally different processes seem to be involved, this has remained unobserved by neurophysiologists for many years.

Before the implications of this research are discussed, however, it is necessary to review briefly some properties of the human brain. As illustrated in Figure A, the human brain is composed of two almost identical halves. Much is currently known about the special functions of the various areas of the brain, and some of this knowledge is summarized in Figure A. In the present context it is the cerebral cortex in particular that is of interest. The control of the senses and of sensory inputs are located in these areas, and thought processes and decision making in particular activate these parts.

An important feature of this almost symmetrically structured brain is the way in which the two brain halves are related to each other. This connection first occurs through the corpus callosum (Figure A), which is a tissue of millions of nerve cells with widely spread connections in the left as well as in the right hemisphere. In animal experimentation and, in some instances, with man, this interconnection can be disrupted. When that is done, it becomes possible to study the specialized functioning of the two hemispheres.

It has been known for many years that sensual impressions received from the environment are dealt with in a hemisphere-specialized fashion. Most of what is received through the right ear or what is

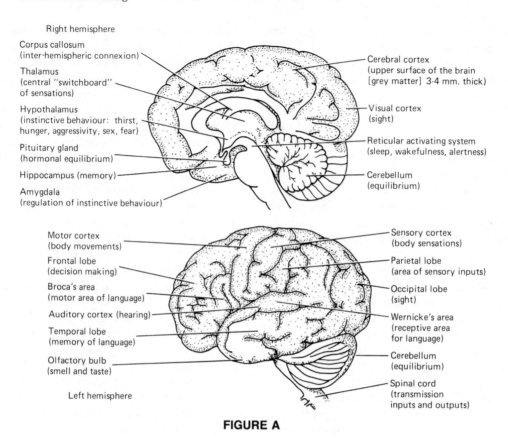

Right hemisphere

Corpus callosum
(inter-hemispheric connexion)

Thalamus
(central "switchboard"
of sensations)

Hypothalamus
(instinctive behaviour: thirst,
hunger, aggressivity, sex, fear)

Pituitary gland
(hormonal equilibrium)

Hippocampus (memory)

Amygdala
(regulation of instinctive behaviour)

Cerebral cortex
(upper surface of the brain
[grey matter] 3-4 mm. thick)

Visual cortex
(sight)

Reticular activating system
(sleep, wakefulness, alertness)

Cerebellum
(equilibrium)

Motor cortex
(body movements)

Frontal lobe
(decision making)

Broca's area
(motor area of language)

Auditory cortex (hearing)

Temporal lobe
(memory of language)

Olfactory bulb
(smell and taste)

Left hemisphere

Sensory cortex
(body sensations)

Parietal lobe
(area of sensory inputs)

Occipital lobe
(sight)

Wernicke's area
(receptive area
for language)

Cerebellum
(equilibrium)

Spinal cord
(transmission
inputs and outputs)

FIGURE A

felt with the right hand is transmitted to the left hemisphere, and in the same way responses made with the right hand or other parts of the right side of the body and controlled by processes occurring in the left brain. A somewhat similar specialization relates to the eyes; however, rather than having the left eye connected with the right brain, and the right eye with the left brain, the specialization is such that all information streaming from the left part of the visual field (defined as what is on the left of the fixation point) is transmitted to the right brain, and vice versa. This specialization of sensual processes is important because it makes it possible in an experimental setting to control what

side of the brain receives the information being transmitted.

In dealing with brain lateralization, a peculiar complication arises, because in some instances of left-handedness the hemispheral specialization is more or less reversed. It is estimated that in approximately one-fourth of the cases of extreme left-handedness, the right brain performs the same functions as those by the left half of the brain in right-handed individuals. It is not known to what extent this reversal is inherited or to what extent it is acquired in early childhood. The phenomenon, however, does give rise to research complications, which sometimes have been avoided by securing right-handed subjects only.

SOURCES OF INFORMATION

As described before, the corpus callosum is the major connecting link between the left and the right hemispheres. Certain extreme cases of epileptic diseases have been successfully treated by cutting through the corpus callosum and, thereby, disconnecting the two brain halves. Most patients who have undergone this kind of surgery seem to function normally afterwards. More thorough examination, however, reveals remarkable differences.

Some of the earliest cases of this kind of surgery were carried out by Bogen and Vogel (1962); studies of the patients' hemispheral, psychological lateralization were carried out by Sperry (1973) and his coworkers. They found, for example, that if a pair of scissors was presented to the left visual field (Figure B), and the individual was asked what was seen, the person answered "scissors." If, on the contrary, the pair of scissors was presented to the left hand or to the left visual field, the patient was not able to report anything back. If, however, the pair of scissors was presented to the left visual field, and the respondent

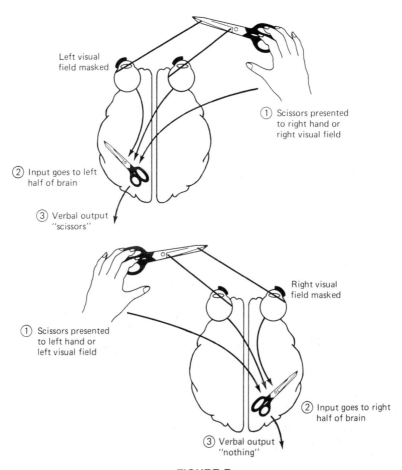

FIGURE B

was asked to pick up, with his left hand, a similar item among the several items placed within reach of his left hand, he would easily pick up the scissors.

Moreover, if the item presented was a wristwatch, and the respondent was asked to select, with his left hand, an item from several that did not include a wristwatch, but included an alarm clock, the respondent would pick up the clock in favor of other items with shapes more similar to the wristwatch. The conclusion from this observation has been that the right brain—being nonverbal—is able to carry out some symbolic information handling.

The observations by Sperry (1973) and Gazzaniga (1977) on patients with intersected brain halves have been of extreme importance to the study of hemispheral lateralization. Moreover, these observations have largely been confirmed by findings from patients with more or less extensive damage to the left and/or to the right brain. Similar observations have been made with patients whose left or right brain has momentarily stopped functioning, either due to drugs or by means of electrical inhibition.

A wealth of interesting findings are reported by Deglin (1976) from Russia. Electroconvulsive therapy (ECT) is a treatment occasionally applied to psychotic patients. By this action, part of the brain is momentarily set out of function by an electric shock. It can be done with the left or right brain, so that it is possible to study the behavior of the patient with only half of the brain functioning. From research on such patients Deglin concludes, regarding the "left-brain person":

> A deterioration has occurred in those aspects of his mental activity which underlie imaginal thinking. Those aspects of his mental activity which underlie abstract, conceptual thinking have been retained

and even improved. This stratification of the psyche is accompanied by an optimistic emotional outlook (p. 10).

Regarding the "right-hemisphere person" Deglin writes:

> The right hemisphere person manifests an impairment in those aspects of mental activity which are the basis of abstract, conceptual thinking while those aspects linked with imaginal thinking have been retained and even improved. This type of stratification of the psyche is accompanied by a negative emotional outlook (p. 13).

A third approach to the study of lateral specialization relies on control of stimulation transmitted to normal individuals, that is, research on persons with intact corpus callosum and normal interaction between the two brain halves. This research has provided findings corresponding to those resulting from the two first approaches. However, it has also been found that in normal individuals the interaction between the two brain halves is extremely strong. It is not that either of the brain halves monopolizes the handling of the various kinds of information, rather it seems to be a matter of relative dominance.

In a review of this research, Kimura (1973) finds that when it comes to visual information the left brain dominates the handling of letters and words, whereas the right brain is superior in tasks, such as location of points in two dimensions, enumeration of dots and forms, matching of slanted lines, and depth perception. Similarly, with regard to auditory information, Kimura reports that the left brain is superior with words, nonsense syllables, and backward speech, whereas the right hemisphere is superior with regard to musical patterns and nonspeech sounds.

Among manual tasks, left-brain

dominance has been observed in connection with skilled movements and free movements during speech. The right brain, on the other hand, has been found superior in locating items that cannot be seen.

NATURE OF HEMISPHERAL SPECIALIZATION

Throughout history, many psychologists, philosophers, and others have pointed at a possible dichotomic structure of the human mind. Some of these dichotomies— with the left-brain term mentioned first— have been pointed out by Bogen (1977):

Rational versus metamorphic (Bruner)

Active versus receptive (Deikman)

Secondary versus primary (Freud)

Realistic versus impulsive (Hilgaard)

Directed versus free (John Hobbes)

Differential versus existential (William James)

Positive versus mythic (Levy-Strauss)

Rational versus intuitive (Maslow)

Sequential versus multiple (Neizer)

Compare these with some of the major differences between right- and left-brain processes as suggested by Ornstein (1973), who maintains that the left brain works sequentially, temporally, verbally, intellectually, causally, logically, and argumentatively, in contrast with the right-brain processes that are more diffuse, spatial, intuitive, and musical.

In summary, the following are some of the major differences between left- and right-brain processes (Lundsgaard 1978):

The human brain—in contrast with the brain of all other species—is significantly more laterally specialized.

The lateral specialization accounts for the flexibility of the human brain, including its ability to use language and symbolic representations.

The left cerebral hemisphere on normal individuals controls speech, arithmetic, and symbolic information handling.

The right hemisphere controls visual as well as auditory (and musical) impressions.

Normally both hemispheres are active together, interacting through the connecting corpus callosum; this may account for the richness of human mental abilities.

Some people are left-brain dominated and others are right-brain dominated.

The extent to which a person becomes left- and/right-brain dominated depends partly on inherited factors and partly on the kind of training, i.e., stimulation, received during childhood.

Left-brain dominated persons tend to rely more heavily on traditional verbal, symbolic problem-solving processes, and right-brain dominated persons are more influenced, and possibly controlled, by spatial, imaginative impressions.

Thus, some individuals are more likely to rely on verbal elements, whereas others may act directly on pictorial representations, storing complete pictures of events and sequences of events that are then utilized in later situations.

WHAT CAN BE MEASURED?

Students of hemispheral lateralization have relied on a number of measurement approaches normally not used by the consumer researcher. One reason for this is the complicated methodological problems associated with the study of hemispheral specialization.

An important methodological question is whether relative hemispheral dominance is an individual trait characterizing a person's overall way of approaching and handling information, or is situational, in that different informational inputs lead to more or less dominating left- or right-brain processes. If the first is true, one may expect to find stable patterns in the way in which different individuals make decisions and apply information—patterns that occur across different situations—though such individual differences need not be invariant through the entire life span of the individual. If, on the other hand, situational differences determine the relative dominance of the left versus right hemisphere, the individual must have the ability to rely on the left as well as on the right brain type of information processing, and some mechanism in the specific situation determines which will occur. This is in line with Hansen (1977), who proposes that consumers can make choices in very different ways depending on situational factors and on the nature of the problem.

Another methodological problem relates to the interaction that occurs between the two brain halves in normal individuals. This interaction makes it difficult to be sure that experimental manipulations aimed at providing information to either of the two brain halves have been successful, and it forces the researcher to use special techniques to ensure that separate right- or left-brain responses are being measured. The hardware used in such studies is, therefore, often complicated. Some approaches require instruments making it possible to control the information transmitted to the experimental subject in a much more minute manner than is normally done in studies of communica-

tion effects. Other approaches rely on highly complicated electronic measurements.

Still other methodological problems follow from the interaction between treatment, measurement, and individual differences. Some methodologies are characterized by the measurements they apply. This is especially so with some of the more "hardware-requiring" methodologies. Here variations in measurement may be studied either among different individuals, or by making several observations of the same individual to study the effect of different treatments. Other methodologies are characterized by their distinctive treatment of the stimulation. Here it becomes possible to study effects of controlled stimulation with a variety of dependent measures. Still other approaches utilize subjects with known individual differences. Patients with known brain damage are extreme cases, but in recent studies individuals with other, less dramatic, differences have been studied. Some of these approaches are discussed in the following sections.

Tachistoscope Technique

In the earliest studies of split-brain patients, a tachistoscope was used for presentation of information either to the left or to the right visual field of the patient. Several devices have been invented for this purpose. Today the most commonly used is illustrated in Figure C. By means of a one-way mirror, it is possible to show pictures in the left or in the right visual field after the respondent has fixed his attention on a particular point. This tachistoscope is also used in the study of normal individual brain functioning.

The technique can be used either for

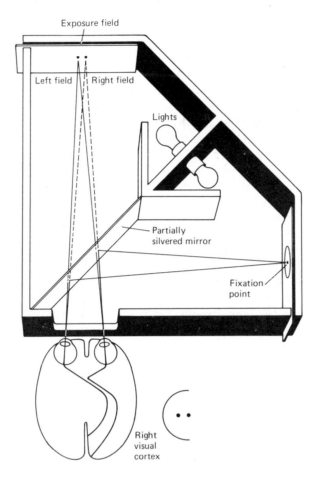

FIGURE C
Two-Field Tachistoscope[1]

[1]The two-field tachistoscope is used for study of visual perception. When the fixation field is lighted, an observer sees a reflection of the field in the partially silvered mirror. He is asked to fixate on a point in the center of the field. Then the fixation-field light is turned off and the exposure-field light is simultaneously turned on for a few milliseconds. The image on the exposure field passes through the partially silvered mirror and is briefly seen by the observer. At the end of the exposure, the fixation-field light comes on and the exposure-field light goes off. By placing the exposure image in the left or right visual field, as desired, the experimenter can selectively stimulate either the right or the left visual cortex.

identification of individual differences in the respondent's use of left- versus right-brain processing, or it can be used to study how different pieces of information give rise to different responses, depending on whether they are presented in the left or in the right visual field.

Dichotic Listening

This is similar to the tachistoscope procedure, except that it uses auditory stimulation. In one use of the technique, two different soundtracks send different messages to the left and to the right ear. This can be done with the use of two earphones and stereo equipment with completely separate left and right soundtracks. For example, two different melodies can be played, one to the left ear and the other to the right ear, and from the respondent's report of what is being heard, the dominating brain half can be identified. Alternatively, one can use words, sentences, nonsense syllables, or figures as signals.

Two procedures are used to eliminate the problem of different individuals having different hearing capacities with the left and right ears. In the first approach, prior to the experiment, the individual adjusts the loudness of the two soundtracks, until s/he judges them to be equal. In the other approach, the same word pairs (or other stimuli pairs) are presented in reverse order to both ears. Following this, the number of correctly identified messages to the right (x) ear and the number of correct words identified by the left ear (y) are counted. A ratio indicating the degree of right- versus left-ear dominance is then computed.

$$\frac{(x - y)}{(x + y)} \cdot 100$$

The larger this ratio is, the more prominent is the right ear, i.e., the left brain.

Like the tachistoscope technique, dichotic listening can be used to identify individual differences, as well as to identify differences in the way in which various kinds of information is handled.

Electroencephalogram (EEG)

Whereas the tachistoscope and the dichotic listening techniques control incoming

stimulation, the EEG technique is unique in terms of the measurements it applies. The EEG measures the amount and pattern of electrical activity in the cerebral cortex, with the use of electrodes placed on the surface of the skull. For a normal relaxed individual, stable (8–13 per second) fluctuation (alpha waves) can be observed. When the individual is activated, for instance by looking at an interesting picture, faster and lower amplitude waves are observed (beta waves).

When EEG is used to study hemispheral differences, the concern is with the pattern of alpha and beta waves in the two hemispheres. The measurements from the side of the right brain are obtained by connecting an electrode at a point a little below the top of the skull to a point at the neck of the right side of the skull. Similarly, information about the left brain is obtained with electrodes located on the left side of the skull.

By studying the frequency with which alpha waves occur in the left and in the right hemisphere, it is possible to learn about the relative use of the two hemispheres when the individual is engaged in different tasks. This procedure has been applied by Appel, Weinstein, and Weinstein (1979) in an attempt to test right/left brain processing when watching commercials. Several problems are connected with the technique, however. First, the results may differ depending on the precise location of the electrodes on the skull. Moreover, this may interact with the type of message being transmitted. Second, it can be extremely difficult to relate the measured fluctuations to more specific aspects of the message being presented. Imagine EEG measures being taken while a 30-second commercial is being aired. Should one compare the average of the left- and right-brain activities during the entire commercial, or should one compare the brain activities occurring while different sections of the commercial are being aired? The latter would relate brain processes to different parts of the commercial, which could have diagnostic value. However, the activity at any given time may be a function of the information received at the same time, or it may be a function of what was received at some earlier point in time.

Also, this technique can be used to study individual, as well as situational, differences. So far, applications have concentrated on identifying different ways of handling incoming information, although findings (Appel, Weinstein, and Weinstein 1979) suggest that individual differences may be established in this fashion.

Emisionstomgraph Technique

When brain activities increase, blood circulation in that part of the brain also increases. When radioactive material is added to the blood, it is possible to measure variations in the intensity of the blood streaming through various parts of the surface of the brain. This emisionstomgraph technique has been developed by Lassen, Ingvar, and Skinhøj (1978) to study blood circulation and brain defects. The technique provides dynamic colored pictures of the intensity of the activity in various areas of the brain, and may have promising implications for the study of hemispheral specialization.

Wechsler Adults Intelligence Scale (WAIS)

The most frequently used intelligence test for adults is WAIS (Freeman 1962). The test, almost half a century old, has been modified several times. It has two parts,

verbal and performance. Although the original purpose of this test was not to measure differences in levels of activity on the two brain halves, it has been suggested that the test does measure aspects of left- as well as right-hemispheral activities.

Some of the test items included in the WAIS battery are particularly suited for testing left-brain abilities, such as, a test measuring verbal ability abstraction, a vocabulary test, and a test measuring arithmetic abilities. Similarly, several items from the performance score are particularly suitable for testing right-brain activities. Among these are the picture completion item (measuring visual abilities), the cube test (measuring visual-spatial abilities and memory), and a puzzle test (measuring visual-synthetic abilities).

Testing for Brain Damage

This is widely used among psychologists. Tests used for this purpose attempt to reveal the extent to which an individual suffers from organic damage to the cortex, resulting in symptoms such as reduced memory, reduced ability to learn, slow thinking, emotional retardedness, unrest, sleepiness, increased disorientation, and inability to make judgments. Some test items used for this purpose are primarily aimed at identifying left-brain activities (Theilgaard 1979).

Tests particularly suited for measuring left-brain capabilities are the "word-pair test," which measures the ability to imprint words by recording how fast and how many word pairs an individual is able to learn, the "copy repetition test," and "the subtraction test," the latter measuring arithmetic abilities. Test items suitable for identifying right-brain capabilities are the Goldstein-Scheerer cube test, measuring the ability to handle abstract visual-spatial patterns, and Andersen's ability gestalt test, measuring visual imprinting and memory.

Stroop Test

In this test the individual is confronted with a perceptual conflict. Thus, if an individual is asked how many figures there are in the sequence below, the correct answer would be five:

44444

To arrive at this answer one would have to rely extensively on left-brain activities, whereas the answer "four" would indicate right-brain activities. Similar conflicts can be constructed between colors and names of colors, and naming of high and low musical pitches. When a sequence of such tests is carried out, individuals may reveal right- or left-brain dominance in their handling of the information. Like the WAIS and the brain-damage tests, it can be used primarily to identify individual differences. Cohen and Martin (1975) have applied this procedure successfully in an attempt to study left- versus right-brain conflicts in interpreting musical impressions.

Conjunctive Lateral Eye Movements (CLEM)

These have been proposed by several authors as a measure of the extent to which the right or the left brain dominates information processing. The background for this is an observation made in studies of eye movements in response to electrical stimulation of the brain. The findings show that the eyes move to the right when the left hemisphere is stimulated, whereas they move to the left when the right half is stimulated. It has been suggested that this can be used to identify differences in hemispheral activity by observing to what side the respondent most frequently looks when thinking over an issue. There is, however, strong disagreement over the validity of the method (Ornstein 1973; Theilgaard 1973). Part of the problem is that the direction in which the eyes are moving may be a function of a very complex interaction among the two brain halves, as well as of the particular test situation.

As discussed earlier, the right hemisphere is not constrained by traditional logic; rather, it is artistic or creative in its way of dealing with impressions. In contrast, the left brain is analytical and systematical. With this background, it is natural to suggest that creativity tests may reveal whether an individual relies more or less on right versus left brain information processing. There is also evidence (Cropley and Field 1969) that what is being measured with creativity tests is very different from what is being measured with traditional IQ tests. So far, however, these measurement techniques have not been used in the study of hemispheral specialization, where they have a potential for identifying individual differences.

The individual's use of the left or right hand in gesticulating during conversation has been suggested to relate to brain dominance (Kimura 1973). Again, however, validation is lacking.

Measurements of the pupil size (pupillometrics) have been used to indicate brain activities (Watson and Gatchel 1979), but not to study differential effects. What is being measured is most frequently believed to be involvement, activity, or engagement in the issue (Hess 1972).

As suggested earlier, many psychologists have proposed dichotomies that more or less directly reflect the kind of differences found between the specialized functions of the left and of the right brain. Therefore, it is not surprising to find that many personality, aptitude, and similar tests include dimensions that may relate to the phenomena discussed here. These tests may provide valuable sources for the researcher trying to develop questionnaire items through which individual differences can be identified.

IMPLICATIONS FOR CONSUMER BEHAVIOR RESEARCH

The findings on hemispheral lateralization of the human brain have implications for the study of consumer behavior. In the following sections of this paper, some of the more obvious implications are discussed—attention processes, pictorial communication, effects of mere exposure, involvement, and individual differences.

Attention Processes

Attention has been studied by observational procedures, such as observation of eye movements and the pupillometer, or based on measures of recall and recognition after tachistoscope exposure. In an excellent review, Broadbent (1977) concludes:

> For what it is worth, therefore, there seems to be sketchy evidence for at least two stages of perceptual selection. The early global, or the low frequency stage packages information from the environment into different segments, each of which can then be attended or rejected. . . .
>
> A later inquiry, or verification stage, works with more detailed information from the original package or segments, and is perhaps more affected by semantic context, by the pleasantness of a word, by co-occurrence probability of detailed features such as sequential probability of letters in words.

One may speculate that the "early global" or "low frequency stage" is predominantly a right-brain process, whereas the later inquiry, or verification stage, implies that the left brain also becomes involved. Moreover, it seems that, whereas the left-brain type of attention can only be maintained for a limited amount of time, the right-brain type of attention is not subject to the same timing process (Kimura 1973). Thus, one can imagine that only if sufficient psychic energy—involvement— is generated, will the extensive inquiry or verification stage occur. In other cases, however, only the first stage is reached, and information is received only in the sense that it gets "packed into different segments."

This suggestion is also in line with the observation by Krugman (1977) that when right hemispheral processes dominate (as in primary attention) recognition is possible, whereas recall requires the involvement of the left-hemispheral type of processes. That is, recognition requires that stored images become activated, whereas recall requires a much higher level of verbal and cognitive activity.

A mechanism like the one just described could, among other things, explain aspects of advertising effects hitherto not understood. The effects of brand names, trade marks, and the like could result primarily from such an elementary unedited storage of total impressions—effects that could be almost proportionate with the number of exposures.

In this connection, one may ask in what form do the informational images formed in the first stage of the attentional processes get stored? Under what conditions does this occur? And, how and when can the information influence subsequent behavior? Additionally, questions must also be answered about the role of forgetting. Do such "unedited" impressions last only a short time? Do they disappear, if they are not reinforced? How frequent are reinforcements needed in order to maintain them?

Pictorial Communication

Very little is understood about the role of pictorial (and musical) material in the communication process. Similarly, the role of design and layout has been only scarcely researched (Hubert and Holbrock 1980; Mitchell 1980). A better understanding and theories of these processes are needed.

Linked to Broadbent's two-step theory of perception and interpreted in terms of hemispheral specialization, a hierarchical theory of picture perception could imply:

Step 1: As in Broadbent's first step of attention, pictorial material is perceived and primarily treated in a holistic fashion in the right hemisphere, where a complete image is stored.

Step 2: a) During interaction between the left and right hemispheres, holistically perceived images are de-

coded, and information relating to relevant attributes is processed and stored, or

b) The images are stored holistically and unedited.

Step 3: In subsequent decisions, the individual may, depending on the situation, rely upon:

a) the encoded—image-like—information stored in the right brain, or

b) the coded attributional information of the left brain.

In Step 3b, choice processes like those assumed in multiattribute models occur (Hansen 1977). In Step 3a, behavior may have great similarity with routinized response behavior (Howard 1977). This suggestion is hypothetical, and much more complicated, or different, brain processes may be involved. Nevertheless, the specialization of the right brain in noncognitive, nonverbal, pictorial, holistic gestalt perception, and of the left brain in verbal, cognitive, symbolic, attributional information processing suggests that the right brain plays a critical role, especially in connection with pictorial information.

Choice Behavior

The previous section has primarily dealt with the special role of right-hemispheral processes in connection with information exposure. There are problems also with regard to the way in which the specialization expresses itself in choice behavior. In this connection, it is worth noting that Olshavsky and Granbois (1979), after reviewing the literature on decision making, conclude: "For many purchases a decision process never occurs, not even on the first purchase."

And, looking for alternative ways in which choices can be explained, they write:

> . . . , they can be made on the basis of surrogates of various types; or they can even occur on a random or superficial basis. Further research, free of the prepurchase decision assumption, may identify still other ways.

Basically, what they are saying is that we can observe choices being made with little or no awareness, seemingly influenced by past information, and without the occurrence of cognitive processes of the kind associated with left-brain activities. Such choices are particularly found in areas where brand loyalty can be observed. Such loyalty occurs where choices are frequently repeated, problems are few, and the individual is not much concerned with a single choice. These, however, are the kinds of conditions discussed before, and the choices may be made primarily based on right-hemispheral activities, where simple recognition of an alternative elicits the choice.

If this proposition is valid, the question arises of how information, received holistically and stored as images, may influence such choices. Here the communication model proposed by Zajonc (1968) is of interest. In his "mere exposure" hypothesis, he suggests that with repeated exposure, stimuli will become more positively evaluated. Further, he maintains that this positive evaluation may result from repeated exposure alone. He compares the evaluations of more and of less frequently used words, and finds a strong positive correlation between exposure and liking, with the more frequently used words being the most

positively evaluated. However, as Zajonc points out, it is not clear whether the most frequently used words are positively evaluated because they are frequent or whether they are used more frequently because they are positively evaluated. Consequently, he turns to studies where exposures have been experimentally manipulated, and shows that subject's liking of nonsense words, figures resembling Chinese characters, and photographs increases with the number of exposures.

It may be that "mere exposure" is a dominant factor when new and uninvolving concepts are at stake. The conditions under which Zajonc has shown the principle to work may very well be where right-brain processing dominates. When involvement is stronger and when stimuli are familiar, stimuli will become associated with known concepts and cognitive processes may take over, which in turn may counteract the "mere exposure effect."

Zajonc (1980) has also shown that positive evaluation following from mere exposure can be established under conditions where we would expect right-brain processes to dominate. Exposing subjects very briefly to stimuli prior to a sorting task, he finds that even though the stimulation is so short that respondents are not aware of its occurrence, they, in the subsequent sorting task, prefer those stimuli to which they had previously been exposed.

The role of emotional conditioning, as discussed by Kroeber-Riel, Hemberle, and von Keitz (1979), may also be seen in this light. They suggest that in some areas:

> The consumer is not interested in the substantial properties such as the ingredients

contained in soup or vermicelli. In general, he will rely upon the fact that the soup purchased comes up to a normal standard of quality, and his attitude towards the product is influenced only very little by means of product specific information and the cognitive attitudinal component.

In these areas, the evaluation of the product is more likely to be controlled by emotional appeals, which can be established by having the product associated with positively loaded images, persons, situations, etc. These are images established in communication situations of low involvement, and images that exert their influence predominantly under the control of right-hemispheral processes.

The Role of Involvement

As early as the 1960s, Krugman (1965) suggested that consumers received information differently depending on whether or not they are involved in the situations in which the information is received. In terms of hemispheral specialization, this should imply that in low-involvement situations right-brain processes dominate, whereas higher degrees of involvement give rise to left-brain processes (Krugman 1977). Therefore, under high-involvement conditions, information processing and deliberate choice making occur, as described in models of decision making and information processing.

Under low-involvement conditions, on the other hand, information is received holistically; pictorial material is received and stored without verbal or similar coding, and possibly emotional impressions are involved. Similarly, in low-involvement situations, choices are made—without any high degree of awareness—based on similarity with situations in the past. Thus, involvement may be a critical variable determining whether left- or right-brain processes dominate. Unfortunately, however, there is no general agreement as to the nature of involvement.

A major question is whether involvement is an enduring characteristic of the individual, describing his/her overall relationship with certain items, products, or groups of items, or whether it is a specific stage of the organism, present in various degrees in different situations. Authors like Lastovicka (1978) and Robertson (1976) discuss involvement in the first sense. They try to identify how individuals are more or less involved with different product categories, assuming that this involvement is relatively stable over time. They also discuss various questionnaire techniques that may be used to quantify this kind of involvement. Sherif, Sherif, and Nebergall's (1965) involvement concept is also of this nature. They assume that under low-involvement conditions, people are willing to accept information that deviates more from their own stand than they are willing to accept under high-involvement conditions.

In the second sense, variations in involvement reflect the extent to which the individual is more or less motivated toward a specific piece of information, product or the like. Here it can be difficult to distinguish between specific motivation, arousal, and involvement. But, it is implied that with high involvement more psychic energy is released for handling incoming information, sorting it out, and making choices. This is the way in which the concept is used by Kroeber-Riel (1979) and by Mitchell (1980).

In the present context, the concept of involvement can be useful as a measure of the degree of individual motivation in a particular information-acquisition or choice situation, and as a determinant of the extent to which left-brain processing will dominate. It has been proposed by Kassarjian and Kassarjian (1979) and Rothschild (1979) that information processing under low-involvement conditions has implications for message frequency. The number of exposures needed before a sufficient amount of learning has occurred may be greater when right-brain processes dominate. Similarly, in instances where involvement is low, it may be advantageous to rely on media that create lower involvement. Television and movies have been suggested to have such properties (Krugman 1965).

Furthermore, when the planned message is not expected to create involvement to any significant degree, an attempt to communicate with long and complicated messages requiring high involvement on the part of the receiver is wasteful. In general, message context may have to differ depending on the extent to which the marketer is communicating with the right and/or the left brain. The use of pictorial material, the use of extensive copy, the complexity of the message, the number of informational items contained in the message, etc., may have to be adjusted depending on the degree of involvement and the nature of the information-handling process.

Individual Differences

Information processing under low-involvement, right-brain dominated attention processes, pictorial-information processing, and mere exposure effects may occur, to varying degrees, for the same individual in different situations. One may,

however, also imagine that individuals differ in the extent to which they, under the same circumstances, rely on right-brain processes. Such individual differences are, in extreme degrees, believed to exist in a number of clinical cases. For instance, schizophrenia has been suggested to be related to extensive right-brain activities; also cases of reduced mental ability related to old age, extensive alcohol abuse, etc., may occur with only little observable damage to right-brain faculties (Wexler 1980).

Others have speculated that qualitative variations in intelligence, and particularly in creativity (Lindzay and Norman 1977), may relate to individual differences in hemispheral lateralization. Here, creativity, intuitive problem recognition, and problem solving are thought to be controlled by right-hemisphere activities.

Eventually, four, rather than two, individual types may exist. One can imagine individuals with more or less extensive left-brain processing, and individuals with more or less extensive right-brain processing. Thereby, four, rather than two, cases arise. With extensive left-brain processing and less extensive right-brain processing (Case 1) versus extensive right-brain processing and limited left-brain processing (Case 2), the dichotomy discussed so far emerges. However, the possibility of simultaneously extensive left- and right-brain processing (Case 3) and simultaneously limited left- and right-brain processing (Case 4) also exists:

	Left Brain	
Right Brain	Active	Less Active
Active	Case 3	Case 2
Less active	Case 1	Case 4

Right-brain dominance influences the reception of information for information storage and for choice behavior. Right-brain dominated persons would act more along the lines discussed in the preceding sections: low involvement information processing and choice behavior would be more frequent, primary attention processes would occur more often, and there would be a tendency to rely more extensively on musical and pictorial impressions.

An Alternative to the Effect Hierarchy Models

The preceding discussion highlighted various aspects of consumer behavior that, when brought together, may constitute an alternative to the traditional decision-making/effect-types of hierarchy models. This can be summarized by the following hypotheses:

H1: Hierarchy-of-effect types of information processing is a typical left-brain phenomenon.

H2: Traditional decision-making behavior as implied in most models of consumer behavior relies primarily on left-brain information processing.

H3: Exposure without awareness or deliberate attention is possible, and is right-brain controlled.

H4: Information storage after exposure without awareness is holistic, with complete images being stored in an uncoded fashion.

H5: Pictures are always (and sometimes only) perceived as a right-brain process.

H6: Repeated exposures without awareness build up attraction or positive tendencies to act toward the object to which one is exposed.

H7: Right-brain processes become more frequent with decreasing involvement and fatigue.

H8: Some individuals are more likely than others to rely on right-brain processes.

IMPLICATIONS FOR UNDERSTANDING THE ROLE OF ADVERTISING

If it is confirmed that even with very low levels of attention some information can still be received, our view of how advertising works must then change. It is possible that a considerable amount of the advertising material to which a person is exposed, and which we normally conclude has no effect, may still be extremely important in forming habits, behavior, and attitudes. This may be a kind of long-run, secondary effect of advertising, the existence of which could support the proposition that the value structure of the messages, more or less unconsciously, is adopted by the receivers, and that this is done almost automatically by consumers, as the defense mechanisms are passive in the low-involvement situations where exposure occurs.

An important question relates to the possible occurrence of individual differences. Can two different personality types be identified, some with dominating right-brain activity and others with dominating left-brain activity? Or should four different types of individuals be considered: some who can use both kinds of information fully, some who are very poor at both kinds, and some who are left- or right-hemispherally specialized? Thus, if consumers differ in relying on left- versus right-brain processes, this could have a dramatic influence on communication strategies. Adaptation to the kinds of information processing and choice behavior that consumers in different segments apply may be very important.

At the extreme, in some product areas a relatively large number of consumers may be left almost untouched by commercial messages. These messages often rely on more extensive left-brain processing, whereas the consumers in question may be much more likely to rely on right-brain information processing.

With regard to public policy issues, individual differences may also be important. Most political information and much information from the public sector is complex, verbal, and not suited for a right-brain dominated type. If such people are numerous, the fact that they rely on completely different kinds of information gives television and the "illustrative" print media an important influence.

Other questions need to be addressed as well. For example, to what extent do the different abilities people have for handling the imaginative versus symbolic depend on the different opportunities they have had for applying different information-processing modes? That is, are some people more thoroughly trained in imaginative information processing, and, if so, does this determine their subsequent personality and their relationship with mass communication?

One may speculate on whether the introduction of the public educational system and the cultural trend in western socieites toward verbal, symbolic, and arithmetic information has caused a general change in the extent to which people rely on left- rather than right-brain informa-tion processing. If so, what role will television and other pictorial mass communications play in the future? Will they cause a reversal shift toward more right-brain dominated behavior, and will this, in turn, cause a change away from that largely symbolic and verbal culture that has characterized the Western World for the last two decades?

Another important implication is concerned with education. In an era where inductive learning has been emphasized by educators at all levels, the traditional lecture has been considered almost the only way of teaching students. In recent years, however, deductive methods have come into focus. Learning by doing and problem-oriented interdisciplinary group teaching have gained widespread interest, and are seen among some educators as the only possible way of teaching. To the extent that the deductive informal teaching process primarily relates to the right brain and the more traditional inductive teaching process primarily communicates to the left brain, it is important to emphasize the need for a mixture of the two approaches (Bogen 1977).

FUTURE RESEARCH STRATEGIES

In a previous section, tentative hypotheses were suggested specifying the more precise nature of the effects of hemispheral specialization. Although these hypotheses are supported by the findings of brain researchers and by those dealing with information handling and choice behavior in other areas, further proof is still needed. It is necessary to derive testable hypotheses from the more complex suggestions discussed in the preceding pages, and to develop methodologies for their testing.

The measurement techniques discussed previously can be used to identify individual differences in the degree to which people rely on the left versus the right hemisphere. Because most of these techniques can be applied only in an experimental setting and with considerable cost associated with each single observation, it is necessary to devise less expensive and less demanding measurement devices. This could be done using elements from the WAIS and from brain-damage testing procedures, in combination with self-rating items, either selected from existing personality and aptitude tests, or constructed with the major differences between right- and left-brain functioning in mind. Such tests, again, could be cross validated with tachistoscope measures, dichotic listening, EEG, and measures of individual differences in lateralization.

The most obvious way of measuring the extent to which different stimuli result in more or less right-brain processing seems to be with the use of EEG measures. Alternatively, measurements could rely on gestures or on the observation of eye movements. As discussed previously, neither of these approaches has been very successful (Ornstein 1973). Thus, the possibility of measuring the dominance of left- or right-brain processes in a specific situation is somewhat less promising than the possibility of identifying individual differences. To overcome this problem, however, one could use a two-step procedure:

- Study the same message (for instance, a combination of pictorial and verbal material) influences of traditional communication-effect measures, such as recognition, recall, learning, attitude,

change, preference, and change with left- versus right-brain dominated individuals.
- Study how different messages (combination of pictures and verbal material) give rise to different response patterns in terms of traditional communication-effect measures. Following this, compare the observed response patterns with those established to be typical for "left-brain receivers" versus "right-brain receivers."

This would make it possible to study differential effects of picture-dominated and verbal dominated messages, with variations in involvement, as well as other message-related variables.

References

Appel, Valentine, Weinstein, Sidney, and Weinstein, Curt (1979), "Brain Activity and Recall of TV Advertising," *Journal of Advertising Research,* 19, 7–15.

Bogen, Joseph E. (1977), "Some Educational Implications of Hemispheric Specialization," in *The Human Brain,* ed. M. C. Wittrock, New York: Prentice-Hall, Inc., pp. 133–52.

_____, and Vogel, Philip J. (1962), "Cerebral Commissurotomy in Man," *Bulletin of Los Angeles Neurological Society,* Bulletin No. 27-8, 169–72.

Broadbent, Donald E. (1977), "The Two Processes of Attention," *American Psychologist,* 32, 109–18.

Cohen, Gillian, and Martin, Michael (1975), "Hemisphere Differences in an Auditory Stroop Test," *Perception and Psychophysics,* 38, 79–83.

Cropley, Al J., and Field, Tate W. (1969), "Achievement in Science and Intellectual Style," *Journal of Applied Psychology,* 53, 132–5.

Deglin, Vadim L. (1976), "Journey Through the Brain," *Unesco Courier,* January, 4–14.

Freeman, Frank S. (1962). *Psychological Testing,* New York: Holt, Rinehart and Winston.

Gazzaniga, Michael S. (1977), "Review of the Split Brain," in *The Human Brain,* ed. M. C. Wittrock, New York: Prentice-Hall, Inc., pp. 89–96.

Hansen, Flemming (1977), "Psychological Models of Consumer Choice," in *A Synthesis of Selected Aspects of Consumer Behavior,* ed. R. Ferber,

Washington, D.C.: U.S. Government Printing Office, pp. 33–67.

Hess, Eckard H. (1972), "Pupillometrics: A Method of Studying Mental, Emotional and Sensory Processes," in *Handbook of Psychophysiology*, eds. N. S. Greenfield and R. A. Sternbach, New York: Holt, Rinehart and Winston.

Howard, John F. (1977), *Consumer Behavior: Theory and Applications*, New York: McGraw-Hill Book Co.

Hubert, Joel, and Holbrock, Morris B. (1980), "The Determinants of Esthetic Value and Growth," in *Advances in Consumer Research, Vol. 7*, ed. Jerry C. Olson, Ann Arbor, MI: Association for Consumer Research.

Kassarjian, Harold H., and Kassarjian, Waltraud M. (1979), "Attitudes under Low Commitment Conditions," in *Attitude Research Plays for High Stakes*, eds. John C. Maloney and Bernard Silverman, Chicago: AMA.

Kimura, Doreen (1973), "The Asymmetry of the Human Brain—Recent Progress in Perception," *Scientific American*, 232, 246–54.

Kroeber-Riel, Werner (1979), "Activation Research: Psychobiological Approaches in Consumer Research," *Journal of Consumer Research*, 5, 240–50.

_____, Hemberle, Gerhard, and von Keitz, Wolfgang (1979), "Product Differentiation by Emotional Conditioning—A Successful Marketing Strategy in Spite of the Critical Consumer?" working paper, International Series, University of the Saarland, Saarbrücken, West Germany.

Krugman, Herbert E. (1965), "The Impact of Television Advertising: Learning without Involvement," *The Public Opinion Quarterly*, 29, 349–56.

_____ (1977), "Memory without Recall, Exposure without Recognition," *Journal of Advertising Research*, 17, 7–12.

_____ (1980), "Substained Viewing of Television," paper presented at The Conference Board, Council on Marketing Research, New York.

Lastovicka, John L. (1978), "Questioning the Concept of Involvement Defined Product Classes," in *Advances in Consumer Research, Vol. 6*, ed. William L. Wilkie, Ann Arbor, MI: Association for Consumer Research, pp. 174–9.

Lassen, Niels A., Ingvar, David H., and Skinhøj, Erik (1978), "Brain Function and Blood Flow," *Scientific American*, October, 50–9.

Lindzay, Peter H., and Norman, Donald A. (1977), *Human Information Processing*, New York: Academic Press.

Lundsgaard, Niels E. (1978), "Psykologiske Funktioners Asymmetriske Representation i den Menneskelige Hjerne," unpublished Ph.D. dissertation at the Copenhagen University, Copenhagen.

Mitchell, Andrew A. (1980), "Using Information Processing Theory to Understand Advertising Effects," in *Advances in Consumer Research, Vol. 7*, ed. Jerry C. Olson, Ann Arbor, MI: Association for Consumer Research.

Olshavsky, Richard W., and Granbois, Donald H., (1979), "Consumer Decision Making—Fact or Fiction?" *Journal of Consumer Research*, 6, 93–100.

Ornstein, Robert E. (1973), *The Nature of Human Consciousness*, New York: Viking Press.

Ottesen, Otto (1980), "Behavioural Paradigms in Advertising Research," working paper, The Copenhagen School of Business Administration and Economics.

Packard, Vance (1957), *The Hidden Persuaders*, New York: Longmans, Green & Co.

Ray, Michael, L. (1976), "Marketing Communication and the Hierarchy of Effects," in *New Models for Communication Research*, ed. P. Clark, New York: Sage Publications, Ltd.

Robertson, Thomas S. (1976), "Low Commitment Consumer Behavior," *Journal of Advertising Research*, 16, 19–24.

Rothschild, Michael L. (1979). "Advertising Strategies for High and Low Involvement Situations," in *Attitude Research Plays for High Stakes*, eds. John C. Maloney and Bernhard Silverman, Chicago: American Marketing Association.

Sherif, Carolyn W., Sherif, Muzafer, and Nebergall, Roger E. (1965), *Attitude and Attitude Change*, Philadelphia: W. B. Saunders, Inc.

Sperry, Roger W. (1973), "Lateral Specialization of Cerebral Function in the Surgically Separated Hemispheres," in *The Psychophysiology of Thinking*, eds. F. J. McGuigan and R. A. Schoonorer, New York: Academic Press, Inc., pp. 209–29.

Theilgaard, Alice (1973), "Psykologiske Funktioners Representation i Hjeren," *Nordisk Psykiatrisk Tidsskft*, 7, 418–26.

_____ (1979), "Demens—Psykologisk Set," *Nordisk Psykiatrisk Tidsskrift*, 33, 398–413.

Watson, Paul J., and Gatchel, Robert J. (1979), "Autonomic Measuring of Advertising," *Journal of Advertising Research*, 19, 15–24.

Wexler, Bruce E. (1980), "Cerebral Laterality and Psychiatry: A Review of the Literature," *American Journal of Psychiatry*, 137, 279–89.

Wittrock, Merlin C. (1977), *The Human Brain*, Englewood Cliffs, N.J.: Prentice-Hall, Inc.

Zajonc, Robert B. (1968), "Attitudinal Effects of Mere Exposure," *Journal of Personality and Social Psychology*, 9, monograph issue.

_____ (1980), "Time and Functions of Mind," *ISR Newsletter*, (Spring), Ann Arbor, MI: University of Michigan, pp. 3–5.

Exercise 35

People are Really Two-Faced

OBJECTIVE To introduce the topic of hemispheral lateralization.

For each of the sets of portraits (1) determine whether portrait A or B is more friendly and (2) determine whether portrait A or B is the more serious. When you have completed this exercise, turn to page 316 for a discussion of this exercise.

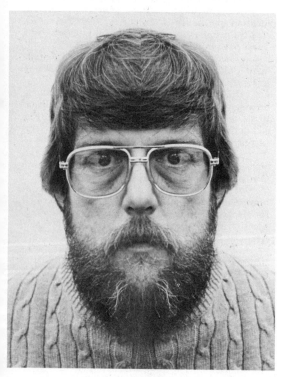

Individual 1
Portrait A

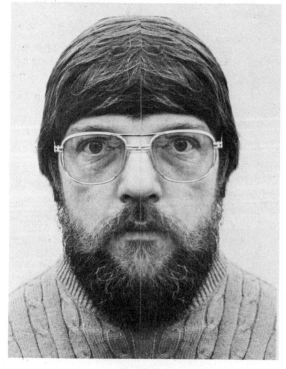

Individual 1
Portrait B

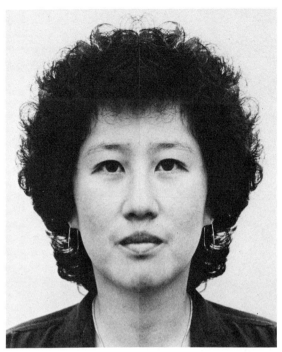

Individual 2
Portrait A

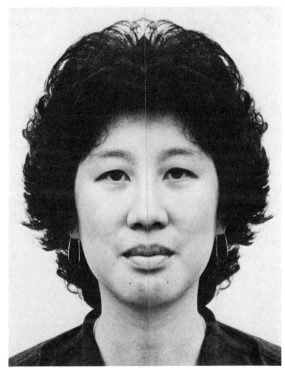

Individual 2
Portrait B

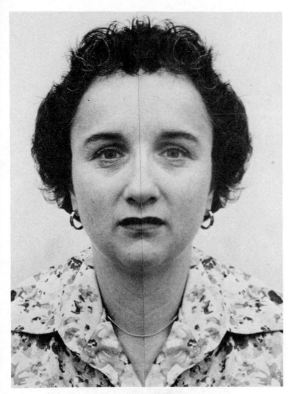

Individual 3
Portrait A

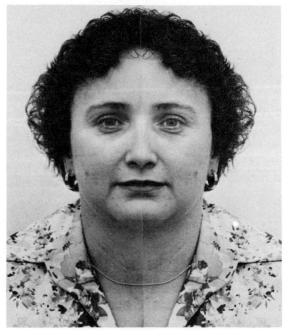

Individual 3
Portrait B

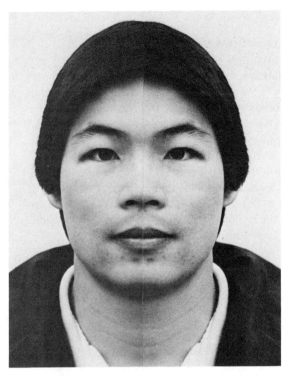

Individual 4
Portrait A

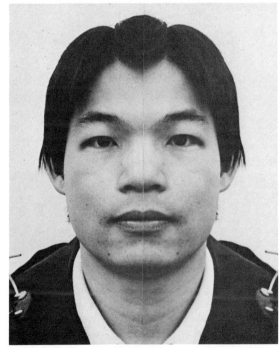

Individual 4
Portrait B

This exercise presented you with composite pictures of individuals. For individual 1, portrait A consisted of two left halves of his face and portrait B consisted of two right halves of his face; for individual 2, portrait B consisted of two right halves of her face and portrait A consisted of two left halves of her face; for individual 3, portrait A consisted of two right halves of her face and portrait B consisted of two left halves of her face; for individual 4, portrait A consisted of two left halves of his face and portrait B consisted of two right halves of his face.

As this exercise shows, the human face is not symmetrical. The right side is our public face and is usually the happier side. The left side is our private face and is usually the more serious. The assymmetry is related to hemispherial specialization. The right brain which controls the left side of the face is the sad hemisphere and the left brain which controls the right side of the face is the happy hemisphere.[1] Shown below are portraits of the "natural whole face" of these four individuals.

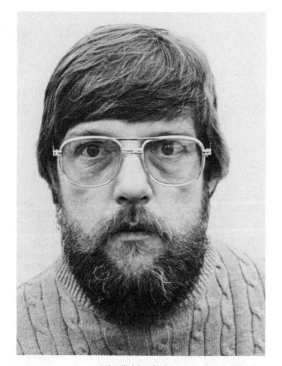

Individual 1

Individual 2

[1]Recommended reading: "Sad Hemisphere, Happy Hemisphere," Marcel Kinsbourne, *Psychology Today,* May 1981, page 92; "People are Really Two-Faced," *Time,* December 11, 1978, pages 126–7.

Individual 3

Individual 4

Exercise 36

Consumer Information Processing

OBJECTIVE To demonstrate the nuances and subtlety of nonverbal communication in consumer information processing

For each set of portraits, indicate the one that you prefer. Your instructor will discuss the interpretations and meanings of your choices.

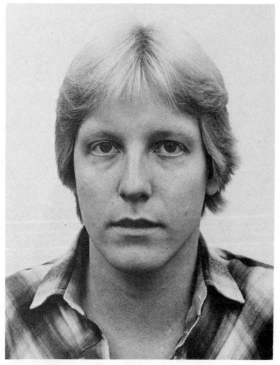

Model A

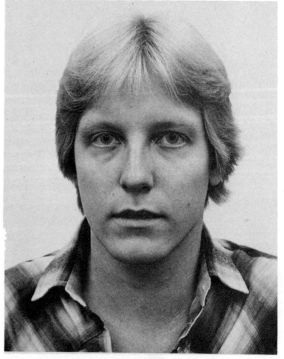

Model A'

Model B

Model B′

Model C

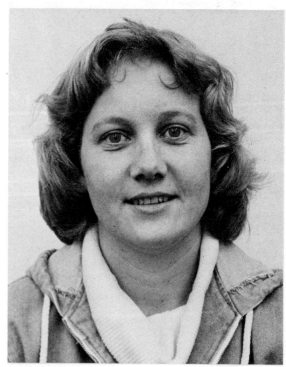

Model C'

320

Model D

Model D'

Model E

Model E′

18

Retail Outlet Selection

Marketers can create images and personalities for retail outlets that encourage desired consumer behavior.

Half the people in the United States do not see a dentist regularly. People fear dentists. But that was before the arrival of the New-Age Dentist whose office is designed to alleviate fear. Mard Naman describes his experience at the New-Age Dentists in the article "The Dawn of New-Age Dentistry." These consumer-oriented dentists show that understanding consumers can go a long way to making unpleasant experiences less unpleasant.

The necessity of creating the appropriate retail outlet for the product is illustrated in the article "Tupperware It Ain't," by Paul Nussbaum. It seems that many people who would never walk into a store front sex shop are, nevertheless, meeting with friends and neighbors in middle-class living rooms to examine sex devices, exotic lotions, and racy underwear. The same products that were perceived as lewd and lascivious are perceived as sources of fun and giggles when the retail outlet is someone's living room.

THE DAWN OF NEW AGE DENTISTRY

The first time I visited the New Age Dentist's office I thought I had accidentally walked into a singles bar. There were ferns everywhere. Redwood ceiling beams. Redwood-framed mirrors. Beautiful dental assistants. Sincere eye contact. Taped music by Gato Barbieri and Linda Ronstadt. A dentist (no white smock) who Explains What He's Doing. Who is not just a technician—no!—but the host for an unusual oral experience.

The dental assistant assigned to me was named Jill. She wore a form-fitting T-shirt; DRILL ME it said across her chest. "Would you like the gas?" Jill asked, smiling. "Sometimes we need to be a little spaced to make it through the world."

"The Dawn of New Age Dentistry," Mard Naman, *New West,* November 19, 1979, p. 15. Reprinted with permission from the November 19, 1979 issue of *New West.* Copyright 1979 by *New West.*

"Turn it up!" I gurgled, with mouth wide open.

The gas, also known as laughing gas, also known as nitrous oxide, is administered via a mini-mask placed over the nose. Its concentration is controlled by mixing it with oxygen. The control switch is numbered from 1 (lightweight) to 5 (knockout potential). You can have whatever strength you want. I wanted it all.

Nitrous oxide has the wonderful ability to make you not care a whole lot that someone is hammering away at your exposed nerve endings. Under its trance you become quite euphoric; Jill was lovely to look at in the first place, but under the seductive influence of nitrous oxide she became a ravishing beauty. I was to spend the next two hours with her hand in my mouth.

The New Age Dentist had trouble

numbing my back teeth. "Have you had this trouble before?" he asked before sticking me with Novocain for the third time. "I don't like to give you so much, but I hate to see people in pain. This should do it," he said, and walked away for a few minutes. "You must have an unusual anatomy," Jill said, laughing.

The gas was giving me a full-tilt glow by now, and Hank Williams had just come on my private headphones. "Hey, good lookin', whaatcha got cookin'?" Time floated by, and I barely noticed the work at hand. My teeth were drilled down, then a series of impressions were made. Jill held the impressions in place while they hardened, all the while sustaining an informative one-way conversation. She told me what a good feeling it was to have a full refrigerator at home. Normally it was quite empty, since she lived alone in a one-bedroom apartment. But friends were visiting for the weekend and she was prepared. "And now," she announced, "I'm going to put some Vaseline on you." "What for?" I asked. "To lubricate, of course."

When the dentist returned from another patient I asked if anyone had ever told him there were a bit too many stimuli for one patient to take. "Well," he said, "we used to show slides. You know, nature scenes and such. And a few patients complained that too much was going on. So we stopped that." It would indeed be difficult, I thought, to watch a slide show while lying in a dentist's chair. I'd have to ask the dentist to get his head out of the way all the time. So I suggested to my dentist that he show Betamax movies in the waiting room. Anything but *Marathon Man*.

As I looked around the cozy living-room setting, I marveled at how things were changing in the world of high-speed drilldom. A few short years ago, going to

the dentist had been, at best, as enjoyable as taking out the garbage, and, at worst, like being attacked with ice picks. But now, here I was, savoring every minute of a gentle dental drama. "With an atmosphere like this," I mentioned to my dentist, through the mist, "you must have patients breaking the door down to get in." "No, no!" he protested. "I'm not working to my capacity, and I've been in practice in San Francisco since 1971. I could work three days a week and see as many patients as I now do in five." "Okay now," he said, getting back to work, "open *real* wide."

But it was no use. The gas had finally affected my ability to perform my only duty. It would be best, everyone agreed, that I be given a "bite block," a small piece of rubber which would prop my mouth open. "It's very comfortable," assured my dentist. "I wish I could join you," whispered Jill.

With the bite block in place, my dentist continued both the work and my education.

The problem, he said, was not necessarily too many dentists for the number of people. "Of all the people you can consider potential patients, 50 percent won't come to a dentist *no matter what you offer them.*" I watched as his jaw tightened. "It's not the money. I'm talking about businessmen who make $50,000 to $60,000 a year. Many can get their health insurance to pay for it, but they won't come. They'd rather let their teeth rot!"

It would probably be the innovative dentists, I guessed, who would get those $60,000-a-year rotten teeth. Good dentistry simply isn't enough anymore. To attract patients, the mouth wizards need to offer something special. Besides sex appeal. (A few weeks later, at a party, I met another New Age practitioner—one who spread dental goodwill *outside* his office. "Well, did you bring the gas?" I asked jokingly. "No," he answered, somewhat taken aback. "You should have told me earlier. I usually carry a travel pack with me.")

Sad to say, not even the New Age Dentist could keep my jaw from aching mightily after his various drugs wore off.

But why dwell on the negative? Why not live for the moment?

For instance: When the New Age Dentist was almost finished, lovely Jill turned off the gas so I could sort of start to straighten out. "Okay," she said through the velvet haze. "I'm going to make one final impression."

There was no doubt in my mind that it was going to be a good one.

TUPPERWARE IT AIN'T

In another era, they would have called this a Tupperware party.

But then they would have sold Tupperware.

A dozen young women, mostly secretaries from a San Diego law firm, are scattered on chairs and cushions throughout the living room of a small bungalow. Red balloons decorate the walls and unobtrusive music plays on the turntable. Sipping punch and munching hors d'oeuvre, these women have gathered to examine and buy sex toys, not kitchen gadgets.

"Emotion Lotion" in a variety of flavors.

Lingerie. Lots of lingerie. Garter belts in passionate colors. And vibrators

with sundry attachments. Fur mitts with natural or artificial fur.

The women don't get to check out everything at once. Ginny Dingman, the 50-year-old entrepreneur who runs Playtime Parties, starts them out slowly. She spreads a red velour cloth on the floor and brings out the soaps and lotions amid nervous laughter.

The business of selling sex accoutrements is booming around the nation these days, and more and more people who would never walk into a storefront sex shop are meeting with friends and neighbors in middle-class living rooms to examine sex devices, exotic lotions and racy underwear.

They are predominantly women, although there are coed and even a few all-male parties.

In Southern California, the phenomenon is "just mushrooming," says San Diego clinical psychologist Javad Emami. Sexologist Marilyn Lawrence of the Institute for the Advanced Study of Human Sexuality in Los Angeles says that there has been a marked growth in interest in the home parties in the past year.

The professional assessments of the parties, and of sex toys, for that matter, vary. Some psychologists decry them as one more sign of a self-centered society's obsession with sex and pleasure. Advocates, though, praise the toys as fun aids toward sexual exploration and fulfillment and the parties as a comfortable way to examine the wares.

For the women at Ginny Dingman's party, though, few of the philosophical questions are a concern. They're here for a good time, and most of them are getting what they came for.

Irene, the hostess for the party, snaps flash pictures of Dingman holding panties that don't have bottoms, of fellow partners fondling feathers and plumes.

A young mother breast-feeds her baby quietly against one wall while her friends examine $17 Velcro-snapped "bonds of love" and a $12 set of body paints.

"How am I going to explain to Mike that I got these at a crystal party?" moans one partygoer. "That's where I told him I was going."

For hostesses like Irene, crystal parties and sex-toy parties have a lot in common. The hostess gets a cut of the night's profits and "premiums" for having the party. For this party, the premiums are books or cassette tapes, readings on the joys of sex and womanhood.

For the sellers like Ginny Dingman, the biggest problem now seems to be keeping control of the business. Dingman, who just started her Playtime Parties a few months ago, finds herself scheduling four and five parties a week. Her dilemma, she says, is whether to continue to run a one-woman show or to set up franchises.

In the Los Angeles area, too, business is booming. One of the leading manufacturers of sex toys, United Sales, now produces $100 kits for home parties with a starter set of everything you need to host. United Sales president Fred Malorrus, whose company sells to a multitude of mail-order firms, figures that at least 500 Los Angeles-area individuals have held home parties in the past few months.

"I think that eventually this should help our business at least 20 percent," Malorrus says of home parties. "The average person won't walk into an adult bookstore, and he's not on the mailing list of most of these places. Their first exposure is at one of these home parties. This way they get a chance to look at the stuff with their next-door neighbor. That way, they get over the shock and the ha-ha-ha-ho-ho-ho business."

And there is a lot of the ha-ha-ha-ho-ho-ho business linked with the selling of sex toys.

"They're just like a bunch of kids at Christmas," says Dingman, who clearly enjoys her role as Santa, but she also acknowledges the need for privacy, even among friends. The party-goers order the toys they want from order blanks passed out at the start of the festivities, and Dingman fills the requests individually in another room. The women take their new wares home in plain brown paper bags. Some leave empty-handed; others spend as much as $30 or $40 for their new pleasures.

Explaining the growth in interest in sex toys and home parties "would be like explaining the Hula-Hoop," says Dr. Rex Beaber of the Family Health Center at the University of California Los Angeles. "Somebody gets an idea, and people come and enjoy themselves."

"Of course, society always has to be psychologically prepared for it, and Southern California is psychologically prepared for anything. I'm convinced that if somebody advocated removing a finger as a social symbol, you could get a significant number of people in Southern California to cut off a finger."

But this phenomenon of sex toy parties seems to be one modern fad that didn't start in California.

"It's not as highly organized here (in Southern California) as it is back East," says United's Malorrus. "It seems like it started in New York—that seems to be where it's coming from."

Exercise 37

Measuring the Store's Image

OBJECTIVE   To provide an opportunity to use an instrument to measure store images.

The consumers' image of the store may very well determine whether or not and to what extent they will patronize the store. This exercise incorporates the use of semantic differential scales[1] to measure store images. As a class or in small groups, choose two stores to compare. Complete a store image profile for each store. Then compute the average rating on each scale for each store among the raters. Consider the marketing implications of the results and their ramifications.

Store #1

Friendly						Unfriendly
Low priced						High priced
Pleasant						Unpleasant
Modern						Old-fashioned
Attractive						Unattractive
Fair						Unfair
Warm						Cold
Good value for money						Poor value for money
Nice place to shop						Not a nice place to shop
Wide selection						Narrow selection
Good advertising						Poor advertising
Good service						Poor service
Reliable						Unreliable
Improving						Falling behind
Pleasant clerks						Unpleasant clerks
Unique store						Store like others
Neat						Untidy

[1]"The Semantic Differential: An Information Source for Designing Retail Patronage Appeals," Robert F. Kelly and Ronald Stephenson, *Journal of Marketing*, Vol. 31, October 1967, p. 45. Printed by the American Marketing Association. Reprinted with permission.

Store #2

Friendly	——	——	——	——	——	Unfriendly
Low priced	——	——	——	——	——	High priced
Pleasant	——	——	——	——	——	Unpleasant
Modern	——	——	——	——	——	Old-fashioned
Attractive	——	——	——	——	——	Unattractive
Fair	——	——	——	——	——	Unfair
Warm	——	——	——	——	——	Cold
Good value for money	——	——	——	——	——	Poor value for money
Nice place to shop	——	——	——	——	——	Not a nice place to shop
Wide selection	——	——	——	——	——	Narrow selection
Good advertising	——	——	——	——	——	Poor advertising
Good service	——	——	——	——	——	Poor service
Reliable	——	——	——	——	——	Unreliable
Improving	——	——	——	——	——	Falling behind
Pleasant clerks	——	——	——	——	——	Unpleasant clerks
Unique store	——	——	——	——	——	Store like others
Neat	——	——	——	——	——	Untidy

Instructions

Profile the average ratings on each of the characteristics for the two stores that your group has rated. Use 0 to indicate the first store's average ratings on the scales below and use X to indicate the second store's average ratings on the scales below. Connect the first store's average ratings with a dashed line ----- and connect the second store's ratings with a solid line ———.

Friendly	——	——	——	——	——	Unfriendly
Low priced	——	——	——	——	——	High priced
Pleasant	——	——	——	——	——	Unpleasant
Modern	——	——	——	——	——	Old-fashioned
Attractive	——	——	——	——	——	Unattractive
Fair	——	——	——	——	——	Unfair
Warm	——	——	——	——	——	Cold
Good value for money	——	——	——	——	——	Poor value for money
Nice place to shop	——	——	——	——	——	Not a nice place to shop
Wide selection	——	——	——	——	——	Narrow selection
Good advertising	——	——	——	——	——	Poor advertising
Good service	——	——	——	——	——	Poor service
Reliable	——	——	——	——	——	Unreliable
Improving	——	——	——	——	——	Falling behind
Pleasant clerks	——	——	——	——	——	Unpleasant clerks
Unique store	——	——	——	——	——	Store like others
Neat	——	——	——	——	——	Untidy

Exercise 38

The Design of Space

OBJECTIVE To illustrate the effect of spatial design on consumer behavior

Analyze the spatial arrangements and atmosphere of the places depicted in the following pictures. First, determine whether the environment encourages or discourages social interaction and, second, determine the elements that suggest the appropriate behaviors.

Picture 1

Picture 2

Picture 3

Picture 4

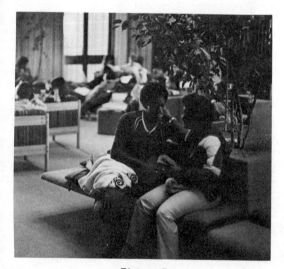

Picture 5

Picture 6

19

Consumerism: Militant Consumer Behavior

The militant consumer behavior of consumerism communicates to marketers that consumers are not satisfied with the functioning of the marketing place. The articles included in this section discuss some of the issues of consumerism.

In the article "Let Them Eat Junk," William Serrin notes that, more than farmers or nutritionists, it is the food scientists aided by marketers who determine what will be on the dinner tables of America. Serrin criticizes food science and marketing for the corruption and decay of the American diet.

In the article "Fast Buck Medicine," Eugene Schoenfeld discusses the effect of third-party payment on emergency-room-care service. Schoenfeld notes that ever since payment for emergency-room care was third partied, it became a money maker. Schoenfeld expresses concern that patient care may suffer when profit making becomes the health profession's main concern.

In the article "Caution: Too Many Health Warnings Could be Counterproductive," Amitai Etzioni suggests that government warnings, labels, and inserts be used sparingly and judiciously to be effective.

In the article "FTC Is Seeking Ways to Decide if Pictures in Advertising Convey False Impressions," Stan Crock reports on the Federal Trade Commission's concern with the nonverbal aspects of advertising. The FTC's authorization to stop deceptive practices has concentrated on the verbal part of advertising. Advertisers, therefore, shy away from making explicit verbal claims for their products and use visual, nonverbal communications to convey meaning.

LET THEM EAT JUNK

Hundreds of men and women laden with plastic shopping bags wander a vast midway of booths. Some wear straw hats, party favors from a turn-of-the-century gala the night before. All around them, on placards hanging from the roof of the Cervantes Convention Exhibition Center in St. Louis, are signs hawking their companies' products.

- Prefabricated pork chops triumph with H & R natural and artificial flavors.
- VD has the scoop on True-to-Life flavors.
- Nutrifox VDD sodium tripolyphosphate is the one for meat-curing applications.
- Now Amazio adds more eye and mouth appeal to processed foods faster than you can say "pregelatinized starches."

These men and women are food scientists. More than farmers, ranchers, or nutritionists, they determine what Americans eat. At a recent convention of the Institute of Food Technologists (IFT), they bustled up and down the corridors between display booths, nibbling on the products that the large food companies hope to place on the nation's dining tables: low-calorie watermelon punch, imitation vanilla cookies, fudge made from artificial chocolate, imitation cream cheese, imitation mozzarella cheese, imitation provolone cheese, sausages made with artificial meat flavor, popcorn flavored with imitation butter, freeze-dried raspberry yogurt chunks, peppermint-flavored mints.

Until the past generation, food scientists concerned themselves largely with techniques of preservation—canning, refrigeration, cellophane wrapping. The technology explosion that occurred during World War II and the decades afterward helped to create an industry more concerned with producing new foods in new forms than with preserving and transporting the existing ones economically and conveniently. Two new practices that had enjoyed immense growth in the 20 years before the war, market research and national advertising, were of great assistance in the birth of what amounted to a whole new enterprise—the modern food industry.

Today Americans spend $260 billion annually on food, almost half of which goes toward the purchase of highly processed items, including convenience and snack foods. We also eat about 40 percent of our meals away from home, spending an additional $105 billion on what is known as the food-service business. Food science is the backbone of this industry as well.

Not long ago the food business, as well as the food-service business, consisted of local entrepreneurs with their own factories, or warehouses, or shops. Today not only the frozen, wrapped, uniform food at the grocery store but also the fast-food restaurants, many of the farms, the food research groups, and even the seeds are controlled by a handful of huge conglomerates with names like General Foods, General Mills, Proctor and Gamble, Kelloggs, along with such nonfood companies as ITT and General Electric. Many of these firms sell literally hundreds of products and spend vast amounts of money on marketing and advertising to convince the public that the new items are somehow different from their predecessors. The lack of competition among these firms has led to charges that food prices are artificially high, as well as, in one case, an FTC antitrust suit. Companies have also been charged with manipulative and deceptive advertising. Critics of the food business are also distressed that the industry has managed almost to saturate the American market and is now looking abroad, especially to the developing nations of the Third World, for new consumers. This internationalization has raised the fear that America will soon be blanketing the world with frozen french fries. But all of these criticisms pale before the essential one: that food-processing companies have succeeded in debasing the American diet.

Just what have technologists done to our food? The answers can be found not only in the foods they put on American plates but in the ideas they put into the minds of American consumers by means of marketing and sales promotion.

"Today's consumers really don't need anything in the way of new products," the research director for Libby, McNeill & Libby, the large Chicago-based food company, told the IFT a few years ago. Nonetheless, he contended, "they are constantly searching for something just a little better or different. . . ." An aggressive company, he pointed out, must capitalize on this. Though one firm might look at a proposed orange-juice product and ask, "Who needs it?" a go-getter, the marketing man suggested, would know better. "A company could come along with an orange-juice product to which an additional color or sweetness . . . or . . . an important nutritional component has been added, and do well in the marketplace."

Enter the food technologist. He can add ingredients that extend the shelf life or keep processed foods stable so that, for example, chocolate pudding doesn't turn into a mess of separated layers of goo, all different colors. He can add substances that produce what the industry calls "fine surface gloss." He can simplify production, saving labor and its costs. Raw foods— milk, meat, eggs, grains, fruits, vegetables—are not important. They exist only to be simulated in the laboratory, with the manufactured copies transformed into new foods, those known in the trade as "fun foods" or "consumer hot buttons." Companies can capitalize on almost any characteristic of these products—the novelty, the taste, the cooking time, a new or unusual container—whatever might pique the fancy of the consumer thumbing through the newspaper food section or strolling the aisles of the supermarket.

"The technology is skewed toward anything that can make a buck and away from anything that improves quality," says James S. Turner, a Washington, D.C. attorney and author of *The Chemical Feast,* a study of the regulatory policies of the Food and Drug Administration. "Nothing is heard from the scientific community about quality. . . . The scientists say to the companies, 'We can improve your sales,' and then they come up with the flavors, colors, and extenders that are added to food substances to make them appear to be food. But it's not food. We don't even know what food is in our society."

The overwhelming dominance of manufactured foods in the American diet belies the idea that we are experiencing a revolution in taste and cooking, a notion largely advanced by food editors and writers. A casual inspection of big-city newspapers and magazines suggests that everyone is puttering around a brick-lined kitchen, a gourmet cookbook in hand, the food processor purring, turning out some delicate, exotic dish. But the reality is that consumers have accepted food technology, and our ever-more homogenized diet is destroying the nation's rich culinary traditions.

Regional and ethnic distinctions are disappearing from American cooking. Food in one neighborhood, city, or state looks and tastes pretty much like food anywhere else. Americans are sitting down to meals largely composed of such items as instant macaroni and cheese, soft white bread, oleomargarine, frozen doughnuts, and Jell-O. "Today it is possible to travel from coast to coast, at any time of year, without feeling any need to change your eating habits," according to a brochure printed by the IFT. "Sophisticated processing and storage techniques, fast transport, and a creative variety of formulated convenience-food products have made it possible to ignore regional and seasonal differences in food production. . . ."

The success of food scientists can be charted by the radical transformation of the American diet in recent years. Consumption of fluid milk, for instance, has slipped more than than 30 percent since 1960; soft drinks are now the nation's number-one beverage. Potato products, largely frozen french fries, became 464 percent more popular between 1910 and 1976, a year in which more fries, in tons, were sold than any other frozen vegetable. In 1940, homemakers bought 50 percent of the flour sold in the United States; today they buy 11 percent. Most flour now goes into processed breads, cakes, pies, and buns sold at grocery stores and fast-food restaurants (40 percent of the beef consumed here is hamburger).

One of the great recent triumphs of food science is Procter and Gamble's potato-chip-like product, Pringles. The baby of several years of research, Pringles are made not from potato slices, like traditional chips, but from a potato paste. They have a salt taste on only one side: Why put taste on both sides, the manufacturer reasoned, when only one will touch the tongue? Without food science, all milk shakes would still contain milk. Many are now made instead from vegetable oils such as coconut or palm, milk-food solids, emulsifiers, flavors, and sugars.

Fast-food restaurants, a booming sector of the economy, depend upon the miracles of modern food science no less than do the drinks and snacks you buy in the grocery store. A firm like Denny's, for example, has some 700 outlets in 41 states, and others scattered across Great Britain and Japan. With labor turnover in the industry running at about 350 percent a year, Denny's must serve foods that can be prepared by almost anyone. Their cooks are not likely to have high culinary skills. Even though Denny's puts pictures on its food containers to make sure employees with limited reading ability can manage the cooking, the chain still relies on food science to make preparation even easier. The foods Denny's chooses are ready for eating when heated to 90 degrees, and are palatable at temperatures between 75 and 105. Though the chain used frozen foods heavily at first, the ballooning costs of refrigeration are dictating a switch to dehydrated foods. In the future, Denny's plans to use foods packaged in retort pouches— flexible aluminum cans whose contents can be quickly warmed under the kitchen faucet. The firm is looking for preportioned servings that will keep for the longest possible time.

Among the long list of accomplishments of modern food science, advances in nutrition cannot be said to rank very high.

A change in public taste has led to a rash of "natural" items, products with some crucial vitamins restored. But food scientists and the companies that they represent do not feel that the diet they have created is deficient in any fundamental way. They do not take well to criticism of it—as one scene at the IFT convention demonstrated. In one part of the program, 400 scientists gathered to watch movies about the health aspects of their business.

Murmurs of approval ran through the audience during the screening of *Chemicals: A Fact of Life,* filmed through the courtesy of the Monsanto Company. *Adventures in Packaging,* by the Package Research Laboratory, enjoyed a similar reception. But the background commentary changed tone with the appearance of the "controversial" films. Food scientists snickered as they watched *The Junk Food Man* and *It's Easy as Selling Candy to a Baby,* made by groups critical of the food-processing industry. In one film, featuring Fat Albert and the Bill Cosby Kids, while Fat Albert wolfs down sweets the viewers are instructed in the dangers of eating sugary foods as well as of snacking. No discussion followed the films. The movies were uniformly ridiculed from the beginning.

Why show them, then? I. D. Wolf, the program's moderator, and a professor of food science from the University of Minnesota, said that the controversial movies were full of "inaccuracies and exaggerations," but that they were representative of the sort of information about processed food now reaching the public. Since laymen might take such charges seriously, she continued, it was up to food scientists to familiarize themselves with them and rebut them.

They have a great deal of rebutting

to do. As Americans have become more concerned about their health, and somewhat more circumspect about what they put into their mouths, allegations like those on the "controversial" films have become common coin. Dr. Michael Jacobson, a well-known food activist and author, claims that the American diet "promotes high blood pressure, strokes, heart disease, obesity, tooth decay, diabetes, and probably certain forms of cancer—surely bowel cancer and breast cancer. Diet is not the only cause of these afflictions, but it is significant. . . . And if you add them all up, they cause half the deaths Americans succumb to annually."

More bad news comes from the Senate Select Committee on Nutrition and Human Needs, which points out that processed food is exceptionally high in sugar and salts. The committee reported that six out of the 10 leading causes of death are linked to over-consumption of fats, cholesterol, sugar, salts, and alcohol.

Food executives often don't take the comments about overweight Americans too seriously. They like to joke that their industry has been so successful at providing wholesome, good-tasting food that the nation's major nutrition problem is obesity. And they are attacking even that condition, the executives say, through edibles that are low in calories.

But food executives do not usually joke when confronted with the allegations about the hazards of their products. Dr. Jack Francis, president-elect of the IFT, concedes that sugar contributes to tooth decay and that high consumption of fats "probably" leads to obesity; but he testily labels other charges "a lot of speculation." Francis calls for more research. And what if further investigation confirms the dangerous consequences of eating processed

food? "What is the alternative?" he asks. "Go back to the diet we had 100 years ago? . . . People aren't going to go back to the salt pork, cabbage, carrots, and potatoes that they ate in New England a century back. We have to feed people, and we have to transport food, and we have to make food delivery as efficient as we possibly can. . . . That means more processing, not less."

The bewildering diversity of canned, frozen, and dehydrated foods on the grocer's shelves gives the mistaken impression that the food business is teeming with small, competitive firms as it was in Francis's "old days," when food meant fresh produce. But as the focus of the food industry has shifted from farm to factory, conglomerates have grown bigger and bigger at the expense of small, independent operators. The number of food companies, according to Carol Tucker Foreman, Assistant Secretary for Food and Consumer Services for the Department of Agriculture, has declined from 44,000 in 1947 to 22,000 in 1972 and is still dropping. Researchers J. M. Connor and Russell C. Parker says that 200 corporations control 63.5 percent of food and tobacco processing sales. They have estimated that monopoly overcharges in the food manufacturing industries totaled $10 billion, or about 6 percent of food sales, in 1975.

Indeed, concentration has become the rule throughout the food business. Farms, the equipment that they use, as well as the crops that they produce, have come more and more under the domination of a shrinking number of conglomerates. Regional supermarket chains have all but eliminated substantial local competition in many cities. The processed-food market is no less concentrated. Campbell's makes 90 percent of our soup. And only four other firms sell us a large majority of many canned fruit and vegetable products.

The billion-dollar food-processing companies not only manufacture hundreds of consumer goods but they have extended their grasp throughout the food business. For example, General Mills sells a long list of cereals, including Wheaties and Cheerios, Betty Crocker cake mixes, Saluto pizza—and owns Red Lobster inns. General Foods has Burger Chef restaurants and markets Maxwell House coffee, Post cereals, Kool-Aid, Jell-O, and Tang. Ralston Purina sells Chicken of the Sea tuna, Chex cereals, and a long list of pet food, and owns the Jack-in-the-Box restaurant chain. Del Monte, which is itself part of the R. J. Reynolds tobacco company, has seed farms and engages in food and agricultural research, agricultural production, transportation, storage and distribution, as well as food processing and service.

One of the crucial tools in the growth of the great food conglomerates has been television advertising. Since many of their products are essentially alike, an advertised image may provide the critical difference in the mind of the consumer. Lay's potato chips, for example, may not differ intrinsically from Wise potato chips; but who could fail to be moved by the sight of Bert Lahr gazing rapturously at Lay's finest? With this kind of clout in mind, food companies have turned heavily to television advertising.

Here, too, government regulatory agencies have stepped in to halt what they consider systematic abuses. Spurred by a series of petitions from public-interest groups, the Federal Communications Commission tried to persuade manufacturers of presweetened cereal, candy, and toys to reduce the numbers of their television commercials to children and to include messages that might mitigate some of the ill effects of their products. Broadcasters and advertisers agreed to decrease slightly the hourly time allotted for advertising on children's TV but have otherwise proved intransigent. The cereal industry has lobbied intensely on the issue, reportedly spending $30 million (peanuts compared to the $600 million spent on children's TV advertising), and has so far staved off further reform.

Action for Children's Television (ACT), a Boston-based group, continues to pressure the FCC. Peggy Charren, the president, argues that children should "be protected from deception in the marketplace the same way adults are. . . . Nobody's ever told a child that Milky Way causes cavities; the message is 'Milky Way at work, rest, or play.' After 10 years of this argument they could at least say, 'at work, rest, or play, and if you don't brush your teeth you're going to get a cavity." ACT would prefer, however, that commercials for sweets be removed from children's TV entirely.

Whatever the marketing strategies and advertising finesse, the food industry faces one apparently intractable problem: America can eat just so many Pringles. The food-processing business has already responded to the problem of satiation by inventing new packages, new slogans, and yet more exotic products. But the national population is stabilizing, and the food companies must look for growth opportunities elsewhere—to pets, for example: Americans now feed 40 million dogs and 30 million cats, whose taste buds remain more or less unexplored territory. Grocery shelf space devoted to pet food has expanded dramatically in the last few years, and dogs now enjoy a variety of comestibles not much less impressive than their masters'.

The biggest growth area of the future is neither new products nor new species, but new countries. General Foods now sells coffee and powdered drinks in Europe, ice cream in Brazil, candy and gum in Mexico, and Tang, that venerable pick-me-up of astronauts, to Japan. Borden's foreign sales account for 20 percent of its total volume. The cereal-makers, with no new mouths to conquer at home, have turned increasingly to the Third World nations of South America and the Middle East. Indeed, the upper crust of the Third World, a vast market full of people who have never so much as seen a frozen apple pie, represents the next great market for many food-processing companies. "The most compelling job," said Kellogg International's Vice-President Charles Tornabene in a *Business Week* interview, "is to change people's food habits." Converting the entire world to the processed-food gospel may prove a daunting task.

In his closing speech to the IFT delegates, William Beers, retired chairman of Kraft, Inc., proposed that underdeveloped nations be encouraged to revamp their food systems into miniature versions of our own. Third World nations, said Beers, "must acquire modern infrastructures—industrial, technological, and marketing." Farmers, said Beers to the cheering scientists, "must be motivated to adopt and use modern agricultural technology." And finally, developing nations must pattern their food marketing systems after our own. Then, he concluded, "there will be demands for new types of processed foods, packaging, transportation, and distribution."

The consequences of selling and aggressively advertising sophisticated food products to Third World consumers have been painfully illustrated in the case of infant formula milk. Most manufacturers of infant formula—Nestlé, Borden, Carnation, and Bristol-Myers, among others—market their product to mothers in developing nations. The companies sent "milk nurses"—employees dressed up as nurses—into maternity wards, where they handed out free samples of the formula. Then the companies launched highly effective advertising campaigns. Mothers in the Ivory Coast were found feeding their children Nescafé after a radio message proclaimed that "Nescafé makes men stronger, women more joyful, and children more intelligent."

Besides taking the message too literally, mothers often do not understand how or simply are not able to use the formula: Once back in the village, clean water may not be available to mix with the formula powder. The instructions may be written in the wrong language, or the mother may be illiterate. Money runs out, they can no longer afford the formula, and they have lost their own ability to nurse. For these reasons, according to INFACT, an anti-formula group, as many as 10 million infants die annually from diseases related to bottle-feeding. But the milk companies have done little to counteract the damage they may have caused.

If the past is any indication, however, the companies will survive these complaints and controversies. The food-processing industry has shown itself to be extraordinarily adaptive. When the American consumer began clamoring for "natural foods," the industry struck "natural" on its labels. While its very success depends on its ability to abolish the past, the industry suggests that its goods have the taste and quality of old-fashioned foods. Running out of Americans to feed, the food business has moved into the Third World, proclaiming itself a force of economic liberation rather than a purveyor of dubious goods.

Of course, the industry is not wholly responsible for the decay of the American diet. After all, no one is forced to choose the laboratory's products over the farm's; no one has to buy orange drink instead of oranges. The industry has found willing customers in the American public.

Yet the questions remain: How do we deal with the technology we have spawned? What kind of food system should we move toward in the future, not only for ourselves but for the rest of the world? Are world hunger and malnutrition to be combated with massive doses of instant junk foods? Unless we choose to confront these questions, we can be assured a steady diet of frozen pizza and cupcakes.

BREAD AND FACTORIES

Enriched flour (barley malt, ferrous sulfate, niacin, thiamine mononitrate, riboflavin), water, corn syrup, partially hydrogenated vegetable shortening (soybean and/or cottonseed and/or palm oil), yeast, salt, soy flour, calcium sulfate, sodium stearoyl-2-lactylate, mono- and diglycerides, whey dicalcium phosphate, potassium bromate, calcium propionate, potassium bromate.

—Ingredients listed on a loaf of bread.

Oxides of nitrogen, chlorine, nitrosyl chloride, chlorine dioxide, benzoyl peroxide, acetone peroxide, azodicarbonamide, plaster of paris.

—Some of the flour additives and processing of chemicals that need not, according to the Code of Federal Regulations, be listed on the package.

Civilization was built on grain. Western civilization used it mainly in the form of bread made of flour, water, a little leaven (yeast), and salt. For the basic loaf, anything else was an adulteration, and the perpetrator was subject to being pilloried in the marketplace.

When bread was well made, the staff of life asked little of the earth. All agriculture was of course organic, and manures and rotation restored the soil. The millstones were turned by people, then by beasts, then by water or wind. The ovens were heated by such fuel as came to hand.

Until the late industrial age, it was common knowledge that bread, like wine, varied in taste and quality with the soil and conditions in which the wheat was grown. Platina, a 15th-century Vatican epicure, wrote that the best bread was made from wheat that grew on hillsides (and indeed the most delicious bread that I ever ate was in a Greek mountain village where the wheat was still sown by hand, nourished with donkey manure, cut by scythes, flailed, and stone-ground). In the mid-19th century, Frederick Law Olmsted observed that the closer he got to the new lands of the frontier, the better the bread tasted. Sylvester Graham, the prophet of whole grain, wrote

> They who have never eaten bread made of wheat recently produced by a pure virgin soil, have but a very imperfect notion of the deliciousness of good bread; such as is often to be met with in the comfortable log houses in our western country.

By 1837, the large millers of the Atlantic Coast were speeding up their mills and shipping tight-packed flour in barrels to all ports. Mary Hooker Cornelius in *The Young Housekeeper's Friend*, published in 1846, wrote:

> Newly ground flour which has never been packed is very superior to barrel flour, so that the people in Western New York, that land of finest wheat, say that the New England people do not know what good flour is.

Mrs. Cornelius was already observing the gradual abandonment of wheat-growing in the older regions along the coast. The industry settled in the Great Plains and gradually expanded into vast, single-crop, mechanized spreads. As the rich soil thinned, increasing amounts of fertilizer and herbicide and pesticide, all synthesized from natural gas and petroleum, had to be applied each year. The result is an enormous crop, a source of national wealth and power, but also a poor-tasting flour.

Already in Graham's time, the mills were bolting out of the wheat all of the bran and much of the germ, which would gum up and scorch if the millstones turned fast. In the next 40 years, steel shears and rollers completed the transformation of flour from a golden, fat, and nourishing food to a lifeless chalk dust. Yeast could barely live on it, so bakers added sugar. From decade to decade, cookbooks added more and more sugar to replace the rich flavor of true flour, creating the addiction to sweetness that now afflicts the American palate. Yeast itself was often replaced by faster chemical leavens, which brought about a national scandal at the turn of the century, involving charges that the public was being poisoned and that officials were being corrupted to let it happen.

Great new strides were achieved in this century. Flour mills were concentrated in a few major grain centers. There they ground the wheat, employing a score of chemicals to keep it from spoiling, packaged it, and shipped it long distances to market.

The neighborhood baker went the way of the town mill. A dwindling number of bread factories dominated the market with heavy advertising, delivering the product in huge vans. Fuel was cheap. The new factory loaf was "improved" to its present condition of wrapped, sliced Styrofoam, dosed with fungicide to prevent mold and with polysorbates to keep it from drying. (The TV commercial for one packaged mix cries "super-moist!" as if that were a virtue.) Permanent shelf life was achieved.

The most advanced bakeries now resemble oil refineries. Flour, water, a score of additives, and huge amounts of yeast, sugar, and water are mixed into a broth that ferments for an hour. More flour is then added, and the dough is extruded into pans, allowed to rise for an hour, then moved through a tunnel oven. The loaves emerge after 18 minutes, to be cooled, sliced, and wrapped.

They call this bread.

A century of complaint about the impoverishment of the staff of life has led the industry to "enrich" it by adding a few of the nutrients it has removed—only a few—and none of the rich array of earthy flavor and body that our forebears loved.

Clinicians recently discovered what the ancients well knew, that roughage was an important element of diet. ITT Continental Baking Company met this need with a loaf that promised added fiber. The government has insisted that the company identify the ingredient more plainly. It is sawdust. We have come to that.

FAST-BUCK MEDICINE

It's six minutes past two on a Monday morning, and I've spent the last two hours trying to save the life of a 58-year-old man stricken with a heart attack. He's comfortable now, but his cardiac nerve tissue is damaged and his heart is beating too slowly. He'll probably need a pacemaker—but none is available in the emergency room of the small hospital in the San Joaquin Valley.

One of the town's two internists suggests transferring the man to Kern Medical Center in Bakersfield, 30 miles away. The ambulance attendants are trained to handle the cardiac emergency, but it's a long drive down Highway 99, and I'll worry about the patient until he reaches the county hospital.

"Fast Buck Medicine," Eugene Schoenfeld, M.D., *New West*, March 13, 1978, pp. 20–22. Reprinted with permission from the March 13, 1979 issue of *New West*. Copyright 1978 by *New West*.

As the ambulance pulls away, a young woman and her three-year-old daughter walk into the emergency room. The mother complains that her daughter woke up crying because of pain in her left ear; a pediatrician had examined her the previous day, diagnosing an ear infection and prescribing an antibiotic, but the child's crying has disturbed the mother's sleep. The pediatrician's office will open in another few hours, but the mother wants something done now. Since antibiotics usually take effect only after one or two days—and since the mother hasn't given the child aspirin for her pain—I advise her to continue the antibiotics and begin giving the child aspirin until the pain and fever subside.

The heart attack victim had never seen the emergency room before, but the mother was a regular customer. She wasn't surprised to see the clerk make out a bill for $36—the minimum emergency room charge, but more than three times the cost of an office visit to the child's pediatrician. And the mother doesn't care about the cost—her family's medical bills are paid by the Medi-Cal program.

The mother and daughter are the bread and butter of the medical industry's newest and fastest-growing enterprise—the franchising of hospital emergency rooms. The average emergency room (known simply as an ER in medical shorthand) is a concession that a hospital turns over to a physician or a doctor-owned company in exchange for a share of the ER profits.

And the profits are considerable. The typical ER in the United States today functions as an around-the-clock drop-in clinic, as well as a crisis center for saving lives. For every patient with a life-threatening health problem—like the heart attack victim—there are a dozen others like the girl with an earache whose complaints are relatively minor and who don't require emergency care.

Most hospitals would not have it any other way. In addition to their share of ER fees—which includes a flat charge per patient visit as well as a percentage of the ER concessionaire's profits—the hospitals also benefit from a steady source of in-patients to fill vacant hospital beds and increased use of other concessions such as x ray and laboratory services. The boom has prompted a sudden proliferation of signs outside local hospitals: "Physician on duty—basic emergency medical care." The California Department of Health now *requires* all hospitals to post these signs so that no individual ER can be accused of advertising—they all advertise. And immediately after one such sign was placed outside a hospital, its ER business doubled.

The patient who uses the ER as a clinic enjoys the luxury of instant and unlimited access to medical care. But the typical ER patient isn't paying for this luxury—at least not directly—since tax money is the chief support for the ER industry. Thanks to Medi-Cal and Medicare payments for ER services, the taxpayer is footing the bill. Since ER charges are so much higher than office visits, medical care for the poor often costs more than for the wealthy.

"If someone wants to pay $40 to have me look at a sore throat, I'm glad to do it," says one of my fellow ER doctors, who gave up his office practice for the highly profitable ER of a nonprofit hospital. "They're paying for the convenience of having a physician available at any time of the day or night."

Emergency medicine, which has always been a potential source of income for doctors and hospitals, became a growth industry only in the 1970s, when physicians found that welfare families could use an ER as a substitute for a family doctor. Just as convalescent hospitals proliferated in the early 1960s, when federal money started paying for nursing care, the franchising of ER concessions flourished when government-sponsored health insurance programs made emergency medicine profitable for doctors and convenient for Medi-Cal and Medicare patients.

Before the boom in emergency medicine, ERs were often staffed by interns fresh out of medical school or graduates of Far Eastern medical mills. Today, emergency medicine is a recognized medical specialty with some 40 residency programs now training approximately 200 ER physicians. The American College of Emergency Physicians (ACEP) publishes its own professional journal, organizes postgraduate educational seminars and establishes "principles of ethical practice." As a result, a growing number of ER concessionaires requires residency training in emergency medicine or ACEP membership when they run classified ads in medical journals for ER staff openings.

A new ER physician who takes a job with a concessionaire can expect a salary of $50,000 to $60,000 a year, along with fringe benefits such as health insurance, paid educational leave and vacations. But the real money in emergency medicine goes to the doctors who operate the ER franchises.

One doctor who held the ER contract for a middle-sized county general hospital in Northern California netted about $200,000 in 1976—$75,000 for his own labor in the ER room, and another $125,000 derived from the earnings of the physicians he hired to cover the hours when he was not on duty. In the parlance of the ER trade, his contract was considered "good" because the hospital's ER sees about 80 patients a day; once an ER's patient load goes over 30 a day, both the concessionaire and the hospital start making money. And $200,000 might be considered a good income, too, but it's not good enough for some physicians in the ER franchising industry.

Another physician-concessionaire in California, for instance, operates thirteen profitable ERs which probably generate about $10 million in physicians' fees each year—and he runs seven more "on spec," hoping they'll also turn profitable someday. And the physician who holds these twenty contracts probably nets $1 million a year from his chain of ERs after paying his physician-employees and other overhead.

Emergency Medical Systems, Inc., is a San Francisco-based corporation that operates 23 ERs throughout Northern California. "They're not McDonalds'," says one physician, referring to a comparison between the booming ER industry and the fast-food franchise. "Compared with some groups, they're just Jack-in-the-Box."

He may be right. An Oakland-based physician group runs more than 40 ERs, mostly in California, and a St. Louis partnership of three doctors oversees a twenty-state chain of about 80 ERs.

"It's hard to see how you can run so many ERs and still maintain good quality control," complains one physician. "You'd have to be totally into business and not give a s--- about medicine anymore. You might have an incompetent staff working for you in Seattle, but never find out because you're sitting in an office a thousand miles away."

Money is certainly not the sole reason that many physicians choose to work in emergency rooms. Although most ER patients have relatively minor health problems, the ER staff often makes the difference between life and death in a true emergency—and they know it. But the physicians who work for ER entrepreneurs have no overhead, no managerial headaches, no nights on call; when their shifts are over, they can simply pick up their coats and leave. Best of all, emergency medicine is never routine. The next case may be an anxious mother with a healthy child or the bloodied victims of an unguarded railroad crossing. In fact, emergency medicine can be a kind of yoga exercise—relaxation, total concentration.

I discovered this unique form of yoga three years ago, when I started working for two doctors who operate three ERs and three outpatient clinics in the San Joaquin Valley. Three times a month, I drive from my home in a Northern California coastal village to the San Francisco airport, where I catch a one-hour flight to Bakersfield. Another car is waiting for me there, and I drive to the ER where I'll work for the next twelve to 60 hours, depending on how much sleep—if any—the patient volume allows.

Rich in oil, crops and country-and-western singers, the Bakersfield area offers little to attract physicians. One weary ER veteran describes Bakersfield as a place where 100,000 Okies and 100,000 Chicanos—all of them boozed up, heavily armed and driving fast cars—compete for 100,000 jobs. Finding a family doctor who will accept Medi-Cal patients is no easy task. In a remote community like Bakersfield, the local ER provides medical care that might not otherwise be available to poor families.

The ER at Bakersfield's San Joaquin Community Hospital—a private hospital affiliated with the Seventh Day Adventist Church—is staffed by the Valley Emergency Medical Group, which was founded in 1973 by Dr. George Flynn and Dr. Fred Kumpel. Today, the ER's well-organized facility and well-trained staff make it possible for a physician to see 70 to 100 patients in a 24-hour shift—and still get a few hours of sleep.

The ER at San Joaquin Community Hospital is small but busy. And it's a good example of how a profitable ER concession operates. A patient visiting the ER pays a physician's fee of $16 or more—the average fee is $22—and an additional $20 charge that goes directly to the hospital for the use of its facilities and staff. Flynn and Kumpel pay the salaries of their physician-employees, and since the ER operates in the black, they pay the hospital a percentage of the gross professional fees.

Of course, a hospital derives other benefits from a busy ER. Heavy use of the ER leads to increased demand for inpatient beds and other hospital services. One

hospital administrator encouraged ER nurses to compete among themselves in a monthly pool to see which shift generated the most patient admissions.

Flynn and Kumpel also operate the ER for the only hospital in Delano—where Medi-Cal covered farm workers constitute most of their patients—and they cover weekend shifts in the ER of the tiny hospital in Tehachapi, a mountain community 40 miles east of Bakersfield. The Delano ER is busiest during the harvest season, but it still fails to show an annual profit. The Tehachapi ER may see as few as twenty patients during a 60-hour weekend, but the hospital is glad to pay the physician's wages and a small management fee; the hospital administration realizes that Tehachapi's four overworked physicians might leave town if the ER did not handle weekend calls.

Not all ER concessions follow the same financial practices. The San Joaquin Community Hospital ER, for instance, pays its physician-employees a flat hourly wage regardless of their patient billings. But the ER at a nearby hospital pays its physicians a percentage of their actual billings. Under such an incentive system, a physician's income rises as he processes more patients. One ER contract-holder estimates that the average professional fee at a hospital using the incentive system is $10 higher than a similar ER paying straight salaries. Since an ER like the one at San Joaquin Community Hospital sees some 28,000 patients a year, the incentive system would add a quarter-million dollars to its gross take. Although some doctors might defend the incentive system as more efficient, it raises serious questions about the motivation of the concessionaire and the physician-employees in treating ER patients. Since volume translates into higher earnings for the employee and higher profits for the contract-holder, the incentive system may tempt doctors to spend less time on each patient in order to see more patients.

Some ER doctors also receive a percentage of the x-ray and laboratory fees generated by their patients—an all-too-common practice in ER concessions. Like the doctor who is tempted to run up his percentage of professional fees by treating more patients, the doctor who shares in x-ray and lab fees may order more of these services than absolutely necessary for the health of the patient.

Last spring, the Florida chapter of the ACEP sponsored a postgraduate seminar on emergency medicine. Salesmen demonstrated the latest examples of nifty medical technology; emergency physicians shared their experience and expertise in handling true medical emergencies. A few days after returning from the conference, I put some newly learned techniques to use in treating a five-year-old whose hand had been caught in a washing machine wringer.

But none of the ACEP seminars dealt with the more prevalent problem of the ER—those weekend and nighttime hours when the ER turns into a pediatric drop-in clinic. Soon ater the wringer accident, I found myself treating a two-month-old boy who had already seen two other physicians that day. The child's pediatrician diagnosed a cold and prescribed aspirin and

fluids; the mother waited until after dark to drive 30 miles to an emergency room for a second opinion. When I saw the baby, he seemed well except for a slight fever and a mild case of dehydration. Had the mother kept the child at home, she could have given him the aspirin and fluids he needed; instead, she ran up more than $100 in medical bills—all to be paid by Medi-Cal.

As long as the medical profession stresses symptomatic rather than preventive treatment—and as long as poor families face the reluctance of doctors in private practice to treat Medi-Cal patients—the ER industry will continue to thrive. In fact, ERs are an accurate microcosm of our modern medical system; franchised medical care is a natural extension of medicine practiced for profit.

A classic study of American medical students once showed that most of them would become business tycoons if they couldn't become doctors. The franchising of ERs offers the physician a perfect opportunity to combine these seemingly disparate interests of the American medicine man.

And with the staggering incomes generated by the modest ER empires that now exist, it may only be a matter of time before the emergency medicine boom attracts the conglomerates. When Gulf + Western or IT&T catches the bug of ER franchising, your local ER may end up on the stock exchange.

CAUTION: TOO MANY HEALTH WARNINGS COULD BE COUNTERPRODUCTIVE

Should the government slap warning labels on products that new scientific data suggest are harmful? The question seemed a very easy one to answer, at first. It seemed clearly in the interest of consumers to get the up-to-date information, right at the shopping counter, that would enable them to make more enlightened purchases. There were certainly precedents in the warnings on cigarette packages, the statements about artificial sweeteners on dietary soft drinks, the requirement that ingredients be listed on food packages. But when I was recently forced to think more systematically about the matter, as a consultant in a study for the Bureau of Alcohol, Firearms and To-

bacco of the U.S. Treasury, I reached a somewhat different conclusion.

BAFT (as everyone calls it) had issued an "advanced notice of proposed rule-making." It solicited information "to decide whether the current regulations should be amended to require a warning label on alcoholic beverage containers regarding the consumption of alcohol by pregnant women." The proposed regulation grew out of several studies that suggested that heavy drinking by a pregnant woman might harm the fetus.

One can safely conclude that BAFT's request for information was not ignored. The agency received 3,000 commentaries, from the liquor industries, wine-growers, consumer groups, individual physicians, and scores of others. Less than 10 percent of those who responded—279, to be exact—favored the labeling; the overwhelming majority opposed it. BAFT then decided to ask a doctor to examine the medical evidence and a sociologist (yours truly) to explore the possible social effects of such labels. We were to advise the agency in preparing the final ruling.

As I waded through the material, piled three and a half feet high on my desk, I received a somewhat frantic call from the Treasury. An "alcohol trade publication" had reported that I was being consulted. I was not to talk with the industry, or consumer advocates, on the matter, but to base my advice solely on the commentaries and data before me. In this way, I was told, the law protects rule-making from undue influence.

I was slightly miffed that anyone would think a Columbia professor could be swayed by special-interest arguments or other inducements. But, on second thought, the law made sense. One should either communicate with none of the parties directly affected by the ruling, or with all of them in an open, public manner. I found no difficulty in staying away from all sides.

My first doubts about the wisdom of the proposed label grew from my impression that the public might already be overwhelmed by warnings. This hypothesis was supported by about two dozen interviews conducted informally with friends, neighbors, people I ran across. "You've got to eat *something*," they told me, typically. "If the water is polluted, the air full of toxins, the bread overloaded with iron, and the peanut butter spoiled by fungus, what is one to consume?"

Furthermore, a survey by public-opinion analyst Daniel Yankelovich suggested that people may not care that much about the quality of their food. The study, presented at the Food Marketing Institute, found that only 15 percent of several groups of women interviewed across the United States (aged 20 to 45, with at least two children living at home, low-middle to middle income) felt strongly about "eating only what is good for them." Four times that many, 60 percent, said they "try for a balanced diet, but don't make a big deal of it." Another 17 percent agreed with the statement that they "eat what they like and don't worry about it." Of course, this did not prove that inflation of warnings was the reason for relative unconcern, but it indirectly suggested that labels as such do not mobilize most people.

In my report to BAFT, I suggested a system of graduated alerts, such as is used in other areas. For example, red flags on beaches signal very dangerous waters; black flags indicate dangerous waters that might be used with caution if one is a good swimmer; and blue flags generally indicate safe waters. Similarly, the city of Los Angeles employs three different alerts to denote levels of smog pollution. During the first stage, children, the elderly, and those with respiratory and cardiac problems are warned to remain indoors, and industries are asked to voluntarily control pollution-producing activities; the more serious second stage warns the public to refrain from strenuous activity, may call for cuts in industrial emission of 20 percent, completely curtails certain activities (such as the unloading of crude oil), and requires some mandatory car pooling. The third and most critical health advisory calls for a "smog holiday," during which all business and industry are shut down and only authorized vehicles are permitted on the roads.

In both cases, extreme alerts are used sparingly, and the various gradations of warning assist the public in distinguishing between higher and lower risks. A similar graduated response seems advisable for consumer products and services. The system could weigh the probability of the danger against the degree of harm (whether the outcome might be a fatality, injury, or only financial loss), and the numbers involved (are most people at risk or only a few). For instance, one could use a black skull and crossbones where there is a very high probability of danger (a proper label for concentrated toxins and high-voltage electricity). Dark-red labels might be used where there is a high probability of danger and/or serious injury (perhaps suitable for cigarette packages). Pale-blue labels might be suitable for lower levels of probability and for lower level of injury (for instance, when a drug is for external use only and will cause upset stomach if ingested). One or more announcements by the proper public authorities could serve as the lowest level of alert.

Applying such a system to the issue at hand, I concluded that data available in the summer of 1978 on the fetal-alcohol syndrome (FAS) seemed to justify a relatively low level of alert. It was not so much that the evidence was rather weak, as early scientific data often are, but that it seemed very uneven. It was strong on the detrimental effects from heavy drinking but very much weaker in trying to prove the harmful effect of moderate drinking on the fetus. (Heavy drinking is defined in the relevant studies as between two and a half to three or more ounces of 100 percent alcohol a day, the equivalent of six drinks.) Based on 58 published cases from 16 different medical centers, it seemed clear that women who frequently drink heavily—or even only occasionally, during "binge drinking"—produce smaller, mentally and physically less-developed children. In

contrast, only one study provided evidence that consumption of alcohol in small amounts might be harmful to the fetus.

Since only a small minority of people drink heavily (the number varies from about 4 to 7 percent, depending on the source and how heavy drinking is defined), it seemed to me that bombarding everyone with labels in order to reach a few was a scattergun approach. Most heavy drinkers are probably addicted (i.e., alcoholic), and therefore it seems very unlikely that they would be deterred by a warning label.

Finally, there was the possibility that a label might actually do harm: if the government requires warnings about the harmful effects if liquor, the industry might, quite justifiably, ask that bottles also list the reported benefits of drinking. Dr. Arthur L. Klatsky, director of the coronary-care unit at Kaiser-Permanente Medical Center in San Francisco, California, is cited as stating that moderate alcohol consumption reduces probability of coronary heart attacks by 30 percent. His conclusion is based on a study of 87,000 patients.

A government label, by itself, seems to imply authoritative approval to some people. Thus, when a required label proclaims that a product contains "the full U.S. recommended daily allowance of vitamin C," many consumers may be led to conclude that the product is somehow more legitimate than even a natural food like an orange. A consulting firm, Paul Fine Associates, wondered if proposed government-approved labels listing the nutrients in synthetic foods were a good idea. "The effect," said the report of a study by the firm, "would be to say to those consumers who have been worried about synthetic foods that they need not worry so long as the products have the proper label.

The rule also says to the public that 'natural' food is not better food."

Did all this mean, I wondered, that one could simply ignore the data on alcohol and pregnant women? Ethically, on the basis of the consumers' right to know, it seemed necessary to at least issue a public warning. Also, it seemed unwise to rely on physicians and other health professionals to alert women to the problem, as several commentaries had suggested. The experience with birth-control pills suggests that doctors tend not to pass along such information. The Food and Drug Administration had initially left this matter to doctors, but reluctantly concluded that it had to reach consumers of contraceptive pills more directly. It required that a warning of the risk of blood clots and heart attacks from the pills be inserted in the packages.

One low-cost method of reaching consumers of alcohol would be to require store-owners who sell liquor to place posters with cautionary warnings in appropriate places on their shelves. The posters could be easily brought up to date as more evidence becomes available. They are also less likely than labels on the bottles to have a legitimating effect, since they are not directly linked with the product, and only call attention to one of its specific features, without attempting to assess its merits and demerits.

I filed my report with BAFT. As this column went to press, the agency was said to be about to reach a conclusion at any moment. In government, this could mean anywhere from two weeks or two years.

Whatever the decision, it will be necessary in the future to use government warnings, labels, and inserts sparingly and judiciously. Otherwise, we might face a Proposition 13-type reaction that could seriously hamper essential government regulation of food and drugs. It is not that studying fetal alcohol syndrome left me opposed to the regulation, but that it made me think that fewer warnings could lead to more effective consumer education and compliance.

FTC IS SEEKING WAYS TO DECIDE IF PICTURES IN ADVERTISING CONVEY FALSE IMPRESSIONS

The familiar pictures in advertisements of couples playing at the beach and cowboys riding the range are posing a thorny question for Federal Trade Commission.

Are the pictures' implicit messages about the products they advertise false, deceptive or misleading in violation of federal laws?

The commission in the past has been concerned primarily with the words used in advertisements. It analyzed claims for products to determine if they could be substantiated. Figuring out whether the un-

stated message of a picture is misleading, however, raises the additional issue of what the unstated message is.

But top officials of the FTC's Bureau of Consumer Protection are wrestling with the question as sophisticated advertisers shy away from making explicit claims for their products and instead use appealing air-brushed photographs of models and tranquil scenes of couples strolling the countryside to sell their goods.

"The media have left the written word behind in a cloud of dust." Albert Kramer, director of the bureau, has said, adding that if regulators don't consider the whole advertisement, they'll have a "very serious problem" assessing whether it's deceptive.

5. _____ _____ _____ _____

6. _____ _____ _____ _____

7. _____ _____ _____ _____

8. _____ _____ _____ _____

9. _____ _____ _____ _____

10. _____ _____ _____ _____

Price Survey Form

Items	Price in Upper-Income Area	Price in Middle-Income Area	Price in Lower-Income Area
1.			
2.			
3.			
4.			
5.			
6.			
7.			
8.			
9.			
10.			

FROLICKING IN THE SURF

In a recent speech, Tracy Westen, the bureau's deputy director, cited an ad for Belair cigarets, which he said is "dominated by a full-page, color photograph of a happy couple frolicking in the surf." The words in the ad, which tell the reader the cigarets take you "all the way to fresh" appear to be "trivial throw aways," Mr. Westen said.

But what is the message of the ad, he asked. Perhaps it is that Belairs will make you "healthy" and "happy," a message that might be deceptive if stated in words, he said.

Because pictures, unlike words, don't have accepted meanings, it's "difficult to agree on the meaning or message communicated by a photograph and thus difficult to agree whether a theme or message in a picture is legally deceptive in FTC terms," Mr. Westen said.

FTC staffers are trying to determine how the impact of the picture can be dealt with. One possibility, according to Dee Pridgen, the bureau's assistant for special projects, is to set up a panel of consumers to see if they agree on the message. Then that message could be reviewed in the same way it would be if it had been presented in words.

TOBACCO DATA SOUGHT

The commission also may seek access to studies by companies or their advertising agencies to see what conclusions they reached about consumer attitudes toward the ads. The FTC currently is seeking such information from the tobacco industry as part of a two-year-old investigation of the industry's advertising practices. The cigaret companies have fought subpoenas from the commission in court and a decision is expected shortly.

Still another possibility, according to Miss Pridgen, is to hire a media expert to assess the effect of ads at a subliminal level. Consumer panels might be unable to articulate the message because "the average person wouldn't know what's going on," she says.

Many advertisements would have difficulty passing the tests, especially ads for such luxury goods as cigarets and alcohol, which use "nonverbal cues or emotional appeals more than others," Miss Pridgen says.

A drive by the FTC might force advertisers to change their ads, she suggests. "We'd like to see them more informative," she adds, citing as models some cigaret advertisements that compare the amount of tar in various brands.

But any attack by the commission on advertising is expected to stir up a storm of protest, possibly including renewed claims the FTC is acting like a "national nanny," a moniker it received when its study of children's advertising was announced several months ago.

COURTS CALLED WORD-ORIENTED

The FTC also may have trouble in court. "We're breaking new ground," Miss Pridgen concedes. "Judges and lawyers just aren't used to thinking" about anything other than the words of an ad. "There also is a question of how literally the message of a picture can be interpreted," she says.

But she defends the staff's efforts, contending that advertisers have forced the commission to take some steps in this direction with their advanced techniques. "If the FTC doesn't explore this area," she says, "its regulations won't have anything to do with the way advertising works.

We'll be nitpicking over words while the media are ahead of us."

The commission is authorized to stop deceptive practices and if it concentrates only on the verbal part of advertising, "we won't be carrying out our mandate," she says.

Exercise 39

You, the Consumer

OBJECTIVE To increase your awareness of your role as a consumer in the marketplace.

The following exercise is designed to make you more aware of your "economic" position in the marketplace as a consumer.

The brand name of the product dominates the product. In some cases, the manufacturer's name may not even be on the package/lable. And even in those cases when the manufacturer's name is available, consumers may make little use of that information. Not knowing who manufacturers what may facilitate the oligopolistic growth of the food industry.

The next time you buy groceries, take a few minutes to examine the products that you bought. Is there any information on the labels that tells you who the manufacturers are? How many different brands did you purchase that are produced by the same manufacturer?

Exercise 40

Consumerism: Caveat Emptor

OBJECTIVE To demonstrate the value of consumer education.

Fresh Horizon Bread is positioned to emphasize its fiber content. What is the component of the fiber content?

Total Cereal and Wheaties Cereal are both manufactured by General Mills. How are the cereals different?

Jiffy Blueberry Muffin Mix features the delicious blueberry muffins on the front of its package. What are the blueberries made of?

Awake is a fruit drink found in the orange juice section of the grocery store. Is Awake an orange juice?

After you have completed this exercise, your instructor will discuss the answers posed in these questions.

Exercise 41

The Economics of Being Poor

OBJECTIVE To arrive at an understanding of the different economic circumstances of the poor and the middle class.

Evidence has lead some scholars of consumer behavior to conclude that the poor pay more. In this exercise you are asked to gather your own evidence and to draw your own conclusions.

Select items and then price these items in retail establishments located in an upper-income area, a middle-income area and in a lower-income area of the city. When you have completed the price survey, compare the price differences and interpret your results.

Price Survey Form

Items	Price in Upper-Income Area	Price in Middle-Income Area	Price in Lower-Income Area
1. _____	_____	_____	_____
2. _____	_____	_____	_____
3. _____	_____	_____	_____
4. _____	_____	_____	_____